A CENTURY
OF THE ESSAY

British and American

EDITED BY DAVID DAICHES

UNIVERSITY LECTURER IN ENGLISH
AT CAMBRIDGE UNIVERSITY

HARCOURT, BRACE AND COMPANY, NEW YORK

1951

CONTENTS

Contents

The Editor

REFLECTIONS
ON THE ESSAY

To WRITE an essay on the essay: the prospect has a certain charm, for the essay is the most self-indulgent of literary forms, and to talk about it calls for an intellectual ease, a relaxed and quizzical attitude, which modern literary critics, whether academic or merely esoteric, generally feel it their duty to avoid. Yet when we think of the essay in this way we are ignoring some of the major forms it has assumed in the last hundred years. The personal or familiar essay—Dr. Johnson's "loose sally"—from Montaigne to Charles Lamb is, I suppose, the essay *par excellence;* it is this kind of essay which established the form as a literary *genre* and gave it its name. Montaigne in 1580 called his confessional discourses *Essais,* that is, attempts, tentative and suggestive remarks, and there is a long line of essay writers who take their cue from him. But the characteristic modern essay is an altogether more serious affair. William James discussing pragmatism, T. S. Eliot appraising Andrew Marvell, Edmund Wilson analyzing A. E. Housman—there is nothing here of the tentative personal confession: these writers are telling the truth as they see it, cogently, urgently, and with high seriousness. The modern essay writer tends to be both more concerned and more *committed* than his predecessor.

Of course, there have been serious philosophical essays from very early times—the Greeks were particularly good at that kind of writing, and it can be found in English literature throughout the seventeenth and eighteenth centuries—but the essay as a recognized literary form, as a kind of writing agreeable for its own sake and enjoyable apart from its message, was a century ago more likely to be the kind of thing done by Montaigne or Abraham Cowley (whose essay, "Of Myself," published posthumously with his other essays in 1668, is one of the first truly confessional short pieces of prose in English) or Addison or Goldsmith or Charles Lamb. While the familiar essay has by no means disappeared in the last hundred years, it has become a thin trickle indeed when compared with the stream of serious critical and philosophical discussions in our time. One might venture a preposterous generalization, and say that ever since the middle of the last century writers have become increasingly worried, have taken themselves and their readers ever more seriously, have more and more lost interest in the light play of ideas, so that the essays they produce are, like Matthew Arnold's or Bertrand Russell's or George Orwell's, searching investigations of troubling problems or earnest exhortations to the gentiles. On the other hand, we have our professional humorists, and Frank Moore Colby, Stephen Leacock, and James Thurber—to cite only three—show what happens when the serious essay becomes very serious: a specialization of function sets in, and the humorous essay becomes a *genre* of its own. Yet even here we must make distinctions: Thurber is very different from, say, the English essayist A. A. Milne or even A. P. Herbert; his humor is often grim, and nobody can say that if he is funny it is because he is not worried.

Western man has become increasingly concerned about himself in the last hundred years (with good cause, it might be added), and this concern is reflected in the growing seriousness of the vast majority of essays. It may be objected that I am here using the term "essay" for two very different kinds of writing, that on the one hand we have the familiar essay, read for its stylistic grace and confessional charm, and on the other we have the serious prose discussion, which can handle any subject, can be of any length, and is often of interest only to those who have a previous interest in the subject handled. Thus, it might be maintained, all that I am saying is that the essay has in some measure given way to the critical discussion, a quite different form of writing, which has existed for a much longer period of time than the essay proper. But the fact is that the line between the professional treatise and the personal chat is a continuous one, and while it is easy enough to distinguish between the extremes, there is a middle ground—the critical essays of Hazlitt, for example—where impressionistic confession and objective exposition of ideas mingle, and even reinforce each other. The element of personality is never wholly absent from any of the discussions included in the present anthology, and so long as that element is present, reinforcing the argument with all kinds of overtones and implied attitudes, the link between the personal essay and the serious monograph is maintained, and we have a right to continue the use of the term "essay."

The serious philosophical essay—Locke's *Essay Concerning Human Understanding,* for example—of the seventeenth or eighteenth century is indeed not an essay in the sense in which I am using the term; but with the growth of periodicals which offered a vehicle for the shorter and less professional prose discussion something of the style and tone of the familiar essay inevitably crept in, so that even T. S. Eliot, for all his repudiation of personality in literature, projects himself in his critical essays in a highly idiosyncratic way, and we see the man reflected in the prose much more immediately and directly than we do in the essays of David Hume or of other professional philosophers. This combination of earnest exposition with revelation—conscious or unconscious—of personality is to be found in the more serious of Addison's *Spectator* essays and is a feature of periodical literature from Addison's day to our own.

There is, however, a difference between the kind of thing that earlier periodical writers were doing and what we often find in modern journals. The growth of specialization has produced more and more specialized periodicals, each addressed to experts, and each using a jargon unintelligible to even the most cultured layman. The decline of the essay in present-day America—and there can be no doubt that, in spite of the fact that good examples of the form can be found without much difficulty, it has declined—is largely due to the decline of the layman, of the non-specialist inquirer, the intelligent and well-read man of large general curiosity. If the essay, however serious and objective in intention, can be defined as a reasonably short prose discussion in which the personality of the author in some degree shapes the style and tone of the argument, and in which the writer's skill in the handling of prose exposition is impressive in its own right and pleasing for the reader to watch in operation, then the treatise in the specialized professional journal today is certainly very far from being an essay: it is most often a set of harsh shorthand notes meant to be translated by the expert reader who can fit it into its context and make sense (if not charm) out of it in relation to that context.

The art of the essay, like that of conversation, has declined in the last century because there are too few people who know enough about enough matters to afford an audience for the attractive discussion which is expert without being specialized. The secret of Dr. Johnson's conversation was that, considering himself an educated man, he had a clearly defined opinion on whatever might be brought to his attention, and was prepared to express it forcefully in the language of educated men, not gracelessly and hermetically in the language of technical experts. The serious prose discussion can only remain an essay if the author is similarly at ease in the world of human thought and is prepared to see the infinite relevance of any particular arguments he might present. That is why Emerson and Arnold and Bertrand Russell and Eliot remain essayists, experts though they are in their way. They write in an atmosphere of luminous intelligence, not in the blinding darkness of technical footnoting.

With human knowledge increasingly broken up into fragments and distributed among experts, the essay which appeals to the "general reader" tends to get ever thinner and triter, talking down to a common ignorance or a common set of prejudices, as far too many newspaper editorials do today. In such an atmosphere, the good essayist renders a very special service: he reminds us of the importance of general intelligence, demonstrating by the example of his own practice that the terms "general" and "intelligence" are not contradictory. The technical expert with his special jargon may be necessary (though this is arguable) if we are to continue to extend the limits of human knowledge in specific areas, but it can be claimed for the essayist that it is he who integrates this knowledge with the pattern of culture of his day, who airs it and demonstrates its relevance to our daily thinking and its general significance in the intellectual climate of our time.

The essayist can perform this function with varying degrees of solemnity. The sense of concern and commitment which we get in Eliot's critical essays is very different from the witty exploitation of ideas we get in an essay by Aldous Huxley, and both these writers have nothing in their tone and attitude that remotely resembles, say, the relaxed and discursive intelligence of Christopher Morley. Yet all are performing a similar kind of service; they are handling ideas effectively in prose in such a way as both to please the reader by the aptness of the expression (by their style, that is to say) and to arouse him to an awareness of the implications for human intelligence of what is being discussed. There is no activity more civilized and more civilizing.

If we can distinguish—at their extremes—between the serious prose discussion addressed to those already interested in the subject and the familiar essay which appeals by the grace with which the author projects his personality, and if we make this distinction only to realize that there is an important middle ground where elements of both come together, we have still left no place for recognition of the kind of essay whose function is simply to demonstrate a certain kind of mastery over prose. The "Character" writers of the seventeenth century, who wrote cleverly phrased descriptions of character types in order to show the aptness of their phrasing, have their heirs in nineteenth-century essayists who are simply professional wielders of a graceful pen. The early Stevenson is often in this category. Stevenson wanted to be a writer before he had anything to say—he even undertook journeys solely in order to be able to write about them skillfully when they were over—and in his earliest phase produced many accomplished essays which, if we take a musical analogy, can be compared to *études* rather than pieces. They are exercises in the handling of English prose, often quite brilliant in their way, and fascinating reading for anyone interested in the potentialities of the medium. This kind of essayist has diminished almost to non-existence, which is a pity, for the essay as *étude* demonstrates and encourages a concern with craftsmanship in exposition of which the present generation stands all too much in need.

One must beware, however, of making too hard and fast a separation between the essay as *étude* and the essay as full composition. Just as the short treatise and the personal essay can merge into each other, so, and to an even

greater degree, the essay as exhibition of mere craftsmanship can transform itself imperceptibly into a significant
treatment of some phase of human thought or experience.
Stevenson wrote "Walking Tours" primarily as an exercise
in English prose; but it emerges as more than that, and we
read it as much for its pleasing rendition of a state of mind
and its effective capturing of the tone of personality as for
the modulation of its prose rhythms. Indeed, modulation
of prose rhythms, or any other aspect of literary craftsmanship, can be seen as effective only to the degree that it gives
life to some content, for the arrangement of words is successful in proportion as it communicates the full implications of what the author has to say. In literature (and
perhaps in music, too) there can never be a pure *étude*.

So one sets up distinctions between different kinds of
essays in order to break them down again. Not, of course,
that these distinctions are unreal: one does not need to
demonstrate that E. B. White is doing something very
different from what Oliver Wendell Holmes did, or even
that the humorous essay of Thurber is very far away, in
tone, style, and general purpose, from the equally (but
differently) humorous essay by Max Beerbohm. But distinctions can be seen and appreciated without the setting
up of rigid categories, even if such categories are helpful
in the initial clearing of one's mind. Let us by all means
read the essays in this collection for what they are, recognizing individuality of style and purpose, noting different
degrees of seriousness, appreciating humor, whimsicality,
gracefulness, profundity, wit, irony, compassion, shrewdness, and whatever other qualities come through to us,
conveyed by the appropriate handling of prose; but there
is no harm, either, in recognizing the common purpose
that runs through even such a disparate group of essays as
this. Here are intelligent and civilized men using the
medium of English prose in order to set ideas happily in a
context of human awareness. The ideas may be deliberately

trivial or preposterous, or they may be profound and challenging, or they may lie anywhere between these extremes. But in each case the author conveys them in appropriate language, organizes them deftly, and presents them in such a way that we can take some delight in the presentation at the same time we respond as intelligent and thoughtful readers to the implications of what is said.

Something in the present state of civilization has made most of us far too defensive about our interests and our pleasures. Do we need to apologize for reading what thoughtful men have said well, whether of description, argument, or self-revelation? Do I need to write another essay explaining the value of this sort of thing? If the reader does not see that the answer to both these questions is a resounding "No!" he is beyond salvation by essays or by any other kind of literature.

Henry D. Thoreau

WHERE I LIVED,
AND WHAT I LIVED FOR

AT a certain season of our life we are accustomed to consider every spot as the possible site of a house. I have thus surveyed the country on every side within a dozen miles of where I live. In imagination I have bought all the farms in succession, for all were to be bought, and I knew their price. I walked over each farmer's premises, tasted his wild apples, discoursed on husbandry with him, took his farm at his price, at any price, mortgaging it to him in my mind; even put a higher price on it,—took everything but a deed of it,—took his word for his deed, for I dearly love to talk,—cultivated it, and him too to some extent, I trust, and withdrew when I had enjoyed it long enough, leaving him to carry it on. This experience entitled me to be regarded as a sort of real-estate broker by my friends. Wherever I sat, there I might live, and the landscape radiated from me accordingly. What is a house but a *sedes,* a seat?—better if a country seat. I discovered many a site for a house not likely to be soon improved, which some might have thought too far from the village, but to my eyes the village was too far from it. Well, there I might live, I said; and there I did live, for an hour, a summer and a winter life, saw how I could let the years run off, buffet the winter through, and see the spring come in. The future inhabitants of this region, wherever they may place their houses, may be sure that they have been anticipated. An afternoon sufficed to lay out the land into orchard, woodlot, and pasture, and to decide what fine oaks or pines should be left to stand before the door, and whence each blasted tree could be seen to the best advantage; and then I let it lie, fallow perchance, for a man is rich in proportion to the number of things which he can afford to let alone.

My imagination carried me so far that I even had the refusal of several farms,—the refusal was all I wanted,— but I never got my fingers burned by actual possession. The nearest that I came to actual possession was when I bought the Hollowell place, and had begun to sort my seeds, and collected materials with which to make a wheelbarrow to carry it on or off with; but before the owner gave me a deed of it, his wife—every man has such a wife— changed her mind and wished to keep it, and he offered me ten dollars to release him. Now, to speak the truth, I had but ten cents in the world, and it surpassed my arithmetic to tell, if I was that man who had ten cents, or who had a farm, or ten dollars, or all together. However, I let him keep the ten dollars and the farm too, for I had carried it far enough; or rather, to be generous, I sold him the farm for just what I gave for it, and, as he was not a rich man, made him a present of ten dollars, and still had my ten cents, and seeds, and materials for a wheelbarrow left. I found thus that I had been a rich man without any damage to my property. But I retained the landscape, and I have since annually carried off what it yielded without a wheelbarrow. With respect to landscapes,—

> I am monarch of all I *survey,*
> My right there is none to dispute.

I have frequently seen a poet withdraw, having enjoyed the most valuable part of a farm, while the crusty farmer supposed that he had got a few wild apples only. Why, the owner does not know it for many years when a poet has put his farm in rhyme, the most admirable kind of invisible fence, has fairly impounded it, milked it, skimmed it, and got all the cream, and left the farmer only the skimmed milk.

The real attractions of the Hollowell farm, to me, were: its complete retirement, being about two miles from the village, half a mile from the nearest neighbor, and separated from the highway by a broad field; its bounding on the river, which the owner said protected it by its fogs from frosts in the spring, though that was nothing to me; the gray color and ruinous state of the house and barn, and the dilapidated fences, which put such an interval between me and the last occupant; the hollow and lichen-covered apple trees, gnawed by rabbits, showing what kind of neighbors I should have; but above all, the recollection I had of it from my earliest voyages up the river when the house was concealed behind a dense grove of red maples, through which I heard the house-dog bark. I was in haste to buy it, before the proprietor finished getting out some rocks, cutting down the hollow apple trees, and grubbing up some young birches which had sprung up in the pasture, or, in short, had made any more of his improvements. To enjoy these advantages I was ready to carry it on; like Atlas, to take the work on my shoulders,—I never heard what compensation he received for that,—and do all those things which had no other motive or excuse but that I might pay for it and be unmolested in my possession of it; for I knew all the while that it would yield the most abundant crop of the kind I wanted if I could only afford to let it alone. But it turned out as I have said.

All that I could say, then, with respect to farming on a large scale (I have always cultivated a garden), was that I had had my seeds ready. Many think that seeds improve with age. I have no doubt that time discriminates between the good and the bad: and when at last I shall plant, I shall be less likely to be disappointed. But I would say to my fellows, once for all, As long as possible live free and uncommitted. It makes but little difference whether you are committed to a farm or the county jail.

Old Cato, whose "De Re Rusticâ" is my "cultivator," says, and the only translation I have seen makes sheer nonsense of the passage, "When you think of getting a farm, turn it thus in your mind, not to buy greedily; nor spare your pains to look at it, and do not think it enough to go round it once. The oftener you go there the more it will please you, if it is good." I think I shall not buy greedily, but go round and round it as long as I live, and be buried in it first, that it may please me the more at last.

The present was my next experiment of this kind, which I purpose to describe more at length; for convenience, putting the experience of two years into one. As I have said, I do not propose to write an ode to dejection, but to brag as lustily as chanticleer in the morning, standing on his roost, if only to wake my neighbors up.

When first I took up my abode in the woods, that is, began to spend my nights as well as days there, which, by accident, was on Independence Day, or the fourth of July, 1845, my house was not finished for winter, but was merely a defence against the rain, without plastering or chimney, the walls being of rough weatherstained boards, with wide chinks, which made it cool at night. The upright white hewn studs and freshly planed door and window casings gave it a clean and airy look, especially in the morning, when its timbers were saturated with dew, so that I fancied that by noon some sweet gum would exude from them. To my imagination it retained throughout the day more or less of this auroral character, reminding me of a certain house on a mountain which I had visited the year before. This was an airy and unplastered cabin, fit to entertain a travelling god, and where a goddess might trail her garments. The winds which passed over my dwelling were such as sweep over the ridges of mountains, bearing the broken strains, or celestial parts only, of terrestrial music. The morning wind forever blows, the poem of creation is uninterrupted; but few are the ears that hear it. Olympus is but the outside of the earth everywhere.

The only house I had been the owner of before, if I except a boat, was a tent, which I used occasionally when making excursions in the summer, and this is still rolled up in my garret; but the boat, after passing from hand to hand, has gone down the stream of time. With this more substantial shelter about me, I had made some progress toward settling in the world. This frame, so slightly clad, was a sort of crystallization around me, and reacted on the builder. It was suggestive somewhat as a picture in outlines. I did not need to go out doors to take the air, for the atmosphere within had lost none of its freshness. It was not so much within doors as behind a door where I sat, even in the rainiest weather. The Harivansa says, "An abode without birds is like a meat without seasoning." Such was not my abode, for I found myself suddenly neighbor to the birds; not by having imprisoned one, but having caged myself near them. I was not only nearer to some of those which commonly frequent the garden and the orchard, but to those wilder and more thrilling songsters of the forest which never, or rarely, serenade a villager,—the wood-thrush, the veery, the scarlet tanager, the field-sparrow, the whippoorwill, and many others.

I was seated by the shore of a small pond, about a mile and a half south of the village of Concord and somewhat higher than it, in the midst of an extensive wood between that town and Lincoln, and about two miles south of that our only field known to fame, Concord Battle Ground; but I was so low in the woods that the opposite shore, half a mile off, like the rest, covered with wood, was my most distant horizon. For the first week, wherever I looked out on the pond it impressed me like a tarn high up on the side of a mountain, its bottom far above the surface of other lakes, and, as the sun arose, I saw it throwing off its mighty clothing of mist, and here and there, by degrees, its soft ripples or its smooth reflecting surface were revealed, while the mists, like ghosts, were stealthily withdrawing in every direction into the woods, as at the breaking up of some noctural conventicle. The very dew seemed to hang upon the trees later into the day than usual, as on the sides of mountains.

This small lake was of most value as a neighbor in the intervals of a gentle rain storm in August, when, both air and water being perfectly still, but the sky overcast, mid-afternoon had all the serenity of evening, and the wood-thrush sang around, and was heard from shore to shore. A lake like this is never smoother than at such a time; and the clear portion of the air above it being shallow and darkened by clouds, the water, full of light, and reflections, becomes a lower heaven itself so much the more important. From a hill top near by, where the wood had recently been cut off, there was a pleasing vista southward across the pond, through a wide indentation in the hills which form the shore there, where their opposite sides sloping toward each other suggested a stream flowing out in that direction through a wooded valley, but stream there was none. That way I looked between and over the near green hills to some distant and higher ones in the horizon, tinged with blue. Indeed, by standing on tiptoe I could catch a glimpse of some of the peaks of the still bluer and more distant mountain ranges in the northwest, those true-blue coins from heaven's own mint, and also of some portion of the village. But in other directions, even from this point, I could not see over or beyond the woods which surrounded me. It is well to have some water in your neighborhood, to give buoyancy to and float the earth. One value even of the smallest well is that when you look into it you see that the earth is not continent but insular. This is as important as that it keeps butter cool. When I looked across the pond from this peak toward the Sudbury meadows, which in time of flood I distinguished elevated perhaps by a mirage in their seething valley, like a coin in a basin, all the earth beyond the pond appeared like a thin crust insulated and floated even by this small sheet of intervening water, and I was reminded that this on which I dwelt was but *dry land*.

Though the view from my door was still more contracted, I did not feel crowded or confined in the least. There was pasture enough for my imagination. The low shrub-oak plateau to which the opposite shore arose, stretched away toward the prairies of the West and the steppes of Tartary, affording ample room for all the roving families of men. "There are none happy in the world but beings who enjoy freely a vast horizon,"—said Damodara, when his herds required new and larger pastures.

Both place and time were changed and I dwelt nearer to those parts of the universe and to those eras in history which had most attracted me. Where I live was as far off as many a region viewed nightly by astronomers. We are wont to imagine rare and delectable places in some remote and more celestial corner of the system, behind the constellation of Cassiopeia's Chair, far from noise and disturbance. I discovered that my house actually had its site in such a withdrawn, but forever new and unprofaned, part of the universe. If it were worth the while to settle in those parts near to the Pleiades or the Hyades, to Aldebaran or Altair, then I was really there, or at an equal remoteness from the life which I had left behind, dwindled and twinkling with as fine a ray to my nearest neighbor, and to be seen only in moonless nights by him. Such was that part of creation where I had squatted:—

There was a shepherd that did live,
    And held his thoughts as high
As were the mounts whereon his flocks
    Did hourly feed him by.

What should we think of the shepherd's life if his flocks always wandered to higher pastures than his thoughts?

Every morning was a cheerful invitation to make my life of equal simplicity, and I may say innocence, with Nature herself. I have been as sincere a worshipper of Aurora as the Greeks. I got up early and bathed in the pond; that was a religious exercise, and one of the best things which I did. They say that characters were engraven on the bathing tub of king Tching-thang to this effect: "Renew thyself completely each day; do it again, and again, and forever again." I can understand that. Morning brings back the heroic ages. I was as much affected by the faint hum of a mosquito making its invisible and unimaginable tour through my apartment at earliest dawn, when I was sitting with door and windows open, as I could be by any trumpet that ever sang of fame. It was Homer's requiem; itself an Iliad and Odyssey in the air, singing its own wrath and wanderings. There was something cosmical about it; a standing advertisement, till forbidden, of the everlasting vigor and fertility of the world. The morning, which is the most memorable season of the day, is the awakening hour. Then there is least somnolence in us; and for an hour, at least, some part of us awakes which slumbers all the rest of the day and night. Little is to be expected of that day, if it can be called a day, to which we are not awakened by our Genius, but by the mechanical nudgings of some servitor, are not awakened by our own newly acquired force and aspirations from within, accompanied by the undulations of celestial music, instead of factory bells, and a fragrance filling the air—to a higher life than we fell asleep from; and thus the darkness bear its fruit, and prove itself to be good, no less than the light. That man who does not believe that each day contains an earlier, more sacred, and auroral hour than he has yet profaned, has despaired of life, and is pursuing a descending and darkening way. After a partial cessation of his sensuous life, the soul of man, or its organs rather, are reinvigorated each day, and his Genius tries again what noble life it can make. All memorable events, I should say, transpire in morning time and in a morning atmosphere. The Vedas say, "All intelligences awake with the morning." Poetry and art, and the fairest and most memorable of the actions of men, date from such an hour. All poets and heroes, like Memnon, are the children of Aurora, and emit their music at sunrise. To him whose elastic and vigorous thought keeps pace with the sun, the day is a perpetual morning. It matters not what the clocks say or the attitudes and labors of men. Morning is when I am awake and there is a dawn in me. Moral reform is the effort to throw off sleep. Why is it that men give so poor an account of their day if they have not been slumbering? They are not such poor calculators. If they had not been overcome with drowsiness they would have performed something. The millions are awake enough for physical labor; but only one in a million is awake enough for effective intellectual exertion, only one in a hundred millions to a poetic or divine life. To be awake is to be alive. I have never yet met a man who was quite awake. How could I have looked him in the face?

We must learn to reawaken and keep ourselves awake, not by mechanical aids, but by an infinite expectation of the dawn, which does not forsake us in our soundest sleep. I know of no more encouraging fact than the unquestionable ability of man to elevate his life by a conscious endeavor. It is something to be able to paint a particular picture, or to carve a statue, and so to make a few objects beautiful; but it is far more glorious to carve and paint the very atmosphere and medium through which we look, which morally we can do. To effect the quality of the day, that is the highest of arts. Every man is tasked to make his life, even in its details, worthy of the contemplation of his most elevated and critical hour. If we refused, or rather used up, such paltry information as we get, the oracles would distinctly inform us how this might be done.

I went to the woods because I wished to live deliberately, to front only the essential facts of life, and see if I could not learn what it had to teach, and not, when I came to die, discover that I had not lived. I did not wish to live what was not life, living is so dear; nor did I wish to practise resignation, unless it was quite necessary. I wanted to live deep and suck out all the marrow of life, to live so sturdily and Spartan-like as to put to rout all that was not life, to cut a broad swath and shave close, to drive life into a corner, and reduce it to its lowest terms, and, if it proved to be mean, why then to get the whole and genuine meanness of it, and publish its meanness to the world; or if it were sublime, to know it by experience, and be able to give a true account of it in my next excursion. For most men, it appears to me, are in a strange uncertainty about it, whether it is of the devil or of God, and have *somewhat hastily* concluded that it is the chief end of man here to "glorify God and enjoy him forever."

Still we live meanly, like ants; though the fable tells us that we were long ago changed into men; like pygmies we fight with cranes; it is error upon error, and clout upon clout, and our best virtue has for its occasion a superfluous and evitable wretchedness. Our life is frittered away by detail. An honest man has hardly need to count more than his ten fingers, or in extreme cases he may add his ten toes, and lump the rest. Simplicity, simplicity, simplicity! I say, let your affairs be as two or three, and not a hundred or a thousand; instead of a million count half a dozen, and keep your accounts on your thumb nail. In the midst of this chopping sea of civilized life, such are the clouds and storms and quicksands and thousand-and-one items to be allowed for, that a man has to live, if he would not founder and go to the bottom and not make his port at all, by dead reckoning, and he must be a great calculator indeed who succeeds. Simplify, simplify. Instead of three meals a day, if it be necessary eat but one; instead of a hundred dishes, five; and reduce other things in proportion. Our life is like a German Confederacy, made up of petty states, with its boundary forever fluctuating, so that even a German cannot tell you how it is bounded at any moment. The nation itself, with all its so-called internal improvements, which, by the way, are all external and superficial, is just such an unwieldy and overgrown establishment, cluttered with furniture and tripped up by its own traps, ruined by luxury and heedless expense, by want of calculation and a worthy aim, as the million households in the land; and the only cure for it as for them is in a rigid economy, a stern and more than Spartan simplicity of life and elevation of purpose. It lives too fast. Men think that it is essential that the *Nation* have commerce, and export ice, and talk through a telegraph, and ride thirty miles an hour, without a doubt, whether *they* do or not; but whether we should live like baboons or like men, is a little uncertain. If we do not get out sleepers, and forge rails, and devote days and nights to the work, but go to tinkering upon our *lives* to improve *them*, who will build railroads? And if railroads are not built, how shall we get to heaven in season? But if we stay at home and mind our business, who will want railroads? We do not ride on the railroad; it rides upon us. Did you ever think what those sleepers are that underlie the railroad? Each one is a man, an Irishman, or a Yankee man. The rails are laid on them, and they are covered with sand, and the cars run smoothly over them. They are sound sleepers, I assure you. And every few years a new lot is laid down and run over; so that, if some have the pleasure of riding on a rail, others have the misfortune to be ridden upon. And when they run over a man that is walking in his sleep, a supernumerary sleeper in the wrong position, and wake him up, they suddenly stop the cars, and make a hue and cry about it, as if this were an exception. I am glad to know that it takes a gang of men for every five miles to keep the sleepers down and level in their beds as it is, for this is a sign that they may sometime get up again.

Why should we live with such hurry and waste of life? We are determined to be starved before we are hungry. Men say that a stitch in time saves nine, and so they take a thousand stitches today to save nine tomorrow. As for work, we haven't any of any consequence. We have the Saint Vitus' dance, and cannot possibly keep our heads still. If I should only give a few pulls at the parish bell-rope, as for a fire, that is, without setting the bell, there is hardly a man on his farm in the outskirts of Concord, notwithstanding that press of engagements which was his excuse so many times this morning, nor a boy, nor a woman, I might almost say, but would forsake all and follow that sound, not mainly to save property from the flames, but, if we will confess the truth, much more to see it burn, since burn it must, and we, be it known, did not set it on fire—or to see it put out, and have a hand in it, if that is done as handsomely; yes, even if it were the parish church itself. Hardly a man takes a half hour's nap after dinner, but when he wakes he holds up his head and asks, "What's the news?" as if the rest of mankind had stood his sentinels. Some give directions to be waked every half hour, doubtless for no other purpose; and then, to pay for it, they tell what they have dreamed. After a night's sleep the news is as indispensable as the breakfast. "Pray tell me anything new that has happened to a man anywhere on this globe,"—and he reads it over his coffee and rolls, that a man has had his eyes gouged out this morning on the Wachito River; never dreaming the while that he lives in the dark unfathomed mammoth cave of this world, and has but the rudiment of an eye himself.

For my part, I could easily do without the post-office. I think that there are very few important communications made through it. To speak critically, I never received more than one or two letters in my life—I wrote this some years ago—that were worth the postage. The penny-post is, commonly, an institution through which you seriously offer a man that penny for his thought which is so often safely offered in jest. And I am sure that I never read any memorable news in a newspaper. If we read of one man robbed, or murdered, or killed by accident, or one house burned, or one vessel wrecked, or one steamboat blown up, or one cow run over on the Western Railroad, or one mad dog killed, or one lot of grasshoppers in the winter,—we never need read of another. One is enough. If you are acquainted with the principle, what do you care for a myriad instances and applications? To a philosopher all news, as it is called, is gossip, and they who edit and read it are old women over their tea. Yet not a few are greedy after this gossip. There was such a rush, as I hear, the other day at one of the offices to learn the foreign news by the last arrival, that several large squares of plate glass belonging to the establishment were broken by the pressure,—news which I seriously think a ready wit might write a twelvemonth or twelve years beforehand with sufficient accuracy. As for Spain, for instance, if you know how to throw in Don Carlos and the Infanta, and Don Pedro and Seville and Granada, from time to time in the right proportions,—they may have changed the names a little since I saw the papers,—and serve up a bull-fight when other entertainments fail, it will be true to the letter, and give us as good an idea of the exact state or ruin of things in Spain as the most succinct and lucid reports under this head in the newspapers: and as for England, almost the last significant scrap of news from that quarter

was the revolution of 1649; and if you have learned the
history of her crops for an average year, you never need
attend to that thing again, unless your speculations are of
a merely pecuniary character. If one may judge who rarely
looks into the newspapers, nothing new does ever happen
in foreign parts, a French revolution not excepted.

What news! how much more important to know what
that is which was never old! "Kieouhe-yu (great dignitary
of the state of Wei) sent a man to Khoung-tseu to know
his news. Khoung-tseu caused the messenger to be seated
near him, and questioned him in these terms: What is
your master doing? The messenger answered with respect:
My master desires to diminish the number of his faults,
but he cannot come to the end of them. The messenger
being gone, the philosopher remarked: What a worthy
messenger! What a worthy messenger!" The preacher,
instead of vexing the ears of drowsy farmers on their day
of rest at the end of the week,—for Sunday is the fit conclusion of an ill-spent week, and not the fresh and brave
beginning of a new one,—with this one other draggletail
of a sermon, should shout with thundering voice,—"Pause!
Avast! Why so seeming fast, but deadly slow?"

Shams and delusions are esteemed for soundest truths,
while reality is fabulous. If men would steadily observe
realities only, and not allow themselves to be deluded,
life, to compare it with such things as we know, would be
like a fairy tale and the Arabian Nights' Entertainments.
If we respected only what is inevitable and has a right to
be, music and poetry would resound along the streets.
When we are unhurried and wise, we perceive that only
great and worthy things have any permanent and absolute
existence,—that petty fears and petty pleasures are but
the shadow of the reality. This is always exhilarating and
sublime. By closing the eyes and slumbering, and consent-
ing to be deceived by shows, men establish and confirm
their daily life of routine and habit everywhere, which still

is built on purely illusory foundations. Children, who play life, discern its true law and relations more clearly than men, who fail to live it worthily, but who think that they are wiser by experience, that is, by failure. I have read in a Hindoo book that "There was a king's son, who, being expelled in infancy from his native city, was brought up by a forester, and, growing up to maturity in that state, imagined himself to belong to the barbarous race with which he lived. One of his father's ministers having discovered him, revealed to him what he was, and the misconception of his character was removed, and he knew himself to be a prince. So soul," continues the Hindoo philosopher, "from the circumstances in which it is placed, mistakes its own character, until the truth is revealed to it by some holy teacher, and then it knows itself to be *Brahme*." I perceive that we inhabitants of New England live this mean life that we do because our vision does not penetrate the surface of things. We think that that *is* which *appears* to be. If a man should walk through this town and see only the reality, where, think you, would the "Mill-dam" go to? If he should give us an account of the realities he beheld there, we should not recognize the place in his description. Look at a meeting-house, or a court-house, or a jail, or a shop, or a dwelling-house, and say what that thing really is before a true gaze, and they would all go to pieces in your account of them. Men esteem truth remote, in the outskirts of the system, behind the farthest star, before Adam and after the last man. In eternity there is indeed something true and sublime. But all these times and places and occasions are now and here. God Himself culminates in the present moment, and will never be more divine in the lapse of all the ages. And we are enabled to apprehend at all what is sublime and noble only by the perpetual instilling and drenching of the reality that surrounds us. The universe constantly and obediently answers to our conceptions; whether we travel fast or slow, the track is laid for us. Let us spend our lives in conceiving then. The poet or the artist never yet had so fair and noble a design but some of his posterity at least could accomplish it.

Let us spend one day as deliberately as Nature, and not be thrown off the track by every nutshell and mosquito's wing that falls on the rails. Let us rise early and fast, or break fast, gently and without perturbation; let company come and let company go, let the bells ring and the children cry,—determined to make a day of it. Why should we knock under and go with the stream? Let us not be upset and overwhelmed in that terrible rapid and whirlpool called a dinner, situated in the meridian shallows. Weather this danger and you are safe, for the rest of the way is down hill. With unrelaxed nerves, with morning vigor, sail by it, looking another way, tied to the mast like Ulysses. If the engine whistles, let it whistle till it is hoarse for its pains. If the bell rings, why should we run? We will consider what kind of music they are like. Let us settle ourselves, and work and wedge our feet downward through the mud and slush of opinion and prejudice, and tradition, and delusion and appearance, that alluvion which covers the globe, through Paris and London, through New York and Boston and Concord, through church and state, through poetry and philosophy and religion, till we come to a hard bottom and rocks in place, which we can call *reality*, and say, This is, and no mistake; and then begin, having a *point d'appui*, below freshet and frost and fire, a place where you might found a wall or a state, or set a lamp-post safely, or perhaps a gauge, not a Nilometer, but a Realometer, that future ages might know how deep a freshet of shams and appearances had gathered from time to time. If you stand right fronting and face to face to a fact, you will see the sun glimmer on both its surfaces, as if it were a cimeter, and feel its sweet edge dividing you through the heart and marrow, and so you will happily conclude your mortal career. Be it life or death, we crave only reality. If we are really dying, let us hear the rattle in our throats and feel cold in the extremities; if we are alive, let us go about our business.

Time is but the stream I go a-fishing in. I drink at it; but while I drink I see the sandy bottom and detect how shallow it is. Its thin current slides away, but eternity remains. I would drink deeper; fish in the sky, whose bottom is pebbly with stars. I cannot count one. I know not the first letter of the alphabet, I have always been regretting that I was not as wise as the day I was born. The intellect is a cleaver; it discerns and rifts its way into the secret of things. I do not wish to be any more busy with my hands than is necessary. My head is hands and feet. I feel all my best faculties concentrated in it. My instinct tells me that my head is an organ for burrowing, as some creatures use their snout and fore-paws, and with it I would mine and burrow my way through these hills. I think that the richest vein is somewhere hereabouts; so by the divining rod and thin rising vapors I judge; and here I will begin to mine.

1854

Oliver Wendell Holmes

THE AUTOCRAT
OF THE BREAKFAST-TABLE

I WAS just going to say, when I was interrupted, that one of the many ways of classifying minds is under the heads of arithmetical and algebraical intellects. All economical and practical wisdom is an extension or variation of the following arithmetical formula: $2 + 2 = 4$. Every philosophical proposition has the more general character of the expression $a + b = c$. We are mere operatives, empirics, and egotists, until we learn to think in letters instead of figures.

They all stared. There is a divinity student lately come among us to whom I commonly address remarks like the above, allowing him to take a certain share in the conversation, so far as assent or pertinent questions are involved. He abused his liberty on this occasion by presuming to say that Leibnitz had the same observation.—No, sir, I replied, he has not. But he said a mighty good thing about mathematics, that sounds something like it, and you found it, *not in the original,* but quoted by Dr. Thomas Reid. I will tell the company what he did say, one of these days.

—If I belong to a Society of Mutual Admiration?—I blush to say that I do not at this present moment. I once did, however. It was the first association to which I ever heard the term applied; a body of scientific young men in a great foreign city who admired their teacher, and to some extent each other. Many of them deserved it; they have become famous since. It amuses me to hear the talk of one of those beings described by Thackeray—

Letters four do form his name—

about a social development which belongs to the very noblest stage of civilization. All generous companies of artists, authors, philanthropists, men of science, are, or ought to be, Societies of Mutual Admiration. A man of genius, or any kind of superiority, is not debarred from admiring the same quality in another, nor the other from returning his admiration. They may even associate together and continue to think highly of each other. And so of a dozen such men, if any one place is fortunate enough to hold so many. The being referred to above assumes several false premises. First, that men of talent necessarily hate each other. Secondly, that intimate knowledge or habitual association destroys our admiration of persons whom we esteemed highly at a distance. Thirdly, that a circle of clever fellows, who meet together to dine and have a good time, have signed a constitutional compact to glorify themselves and to put down him and the fraction of the human race not belonging to their number. Fourthly, that it is an outrage that he is not asked to join them.

Here the company laughed a good deal, and the old gentleman who sits opposite said: "That's it! that's it!"

I continued, for I was in the talking vein. As to clever people's hating each other, I think *a little* extra talent does sometimes make people jealous. They become irritated by perpetual attempts and failures, and it hurts their tempers and dispositions. Unpretending mediocrity is good, and genius is glorious; but a weak flavor of genius in an essentially common person is detestable. It spoils the grand neutrality of a commonplace character, as the rinsings of an unwashed wine-glass spoil a draught of fair water. No wonder the poor fellow we spoke of, who always belongs to this class of slightly flavored mediocrities, is puzzled and vexed by the strange sight of a dozen men of capacity working and playing together in harmony. He and his fellows are always fighting. With them familiarity naturally breeds contempt. If they ever praise each other's bad drawings, or broken-winded novels, or spavined verses, nobody ever supposed it was from admiration; it was simply a contract between themselves and a publisher or dealer.

If the Mutuals have really nothing among them worth admiring, that alters the question. But if they are men with noble powers and qualities, let me tell you that, next to youthful love and family affections, there is no human sentiment better than that which unites the Societies of Mutual Admiration. And what would literature or art be without such associations? Who can tell what we owe to the Mutual Admiration Society of which Shakespeare, and Ben Jonson, and Beaumont and Fletcher were members? Or to that of which Addison and Steele formed the centre, and which gave us the Spectator? Or to that where Johnson, and Goldsmith, and Burke, and Reynolds, and Beauclerk, and Boswell, most admiring among all admirers, met together? Was there any great harm in the fact that the Irvings and Paulding wrote in company? or any unpardonable cabal in the literary union of Verplanck and Bryant and Sands and as many more as they chose to associate with them?

The poor creature does not know what he is talking about when he abuses this noblest of institutions. Let him inspect its mysteries through the knot-hole he has secured, but not use that orifice as a medium for his pop-gun. Such a society is the crown of a literary metropolis; if a town has not material for it, and spirit and good feeling enough to organize it, it is a mere caravansary, fit for a man of genius to lodge in, but not to live in. Foolish people hate and dread and envy such an association of men of varied powers and influence, because it is lofty, serene, impregnable, and, by the necessity of the case, exclusive. Wise ones are prouder of the title M.S.M.A. than of all their other honors put together.

—All generous minds have a horror of what are commonly called "facts." They are the brute beasts of the intellectual domain. Who does not know fellows that always have an ill-conditioned fact or two which they lead after them into decent company like so many bull-dogs, ready to let them slip at every ingenious suggestion, or convenient generalization, or pleasant fancy? I allow no "facts" at this table. What! Because bread is good and wholesome, and necessary and nourishing, shall you thrust a crumb into my windpipe while I am talking? Do not these muscles of mine represent a hundred loaves of bread? and is not my thought the abstract of ten thousand of these crumbs of truth with which you would choke off my speech?

[The above remark must be conditioned and qualified for the vulgar mind. The reader will, of course, understand the precise amount of seasoning which must be added to it before he adopts it as one of the axioms of his life. The speaker disclaims all responsibility for its abuse in incompetent hands.]

This business of conversation is a very serious matter. There are men whom it weakens one to talk with an hour more than a day's fasting would do. Mark this which I am going to say, for it is as good as a working professional man's advice, and costs you nothing: It is better to lose a pint of blood from your veins than to have a nerve tapped. Nobody measures your nervous force as it runs away, nor bandages your brain and marrow after the operation.

There are men of *esprit* who are excessively exhausting to some people. They are the talkers who have what may be called *jerky* minds. Their thoughts do not run in the natural order of sequence. They say bright things on all possible subjects, but their zigzags rack you to death. After a jolting half-hour with one of these jerky companions, talking with a dull friend affords great relief. It is like taking the cat in your lap after holding a squirrel.

What a comfort a dull but kindly person is, to be sure, at times! A ground-glass shade over a gaslamp does not bring more solace to our dazzled eyes than such a one to our minds.

"Do not dull people bore you?" said one of the lady-boarders,—the same who sent me her autograph-book last week with a request for a few original stanzas, not remembering that "The Pactolian" pays me five dollars a line for everything I write in its columns.

"Madam," said I (she and the century were in their teens together), "all men are bores, except when we want them. There never was but one man whom I would trust with my latch-key."

"Who might that favored person be?"

"Zimmermann." *

—The men of genius that I fancy most, have erectile heads like the cobra-di-capello. You remember what they tell of William Pinkney, the great pleader; how in his eloquent paroxysms the veins of his neck would swell and his face flush and his eyes glitter, until he seemed on the verge of apoplexy. The hydraulic arrangements for supplying the brain with blood are only second in importance to its own organization. The bulbous-headed fellows who steam well when they are at work are the men that draw big audiences and give us marrowy books and pictures. It is a good sign to have one's feet grow cold when he is writing. A great writer and speaker once told me that he often wrote with his feet in hot water; but for this, *all* his

* The *Treatise on Solitude* is not so frequently seen lying about on library tables as in our younger days. I remember that I always respected the title and let the book alone.

blood would have run into his head, as the mercury some-times withdraws into the ball of a thermometer.

—You don't suppose that my remarks made at this table are like so many postage-stamps, do you,—each to be only once uttered? If you do, you are mistaken. He must be a poor creature who does not often repeat himself. Imagine the author of the excellent piece of advice, "Know thy-self," never alluding to that sentiment again during the course of a protracted existence! Why, the truths a man carries about with him are his tools; and do you think a carpenter is bound to use the same plane but once to smooth a knotty board with, or to hang up his hammer after it has driven its first nail? I shall never repeat a con-versation, but an idea often. I shall use the same types when I like, but not commonly the same stereotypes. A thought is often original, though you have uttered it a hundred times. It has come to you over a new route, by a new and express train of associations.

Sometimes, but rarely, one may be caught making the same speech twice over, and yet be held blameless. Thus, a certain lecturer, after performing in an inland city, where dwells a *Littératrice* of note, was invited to meet her and others over the social teacup. She pleasantly referred to his many wanderings in his new occupation. "Yes," he replied, "I am like the Huma,* the bird that never lights, being always in the cars, as he is always on the wing."— Years elapsed. The lecturer visited the same place once more for the same purpose. Another social cup after the lecture, and a second meeting with the distinguished lady. "You are constantly going from place to place," she said.

* It was an agreeable incident of two consecutive visits to Hart-ford, Conn., that I met there the late Mrs. Sigourney. The sec-ond meeting recalled the first, and with it the allusion to the Huma, which bird is the subject of a short poem by another New England authoress, which may be found in Mr. Griswold's collection.

—"Yes," he answered, "I am like the Huma,"—and finished the sentence as before.

What horrors, when it flashed over him that he had made this fine speech, word for word, twice over! Yet it was not true, as the lady might perhaps have fairly inferred, that he had embellished his conversation with the Huma daily during that whole interval of years. On the contrary he had never once thought of the odious fowl until the recurrence of precisely the same circumstances brought up precisely the same idea. He ought to have been proud of the accuracy of his mental adjustments. Given certain factors, and a sound brain should always evolve the same fixed product with the certainty of Babbage's calculating machine.

—What a satire, by the way, is that machine on the mere mathematician! A Frankenstein monster, a thing without brains and without heart, too stupid to make a blunder; which turns out results like a cornsheller, and never grows any wiser or better, though it grind a thousand bushels of them!

I have an immense respect for a man of talents *plus* "the mathematics." But the calculating power alone should seem to be the least human of qualities, and to have the smallest amount of reason in it; since a machine can be made to do the work of three or four calculators, and better than any one of them. Sometimes I have been troubled that I had not a deeper intuitive apprehension of the relations of numbers. But the triumph of the ciphering hand-organ has consoled me. I always fancy I can hear the wheels clicking in a calculator's brain. The power of dealing with numbers is a kind of "detached lever" arrangement, which may be put into a mighty poor watch. I suppose it is about as common as the power of moving the ears voluntarily, which is a moderately rare endowment.

—Little localized powers, and little narrow streaks of

specialized knowledge, are things men are very apt to be conceited about. Nature is very wise; but for this encouraging principle how many small talents and little accomplishments would be neglected! Talk about conceit as much as you like, it is to human character what salt is to the ocean; it keeps it sweet, and renders it endurable. Say rather it is like the natural unguent of the sea-fowl's plumage, which enables him to shed the rain that falls on him and the wave in which he dips. When one has had *all* his conceit taken out of him, when he has lost *all* his illusions, his feathers will soon soak through, and he will fly no more.

"So you admire conceited people, do you?" said the young lady who has come to the city to be finished off for —the duties of life.

I am afraid you do not study logic at your school, my dear. It does not follow that I wish to be pickled in brine because I like a salt-water plunge at Nahant. I say that conceit is just as natural a thing to human minds as a centre is to a circle. But little-minded people's thoughts move in such small circles that five minutes' conversation gives you an arc long enough to determine their whole curve. An arc in the movement of a large intellect does not soon betray it. The highest thought, that is, is the most seemingly impersonal; it does not obviously imply any individual centre.

Audacious self-esteem, with good ground for it, is always imposing. What resplendent beauty that must have been which could have authorized Phryne to "peel" in the way she did! What fine speeches are those two: *"Non omnis moriar,"* and "I have taken all knowledge to be my province"! Even in common people, conceit has the virtue of making them cheerful; the man who thinks his wife, his baby, his house, his horse, his dog, and himself severally unequalled, is almost sure to be a good-humored person, though liable to be tedious at times.

—What are the great faults of conversation? Want of ideas, want of words, want of manners, are the principal ones, I suppose you think. I don't doubt it, but I will tell you what I have found spoil more good talks than any-thing else;—long arguments on special points between people who differ on the fundamental principles upon which these points depend. No men can have satisfactory relations with each other until they have agreed on certain *ultimata* of belief not to be disturbed in ordinary conver-sation, and unless they have sense enough to trace the secondary questions depending upon these ultimate beliefs to their source. In short, just as a written constitution is essential to the best social order, so a code of finalities is a necessary condition of profitable talk between two persons. Talking is like playing on the harp; there is as much in laying the hand on the strings to stop their vibrations as in twanging them to bring out their music.

—Do you mean to say the pun-question is not clearly settled in your minds? Let me lay down the law upon the subject. Life and language are alike sacred. Homicide and *verbicide*—that is, violent treatment of a word with fatal results to its legitimate meaning, which is its life— are alike forbidden. Manslaughter, which is the meaning of the one, is the same as man's laughter, which is the end of the other. A pun is *primâ facie* an insult to the person you are talking with. It implies utter indifference to or sublime contempt for his remarks, no matter how serious. I speak of total depravity, and one says all that is written on the subject is deep raving. I have committed my self-respect by talking with such a person. I should like to commit him, but cannot, because he is a nuisance. Or I speak of geological convulsions, and he asks me what was the cosine of Noah's ark; also, whether the Deluge was not a deal huger than any modern inundation.

A pun does not commonly justify a blow in return. But if a blow were given for such cause, and death ensued, the jury would be judges both of the facts and of the pun, and might, if the latter were of an aggravated character, return a verdict of justifiable homicide. Thus, in a case lately decided before Miller, J., Doe presented Roe a subscription paper, and urged the claims of suffering humanity. Roe replied by asking, When charity was like a top? It was in evidence that Doe preserved a dignified silence. Roe then said, "When it begins to hum." Doe then—and not till then—struck Roe, and his head happening to hit a bound volume of the Monthly Rag-Bag and Stolen Miscellany, intense mortification ensued, with a fatal result. The chief laid down his notions of the law to his brother justices, who unanimously replied, "Jest so." The chief rejoined, that no man should jest so without being punished for it, and charged for the prisoner, who was acquitted, and the pun ordered to be burned by the sheriff. The bound volume was forfeited as a deodand, but not claimed.

People that make puns are like wanton boys that put coppers on the railroad tracks. They amuse themselves and other children, but their little trick may upset a freight train of conversation for the sake of a battered witticism.

I will thank you, B. F., to bring down two books, of which I will mark the places on this slip of paper. (While he is gone, I may say that this boy, our landlady's youngest, is called BENJAMIN FRANKLIN, after the celebrated philosopher of that name. A highly merited compliment.)

I wished to refer to two eminent authorities. Now be so good as to listen. The great moralist says: "To trifle with the vocabulary which is the vehicle of social intercourse is to tamper with the currency of human intelligence. He who would violate the sanctities of his mother tongue would invade the recesses of the paternal till without remorse, and repeat the banquet of Saturn without an indigestion."

And, once more, listen to the historian. "The Puritans hated puns. The Bishops were notoriously addicted to them. The Lords Temporal carried them to the verge of license. Majesty itself must have its Royal quibble. 'Ye be burly, my Lord of Burleigh,' said Queen Elizabeth, 'but ye shall make less stir in our realm than my Lord of Leicester.' The gravest wisdom and the highest breeding lent their sanction to the practice. Lord Bacon playfully declared himself a descendant of 'Og, the King of Bashan.' Sir Philip Sidney, with his last breath, reproached the soldier who brought him water, for wasting a casque full upon a dying man. A courtier, who saw Othello performed at the Globe Theatre, remarked, that the blackamoor was a brute, and not a man. 'Thou hast reason,' replied a great Lord, 'according to Plato his saying; for this be a two-legged animal *with* feathers.' The fatal habit became universal. The language was corrupted. The infection spread to the national conscience. Political double-dealings naturally grew out of verbal double meanings. The teeth of the new dragon were sown by the Cadmus who introduced the alphabet of equivocation. What was levity in the time of the Tudors grew to regicide and revolution in the age of the Stuarts."

Who was that boarder that just whispered something about the Macaulay-flowers of literature?—There was a dead silence.—I said calmly, I shall henceforth consider any interruption by a pun as a hint to change my boarding-house. Do not plead my example. If I have used any such, it has been only as a Spartan father would show up a drunken helot. We have done with them.

—If a logical mind ever found out anything with its logic?—I should say that its most frequent work was to build a *pons asinorum* over chasms which shrewd people can bestride without such a structure. You can hire logic, in the shape of a lawyer, to prove anything that you want to prove. You can buy treatises to show that Napoleon never lived, and that no battle of Bunker-hill was ever fought. The great minds are those with a wide span, which couple truths related to, but far removed from, each other. Logicians carry the surveyor's chain over the track of which these are the true explorers. I value a man mainly for his primary relations with truth, as I understand truth,—not for any secondary artifice in handling his ideas. Some of the sharpest men in argument are notoriously unsound in judgment. I should not trust the counsel of a clever debater, any more than that of a good chess-player. Either may of course advise wisely, but not necessarily because he wrangles or plays well.

The old gentleman who sits opposite got his hand up, as a pointer lifts his forefoot, at the expression, "his relations with truth, as I understand truth," and when I had done, sniffed audibly, and said I talked like a transcendentalist. For his part, common sense was good enough for him.

Precisely so, my dear sir, I replied; common sense, *as you understand it*. We all have to assume a standard of judgment in our own minds, either of things or persons. A man who is willing to take another's opinion has to exercise his judgment in the choice of whom to follow, which is often as nice a matter as to judge of things for one's self. On the whole, I had rather judge men's minds by comparing their thoughts with my own, than judge of thoughts by knowing who utter them. I must do one or the other. It does not follow, of course, that I may not recognize another man's thoughts as broader and deeper than my own; but that does not necessarily change my opinion, otherwise this would be at the mercy of every superior mind that held a different one. How many of our most cherished beliefs are like those drinking-glasses of the ancient pattern, that serve us well so long as we keep them in our hand, but spill all if we attempt to set them down! I have sometimes compared conversation to the

Italian game of *mora,* in which one player lifts his hand with so many fingers extended, and the other gives the number if he can. I show my thought, another his, if they agree, well; if they differ, we find the largest common factor, if we can, but at any rate avoid disputing about remainders and fractions, which is to real talk what tuning an instrument is to playing on it.

—What if, instead of talking this morning, I should read you a copy of verses, with critical remarks by the author? Any of the company can retire that like.

ALBUM VERSES

When Eve had led her lord away,
  And Cain had killed his brother,
The stars and flowers, the poets say,
  Agreed with one another.

To cheat the cunning tempter's art,
  And teach the race its duty,
By keeping on its wicked heart
  Their eyes of light and beauty.

A million sleepless lids, they say,
  Will be at least a warning;
And so the flowers would watch by day,
  The stars from eve to morning.

On hill and prairie, field and lawn,
  Their dewy eyes upturning,
The flowers still watch from reddening dawn
  Till western skies are burning.

Alas! each hour of daylight tells
  A tale of shame so crushing,
That some turn white as sea-bleached shells,
  And some are always blushing.

But when the patient stars look down
   On all their light discovers,
The traitor's smile, the murderer's frown,
   The lips of lying lovers,

They try to shut their saddening eyes,
   And in the vain endeavor
We see them twinkling in the skies,
   And so they wink forever.

What do *you* think of these verses, my friends?—Is that piece an impromptu? said my landlady's daughter. (Aet. 19+. Tender-eyed blond. Long ringlets. Cameo pin. Gold pencil-case on a chain. Locket. Bracelet. Album. Autograph book. Accordeon. Reads Byron, Tupper, and Sylvanus Cobb, Junior, while her mother makes the puddings. Says "Yes?" when you tell her anything.)—*Oui et non, ma petite,*—Yes and no, my child. Five of the seven verses were written off-hand; the other two took a week, —that is, were hanging round the desk in a ragged, forlorn, unrhymed condition as long as that. All poets will tell you just such stories. *C'est le* DERNIER *pas qui coute.* Don't you know how hard it is for some people to get out of a room after their visit is really over? They want to be off, and you want to have them off, but they don't know how to manage it. One would think they had been built in your parlor or study, and were waiting to be launched. I have contrived a sort of ceremonial inclined plane for such visitors, which being lubricated with certain smooth phrases, I back them down, metaphorically speaking, stern-foremost, into their "native element," the great ocean of out-doors. Well, now, there are poems as hard to get rid of as these rural visitors. They come in glibly, use up all the serviceable rhymes, *day, ray, beauty, duty, skies, eyes, other, brother, mountain, fountain,* and the like; and so they go on until you think it is time for the wind-up, and the wind-up won't come on any terms. So they lie about until you get sick of the sight of them, and end by thrusting some cold scrap of a final couplet upon them, and turning them out of doors. I suspect a good many "impromptus" could tell just such a story as the above.—Here turning to our landlady I used an illustration which pleased the company much at the time, and has since been highly commended. "Madam," I said, "you can pour three gills and three quarters of honey from that pint jug, if it is full, in less than one minute; but, Madam, you could not empty that last quarter of a gill, though you were turned into a marble Hebe, and held the vessel upside down for a thousand years."

One gets tired to death of the old, old rhymes, such as you see in that copy of verses,—which I don't mean to abuse, or to praise either. I always feel as if I were a cobbler, putting new top-leathers to an old pair of boot-soles and bodies, when I am fitting sentiments to these venerable jingles.

. . . . youth
. . . . morning
. . . . truth
. . . . warning

Nine tenths of the "Juvenile Poems" written spring out of the above musical and suggestive coincidences.

"Yes?" said our landlady's daughter.

I did not address the following remark to her, and I trust, from her limited range of reading, she will never see it; I said it softly to my next neighbor.

When a young female wears a flat circular sidecurl, gummed on each temple,—when she walks with a male, not arm in arm, but his arm against the back of hers,—and when she says "Yes?" with the note of interrogation, you are generally safe in asking her what wages she gets, and who the "feller" was you saw her with.

"What were you whispering?" said the daughter of the house, moistening her lips, as she spoke, in a very engaging manner.

"I was only laying down a principle of social diagnosis."

"Yes?"

—It is curious to see how the same wants and tastes find the same implements and modes of expression in all times and places. The young ladies of Otaheite, as you may see in Cook's Voyages, had a sort of crinoline arrangement fully equal in radius to the largest spread of our own lady-baskets. When I fling a Bay-State shawl over my shoulders, I am only taking a lesson from the climate which the Indian had learned before me. A blanket-shawl we call it, and not a plaid; and we wear it like the aborigines, and not like the Highlanders.

—We are the Romans of the modern world,—the great assimilating people. Conflicts and conquests are of course necessary accidents with us, as with our prototypes. And so we come to their style of weapon. Our army sword is the short, stiff, pointed *gladius* of the Romans; and the American bowie-knife is the same tool, modified to meet the daily wants of civil society. I announce at this table an axiom not to be found in Montesquieu or the journals of Congress:—

The race that shortens its weapons lengthens its boundaries.

Corollary. It was the Polish *lance* that left Poland at last with nothing of her own to bound.

Dropped from her nerveless grasp the *shattered spear!*

What business had Sarmatia to be fighting for liberty with a fifteen-foot pole between her and the breasts of her enemies? If she had but clutched the old Roman and young American weapon, and come to close quarters, there might have been a chance for her; but it would have spoiled the best passage in "The Pleasures of Hope."

—Self-made men?—Well, yes. Of course every body likes and respects self-made men. It is a great deal better to be made in that way than not to be made at all. Are any of you younger people old enough to remember that Irishman's house on the marsh at Cambridgeport, which house he built from drain to chimney-top with his own hands? It took him a good many years to build it, and one could see that it was a little out of plumb, and a little wavy in outline, and a little queer and uncertain in general aspect. A regular hand could certainly have built a better house; but it was a very good house for a "self-made" carpenter's house, and people praised it, and said how remarkably well the Irishman had succeeded. They never thought of praising the fine blocks of houses a little farther on.

Your self-made man, whittled into shape with his own jack-knife, deserves more credit, if that is all, than the regular engine-turned article, shaped by the most approved pattern, and French-polished by society and travel. But as to saying that one is every way the equal of the other, that is another matter. The right of strict social discrimination of all things and persons, according to their merits, native or acquired, is one of the most precious republican privileges. I take the liberty to exercise it when I say that, *other things being equal,* in most relations of life I prefer a man of family.

What do I mean by a man of family?—O, I'll give you a general idea of what I mean. Let us give him a first-rate fit out; it costs us nothing.

Four or five generations of gentlemen and gentlewomen; among them a member of his Majesty's Council for the Province, a Governor or so, one or two Doctors of Divinity, a member of Congress, not later than the time of long boots with tassels.

Family portraits. The member of the Council, by Smibert. The great merchant-uncle, by Copley, full

length, sitting in his arm-chair, in a velvet cap and flowered
robe, with a globe by him, to show the range of his commercial transactions, and letters with large red seals lying
round, one directed conspicuously to The Honorable, etc.,
etc. Great-grandmother by the same artist; brown satin,
lace very fine, hands superlative; grand old lady, stiffish,
but imposing. Her mother, artist unknown; flat, angular,
hanging sleeves; parrot on fist. A pair of Stuarts, viz., 1. A
superb, full-blown, mediaeval gentleman, with a fiery dash
of Tory blood in his veins, tempered down with that of a
fine old rebel grandmother, and warmed up with the best
of old India Madeira; his face is one flame of ruddy sunshine; his ruffled shirt rushes out of his bosom with an
impetuous generosity, as if it would drag his heart after
it; and his smile is good for twenty thousand dollars to
the Hospital, besides ample bequests to all relatives and
dependants. 2. Lady of the same; remarkable cap; high
waist, as in time of Empire; bust *à la Josephine;* wisps of
curls, like celery-tips, at sides of forehead; complexion
clear and warm, like rose-cordial. As for the miniatures
by Malbone, we don't count them in the gallery.

Books, too, with the names of old college-students in
them,—family names;—you will find them at the head of
their respective classes in the days when students took rank
on the catalogue from their parents' condition. Elzevirs,
with the Latinized appellations of youthful progenitors,
and *Hic liber est meus* on the title-page. A set of Hogarth's
original plates. Pope, original edition, 15 volumes, London,
1717. Barrow on the lower shelves, in folio. Tillotson on
the upper, in a little dark platoon of octo-decimos.

Some family silver; a string of wedding and funeral
rings; the arms of the family curiously blazoned; the same
in worsted, by a maiden aunt.

If the man of family has an old place to keep these
things in, furnished with claw-footed chairs and black

mahogany tables, and tall bevel-edged mirrors, and stately upright cabinets, his outfit is complete.

No, my friends, I go (always, other things being equal) for the man who inherits family traditions and the cumulative humanities of at least four or five generations. Above all things, as a child, he should have tumbled about in a library. All men are afraid of books, who have not handled them from infancy. Do you suppose our dear *didascalos* * over there ever read *Poli Synopsis,* or consulted *Castelli Lexicon,* while he was growing up to their stature? Not he; but virtue passed through the hem of their parchment and leather garments whenever he touched them, as the precious drugs sweated through the bat's handle in the Arabian story. I tell you he is at home wherever he smells the invigorating fragrance of Russia leather. No self-made man feels so. One may, it is true, have all the antecedents I have spoken of, and yet be a boor or a shabby-fellow. One may have none of them, and yet be fit for councils and courts. Then let them change places. Our social arrangement has this great beauty, that its strata shift up and down as they change specific gravity, without being clogged by layers of prescription. But I still insist on my democratic liberty of choice, and I go for the man with the gallery of family portraits against the one with the twenty-five-cent daguerreotype, unless I find out that the last is the better of the two.

1857

* "Our dear *didascalos*" was meant for Professor James Russell Lowell, now Minister to England. It requires the union of exceptional native gifts and generations of training to bring the "natural man" of New England to the completeness of scholarly manhood, such as that which adds new distinction to the name he bears, already remarkable for its successive generations of eminent citizens.

"Self-made" is imperfectly made, or education is a superfluity and a failure.

Ralph Waldo Emerson

ILLUSIONS

SOME years ago, in company with an agreeable party, I spent a long summer day in exploring the Mammoth Cave in Kentucky. We traversed, through spacious galleries affording a solid masonry foundation for the town and county overhead, the six or eight black miles from the mouth of the cavern to the innermost recess which tourists visit,—a niche or grotto made of one seamless stalactite, and called, I believe, Serena's Bower. I lost the light of one day. I saw high domes and bottomless pits; heard the voice of unseen waterfalls; paddled three quarters of a mile in the deep Echo River, whose waters are peopled with the blind fish; crossed the streams "Lethe" and "Styx"; plied with music and guns the echoes in these alarming galleries; saw every form of stalagmite and stalactite in the sculptured and fretted chambers;—icicle, orange-flower, acanthus, grapes and snowball. We shot Bengal lights into the vaults and groins of the sparry cathedrals and examined all the masterpieces which the four combined engineers, water, limestone, gravitation and time, could make in the dark.

The mysteries and scenery of the cave had the same dignity that belongs to all natural objects, and which shames the fine things to which we foppishly compare them. I remarked especially the mimetic habit with which nature, on new instruments, hums her old tunes, making night to mimic day, and chemistry to ape vegetation. But I then took notice and still chiefly remember that the best thing which the cave had to offer was an illusion. On arriving at what is called the "Star-Chamber," our lamps were taken from us by the guide and extinguished or put aside, and, on looking upwards, I saw or seemed to see the night heaven thick with stars glimmering more or less brightly over our heads, and even what seemed a comet flaming among them. All the party were touched with astonishment and pleasure. Our musical friends sung with much feeling a pretty song, "The stars are in the quiet sky," etc., and I sat down on the rocky floor to enjoy the serene picture. Some crystal specks in the black ceiling high overhead, reflecting the light of a half-hid lamp, yielded this magnificent effect.

I own I did not like the cave so well for eking out its sublimities with this theatrical trick. But I have had many experiences like it, before and since; and we must be content to be pleased without too curiously analyzing the occasions. Our conversation with nature is not just what it seems. The cloud-rack, the sunrise and sunset glories, rainbows and Northern Lights are not quite so spheral as our childhood thought them, and the part our organization plays in them is too large. The senses interfere everywhere and mix their own structure with all they report of. Once we fancied the earth a plane, and stationary. In admiring the sunset we do not yet deduct the rounding, coördinating, pictorial powers of the eye.

The same interference from our organization creates the most of our pleasure and pain. Our first mistake is the belief that the circumstance gives the joy which we give to the circumstance. Life is an ecstasy. Life is sweet as nitrous oxide; and the fisherman dripping all day over a cold pond, the switchman at the railway intersection, the farmer in the field, the Negro in the rice-swamp, the fop in the street, the hunter in the woods, the barrister with

the jury, the belle at the ball, all ascribe a certain pleasure
to their employment, which they themselves give it.
Health and appetite impart the sweetness to sugar, bread
and meat. We fancy that our civilization has got on far,
but we still come back to our primers.

We live by our imaginations, by our admirations, by
our sentiments. The child walks amid heaps of illusions,
which he does not like to have disturbed. The boy, how
sweet to him is his fancy! how dear the story of barons
and battles! What a hero he is, whilst he feeds on his
heroes! What a debt is his to imaginative books! He has
no better friend or influence than Scott, Shakespeare, Plu-
tarch, and Homer. The man lives to other objects, but
who dare affirm that they are more real? Even the prose
of the streets is full of refractions. In the life of the dreariest
alderman, fancy enters into all details and colours them
with rosy hue. He imitates the air and actions of people
whom he admires, and is raised in his own eyes. He pays
a debt quicker to a rich man than to a poor man. He wishes
the bow and compliment of some leader in the state or in
society; weighs what he says; perhaps he never comes
nearer to him for that, but dies at last better contented
for this amusement of his eyes and his fancy.

The world rolls, the din of life is never hushed. In
London, in Paris, in Boston, in San Francisco, the carnival,
the masquerade is at its height. Nobody drops his domino.
The unities, the fictions of the piece it would be an impertinence to break. The chapter of fascinations is very
long. Great is paint; nay, God is the painter; and we
rightly accuse the critic who destroys too many illusions.
Society does not love its unmaskers. It was wittily if somewhat bitterly said by D'Alembert, *"qu'un état de vapeur
était un état très fâcheux, parcequ'il nous faisait voir les
choses comme elles sont."* I find men victims of illusion
in all parts of life. Children, youths, adults and old men,
all are led by one bauble or another. Yoganidra, the god-

dess of illusion, Proteus, or Momus, or Gylfi's Mocking, —for the Power has many names,—is stronger than the Titans, stronger than Apollo. Few have overheard the gods or surprised their secret. Life is a succession of lessons which must be lived to be understood. All is riddle, and the key to a riddle is another riddle. There are as many pillows of illusion as flakes in a snow-storm. We wake from one dream into another dream. The toys to be sure are various, and are graduated in refinement to the quality of the dupe. The intellectual man requires a fine bait; the sots are easily amused. But everybody is drugged with his own frenzy, and the pageant marches at all hours, with music and banner and badge.

Amid the joyous troop who give in to the charivari, comes now and then a sad-eyed boy whose eyes lack the requisite refractions to clothe the show in due glory, and who is afflicted with a tendency to trace home the glittering miscellany of fruits and flowers to one root. Science is a search after identity, and the scientific whim is lurking in all corners. At the State Fair a friend of mine complained that all the varieties of fancy pears in our orchards seem to have been selected by somebody who had a whim for a particular kind of pear, and only cultivated such as had that perfume; they were all alike. And I remember the quarrel of another youth with the confectioners, that when he racked his wit to choose the best comfits in the shops, in all the endless varieties of sweetmeat he could find only three flavors, or two. What then? Pears and cakes are good for something; and because you unluckily have an eye or nose too keen, why need you spoil the comfort which the rest of us find in them? I knew a humorist who in a good deal of rattle had a grain or two of sense. He shocked the company by maintaining that the attributes of God were two,—power and risibility,—and that it was the duty of every pious man to keep up the comedy. And I have known gentlemen of great stake in the community, but whose sympathies were cold,—presidents of colleges and governors and senators,—who held themselves bound to sign every temperance pledge, and act with Bible societies and missions and peace-makers, and cry *Hist-a-boy!* to every good dog. We must not carry comity too far, but we all have kind impulses in this direction. When the boys come into my yard for leave to gather horse-chestnuts, I own I enter into nature's game and affect to grant the permission reluctantly, fearing that any moment they will find out the imposture of that showy chaff. But this tenderness is quite unnecessary; the enchantments are laid on very thick. Their young life is thatched with them. Bare and grim to tears is the lot of the children in the hovel I saw yesterday; yet not the less they hung it round with frippery romance, like the children of the happiest fortune, and talked of "the dear cottage where so many joyful hours had flown." Well, this thatching of hovels is the custom of the country. Women, more than all, are the element and kingdom of illusion. Being fascinated, they fascinate. They see through Claude-Lorraines. And how dare any one, if he could, pluck away the *coulisses,* stage effects and ceremonies, by which they live? Too pathetic, too pitiable, is the region of affection, and its atmosphere always liable to *mirage.*

We are not very much to blame for our bad marriages. We live amid hallucinations; and this especial trap is laid to trip up our feet with, and all are tripped up first or last. But the mighty Mother who had been so sly with us, as if she felt that she owed us some indemnity, insinuates into the Pandora-box of marriage some deep and serious benefits and some great joys. We find delight in the beauty and happiness of children that makes the heart too big for the body. In the worst-assorted connections there is ever some mixture of true marriage. Teague and his jade get some just relations of mutual respect, kindly observation, and fostering of each other; learn something, and would carry themselves wiselier if they were now to begin.

'Tis fine for us to point at one or another fine madman, as if there were any exempts. The scholar in his library is none. I, who have all my life heard any number of orations and debates, read poems and miscellaneous books, conversed with many geniuses, am still the victim of any new page; and if Marmaduke, or Hugh, or Moosehead, or any other, invent a new style of mythology, I fancy that the world will be all brave and right if dressed in these colours, which I had not thought of. Then at once I will daub with this new paint; but it will not stick. 'Tis like the cement which the peddler sells at the door; he makes broken crockery hold with it, but you can never buy of him a bit of the cement which will make it hold when he is gone.

Men who make themselves felt in the world avail themselves of a certain fate in their constitution which they know how to use. But they never deeply interest us unless they lift a corner of the curtain, or betray, never so slightly, their penetration of what is behind it. 'Tis the charm of practical men that outside of their practicality are a certain poetry and play, as if they led the good horse Power by the bridle, and preferred to walk, though they can ride so fiercely. Bonaparte is intellectual, as well as Caesar; and the best soldiers, sea-captains and railway men have a gentleness when off duty, a good-natured admission that there are illusions, and who shall say that he is not their sport? We stigmatize the cast-iron fellows who cannot so detach themselves, as "dragon-ridden," "thunder-stricken," and fools of fate, with whatever powers endowed.

Since our tuition is through emblems and indirections, it is well to know that there is method in it, a fixed scale and rank above rank in the phantasms. We begin low with coarse masks and rise to the most subtle and beautiful. The red men told Columbus "they had an herb which took away fatigue;" but he found the illusion of "arriving from the east at the Indies" more composing to his lofty spirit than any tobacco. Is not our faith in the impenetrability of matter more sedative than narcotics? You play with jackstraws, balls, bowls, horse and gun, estates and politics; but there are finer games before you. Is not time a pretty toy? Life will show you masks that are worth all your carnivals. Yonder mountain must migrate into your mind. The fine star-dust and nebulous blur in Orion, "the portentous year of Mizar and Alcor," must come down and be dealt with in your household thought. What if you shall come to discern that the play and playground of all this pompous history are radiations from yourself, and that the sun borrows his beams? What terrible questions we are learning to ask! The former men believed in magic, by which temples, cities and men were swallowed up, and all trace of them gone. We are coming on the secret of a magic which sweeps out of men's minds all vestige of theism and beliefs which they and their fathers held and were framed upon.

There are deceptions of the senses, deceptions of the passions, and the structural, beneficent illusions of sentiment and of the intellect. There is the illusion of love, which attributes to the beloved person all which that person shares with his or her family, sex, age or condition, nay, with the human mind itself. 'Tis these which the lover loves, and Anna Matilda gets the credit of them. As if one shut up always in a tower, with one window through which the face of heaven and earth could be seen, should fancy that all the marvels he beheld belonged to that window. There is the illusion of time, which is very deep; who has disposed of it?—or come to the conviction that what seems the *succession* of thought is only the distribution of wholes into casual series? The intellect sees that every atom carries the whole of nature; that the mind opens to omnipotence; that, in the endless striving and ascents, the metamorphosis is entire, so that the soul doth not know itself in its own act when that act is perfected. There is illusion that shall deceive even the elect. There is illusion that shall deceive even the performer of the miracle. Though he make his body, he denies that he makes it. Though the world exist from thought, thought is daunted in presence of the world. One after the other we accept the mental laws, still resisting those which follow, which however must be accepted. But all our concessions only compel us to new profusion. And what avails it that science has come to treat space and time as simply forms of thought, and the material world as hypothetical, and withal our pretension of *property* and even of self-hood are fading with the rest, if, at the last, even our thoughts are not finalities, but the incessant flowing and ascension reach these also, and each thought which yesterday was a finality, today is yielding to a larger generalization?

With such volatile elements to work in, 'tis no wonder if our estimates are loose and floating. We must work and affirm, but we have no guess of the value of what we say or do. The cloud is now as big as your hand, and now it covers a county. That story of Thor, who was set to drain the drinking-horn in Asgard and to wrestle with the old woman and to run with the runner Lok, and presently found that he had been drinking up the sea, and wrestling with Time, and racing with Thought,—describes us, who are contending, amid these seeming trifles, with the supreme energies of nature. We fancy we have fallen into bad company and squalid condition, low debts, shoe-bills, broken glass to pay for, pots to buy, butcher's meat, sugar, milk and coal. "Set me some great task, ye gods! and I will show my spirit." "Not so," says the good Heaven; "plod and plough, vamp your old coats and hats, weave a shoestring; great affairs and the best wine by and by." Well, 'tis all phantasm; and if we weave a yard of tape in all humility and as well as we can, long hereafter we shall see it was no cotton tape at all but some galaxy which we braided, and that the threads were Time and Nature.

We cannot write the order of the variable winds. How can we penetrate the law of our shifting moods and susceptibility? Yet they differ as all and nothing. Instead of the firmament of yesterday, which our eyes require, it is today an egg-shell which coops us in; we cannot even see what or where our stars of destiny are. From day to day the capital facts of human life are hidden from our eyes. Suddenly the mist rolls up and reveals them, and we think how much good time is gone that might have been saved had any hint of these things been shown. A sudden rise in the road shows us the system of mountains, and all the summits, which have been just as near us all the year, but quite out of mind. But these alternations are not without their order, and we are parties to our various fortune. If life seem a succession of dreams, yet poetic justice is done in dreams also. The visions of good men are good; it is the undisciplined will that is whipped with bad thoughts and bad fortunes. When we break the laws, we lose our hold on the central reality. Like sick men in hospitals, we change only from bed to bed, from one folly to another; and it cannot signify much what becomes of such castaways, wailing, stupid, comatose creatures, lifted from bed to bed, from the nothing of life to the nothing of death.

In this kingdom of illusions we grope eagerly for stays and foundations. There is none but a strict and faithful dealing at home and a severe barring out of all duplicity or illusion there. Whatever games are played with us, we must play no games with ourselves, but deal in our privacy with the last honesty and truth. I look upon the simple and childish virtues of veracity and honesty as the root of all that is sublime in character. Speak as you think, be what you are, pay your debts of all kinds. I prefer to be owned as sound and solvent, and my word as good as my bond, and to be what cannot be skipped, or dissipated, or undermined, to all the *éclat* in the universe. This reality is the foundation of friendship, religion, poetry and art. At the top or at the bottom of all illusions, I set the cheat which still leads us to work and live for appearances; in spite of our conviction, in all sane hours, that it is what we really are that avails with friends, with strangers, and with fate or fortune.

One would think from the talk of men that riches and poverty were a great matter; and our civilization mainly respects it. But the Indians say that they do not think the white man, with his brow of care, always toiling, afraid of heat and cold, and keeping within doors, has any advantage of them. The permanent interest of every man is never to be in a false position, but to have the weight of nature to back him in all that he does. Riches and poverty are a thick or thin costume; and our life—the life of all of us—identical. For we transcend the circumstance continually and taste the real quality of existence; as in our employments, which only differ in the manifestations but express the same laws; or in our thoughts, which wear no silks and taste no ice-creams. We see God face to face every hour, and know the savor of nature.

The early Greek philosophers Heraclitus and Xenophanes measured their force on this problem of identity. Diogenes of Apollonia said that unless the atoms were made of one stuff, they could never blend and act with one another. But the Hindoos, in their sacred writings, express the liveliest feeling, both of the essential identity and of that illusion which they conceive variety to be. "The notions, '*I am*,' and '*This is mine*,' which influence mankind, are but delusions of the mother of the world. Dispel, O Lord of all creatures! the conceit of knowledge which proceeds from ignorance." And the beatitude of man they hold to lie in being freed from fascination.

The intellect is stimulated by the statement of truth in

a trope, and the will by clothing the laws of life in illusions. But the unities of Truth and of Right are not broken by the disguise. There need never be any confusion in these. In a crowded life of many parts and performers, on a stage of nations, or in the obscurest hamlet in Maine or California, the same elements offer the same choices to each new comer, and, according to his election, he fixes his fortune in absolute Nature. It would be hard to put more mental and moral philosophy than the Persians have thrown into a sentence,—

> Fooled thou must be, though wisest of the wise:
> Then be the fool of virtue, not of vice.

There is no chance and no anarchy in the universe. All is system and gradation. Every god is there sitting in his sphere. The young mortal enters the hall of the firmament; there is he alone with them alone, they pouring on him benedictions and gifts, and beckoning him up to their thrones. On the instant, and incessantly, fall snow-storms of illusions. He fancies himself in a vast crowd which sways this way and that and whose movement and doings he must obey: he fancies himself poor, orphaned, insignificant. The mad crowd drives hither and thither, now furiously commanding this thing to be done, now that. What is he that he should resist their will, and think or act for himself? Every moment new changes and new showers of deceptions to baffle and distract him. And when, by and by, for an instant, the air clears and the cloud lifts a little, there are the gods still sitting around him on their thrones,—they alone with him alone.

1860

Walter Bagehot

LADY MARY WORTLEY MONTAGU

NOTHING is so transitory as second-class fame. The name of Lady Mary Wortley Montagu is hardly known to the great mass of ordinary English readers. A generation has arisen which has had time to forget her. Yet only a few years since, an allusion to the "Lady Mary" would have been easily understood by every well-informed person; young ladies were enjoined to form their style upon hers; and no one could have anticipated that her letters would seem in 1862 as different from what a lady of rank would then write or publish as if they had been written in the times of paganism. The very change, however, of popular taste and popular morality gives these letters now a kind of interest. The farther and the more rapidly we have drifted from where we once lay, the more do we wish to learn what kind of port it was. We venture, therefore, to recommend the letters of Lady Mary Wortley Montagu as an instructive and profitable study, not indeed to the youngest of young ladies, but to those maturer persons of either sex "who have taken all knowledge to be their province," and who have commenced their reading in "universality" by an assiduous perusal of Parisian fiction.

It is, we admit, true that these letters are not at the present day very agreeable reading. What our grandfathers and grandmothers thought of them it is not so easy to say. But it now seems clear that Lady Mary was that most miserable of human beings, an ambitious and wasted woman; that she brought a very cultivated intellect into a very cultivated society; that she gave to that society what it was most anxious to receive, and received from it all which it had to bestow;—and yet that this all was to her as nothing. The high intellectual world of England has never been so compact, so visible in a certain sense, so enjoyable, as it was in her time. She had a mind to understand it, beauty to adorn it, and wit to amuse it; but she chose to pass a great part of her life in exile, and returned at last to die at home among a new generation, whose name she hardly knew, and to whom she herself was but a spectacle and a wonder.

Lady Mary Pierrepont—for that was by birth her name—belonged to a family which had a traditional reputation for ability and cultivation. The *Memoirs of Lucy Hutchinson*—almost the only legacy that remains to us from the first generation of refined Puritans, the only book, at any rate, which effectually brings home to us how different they were in taste and in temper from their more vulgar and feeble successors—contains a curious panegyric on *wise William* Pierrepont, to whom the Parliamentary party resorted as an oracle of judgment, and whom Cromwell himself, if tradition may be trusted, at times condescended to consult and court. He did not, however, transmit much of his discretion to his grandson, Lady Mary's father. This nobleman, for he inherited from an elder branch of the family both the marquisate of Dorchester and the dukedom of Kingston, was a mere man "about town," as the homely phrase then went, who passed a long life of fashionable idleness interspersed with political intrigue, and who signalized his old age by marrying a young beauty of fewer years than his youngest daughter, who, as he very likely knew, cared nothing for him and much for another person. He had the "grand air," however, and he expected his children, when he visited them, to kneel down immediately and ask his blessing, which, if his character was what is said, must have been *very* valuable. The only attention he ever (that we know of) bestowed on Lady Mary was a sort of theatrical outrage, pleasant enough to her at the time, but scarcely in accordance with the educational theories in which we now believe. He was a member of the Kit-Cat, a great Whig club, the Brooks's of Queen Anne's time, which, like Brooks's, appears not to have been purely political, but to have found time for occasional relaxation and for somewhat unbusiness-like discussions. They held annually a formal meeting to arrange the female toasts for that year; and we are told that "a whim seized" her father "to nominate" Lady Mary, "then not eight years old, a candidate; alleging that she was far prettier than any lady on their list. The other members demurred, because the rules of the club forbade them to elect a beauty whom they had never seen. 'Then you shall see her,' cried he; and in the gaiety of the moment sent orders home to have her finely dressed and brought to him at the tavern, where she was received with acclamations, her claim unanimously allowed, her health drunk by every one present, and her name engraved in due form upon a drinking-glass. The company consisting of some of the most eminent men in England, she went from the lap of one poet, or patriot, or statesman, to the arms of another, was feasted with sweetmeats, overwhelmed with caresses, and what perhaps already pleased her better than either, heard her wit and beauty loudly extolled on every side. Pleasure, she said, was too poor a word to express her sensations: they amounted to ecstasy: never again, throughout her whole future life, did she pass so happy a day. Nor, indeed, could she; for the love of admiration, which this scene was calculated to excite or increase, could never again be so fully gratified; there is always some alloying ingredient in the cup, some drawback upon the triumphs, of grown people. Her father carried on the frolic, and, we may conclude, confirmed the taste, by having her picture painted for the club-room, that she might be enrolled a regular toast." Perhaps some young ladies of more than eight years old would not much object to have lived in those times. Fathers may be wiser now than they were then, but they rarely make themselves so thoroughly agreeable to their children. This stimulating education would leave a weak and vain girl still more vain and weak; but it had not that effect on Lady Mary. Vain she probably was, and her father's boastfulness perhaps made her vainer; but her vanity took an intellectual turn. She read vaguely and widely; she managed to acquire some knowledge—how much is not clear—of Greek and Latin, and certainly learned with sufficient thoroughness French and Italian. She used to say that she had the worst education in the world, and that it was only by the "help of an uncommon memory and indefatigable labour" that she had acquired her remarkable attainments. Her father certainly seems to have been capable of any degree of inattention and neglect; but we should not perhaps credit too entirely all the legends which an old lady recounted to her grandchildren of the intellectual difficulties of her youth.

She seems to have been encouraged by her grandmother, one of the celebrated Evelyn family, whose memory is thus enigmatically but still expressively enshrined in the diary of the author of *Sylva:*—"Under this date," we are informed, "of the 2nd of July, 1649, he records a day spent at Godstone, where Sir John" (this lady's father) "was on a visit with his daughter"; and he adds: "Mem. The prodigious memory of Sir John of Wilts's daughter, since married to Mr. W. Pierrepont." The lady who was thus formidable in her youth deigned in her old age to write frequently, as we should now say,—to open a "regular commerce" of letters, as was said in that age—with Lady Mary when quite a girl, which she always believed to have been beneficial to her, and probably believed rightly; for she was intelligent enough to comprehend what was said to her, and the old lady had watched many changes in many things.

Her greatest intellectual guide, at least so in after life she used to relate, was Mr. Wortley, whom she afterwards married. "When I was young," she said, "I was a great admirer of Ovid's *Metamorphoses,* and that was one of the chief reasons that set me upon the thoughts of stealing the Latin language. Mr. Wortley was the only person to whom I communicated my design, and he encouraged me in it. I used to study five or six hours a day for two years in my father's library; and so got that language, whilst everybody else thought I was reading nothing but novels and romances." She perused, however, some fiction also; for she possessed, till her death, the whole library of Mrs. Lennox's *Female Quixote,* a ponderous series of novels in folio, in one of which she had written, in her fairest youthful hand, the names and characteristic qualities of "the beautiful Diana, the volatile Clemene, the melancholy Doris, Celadon the faithful, Adamas the wise, and so on, forming two columns."

Of Mr. Wortley's character it is not difficult, from the materials before us, to decipher the features; he was a slow man, with a taste for quick companions. Swift's diary to Stella mentions an evening spent over a bottle of old wine with Mr. Wortley and Mr. Addison. Mr. Wortley was a rigid Whig, and Swift's transition to Toryism soon broke short that friendship. But with Addison he maintained an intimacy which lasted during their joint lives, and survived the marriages of both. With Steele likewise he was upon the closest terms, is said to have written some papers in the *Tatler* and *Spectator;* and the second volume of the former is certainly dedicated to him in affectionate and respectful terms.

Notwithstanding, however, these conspicuous testimonials to high ability, Mr. Wortley was an orderly and dull person. Every letter received by him from his wife during five and twenty years of absence, was found, at his death, carefully endorsed with the date of its arrival, and with a *synopsis* of its contents. "He represented," we are told, "at various times, Huntingdon, Westminster, and Peterborough in Parliament, and appears to have been a member of that class who win respectful attention by sober and business-like qualities; and his name is constantly found in the drier and more formal part of the politics of the time." He answered to the description given more recently of a similar person: "Is not," it was asked, "Sir John—a very methodical person?" "Certainly he is," was the reply, "he files his invitations to dinner." The Wortley papers, according to the description of those who have inspected them, seem to contain the accumulations of similar documents during many years. He hoarded money, however, to more purpose, for he died one of the richest commoners in England; and a considerable part of the now marvellous wealth of the Bute family seems at first to have been derived from him.

Whatever good qualities Addison and Steele discovered in Mr. Wortley, they were certainly not those of a good writer. We have from his pen and from that of Lady Mary a description of the state of English politics during the three first years of George III., and any one who wishes to understand how much readability depends upon good writing would do well to compare the two. Lady Mary's is a clear and bright description of all the superficial circumstances of the time; Mr. Wortley's is equally superficial, often unintelligible and always lumbering, and scarcely succeeds in telling us more than that the writer was wholly unsuccessful in all which he tried to do. As to Mr. Wortley's contributions to the periodicals of his time, we may suspect that the jottings preserved at London are all which he ever wrote of them and that the style and

arrangement were supplied by more skilful writers. Even
a county member might furnish headings for the *Saturday
Review*. He might say: "*Trent* British vessel—Americans
always intrusive—Support Government—Kill all that is
necessary."

What Lady Mary discovered in Mr. Wortley it is easier
to say and shorter, for he was very handsome. If his
portrait can be trusted, there was a placid and business-like
repose about him, which might easily be attractive to a
rather excitable and wild young lady, especially when
combined with imposing features and a quiet, sweet expression. He attended *to her* also. When she was a girl of
fourteen, he met her at a party, and evinced his admiration. And a little while later, it is not difficult to fancy
that a literary young lady might be much pleased with a
good-looking gentleman not uncomfortably older than
herself, yet having a place in the world, and well known
to the literary men of the age. He was acquainted with the
classics too, or was supposed to be so; whether it was a
consequence of or a preliminary to their affections, Lady
Mary wished to know the classics also.

Bishop Burnet was so kind as to superintend the singular studies—for such they were clearly thought—of this
aristocratic young lady; and the translation of the *Enchi-
ridion* of Epictetus, which he revised, is printed in this
edition of her works. But even so grave an undertaking
could not wholly withdraw her from more congenial pursuits. She commenced a correspondence with Miss Wortley,
Mr. Wortley's unmarried sister, which still remains,
though Miss Wortley's letters are hardly to be called hers,
for her brother composed, and she merely copied them.
The correspondence is scarcely in the sort of English or in
the tone which young ladies, we understand, now use.

"It is as impossible [says Miss Wortley] for my dearest
Lady Mary to utter thought that can seem dull as to put

on a look that is not beautiful. Want of wit is a fault that those who envy you most would not be able to find in your compliments. To me they seem perfect, since repeated assurances of your kindness forbid me to question their sincerity. You have often found that the most angry, nay, the most neglectful air you can assume, has made as deep a wound as the kindest; and these lines of yours, that you tax with dulness (perhaps because they were writ when you was not in a right humour, or when your thoughts were elsewhere employed), are so far from deserving the imputation, that the very turn of your expression, had I forgot the rest of your charms, would be sufficient to make me lament the only fault you have—your inconstancy."

To which the reply is:

"I am infinitely obliged to you, my dear Mrs. Wortley, for the wit, beauty, and other fine qualities you so generously bestow upon me. Next to receiving them from heaven, you are the person from whom I would choose to receive gifts and graces: I am very well satisfied to owe them to your own delicacy of imagination, which represents to you the idea of a fine lady, and you have good nature enough to fancy I am she. All this is mighty well, but you do not stop there; imagination is boundless. After giving me imaginary wit and beauty, you give me imaginary passions; and you tell me I'm in love: if I am it is a perfect sin of ignorance, for I don't so much as know the man's name: I have been studying these three hours, and cannot guess who you mean. I passed the days of Nottingham races [at] Thoresby without seeing, or even wishing to see, one of the sex. Now, if I am in love, I have very hard fortune to conceal it so industriously from my own knowledge, and yet discover it so much to other people. 'Tis against all form to have such a passion as that, without giving one sign for the matter. Pray tell me the name of him I love, that I may (according to the laudable custom of lovers) sigh to the woods and groves hereabouts, and teach it to the echo."

After some time Miss Wortley unfortunately died, and there was an obvious difficulty in continuing the correspondence without the aid of an appropriate sisterly screen. Mr. Wortley seems to have been tranquil and condescending; perhaps he thought placid tactics would be most effective, for Lady Mary was not so calm. He sent her some *Tatlers,* and received, by way of thanks, the following tolerably encouraging letter:

"To Mr. Wortley Montagu.

"I am surprised at one of the *Tatlers* you send me; is it possible to have any sort of esteem for a person one believes capable of having such trifling inclinations? Mr. Bickerstaff has very wrong notions of our sex. I can say there are some of us that despise charms of show, and all the pageantry of greatness, perhaps with more ease than any of the philosophers. In contemning the world, they seem to take pains to contemn it; we despise it, without taking the pains to read lessons of morality to make us do it. At least I know I have always looked upon it with contempt, without being at the expense of one serious reflection to oblige me to it. I carry the matter yet farther; was I to choose of two thousand pounds a year or twenty thousand, the first would be my choice. There is something of an unavoidable *embarras* in making what is called a great figure in the world; [it] takes off from the happiness of life; I hate the noise and hurry inseparable from great estates and titles, and look upon both as blessings that ought to be given to fools, for 'tis only to them that they are blessings. The pretty fellows you speak of, I own, entertain me sometimes; but is it impossible to be diverted with what one despises? I can laugh at a puppet-show; at the same time I know there is nothing in it worth my attention or regard. General notions are generally wrong.

Ignorance and folly are thought the best foundations for virtue, as if not knowing what a good wife is was necessary to make one so. I confess that can never be my way of reasoning; as I always forgive an *injury* when I think it not done out of malice, I can never think myself *obliged* by what is done without design. Give me leave to say it (I know it sounds vain), I know how to make a man of sense happy; but then that man must resolve to contribute something towards it himself. I have so much esteem for you, I should be very sorry to hear you was unhappy; but for the world I would not be the instrument of making you so; which (of the humour you are) is hardly to be avoided if I am your wife. You distrust me—I can neither be easy, nor loved, where I am distrusted. Nor do I believe your passion for me is what you pretend it; at least I am sure was I in love I could not talk as you do. Few women would have spoke so plainly as I have done; but to dissemble is among the things I never do. I take more pains to approve my conduct to myself than to the world; and would not have to accuse myself of a minute's deceit. I wish I loved you enough to devote myself to be for ever miserable, for the pleasure of a day or two's happiness. I cannot resolve upon it. You must think otherwise of me, or not at all.

"I don't enjoin you to burn this letter. I know you will. 'Tis the first I ever writ to one of your sex, and shall be the last. You must never expect another. I resolve against all correspondence of the kind; my resolutions are seldom made, and never broken."

Mr. Wortley, however, still grumbled. He seems to have expected a young lady to do something even more decisive than ask him to marry her. He continued to hesitate and pause. The lady in the comedy says, "What right has a man to intend unless he states his intentions?" and Lady Mary's biographers are entirely of that opinion.

They think her exceedingly ill-used, and Mr. Wortley exceedingly to blame. And so it may have been; certainly a love-correspondence is rarely found where activity and intrepidity on the lady's side so much contrasts with quiescence and timidity on the gentleman's. If, however, we could summon him before us, probably Mr. Wortley would have something to answer on his own behalf. It is tolerably plain that he thought Lady Mary too excitable. "Certainly," he doubtless reasoned, "she is a handsome young lady, and very witty; but beauty and wit are dangerous as well as attractive. Vivacity is delightful; but my esteemed friend Mr. Addison has observed that excessive quickness of parts is not unfrequently the cause of extreme rapidity in action. Lady Mary makes love to me before marriage, and I like it; but may she not make love also to some one else after marriage? and then I shall not like it." Accordingly he writes to her timorously as to her love of pleasure, her love of romantic reading, her occasional toleration of younger gentlemen and quicker admirers. At last, however, he proposed; and, so far as the lady was concerned, there was no objection.

We might have expected, from a superficial view of the facts, that there would have been no difficulty either on the side of her father. Mr. Wortley died one of the richest commoners in England; was of the first standing in society, of good family, and he had apparently, therefore, money to settle and station to offer to his bride. And he did offer both. He was ready to settle an ample sum on Lady Mary, both as his wife and as his widow, and was anxious that, if they married, they should live in a manner suitable to her rank and his prospects. But nevertheless there was a difficulty. The *Tatler* had recently favoured its readers with dissertations upon social ethics not altogether dissimilar to those with which the *Saturday Review* frequently instructs its readers. One of those dissertations contained an elaborate exposure of the folly of settling your estate upon your unborn children. The arguments were of a sort very easily imaginable. "Why," it was said, "should you give away that which you have to a person whom you do not know; whom you may never see; whom you may not like when you do see; who may be undutiful, unpleasant, or idiotic? Why, too, should each generation surrender its due control over the next? When the family estate is settled, men of the world know that the father's control is gone, for disinterested filial affection is an unfrequent though doubtless possible virtue; but so long as *property* is in suspense, all expectants will be attentive to those who have it in their power to give or not to give it." These arguments had converted Mr. Wortley, who is said even to have contributed notes for the article, and they seem to have converted Lady Mary also. She was to have her money, and the most plain-spoken young ladies do not commonly care to argue much about the future provision for their possible children; the subject is always delicate and a little frightful, and, on the whole, must be left to themselves. But Lord Dorchester, her father, felt it his duty to be firm. It is an old saying that "you never know where a man's conscience may turn up," and the advent of ethical feeling was in this case even unusually beyond calculation. Lord Dorchester had never been an anxious father, and was not now going to be a liberal father. He never cared much about Lady Mary, except in so far as he could himself gain *éclat* by exhibiting her youthful beauty, and he was not now at her marriage about to do at all more than was necessary and decent in his station. It was not therefore apparently probable that he would be irritatingly obstinate respecting the income of his daughter's children. He was so, however. He deemed it a duty to see that "*his* grandchild never should be a beggar," and, for what reason does not so clearly appear, wished that his eldest male grandchild should be immensely richer than all his other grandchildren. The old feudal aristocrat, often in modern

Europe so curiously disguised in the indifferent exterior of a careless man of the world, was, as became him, dictatorial and unalterable upon the duty of founding a family. Though he did not care much for his daughter, he cared much for the position of his daughter's eldest son. He had probably stumbled on the fundamental truth that "girls were girls, and boys were boys," and was disinclined to disregard the rule of primogeniture by which he had obtained his marquisate, and from which he expected a dukedom.

Mr. Wortley, however, was through life a man, if eminent in nothing else, eminent at least in obstinacy. He would not give up the doctrine of the *Tatler* even to obtain Lady Mary. The match was accordingly abandoned, and Lord Dorchester looked out for and found another gentleman who he proposed to make his son-in-law; for he believed, according to the old morality, "that it was the duty of the parents to find a husband for a daughter, and that when he was found, it was the daughter's duty to marry him." It was as wrong in her to attempt to choose as in him to neglect to seek. Lady Mary was, however, by no means disposed to accept this passive theory of female obligation. She *had* sought and chosen; and to her choice she intended to adhere. The conduct of Mr. Wortley would have offended some ladies, but it rather augmented her admiration. She had exactly that sort of irritable intellect which sets an undue value on new theories of society and morality, and is pleased when others do so too. She thought Mr. Wortley was quite right not to "defraud himself for a possible infant," and admired his constancy and firmness. She determined to risk a step, as she herself said, unjustifiable to her own relatives, but which she nevertheless believed that she could justify to herself. She decided on eloping with Mr. Wortley.

Before, however, taking this audacious leap, she looked a little. Though she did not object to the sacrifice of the customary inheritance of her contingent son, she by no means approved of sacrificing the settlement which Mr. Wortley had undertaken at a prior period of the negotiation to make upon herself. And according to common sense, she was undoubtedly judicious. She was going from her father, and foregoing the money which he had promised her; and therefore it was not reasonable that, by going *to* her lover, she should forfeit also the money which *he* had promised her. And there is nothing offensive in her mode of expression. "'Tis something odd for a woman that brings nothing to expect anything; but after the way of my education, I dare not pretend to live but in some degree suitable to it. I had rather die than return to a dependency upon relations I have disobliged. Save me from that fear, if you love me. If you cannot, or think I ought not to expect it, be sincere and tell me so. 'Tis better I should not be yours at all, than, for a short happiness, involve myself in ages of misery. I hope there will never be occasion for this precaution; but, however, 'tis necessary to make it." But true and rational as all this seems, perhaps it is still truer and still more rational to say that if a woman has not sufficient confidence in her lover to elope with him without a previous promise of a good settlement, she had better not elope with him at all. After all, if he declines to make the stipulated settlement, the lady will have either to return to her friends or to marry without it, and she would have the full choice between these satisfactory alternatives, even if she asked no previous promise from her lover. At any rate, the intrusion of coarse money among the refined materials of romance is, in this case, even more curious and remarkable than usual.

After some unsuccessful attempts, Lady Mary and Mr. Wortley did elope and did marry, and, after a certain interval, of course, Lord Dorchester received them, notwithstanding their contempt of his authority, into some sort of favour and countenance. They had probably saved him money by their irregularity, and economical frailties are rarely judged severely by men of fashion who are benefited by them. Lady Mary, however, was long a little mistrusted by her own relations, and never seems to have acquired much family influence; but her marriage was not her only peculiarity, or the only one which impartial relations might dislike.

The pair appear to have been for a little while tolerably happy. Lady Mary was excitable, and wanted letters when absent, and attention when present: Mr. Wortley was heavy and slow; could not write letters when away, and seemed torpid in her society when at home. Still, these are common troubles. Common, too, is the matrimonial correspondence upon baby's deficiency in health, and on Mrs. Behn's opinion that "the cold bath is the best medicine for weak children." It seems an odd end to a deferential perusal of Latin authors in girlhood, and to a spirited elopement with the preceptor in after years; but the transition is only part of the usual irony of human life.

The world, both social and political, into which Lady Mary was introduced by her marriage was singularly calculated to awaken the faculties, to stimulate the intellect, to sharpen the wit, and to harden the heart of an intelligent, witty, and hard-headed woman. The world of London—even the higher world—is now too large to be easily seen, or to be pithily described. The elements are so many, their position is so confused, the display of their mutual counteraction is so involved, that many years must pass away before even a very clever woman can thoroughly comprehend it all. She will cease to be young and handsome long ere she does comprehend it. And when she at last understands it, it does not seem a fit subject for concise and summary wit. Its evident complexity refuses to be condensed into pithy sayings and brilliant *bons-mots*. It has fallen into the hands of philosophers, with less brains perhaps than the satirists of our fathers, but with more anxiety to tell the whole truth, more toleration for the many-sidedness of the world, with less of sharp conciseness, but, perhaps, with more of useful completeness. As are the books, so are the readers. People do not wish to read satire nowadays. The epigrams even of Pope would fall dull and dead upon this serious and investigating time. The folly of the last age affected levity; the folly of this, as we all know, encases itself in ponderous volumes, which defy refutation, in elaborate arguments which prove nothing, in theories which confuse the uninstructed, and which irritate the well-informed. The folly of a hundred years since was at least the folly of Vivien, but ours is the folly of Merlin:

> *You* read the book, my pretty Vivien,
> And none can read the text, not even I,
> And none can read the comments but myself—
> Oh, the results are simple! *

Perhaps people did not know then as much as they know now: indisputably they knew nothing like so much in a superficial way *about* so many things; but they knew far more correctly where their knowledge began and where it stopped; what they thought and why they thought it: they had readier illustrations and more summary phrases; they could say at once what it *came to,* and to what action it should lead.

The London of the eighteenth was an aristocratic world, which lived to itself, which displayed the virtues and developed the vices of an aristocracy which was under little fear of external control or check; which emancipated itself from the control of the crown; which had not fallen under the control of the *bourgeoisie;* which saw its own life, and saw that, according to its own maxims, it was good. Public opinion now rules, and it is an opinion which constrains

* Tennyson: "Merlin and Vivien."

the conduct, and narrows the experience, and dwarfs the violence, and minimizes the frankness of the highest classes, while it diminishes their vices, supports their conscience, and precludes their grossness. There was nothing like this in the last century, especially in the early part of it. The aristocracy came to town from their remote estates —where they were uncontrolled by any opinion or by an equal society, and where the eccentricities and personalities of each character were fostered and exaggerated—to a London which was like a large country town, in which everybody of rank knew everybody of rank, where the eccentricities of each rural potentate came into picturesque collision with the eccentricities of other rural potentates, where the most minute allusions to the peculiarities and the career of the principal persons were instantly understood, where squibs were on every table, and where satire was in the air. No finer field of social observation could be found for an intelligent and witty woman. Lady Mary understood it at once.

Nor was the political life of the last century so unfavourable to the influence and so opposed to the characteristic comprehension of women as our present life. We are now ruled by political discussion and by a popular assembly, by leading articles, and by the House of Commons. But women can scarcely ever compose leaders, and no woman sits in our representative chamber. The whole tide of abstract discussion, which fills our mouths and deafens our ears, the whole complex accumulation of facts and figures to which we refer everything, and which we apply to everything, is quite unfemale. A lady has an insight into what she sees; but how will this help her with the case of the *Trent,* with the proper structure of a representative chamber, with Indian finance or parliamentary reform? Women are clever, but cleverness of itself is nothing at present. A sharp Irish writer described himself "as bothered entirely by the want of preliminary information"; women are in the same difficulty now. Their nature may hereafter change, as some sanguine advocates suggest. But the visible species certainly have not the intellectual providence to acquire the vast stores of dry information which alone can enable them to judge adequately of our present controversies. We are ruled by a machinery of oratory and discussion, in which women have no share, and which they hardly comprehend: we are engaged on subjects which need an arduous learning, to which they have no pretensions.

In the last century much of this was very different. The court still counted for much in English politics. The House of Commons was the strongest power in the State machine, but it was not so immeasurably the strongest power as now. It was absolutely supreme within its sphere, but the sphere was limited. It could absolutely control the money, and thereby the policy, of the State. Whether there should be peace or war, excise or no excise, it could and did despotically determine. It was supreme in its choice of *measures*. But, on the other hand, it had only a secondary influence in the choice of *persons*. Who the Prime Minister was to be, was a question not only theoretically determinable, but in fact determined by the Sovereign. The House of Commons could despotically impose two conditions: first, that the Prime Minister should be a man of sufficient natural ability, and sufficient parliamentary experience, to conduct the business of his day; secondly, that he should adopt the policy which the nation wished. But, subject to a conformity with these prerequisites, the selection of the king was nearly uncontrolled. Sir Robert Walpole was the greatest master of parliamentary tactics and political business in his generation; he was a statesman of wide views and consummate dexterity; but these intellectual gifts, even joined to immense parliamentary experience, were not alone sufficient to make him and to keep him Prime Minister of England. He also maintained, during two reigns, a complete system of court-strategy. During the reign of George II. he kept a *queen-watcher*. Lord Hervey, one of the cleverest men in England, the keenest observer, perhaps, in England, was induced by very dexterous management to remain at court during many years—to observe the queen, to hint to the queen, to remove wrong impressions from the queen, to confirm the Walpolese predilections of the queen, to report every incident to Sir Robert. The records of politics tell us few stranger tales than that it should have been necessary for the Sir Robert Peel of the age to hire a sub-ordinate as safe as Eldon, and as witty as Canning, for the sole purpose of managing a clever German woman, to whom the selection of a Prime Minister was practically entrusted. Nor was this the only court-campaign which Sir Robert had to conduct, or in which he was successful. Lady Mary who hated him much, has satirically described the foundation upon which his court favour rested during the reign of George I.:

"The new court with all their train was arrived before I left the country. The Duke of Marlborough was returned in a sort of triumph, with the apparent merit of having suffered for his fidelity to the succession, and was reinstated in his office of general, etc. In short, all people who had suffered any hardship or disgrace during the late ministry would have it believed that it was occasioned by their attachment to the House of Hanover. Even Mr. Walpole, who had been sent to the Tower for a piece of bribery proved upon him, was called a confessor to the cause. But he had another piece of good luck that yet more con-tributed to his advancement; he had a very handsome sister, whose folly had lost her reputation in London; but the yet greater folly of Lord Townshend, who happened to be a neighbour in Norfolk to Mr. Walpole, had occasioned his being drawn in to marry her some months before the queen died.

"Lord Townshend had that sort of understanding which commonly makes men honest in the first part of their lives; they follow the instructions of their tutor, and, till somebody thinks it worth their while to show them a new path, go regularly on in the road where they are set. Lord Townshend had then been many years an excellent husband to a sober wife, a kind master to all his servants and dependents, a serviceable relation wherever it was in his power, and followed the instinct of nature in being fond of his children. Such a sort of behaviour, without any glaring absurdity, either in prodigality or avarice, always gains a man the reputation of reasonable and honest; and this was his character when the Earl of Godolphin sent him envoy to the States, not doubting but he would be faithful to his orders, without giving himself the trouble of criticizing on them, which is what all ministers wish in an envoy. Robotun, a French refugee (secretary to Bernstoff, one of the Elector of Hanover's ministers), happened then to be at the Hague, and was civilly received at Lord Townshend's, who treated him at his table with the English hospitality, and he was charmed with a reception which his birth and education did not entitle him to. Lord Townshend was recalled when the queen changed her ministry; his wife died, and he retired into the country where (as I have said before) Walpole had art enough to make him marry his sister Dolly. At that time, I believe, he did not propose much more advantage by the match than to get rid of a girl that lay heavy on his hands.

"When King George ascended the throne, he was surrounded by all his German ministers and playfellows, male and female. Baron Goritz was the most considerable among them both for birth and fortune. He had managed the king's treasury thirty years with the utmost fidelity and economy; and had the true German honesty, being a plain, ·

sincere, and unambitious man. Bernstoff, the secretary, was of a different turn. He was avaricious, artful, and designing; and had got his share in the king's councils by bribing his women. Robotun was employed in these matters, and had the sanguine ambition of a Frenchman. He resolved there should be an English ministry of his choosing; and knowing none of them personally but Townshend, he had not failed to recommend him to his master, and his master to the king, as the only proper person for the important post of Secretary of State; and he entered upon that office with universal applause, having at that time a very popular character, which he might possibly have retained for ever if he had not been entirely governed by his wife and her brother R. Walpole, whom he immediately advanced to be paymaster, esteemed a post of exceeding profit, and very necessary for his indebted estate."

And it is indisputable that Lord Townshend, who thought he was a very great statesman, and who began as the patron of Sir Robert Walpole, nevertheless was only his court-agent—the manager on his behalf of the king and of the king's mistresses.

We need not point out at length, for the passage we have cited of itself indicates, how well suited this sort of politics is to the comprehension and to the pen of a keen-sighted and witty woman.

Nor was the court the principal improver of the London society of the age. The House of Commons was then a part of society. This separate, isolated, aristocratic world, of which we have spoken, had an almost undisputed command of both Houses in the Legislature. The letter of the constitution did not give it them, and no law appointed that it should be so. But the aristocratic class were by far the most *eligible* part of the nation. Even in the boroughs, where there was universal suffrage, or something near it, they were the favourites. Accordingly, they gave the tone to the House of Commons; they required the small community of members who did not belong to their order to conform as far as they could to their usages, and to guide themselves by their code of morality and of taste. In the main the House of Commons obeyed these injunctions, and it was repaid by being incorporated within the aristocratic world: it became not only the council of the nation, but the debating-club of fashion. That which was "received" modified the recipient. The remains of the aristocratic society, wherever we find them, are penetrated not only with an aristocratic but with a political spirit. They breathe a sort of atmosphere of politics. In the London of the present day, the vast miscellaneous *bourgeois* London, we all know that this is not so. "In the country," said a splenetic observer, "people talk politics; at London dinners you talk nothing; between two pillars of crinoline you eat and are resigned." A hundred and fifty years ago, as far as our rather ample materials inform us, people in London talked politics just as they now talk politics in Worcestershire; and being on the spot, and cooped up with politicians in a small social world, their talk was commonly better. They knew the people of whom they spoke, even if they did not know the subjects with which they were concerned.

No element is better fitted to counteract the characteristic evil of an aristocratic society. The defect of such societies in all times has been frivolity. All talk has tended to become gossip; it has ceased to deal with important subjects, and has devoted itself entirely to unimportant incidents. Whether the Duc de —— has more or less prevailed with the Marquise de —— is a sort of common form into which any details may be fitted, and any names inserted. The frivolities of gallantry—never very important save to some woman who has long been dead—fill the records of all aristocracies who lived under a despotism, who had no political authority, no daily political cares. The aristocracy of England in the last century was, at any rate, exempt from *this* reproach. There is in the records of it not only an intellectuality, which would prove little—for every clever describer, by the subtleties of his language and the arrangement of his composition, gives a sort of intellectuality even to matters which have no pretension to it themselves—but likewise a pervading medium of political discussion. The very language in which they are written is the language of political business. Horace Walpole was certainly by nature no politician and no orator; yet no discerning critic can read a page of his voluminous remains without feeling that the writer has through life lived with politicians. A keen, observant mind, not naturally political, but capable of comprehending and viewing any subject which was brought before it, has chanced to have this particular subject—politics—presented to it for a lifetime; and all its delineations, all its efforts, all its thoughts, reflect it, and are coloured by it. In all the records of the eighteenth century the tonic of business is seen to combat the relaxing effect of habitual luxury.

This element, too, is favourable to a clever woman. The more you can put before such a person the greater she will be; the less her world, the less she is. If you place the most keen-sighted lady in the midst of the pure futilities and unmitigated flirtations of an aristocracy, she will sink to the level of those elements, and will scarcely seem to wish for anything more, or to be competent for anything higher. But if she is placed in an intellectual atmosphere, in which political or other important subjects are concurrently passing, you will probably find that she can talk better upon them than you can, without your being able to explain whence she derived either her information or her talent.

The subjects, too, which were discussed in the political society of the last age were not so inscrutable to women as our present subjects; and even when there were great difficulties they were more on a level with men in the discussion of them than they now are. It was no disgrace to be destitute of preliminary information at a time in which there were no accumulated stores from which such information could be derived. A lightening element of female influence is therefore to be found through much of the politics of the eighteenth century.

Lady Mary entered easily into all this world, both social and political. She had beauty for the fashionable, satire for the witty, knowledge for the learned, and intelligence for the politician. She was not too refined to shrink from what we now consider the coarseness of that time. Many of her verses themselves are scarcely adapted for our decorous pages. Perhaps the following give no unfair idea of her ordinary state of mind:

TOWN ECLOGUES

Roxana; or, The Drawing-Room

Roxana, from the court retiring late,
Sigh'd her soft sorrows at St. James's Gate.
Such heavy thoughts lay brooding in her breast,
Not her own chairmen with more weight oppress'd;
They groan the cruel load they're doom'd to bear;
She in these gentle sounds express'd her care.
   "Was it for this that I these roses wear?
For this new-set the jewels for my hair?
Ah! Princess! with what zeal have I pursued!
Almost forgot the duty of a prude.
Thinking I never could attend too soon,
I've miss'd my prayers, to get me dress'd by noon.
For thee, ah! what for thee did I resign!
My pleasures, passions, all that e'er was mine.
I sacrific'd both modesty and ease,
Left operas and went to filthy plays;

Double-entendres shock my tender ear;
Yet even this for thee I choose to bear.
In glowing youth, when nature bids be gay,
And every joy of life before me lay,
By honour prompted, and by pride restrain'd,
The pleasures of the young my soul disdain'd:
Sermons I sought, and with a mien severe
Censur'd my neighbours, and said daily prayer.
   "Alas! how chang'd—with the same sermon-mien
That once I pray'd, the *What d'ye call't* * I've seen.
Ah! cruel Princess, for thy sake I've lost
That reputation which so dear had cost:
I, who avoided every public place,
When bloom and beauty bade me show my face,
Now near thee constant every night abide
With never-failing duty by thy side;
Myself and daughters standing on a row,
To all the foreigners a goodly show!
Oft had your drawing-room been sadly thin,
And merchants' wives close by the chair been seen,
Had not I amply filled the empty space,
And saved your highness from the dire disgrace.
   "Yet Coquetilla's artifice prevails,
When all my merit and my duty fails;
That Coquetilla, whose deluding airs
Corrupt our virgins, still our youth ensnares;
So sunk her character, so lost her fame,
Scarce visited before your highness came:
Yet for the bed-chamber 'tis her you choose,
When zeal and fame and virtue you refuse.
Ah! worthy choice! not one of all your train
Whom censure blasts not, and dishonours stain!
Let the nice hind now suckle dirty pigs,
And the proud pea-hen hatch the cuckoo's eggs!

   * A mock-tragedy by Gay.

Let Iris leave her paint and own her age,
And grave Suffolka wed a giddy page!
A greater miracle is daily view'd,
A virtuous Princess with a court so lewd.
  "I know thee, Court! with all thy treach'rous wiles,
Thy false caresses and undoing smiles!
Ah! Princess, learn'd in all the courtly arts,
To cheat our hopes, and yet to gain our hearts!
  "Large lovely bribes are the great statesman's aim;
And the neglected patriot follows fame.
The Prince is ogled; some the King pursue;
But your Roxana only follows you.
Despis'd Roxana, cease, and try to find
Some other, since the Princess proves unkind:
Perhaps it is not hard to find at court,
If not a greater, a more firm support."

There was every kind of rumour as to Lady Mary's own
conduct, and we have no means of saying whether any
of these rumours were true. There is no evidence against
her which is worthy of the name. So far as can be proved,
she was simply a gay, witty, bold-spoken, handsome
woman, who made many enemies by unscrupulous speech,
and many friends by unscrupulous flirtation. We may believe, but we cannot prove, that she found her husband
tedious, and was dissatisfied that his slow, methodical,
borné mind made so little progress in the political world,
and understood so little of what really passed there. Unquestionably she must have much preferred talking to
Lord Hervey to talking with Mr. Montagu. But we must
not credit the idle scandals of a hundred years since, because they may have been true, or because they appear
not inconsistent with the characters of those to whom they
relate. There were legends against every attractive and
fashionable woman in that age, and most of the legends
were doubtless exaggerations and inventions. We cannot

know the truth of such matters now, and it would hardly be worth searching into if we could; but the important fact is certain, Lady Mary lived in a world in which the worst rumours were greedily told, and often believed, about her and others; and the moral refinement of a woman must always be impaired by such a contact.

Lady Mary was so unfortunate as to incur the partial dislike of one of the great recorders of that age, and the bitter hostility of the other. She was no favourite with Horace Walpole, and the bitter enemy of Pope. The first is easily explicable. Horace Walpole never loved his father, but recompensed himself by hating his father's enemies. No one connected with the opposition to Sir Robert is spared by his son, if there be a fair opportunity for unfavourable insinuation. Mr. Wortley Montagu was the very man for a grave mistake. He made the very worst that could be made in that age. He joined the party of constitutional exiles on the Opposition bench, who had no real objection to the policy of Sir Robert Walpole; who, when they had a chance, adopted that policy themselves; who were discontented because they had no power, and he had all the power. Probably too, being a man eminently respectable, Mr. Montagu was frightened at Sir Robert's unscrupulous talk and not very scrupulous actions. At any rate, he opposed Sir Robert; and thence many a little observation of Horace Walpole's against Lady Mary.

Why Pope and Lady Mary quarrelled is a question on which much discussion has been expended, and on which a judicious German professor might even now compose an interesting and exhaustive monograph. A curt English critic will be more apt to ask, "Why they should *not* have quarrelled?" We know that Pope quarrelled with almost every one; we know that Lady Mary quarrelled or half quarrelled with most of her acquaintances. Why, then, should they not have quarrelled with one another?

It is certain that they were very intimate at one time;

for Pope wrote to her some of the most pompous letters of compliment in the language. And the more intimate they were to begin with, the more sure they were to be enemies in the end. Human nature will not endure that sort of proximity. An irritable, vain poet, who always fancies that people are trying to hurt him, whom no argument could convince that every one is not perpetually thinking about him, cannot long be friendly with a witty woman of unscrupulous tongue, who spares no one, who could sacrifice a good friend for a bad *bon-mot,* who thinks of the person whom she is addressing, not of those about whom she is speaking. The natural relation of the two is that of victim and torturer, and no other will long continue. There appear also to have been some money matters (of all things in the world) between the two. Lady Mary was entrusted by Pope with some money to use in speculation during the highly fashionable panic which derives its name from the South-Sea Bubble,—and as of course it was lost, Pope was very angry. Another story goes that Pope made serious love to Lady Mary, and that she laughed at him; upon which a very personal, and not always correct, controversy has arisen as to the probability or improbability of Pope's exciting a lady's feelings. Lord Byron took part in it with his usual acuteness and incisiveness, and did not leave the discussion more decent than he found it. Pope doubtless was deformed, and had not the large red health that uncivilized women admire; yet a clever lady might have taken a fancy to him, for the little creature knew what he was saying. There is, however, no evidence that Lady Mary did so. We only know that there was a sudden coolness or quarrel between them, and that it was the beginning of a long and bitter hatred.

In their own times Pope's sensitive disposition probably gave Lady Mary a great advantage. Her tongue perhaps gave him more pain than his pen gave her. But in later times she has fared the worst. What between Pope's sarcasms and Horace Walpole's anecdotes, Lady Mary's reputation has suffered very considerably. As we have said, her offences are *non proven;* there is no evidence to convict her; but she is likely to be condemned upon the general doctrine that a person who is accused of much is probably guilty of something.

During many years Lady Mary continued to live a distinguished fashionable and social life, with a single remarkable break. This interval was her journey to Constantinople. The powers that then were, thought fit to send Mr. Wortley as ambassador to Constantinople, and his wife accompanied him. During that visit she kept a journal, and wrote sundry real letters, out of which, after her return, she composed a series of unreal letters as to all she saw and did in Turkey, and on the journey there and back, which were published, and which are still amusing, if not always select, reading. The Sultan was not then the "dying man"; he was the "Grand Turk." He was not simply a potentate to be counted with, but a power to be feared. The appearance of a Turkish army on the Danube had in that age much the same effect as the appearance of a Russian army now. It was an object of terror and dread. A mission at Constantinople was not then a *bureau* for interference in Turkey, but a serious office for transacting business with a great European power. A European ambassador at Constantinople now presses on the Government there impracticable reforms; he then asked for useful aid. Lady Mary was evidently impressed by the power of the country in which she sojourned; and we observe in her letters evident traces of the notion that the Turk was the dread of Christendom,—which is singular now, when the Turk is its *protégé*.

Lady Mary had another advantage too. Many sorts of books make steady progress; a scientific treatise published now is sure to be fuller and better than one on the same subject written long ago. But with books of travel in a stationary country the presumption is the contrary. In that case the old book is probably the better book. The first traveller writes out a plain straightforward description of the most striking objects with which he meets; he believes that his readers know nothing of the country of which he is writing, for till he visited it he probably knew nothing himself; and, if he is sensible, he describes simply and clearly all which most impresses him. He has no motive for not dwelling upon the principal things, and most likely will do so, as they are probably the most conspicuous. The second traveller is not so fortunate. He is always in terror of the traveller who went before. He fears the criticism,— "This is all very well, *but* we knew the whole of it before. No. 1 said that at page 103." In consequence he is timid. He picks and skips. He fancies that you are acquainted with all which is great and important, and he dwells, for your good and to your pain, upon that which is small and unimportant. For ordinary readers no result can be more fatal. They perhaps never read—they certainly do not remember—anything upon the subject. The curious *minutiae,* so elaborately set forth, are quite useless, for they have not the general framework in which to store them. Not knowing much of the first traveller's work, that of the second is a supplement to a treatise with which they are unacquainted. In consequence they do not read it. Lady Mary made good use of her position in the front of the herd of tourists. She told us what she saw in Turkey—all the best of what she saw, and all the most remarkable things—and told it very well.

Nor was this work the only fruit of her Turkish travels; she brought home the notion of inoculation. Like most improvers, she was roughly spoken to. Medical men were angry because the practice was not in their books, and conservative men were cross at the agony of a new idea. Religious people considered it wicked to have a disease which Providence did not think fit to send you; and simple people "did not like to make themselves ill of their own accord." She triumphed, however, over all obstacles; inoculation, being really found to lengthen life and save complexions, before long became general.

One of the first patients upon whom Lady Mary tried the novelty was her own son, and many considerate people thought it "worthy of observation" that he turned out to be a scamp. When he ran away from school, the mark of inoculation, then rare, was used to describe him, and after he was recovered, he never did anything that was good. His case seems to have been the common one in which Nature (as we speak) requites herself for the strong-headedness of several generations by the weakness of one. His father's and his mother's family had been rather able for some generations; the latter remarkably so. But this boy had always a sort of practical imbecility. He was not stupid, but he never did anything right. He exemplified another curious trait of Nature's practice. Mr. Montagu was obstinate, though sensible; Lady Mary was flighty, though clever. Nature combined the defects. Young Edward Montagu was both obstinate and flighty. The only pleasure he can ever have given his parents was the pleasure of *feeling* their own wisdom. He showed that they were right before marriage in not settling the paternal property upon him, for he ran through every shilling he possessed. He was not sensible enough to keep his property, and just not fool enough for the law to take it from him.

After her return from Constantinople, Lady Mary continued to lead the same half-gay and half-literary life as before; but at last she did not like it. Various ingenious inquirers into antiquated *minutiae* have endeavoured, without success, to discover reasons of detail which might explain her dissatisfaction. They have suggested that some irregular love-affair was unprosperous, and hinted that she and her husband were not on good terms. The love-affair, however, when looked for, cannot be found; and though she and her husband would appear to have been but distantly related, they never had any great quarrel which we know of. Neither seems to have been fitted to give the other much pleasure, and each had the fault of which the other was most impatient. Before marriage Lady Mary had charmed Mr. Montagu, but she had also frightened him; after marriage she frightened, but did not charm him. He was formal and composed; she was flighty and *outrée*. "What *will* she do next?" was doubtless the poor man's daily feeling; and "Will he ever do anything?" was probably also hers. Torpid business, which is always going on, but which never seems to come to anything, is simply aggravating to a clever woman. Even the least impatient lady can hardly endure a perpetual process for which there is little visible and nothing theatrical to show; and Lady Mary was by no means the least impatient. But there was no abrupt quarrel between the two; and a husband and wife can generally manage to continue to live together during a second twenty years. These reasons of detail are scarcely the reasons for Lady Mary's wishing to break away from the life to which she had so long been used. Yet there was clearly some reason, for Lady Mary went abroad, and stayed there during many years.

We believe that the cause was not special and peculiar to the case, but general, and due to the invariable principles of human nature, at all times and everywhere. If historical experience proves anything, it proves that the earth is not adapted for a life of mere intellectual pleasure. The life of a brute on earth, though bad, is possible. It is not even difficult to many persons to destroy the higher part of their nature by a continual excess in sensual pleasure. It is even more easy and possible to dull all the soul and most of the mind by a vapid accumulation of torpid comfort. Many of the middle classes spend their whole lives in a constant series of petty pleasures, and an undeviating pursuit of small material objects. The gross pursuit of pleasure, and the tiresome pursuit of petty comfort, are quite suitable to such "a being as man in such a world as the present one." What is not possible is to combine the pursuit of pleasure and the enjoyment of comfort with the characteristic pleasures of a strong mind. If you wish for luxury, you must not nourish the inquisitive instinct. The great problems of human life are in the air; they are without us in the life we see, within us in the life we feel. A quick intellect feels them in a moment. It says, "Why am I here? What is pleasure, that I desire it? What is comfort, that I seek it? What are carpets and tables? What is the lust of the eye? What is the pride of life, that they should satisfy *me?* I was not made for such things. I hate them, because I have liked them; I loathe them, because it seems that there is nothing else for me." An impatient woman's intellect comes to this point in a moment; it says, "Society is good, but I have seen society. What is the use of talking, or hearing *bons-mots?* I have done both till I am tired of doing either. I have laughed till I have hated them for being such fools. As for instruction, I have seen the men of genius of my time; and they tell me nothing,—nothing of what I want to know. They are choked with intellectual frivolities. They cannot say 'whence I came, and whither I go.' What do they know of themselves? It is not from literary people that we can learn anything; more likely, they will copy, or try to copy, the manners of lords, and make ugly love, in bad imitation of those who despise them." Lady Mary felt this, as we believe. She had seen all the world of England and it did not *satisfy*. She turned abroad, not in pursuit of definite good, nor from fear of particular evil, but from a vague wish for some great change—from a wish to escape from a life which harassed the soul, but did not calm it; which awakened the intellect without answering its questions.

She lived abroad for more than twenty years, at Avignon

and Venice and elsewhere; and during that absence she wrote the letters which compose the greater part of her works. And there is no denying that they are good letters. The art of note-writing may become classical—it is for the present age to provide models of that sort of composition —but letters have perished. Nobody but a bore now takes pains enough to make them pleasant; and the only result of a bore's pains is to make them unpleasant. The correspondence of the present day is a continual labour without any visible achievement. The dying penny-a-liner said with emphasis: "That which I have written has perished." We might all say so of the mass of petty letters we write. They are a heap of small atoms, each with some interest individually, but with no interest as a whole; all the items concern us, but they all add up to nothing. In the last century, cultivated people who sat down to write a letter took plains to have something to say, and took pains to say it. The postage was perhaps ninepence; and it would be impudent to make a correspondent pay ninepence for nothing. Still more impudent was it, *after* having made him pay ninepence, to give him the additional pain of making out what was half expressed. People, too, wrote to one another then, not unfrequently, who had long been separated, and who required much explanation and many details to make the life of each intelligible to the other. The correspondence of the nineteenth century is like a series of telegrams with amplified headings. There is not more than one idea; and that idea comes soon, and is soon over. The best correspondence of the last age is rather like a good light article,—in which the points are studiously made,—in which the effort to make them is studiously concealed,—in which a series of selected circumstances is set forth,—in which you feel, but are not told, that the principle of the writer's selection was to make his composition pleasant.

In letter-writing of this kind Lady Mary was very skilful. She has the highest merit of letter-writing—she is concise without being affected. Fluency, which a great orator pronounced to be the curse of orators, is at least equally the curse of writers. There are many people, many ladies especially, who can write letters at any length, in any number, and at any time. We may be quite sure that the letters so written are not good letters. Composition of any sort implies consideration; you must see where you are going before you can go straight, or can pick your steps as you go. On the other hand, too much consideration is unfavourable to the ease of letter-writing, and perhaps of all writing. A letter too much studied wants flow; it is a museum of hoarded sentences. Each sentence sounds effective; but the whole composition wants vitality. It was written with the memory instead of the mind; and every reader feels the effect, though only the critical reader can detect the cause. Lady Mary understood all this. She said what she had to say in words that were always graphic and always sufficiently good, but she avoided curious felicity. Her expressions seemed choice, but not chosen.

At the end of her life Lady Mary pointed a subordinate but not a useless moral. The masters of mundane ethics observe that "you should stay in the world, or stay out of the world." Lady Mary did neither. She went out and tried to return. Horace Walpole thus describes the result:

"Lady Mary Wortley is arrived; I have seen her; I think her avarice, her art, and her vivacity are all increased. Her dress, like her language, is a *galimatias* of several countries; the groundwork rags, and the embroidery nastiness. She needs no cap, no handkerchief, no gown, no petticoat, and no shoes. An old black laced hood represents the first; the fur of a horseman's coat, which replaces the third, serves for the second; a dimity petticoat is deputy and officiates for the fourth; and slippers act the part of the last. When I was at Florence, and she was expected there, we were drawing *sortes Virgilianas* for her; we literally drew

Insanam vatem aspicies.

It would have been a stranger prophecy now even than it was then."

There is a description of what the favourite of society becomes after leaving it for years, and after indulging eccentricities for years! There is a commentary on the blunder of exposing yourself in your old age to young people, to whom you have always been a tradition and a name! Horace Walpole doubtless painted up a few trivialities a little. But one of the traits is true. Lady Mary lived before the age in which people waste half their lives in washing the whole of their persons.

Lady Mary did not live long after her return to England. Horace Walpole's letter is written on the 2nd February 1762, and she died on the 21st August in the same year. Her husband had died just before her return, and perhaps, after so many years, she would not have returned unless he had done so. *Requiescat in pace;* for she quarrelled all her life.

1862

Matthew Arnold

PREFACE TO ESSAYS
IN CRITICISM, FIRST SERIES

SEVERAL of the Essays which are here collected and reprinted had the good or the bad fortune to
be much criticized at the time of their first appearance. I
am not now going to inflict upon the reader a reply to
those criticisms; for one or two explanations which are
desirable, I shall elsewhere, perhaps, be able some day to
find an opportunity; but, indeed, it is not in my nature,—
some of my critics would rather say, not in my power,—
to dispute on behalf of any opinion, even my own, very
obstinately. To try and approach truth on one side after
another, not to strive or cry, nor to persist in pressing forward, on any one side, with violence and self-will,—it is
only thus, it seems to me, that mortals may hope to gain
any vision of the mysterious Goddess, whom we shall
never see except in outline, but only thus even in outline.
He who will do nothing but fight impetuously towards
her on his own, one, favorite, particular line, is inevitably
destined to run his head into the folds of the black robe in
which she is wrapped.

So it is not to reply to my critics that I write this Preface,
but to prevent a misunderstanding, of which certain
phrases that some of them use make me apprehensive. Mr.
Wright, one of the many translators of Homer, has
published a letter to the Dean of Canterbury, complaining
of some remarks of mine, uttered now a long while ago, on

his version of the *Iliad*. One cannot be always studying
one's own works, and I was really under the impression,
till I saw Mr. Wright's complaint, that I had spoken of
him with all respect. The reader may judge of my astonishment, therefore, at finding, from Mr. Wright's
pamphlet, that I had "declared with much solemnity that
there is not any proper reason for his existing." That I
never said; but, on looking back at my Lectures on
Translating Homer, I find that I did say, not that Mr.
Wright, but that Mr. Wright's version of the *Iliad*, repeating in the main the merits and defects of Cowper's
version, as Mr. Sotheby's repeated those of Pope's version,
had, if I might be pardoned for saying so, no proper
reason for existing. Elsewhere I expressly spoke of the
merit of his version; but I confess that the phrase, qualified as I have shown, about its want of a proper reason for
existing, I used. Well, the phrase had, perhaps, too much
vivacity; we have all of us a right to exist, we and our
works; an unpopular author should be the last person to
call in question this right. So I gladly withdraw the
offending phrase, and I am sorry for having used it; Mr.
Wright, however, would perhaps be more indulgent to
my vivacity, if he considered that we are none of us
likely to be lively much longer. My vivacity is but the
last sparkle of flame before we are all in the dark, the last
glimpse of color before we all go into drab,—the drab of
the earnest, prosaic, practical, austerely literal future. Yes,
the world will soon be the Philistines'! and then, with
every voice, not of thunder, silenced, and the whole earth
filled and ennobled every morning by the magnificent
roaring of the young lions of the *Daily Telegraph,* we shall
all yawn in one another's faces with the dismalest, the
most unimpeachable gravity.

But I return to my design in writing this Preface. That
design was, after apologizing to Mr. Wright for my vivacity of five years ago, to beg him and others to let me

bear my own burdens, without saddling the great and famous University to which I have the honor to belong with any portion of them. What I mean to deprecate is such phrases as "his professorial assault," "his assertions issued *ex cathedra,*" "the sanction of his name as the representative of poetry," and so on. Proud as I am of my connection with the University of Oxford, I can truly say that, knowing how unpopular a task one is undertaking when one tries to pull out a few more stops in that powerful but at present somewhat narrow-toned organ, the modern Englishman, I have sought always to stand by myself, and to compromise others as little as possible. Besides this, my native modesty is such that I have always been shy of assuming the honorable style of Professor, because this is a title I share with so many distinguished men,—Professor Pepper, Professor Anderson, Professor Frickel, and others,—who adorn it, I feel, much more than I do.

However, it is not merely out of modesty that I prefer to stand alone, and to concentrate on myself, as a plain citizen of the republic of letters, and not as an office-bearer in a hierarchy, the whole responsibility for all I write; it is much more out of genuine devotion to the University of Oxford, for which I feel, and always must feel, the fondest, the most reverential attachment. In an epoch of dissolution and transformation, such as that on which we are now entered, habits, ties, and associations are inevitably broken up, the action of individuals becomes more distinct, the shortcomings, errors, heats, disputes, which necessarily attend individual action, are brought into greater prominence. Who would not gladly keep clear, from all these passing clouds, an august institution which was there before they arose, and which will be there when they have blown over?

It is true, the *Saturday Review* maintains that our epoch of transformation is finished; that we have found our philosophy; that the British nation has searched all anchorages for the spirit, and has finally anchored itself, in the fulness of perfected knowledge, on Benthamism. This idea at first made a great impression on me; not only because it is so consoling in itself, but also because it explained a phenomenon which in the summer of last year had, I confess, a good deal troubled me. At that time my avocations led me to travel almost daily on one of the Great Eastern Lines,—the Woodford Branch. Every one knows that the murderer, Müller, perpetrated his detestable act on the North London Railway, close by. The English middle class, of which I am myself a feeble unit, travel on the Woodford Branch in large numbers. Well, the demoralization of our class,—the class which (the newspapers are constantly saying it, so I may repeat it without vanity) has done all the great things which have ever been done in England,—the demoralization, I say, of our class, caused by the Bow tragedy, was something bewildering. Myself a transcendentalist (as the *Saturday Review* knows), I escaped the infection; and, day after day, I used to ply my agitated fellow-travellers with all the consolations which my transcendentalism would naturally suggest to me. I reminded them how Caesar refused to take precautions against assassination, because life was not worth having at the price of an ignoble solicitude for it. I reminded them what insignificant atoms we all are in the life of the world. "Suppose the worst to happen," I said, addressing a portly jeweller from Cheapside; "suppose even yourself to be the victim; *il n'y a pas d'homme nécessaire*. We should miss you for a day or two upon the Woodford Branch; but the great mundane movement would still go on, the gravel walks of your villa would still be rolled, dividends would still be paid at the Bank, omnibuses would still run, there would still be the old crush at the corner of Fenchurch Street." All was of no avail. Nothing could moderate, in the bosom of the great English middle class, their passionate, absorbing, almost bloodthirsty clinging to life. At the moment I thought this over-concern a little unworthy; but the *Saturday Review* suggests a touching explanation of it. What I took for the ignoble clinging to life of a comfortable worldling, was, perhaps, only the ardent longing of a faithful Benthamite, traversing an age still dimmed by the last mists of transcendentalism, to be spared long enough to see his religion in the full and final blaze of its triumph. This respectable man, whom I imagined to be going up to London to serve his shop, or to buy shares, or to attend an Exeter Hall meeting, or to assist at the deliberations of the Marylebone Vestry, was even, perhaps, in real truth, on a pious pilgrimage, to obtain from Mr. Bentham's executors a secret bone of his great, dissected master.

And yet, after all, I cannot but think that the *Saturday Review* has here, for once, fallen a victim to an idea,—a beautiful but deluding idea,—and that the British nation has not yet, so entirely as the reviewer seems to imagine, found the last word of its philosophy. No, we are all seekers still! seekers often make mistakes, and I wish mine to redound to my own discredit only, and not to touch Oxford. Beautiful city! so venerable, so lovely, so unravaged by the fierce intellectual life of our century, so serene!

There are our young barbarians, all at play!

And yet, steeped in sentiment as she lies, spreading her gardens to the moonlight, and whispering from her towers the last enchantments of the Middle Age, who will deny that Oxford, by her ineffable charm, keeps ever calling us nearer to the true goal of all of us, to the ideal, to perfection,—to beauty, in a word, which is only truth seen from another side?—nearer, perhaps, than all the science of Tübingen. Adorable dreamer, whose heart has been so romantic! who hast given thyself so prodigally, given thyself to sides and to heroes not mine, only never to the Philistines! home of lost causes, and forsaken beliefs, and unpopular names, and impossible loyalties! what example could ever so inspire us to keep down the Philistine in ourselves, what teacher could ever so save us from that bondage to which we are all prone, that bondage which Goethe, in his incomparable lines on the death of Schiller, makes it his friend's highest praise (and nobly did Schiller deserve the praise) to have left miles out of sight behind him;—the bondage of *"was uns alle bändigt, das Gemeine!"* She will forgive me, even if I have unwittingly drawn upon her a shot or two aimed at her unworthy son; for she is generous, and the cause in which I fight is, after all, hers. Apparitions of a day, what is our puny warfare against the Philistines, compared with the warfare which this queen of romance has been waging against them for centuries, and will wage after we are gone?

1865

Robert Louis Stevenson

WALKING TOURS

IT must not be imagined that a walking tour, as some would have us fancy, is merely a better or worse way of seeing the country. There are many ways of seeing landscape quite as good; and none more vivid, in spite of canting dilettantes, than from a railway train. But landscape on a walking tour is quite accessory. He who is indeed of the brotherhood does not voyage in quest of the picturesque, but of certain jolly humours—of the hope and spirit with which the march begins at morning, and the peace and spiritual repletion of the evening's rest. He cannot tell whether he puts his knapsack on, or takes it off, with more delight. The excitement of the departure puts him in key for that of the arrival. Whatever he does is not only a reward in itself, but will be further rewarded in the sequel; and so pleasure leads on to pleasure in an endless chain. It is this that so few can understand; they will either be always lounging or always at five miles an hour; they do not play off the one against the other, prepare all day for the evening, and all evening for the next day. And, above all, it is here that your overwalker fails of comprehension. His heart rises against those who drink their curaçoa in liqueur glasses, when he himself can swill it in a brown john. He will not believe that the flavour is more delicate in the smaller dose. He will not believe that to walk this unconscionable distance is merely to stupefy and brutalise himself, and come to his inn, at night, with a sort of frost on his five wits, and a starless night of darkness in his spirit. Not for him the mild luminous evening of the temperate walker! He has nothing left of man but a physical need for bedtime and a double nightcap; and even his pipe, if he be a smoker, will be savourless and disenchanted. It is the fate of such an one to take twice as much trouble as is needed to obtain happiness, and miss the happiness in the end; he is the man of the proverb, in short, who goes further and fares worse.

Now, to be properly enjoyed, a walking tour should be gone upon alone. If you go in a company, or even in pairs, it is no longer a walking tour in anything but name; it is something else, and more in the nature of a picnic. A walking tour should be gone upon alone, because freedom is of the essence; because you should be able to stop and go on, and follow this way or that, as the freak takes you; and because you must have your own pace, and neither trot alongside a champion walker, nor mince in time with a girl. And then you must be open to all impressions and let your thoughts take colour from what you see. You should be as a pipe for any wind to play upon. "I cannot see the wit," says Hazlitt, "of walking and talking at the same time. When I am in the country, I wish to vegetate like the country," which is the gist of all that can be said upon the matter. There should be no cackle of voices at your elbow, to jar on the meditative silence of the morning. And so long as a man is reasoning he cannot surrender himself to that fine intoxication that comes of much motion in the open air, that begins in a sort of dazzle and sluggishness of the brain, and ends in a peace that passes comprehension.

During the first day or so of any tour there are moments of bitterness, when the traveller feels more than coldly towards his knapsack, when he is half in a mind to throw it bodily over the hedge and, like Christian on a similar

òccasion, "give three leaps and go on singing." And yet it
soon acquires a property of easiness. It becomes magnetic;
the spirit of the journey enters into it. And no sooner have
you passed the straps over your shoulder than the lees of
sleep are cleared from you, you pull yourself together with
a shake, and fall at once into your stride. And surely, of
all possible moods, this, in which a man takes the road, is
the best. Of course, if he *will* keep thinking of his anxieties,
if he *will* open the merchant Abudah's chest and walk arm
in arm with the hag—why, wherever he is, and whether
he walk fast or slow, the chances are that he will not be
happy. And so much the more shame to himself! There
are perhaps thirty men setting forth at the same hour, and
I would lay a large wager there is not another dull face
among the thirty. It would be a fine thing to follow, in a
coat of darkness, one after another of these wayfarers,
some summer morning, for the first few miles upon the
road. This one, who walks fast, with a keen look in his
eyes, is all concentrated in his own mind; he is up at his
loom, weaving and weaving, to set the landscape to words.
This one peers about, as he goes, among the grasses; he
waits by the canal to watch the dragon-flies; he leans on
the gate of the pasture, and cannot look enough upon the
complacent kine. And here comes another talking, laughing, and gesticulating to himself. His face changes from
time to time, as indignation flashes from his eyes or anger
clouds his forehead. He is composing articles, delivering
orations, and conducting the most impassioned inter-
views, by the way. A little farther on, and it is as like as
not he will begin to sing. And well for him, supposing him
to be no great master in that art, if he stumble across no
stolid peasant at a corner; for on such an occasion, I
scarcely know which is the more troubled, or whether it is
worse to suffer the confusion of your troubadour or the
unfeigned alarm of your clown. A sedentary population,
accustomed, besides, to the strange mechanical bearing of

the common tramp, can in no wise explain to itself the gaiety of these passers-by. I knew one man who was arrested as a runaway lunatic because, although a full-grown person with a red beard, he skipped as he went like a child. And you would be astonished if I were to tell you all the grave and learned heads who have confessed to me that, when on walking tours, they sang—and sang very ill—and had a pair of red ears when, as described above, the inauspicious peasant plumped into their arms from round a corner. And here, lest you should think I am exaggerating, is Hazlitt's own confession, from his essay *On Going a Journey*, which is so good that there should be a tax levied on all who have not read it:—

"Give me the clear blue sky over my head," says he, "and the green turf beneath my feet, a winding road before me, and a three hours' march to dinner—and then to thinking! It is hard if I cannot start some game on these lone heaths. I laugh, I run, I leap, I sing for joy."

Bravo! After that adventure of my friend with the policeman, you would not have cared, would you, to publish that in the first person? But we have no bravery nowadays, and, even in books, must all pretend to be as dull and foolish as our neighbours. It was not so with Hazlitt. And notice how learned he is (as, indeed, throughout the essay) in the theory of walking tours. He is none of your athletic men in purple stockings, who walk their fifty miles a day: three hours' march is his ideal. And then he must have a winding road, the epicure!

Yet there is one thing I object to in these words of his, one thing in the great master's practice that seems to me not wholly wise. I do not approve of that leaping and running. Both of these hurry the respiration; they both shake up the brain out of its glorious open-air confusion; and they both break the pace. Uneven walking is not so agreeable to the body, and it distracts and irritates the mind. Whereas, when once you have fallen into an equable stride, it requires no conscious thought from you to keep it up, and yet it prevents you from thinking earnestly of anything else. Like knitting, like the work of a copying clerk, it gradually neutralises and sets to sleep the serious activity of the mind. We can think of this or that, lightly and laughingly, as a child thinks, or as we think in a morning doze; we can make puns or puzzle out acrostics, and trifle in a thousand ways with words and rhymes; but when it comes to honest work, when we come to gather ourselves together for an effort, we may sound the trumpet as loud and long as we please; the great barons of the mind will not rally to the standard, but sit, each one, at home, warming his hands over his own fire and brooding on his own private thought!

In the course of a day's walk, you see, there is much variance in the mood. From the exhilaration of the start, to the happy phlegm of the arrival, the change is certainly great. As the day goes on, the traveller moves from the one extreme towards the other. He becomes more and more incorporated with the material landscape, and the open-air drunkenness grows upon him with great strides, until he posts along the road, and sees everything about him, as in a cheerful dream. The first is certainly brighter, but the second stage is the more peaceful. A man does not make so many articles towards the end, nor does he laugh aloud; but the purely animal pleasures, the sense of physical wellbeing, the delight of every inhalation, of every time the muscles tighten down the thigh, console him for the absence of the others, and bring him to his destination still content.

Nor must I forget to say a word on bivouacs. You come to a milestone on a hill, or some place where deep ways meet under trees; and off goes the knapsack, and down you sit to smoke a pipe in the shade. You sink into yourself, and the birds come round and look at you, and your smoke dissipates upon the afternoon under the blue dome of heaven; and the sun lies warm upon your feet, and the cool air visits your neck and turns aside your open shirt. If you are not happy, you must have an evil conscience. You may dally as long as you like by the roadside. It is almost as if the millennium were arrived, when we shall throw our clocks and watches over the house-top, and remember time and seasons no more. Not to keep hours for a lifetime is, I was going to say, to live for ever. You have no idea, unless you have tried it, how endlessly long is a summer's day, that you measure out only by hunger, and bring to an end only when you are drowsy. I know a village where there are hardly any clocks, where no one knows more of the days of the week than by a sort of instinct for the *fête* on Sundays, and where only one person can tell you the day of the month, and she is generally wrong; and if people were aware how slow Time journeyed in that village, and what armfuls of spare hours he gives, over and above the bargain, to its wise inhabitants, I believe there would be a stampede out of London, Liverpool, Paris, and a variety of large towns, where the clocks lose their heads, and shake the hours out each one faster than the other, as though they were all in a wager. And all these foolish pilgrims would each bring his own misery along with him, in a watch-pocket! It is to be noticed, there were no clocks and watches in the much-vaunted days before the flood. It follows, of course, there were no appointments, and punctuality was not yet thought upon. "Though ye take from a covetous man all his treasure," says Milton, "he has yet one jewel left; ye cannot deprive him of his covetousness." And so I would say of a modern man of business, you may do what you will for him, put him in Eden, give him the elixir of life —he has still a flaw at heart, he still has his business habits. Now, there is no time when business habits are more mitigated than on a walking tour. And so during these halts, as I say, you will feel almost free.

But it is at night, and after dinner, that the best hour comes. There are no such pipes to be smoked as those that follow a good day's march; the flavour of the tobacco is a thing to be remembered, it is so dry and aromatic, so full and so fine. If you wind up the evening with grog, you will own there was never such grog; at every sip a jocund tranquility spreads about your limbs, and sits easily in your heart. If you read a book—and you will never do so save by fits and starts—you find the language strangely racy and harmonious; words take a new meaning; single sentences possess the ear for half an hour together; and the writer endears himself to you, at every page, by the nicest coincidence of sentiment. It seems as if it were a book you had written yourself in a dream. To all we have read on such occasions we look back with special favour. "It was on the 10th of April 1798," says Hazlitt, with amorous precision, "that I sat down to a volume of the new *Heloïse,* at the Inn at Llangollen, over a bottle of sherry and a cold chicken." I should wish to quote more, for though we are mighty fine fellows nowadays, we cannot write like Hazlitt. And talking of that, a volume of Hazlitt's essays would be a capital pocket-book on such a journey; so would a volume of Heine's songs; and for *Tristram Shandy* I can pledge a fair experience.

If the evening be fine and warm, there is nothing better in life than to lounge before the inn door in the sunset, or lean over the parapet of the bridge, to watch the weeds and the quick fishes. It is then, if ever, that you taste joviality to the full significance of that audacious word. Your muscles are so agreeably slack, you feel so clean and so strong and so idle that whether you move or sit still, whatever you do is done with pride and a kingly sort of pleasure. You fall in talk with anyone, wise or foolish, drunk or sober. And it seems as if a hot walk purged you, more than of anything else, of all narrowness and pride, and left curiosity to play its part freely, as in a child or a man of science. You lay aside all your own hobbies, to watch provincial humours develop themselves before you, now as a laughable farce, and now grave and beautiful like an old tale.

Or perhaps you are left to your own company for the night, and surly weather imprisons you by the fire. You may remember how Burns, numbering past pleasures, dwells upon the hours when he has been "happy thinking." It is a phrase that may well perplex a poor modern girt about on every side by clocks and chimes, and haunted, even at night, by flaming dial-plates. For we are all so busy, and have so many far-off projects to realise, and castles in the fire to turn into solid, habitable mansions on a gravel soil, that we can find no time for pleasure trips into the Land of Thought and among the Hills of Vanity. Changed times, indeed, when we must sit all night, beside the fire, with folded hands; and a changed world for most of us, when we find we can pass the hours without discontent, and be happy thinking. We are in such haste to be doing, to be writing, to be gathering gear, to make our voice audible a moment in the derisive silence of eternity, that we forget that one thing, of which these are but the parts—namely to live. We fall in love, we drink hard, we run to and fro upon the earth like frightened sheep. And now you are to ask yourself if, when all is done, you would not have been better to sit by the fire at home, and be happy thinking. To sit still and contemplate,—to remember the faces of women without desire, to be pleased by the great deeds of men without envy, to be everything and everywhere in sympathy, and yet content to remain where and what you are—is not this to know both wisdom and virtue, and to dwell with happiness? After all, it is not they who carry flags, but they who look upon it from a private chamber who have the fun of the procession. And once you are at that, you are in the very humour of all social heresy. It is no time for shuffling, or for big empty words. If you ask yourself what you mean by fame, riches, or learning, the answer is far to seek; and you go back into that kingdom of light imaginations, which seem so vain in the eyes of Philistines perspiring after wealth, and so momentous to those who are stricken with the disproportions of the world, and in the face of the gigantic stars, cannot stop to split differences between two degrees of the infinitesimally small, such as a tobacco pipe or the Roman Empire, a million of money or a fiddlestick's end.

You lean from the window, your last pipe reeking whitely into the darkness, your body full of delicious pains, your mind enthroned in the seventh circle of content; when suddenly the mood changes, the weather-cock goes about, and you ask yourself one question more: whether, for the interval, you have been the wisest philosopher or the most egregious of donkeys? Human experience is not yet able to reply; but at least you have had a fine moment, and looked down upon all the kingdoms of the earth. And whether it was wise or foolish, tomorrow's travel will carry you, body and mind, into some different parish of the infinite.

1876

Andrew Lang

GOLF

WHILE pheasant-shooters are enjoying the first day of the season, the votaries of a sport not less noble, though less noisy, are holding the great festival of their year. The autumn meeting of the Royal and Ancient Golf Club of St. Andrews is in full swing, and the words will suggest pleasant memories to many a golfer. Golf is not one of the more brilliant and famous pastimes of the day, though it yields to none in antiquity and in unassuming merit. The names of the winners of the gold medal and of the silver cross are not telegraphed all over the world as widely as Mr. Tennyson's hero wished the news that Maud had accepted him to be. The red man may possibly "dance beneath his red cedar tree" at the tidings of the event of one of our great horse-races, or great university matches. At all events, even if the red man preserves his usual stoicism of demeanour, his neighbours, the pale-faces, like to know all about the result of many English sports the moment they are decided. Golf, as we have said, excites less general enthusiasm; but in people who love it at all, the love is burning, consuming; they will talk golf-shop in season and out of season. Few persons, perhaps, will call golf the very first and queen of games. Cricket exercises more faculties of body, and even of mind, for does not the artful bowler "bowl with his head"? Football demands an extraordinary personal courage, and implies the existence of a fierce delight in battle with one's peers. Tennis, with all its merits, is a game for the few, so rare are tennis-courts and so expensive the pastime. But cricketers, football-players, tennis-players, would all give golf the second place after their favourite exercise; and just as Themistocles was held to be the best Greek general, because each of his fellows placed him second, so golf may assert a right to be thought the first of games. One great advantage it certainly has—it is a game for "men" of all ages, from eight, or even younger, to eighty. The links of St. Andrews are probably cleared just now of the little lads and the veterans; they make room for the heroes, the medalists, the great players—Mr. Mackay, Mr. Lamb, Mr. Leslie Balfour, and the rest. But at ordinary times there are always dozens of tiny boys in knicker-bockers and scarlet stockings, who "drive out" the first hole in some twenty strokes of their little clubs, and who pass much of their time in fishing for their lost balls in the muddy burn. As for the veterans "on the threshold of old age," it is pleasant to watch their boyish eagerness, the swaying of their bodies as they watch the short flight of their longest hits; their delight when they do manage to hit further than the sand-pit, or "bunker," which is named after the nose of a long-dead principal of the university; their caution, nay, their almost tedious delay in the process of putting, that is, of hitting the ball over the "green" into the neighbouring hole. They can still do their round, or their two rounds, five or ten miles' walking a day; and who can speak otherwise than well of a game which is not too strenuous for healthy age or tender childhood, and yet allows an athlete of twenty-three to put out all his strength?

Golf is a thoroughly national game; it is as Scotch as haggis, cockie-leekie, high cheek-bones, or rowanberry jam. A spurious imitation, or an arrested development of the sport, exists in the south of France, where a ball is knocked along the roads to a fixed goal. But this is natur-

ally very poor fun compared to the genuine game as
played on the short turf besides the grey northern sea on
the coast of Fife. Golf has been introduced of late years into
England and is played at Westward Ho, at Wimbledon,
at Blackheath (the oldest club), at Liverpool, over Cowley
Marsh, near Oxford, and in many other places. It is, therefore, no longer necessary to say that golf is not a highly
developed and scientific sort of hockey, or bandy-ball.
Still, there be some to whom the processes of the sport are
a mystery, and who would be at a loss to discriminate a
niblick from a bunker-iron. The thoroughly equipped
golf-player needs an immense variety of weapons, or implements, which are carried for him by his caddie—a youth or
old man, who is, as it were, his esquire, who sympathizes
with him in defeat, rejoices in his success, and aids him
with such advice as his superior knowledge of the ground
suggests. The class of human beings known as caddies are
the offspring of golf, and have peculiar traits which distinguish them from the professional cricketer, the water-
man, the keeper, the gillie, and all other professionals. It is
not very easy to account for their little peculiarities. One
thing is certain—that when golf was introduced by
Scotchmen into France, and found a home at Pau, in the
shadow of the Pyrenees, the French caddie sprang, so to
speak, from the ground, the perfect likeness of his Scottish brother. He was just as sly, just as importunate in
his demands to be employed, just as fond of "putting at
short holes," more profane, and every bit as contemptuous
of all non-golf-playing humanity as the boyish Scotch
caddies, in whom contempt has reversed the usual process,
and bred familiarity with all beginners.

The professional cricketer can instruct an unskilled
amateur, can take his ill-guarded wicket, and make him
"give chances" all over the field, without bursting into
yells of unseemly laughter. But the little caddie cannot restrain his joy when the tyro at golf, after missing his ball

some six times, ultimately dashes off the head of his club against the ground. Nor is he less exuberant when his patron's ball is deep in a "bunker," or sand-pit, where the wretch stands digging at it with an iron, hot, helpless, and wrathful. And yet golf is a sport not learned in a day, and caddies might be more considerate. The object of the game is to strike the small guttapercha ball into a hole about five inches wide, distant from the striker about three hundred yards, and separated from him by rough grass and smooth sand-pits, furze bushes, and perhaps a road or a brook. He who, of two players, gets his ball into the hole in the smallest number of strokes is the winner of that hole, and the party then play towards the next hole. All sorts of skill are needed—strength and adroitness, and a certain supple "swing" of the body, are wanted to send the ball "sure and far" in the "driving" part of the game. Nothing is so pleasant as a clean "drive." The sensation is like that of hitting a ball to square-leg, fair and full, at cricket. Then the golfer must have the knack to lift his ball out of deep sand with the "iron," and to strike it deftly "a half-shot" up to the hole with the "cleek;" and, lastly, coolness and a good eye when he "putts" or hits his ball actually up to the very hole.

Any degree of skill in these varied feats makes golf a delightful game, if the opponents are well matched. Nor are the charms of scenery wanting at St. Andrews, the headquarters of the sport. There is no more picturesque town in Scotland than the little university city. From the plain of the estuary of the river Eden, across the long leagues of marsh land and the stretches of golden sand and brown, the towers of St. Andrews—for it is a town of many towers—are seen breaking the sky-line. Built on a windy headland, running out to the grey northern sea, it reaches the water with an ancient pier of rugged stone. Immediately above is the site of a chapel of immemorial age, and above that again are the ruins of the cathedral—

gaunt spires with broken tracery, standing where once the burnished roof of copper flashed far across the deep. The high street winds from the cathedral precinct past an old house of Queen Mary Stuart, past ruined chapels of St. Leonard's, and the university chapel with its lovely spire, down to the shores of the bay; and along the bay run the famous "links," where the royal and ancient game has its cradle and home. Other links, as Prestwick, or North Berwick, may vie with those of St. Andrews in extent, or in the smoothness of the putting greens, or in the number and hardness of the "hazards," or difficult places; but none offer so wide and varied an extent of scenery, from the melancholy stretch of the parallel sands to the hills in the west, the golden glitter of the beach, beneath the faint aerial blue of the still more distant hills across the firth, while behind is the city set on its cliffs, and proud with its crown of spires. The reflected sunset lingers on the walls and crags and towers, that shine imaged in the wet sands, the after-glow hangs over the eastern sky, and these have their charm; but their charm yields to that of golf. It is a sign that a man has lost heart and hope when he dilates on the beauty of the scenery, and abstracts his attention from what alone would interest him were he winning— the "lie" of his ball. Who can stop to think of the beauties of nature, when he and his antagonist are equal, and there are only two more holes left to play in the match for the medal? It is a serious moment; not one of the little crowd of observers, the gallery that accompany the players, dares to speak, or even cough. The caddie who sneezes is lost, for he will be accused of distracting his master's attention. The ladies begin to appear in the background, ready to greet the players, and to tell the truth, are not very welcome to the nervous golfer. Everything turns on half an inch of leather in a "drive," or a stiff blade of grass in a putt, and the interest is wound up to a really breathless pitch. Happy he is who does not in his excitement "top" his ball into the neighboring brook, or "heel" it and send it devious down to the depths of ocean. Happy is he who can "hole out the last hole in four" beneath the eyes of the ladies. Striding victorious into the hospitable club, where beer awaits him, he need not envy the pheasant-slayer who has slain his hundreds.

1889

Walter Pater

SHAKESPEARE'S ENGLISH KINGS

A brittle glory shineth in this face:
As brittle as the glory is the face.

THE English plays of Shakespeare needed but the completion of one unimportant interval to possess the unity of a popular chronicle from Richard the Second to Henry the Eighth, and possess, as they actually stand, the unity of a common motive in the handling of the various events and persons which they bring before us. Certain of his historic dramas, not English, display Shakespeare's mastery in the development of the heroic nature amid heroic circumstances; and had he chosen, from English history, to deal with Coeur-de-Lion or Edward the First, the innate quality of his subject would doubtless have called into play something of that profound and sombre power which in *Julius Caesar* and *Macbeth* has sounded the depths of mighty character. True, on the whole, to fact, it is another side of kingship which he has made prominent in his English histories. The irony of kingship—average human nature, flung with a wonderfully pathetic effect into the vortex of great events; tragedy of everyday quality heightened in degree only by the conspicuous scene which does but make those who play their parts there conspicuously unfortunate; the utterance

of common humanity straight from the heart, but refined
like other common things for kingly uses by Shakespeare's
unfailing eloquence: such, unconsciously for the most part,
though palpably enough to the careful reader, is the conception under which Shakespeare has arranged the lights
and shadows of the story of the English kings, emphasizing merely the light and shadow inherent in it, and keeping very close to the original authorities, not simply in the
general outline of these dramatic histories but sometimes
in their very expression. Certainly the history itself, as he
found it in Hall, Holinshed, and Stowe, those somewhat
picturesque old chroniclers who had themselves an eye for
the dramatic "effects" of human life, has much of this
sentiment already about it. What he did not find there was
the natural prerogative—such justification, in kingly, that
is to say, in exceptional, qualities, of the exceptional position, as makes it practicable in the result. It is no *Henriade*
he writes, and no history of the English people, but the
sad fortunes of some English kings as conspicuous examples of the ordinary human condition. As in a children's
story, all princes are in extremes. Delightful in the sunshine above the wall into which chance lifts the flower
for a season, they can but plead somewhat more touchingly
than others their everyday weakness in the storm. Such is
the motive that gives unity to these unequal and intermittent contributions toward a slowly evolved dramatic chronicle, which it would have taken many days to rehearse; a
not distant story from real life still well remembered in its
general course, to which people might listen now and
again, as long as they cared, finding human nature at
least wherever their attention struck ground in it.

He begins with John, and allows indeed to the first of
these English kings a kind of greatness, making the development of the play centre in the counter-action of his
natural gifts—that something of heroic force about him—
by a madness which takes the shape of reckless impiety,

forced especially on men's attention by the terrible circumstances of his end, in the delineation of which Shakespeare triumphs, setting, with true poetic tact, this incident of the king's death, in all the horror of a violent one, amid a scene delicately suggestive of what is perennially peaceful and genial in the outward world. Like the sensual humours of Falstaff in another play, the presence of the bastard Faulconbridge, with his physical energy and his unmistakable family likeness—"those limbs which Sir Robert never holp to make" *—contributes to an almost coarse assertion of the force of nature, of the somewhat ironic preponderance of nature and circumstance over men's artificial arrangements, to the recognition of a certain potent natural aristocracy, which is far from being always identical with that more formal, heraldic one. And what is a coarse fact in the case of Faulconbridge becomes a motive of pathetic appeal in the wan and babyish Arthur. The magic with which nature models tiny and delicate children to the likeness of their rough fathers is nowhere more justly expressed than in the words of King Philip.—

Look here upon thy brother Geoffrey's face!
These eyes, these brows were moulded out of his:
This little abstract doth contain that large
Which died in Geoffrey; and the hand of time
Shall draw this brief into as huge a volume.

It was perhaps something of a boyish memory of the shocking end of his father that had distorted the piety of Henry the Third into superstitious terror. A frightened soul, himself touched with the contrary sort of religious madness, doting on all that was alien from his father's huge ferocity, on the genialities, the soft gilding, of life,

* *Elinor.* Do you not read some tokens of my son (Coeur-de-Lion)
　　　In the large composition of this man?

on the genuine interests of art and poetry, to be credited
more than any other person with the deep religious expression of Westminster Abbey, Henry the Third picturesque
though useless, but certainly touching, might have furnished Shakespeare, had he filled up this interval in his
series, with precisely the kind of effect he tends towards in
his English plays. But he found it completer still in the
person and story of Richard the Second, a figure—"that
sweet lovely rose"—which haunts Shakespeare's mind, as
it seems long to have haunted the minds of the English
people, as the most touching of all examples of the irony
of kingship.

Henry the Fourth—to look for a moment beyond our
immediate subject, in pursuit of Shakespeare's thought—
is presented, of course, in general outline, as an impersona-
tion of "surviving force:" he has a certain amount of king-
craft also, a real fitness for great opportunity. But still
true to his leading motive, Shakespeare, in *King Henry the
Fourth,* has left the high-water mark of his poetry in the
soliloquy which represents royalty longing vainly for the
toiler's sleep; while the popularity, the showy heroism,
of Henry the Fifth, is used to give emphatic point to the
old earthy commonplace about "wild oats." The wealth
of homely humour in these plays, the fun coming straight
home to all the world, of Fluellen especially in his unconscious interview with the king, the boisterous earthi-
ness of Falstaff and his companions, contribute to the same
effect. The keynote of Shakespeare's treatment is indeed
expressed by Henry the Fifth himself, the *greatest* of
Shakespeare's kings.—"Though I speak it to you," he says
incognito, under cover of night, to a common soldier on
the field, "I think the king is but a man, as I am: the
violet smells to him as it doth to me: all his senses have
but human conditions; and though his affections be higher
mounted than ours yet when they stoop they stoop with
like wing." And, in truth, the really kingly speeches

which Shakespeare assigns to him, as to other kings weak enough in all but speech, are but a kind of flowers, worn for, and effective only as personal embellishment. They combine to one result with the merely outward and ceremonial ornaments of royalty, its pageantries, flaunting so naively, so credulously, in Shakespeare, as in that old medieval time. And then, the force of Hotspur is but transient youth, the common heat of youth, in him. The character of Henry the Sixth again, *roi fainéant,* with La Pucelle * for his counterfoil, lay in the direct course of Shakespeare's design: he has done much to fix the sentiment of the "holy Henry." Richard the Third, touched, like John, with an effect of real heroism, is spoiled like him by something of criminal madness, and reaches his highest level of tragic expression when circumstances reduce him to terms of mere human nature.—

> A horse! A horse! My kingdom for a horse!

The Princes in the Tower recall to mind the lot of young Arthur:—

> I'll go with thee,
> And find the inheritance of this poor child,
> His little kingdom of a forced grave.

And when Shakespeare comes to Henry the Eighth, it is not the superficial though very English splendour of the king himself, but the really potent and ascendant nature of the butcher's son on the one hand, and Katharine's subdued reproduction of the sad fortunes of Richard the second on the other, that define his central interest.†

* Perhaps the one person of *genius* in these English plays.
> The spirit of deep prophecy she hath,
> Exceeding the nine Sibyls of old Rome:
> What's past and what's to come she can descry.

† Proposing in this paper to trace the leading sentiment in Shakespeare's English Plays as a sort of *popular dramatic chronicle,* I have left untouched the question how much (or, in the case

With a prescience of the Wars of the Roses, of which his errors were the original cause, it is Richard who best exposes Shakespeare's own constant sentiment concerning war, and especially that sort of civil war which was then recent in English memories. The soul of Shakespeare, certainly, was not wanting in a sense of the magnanimity of warriors. The grandiose aspects of war, its magnificent apparelling, he records monumentally enough— the "dressing of the lists," the lion's heart, its unfaltering haste thither in all the freshness of youth and morning.—

> Not sick although I have to do with death—
> The sun doth gild our armour: Up, my Lords!—
> I saw young Harry with his beaver on,
> His cuisses on his thighs, gallantly arm'd,
> Rise from the ground like feather'd Mercury.

Only, with Shakespeare, the afterthought is immediate:—

> They come like sacrifices in their trim.

> —Will it never be today? I will trot tomorrow a mile, and
> my way shall be paved with English faces.

This sentiment Richard reiterates very plaintively, in association with the delicate sweetness of the English fields, still sweet and fresh, like London and her other fair towns in that England of Chaucer, for whose soil the exiled Bolingbroke is made to long so dangerously, while Richard on his return from Ireland salutes it—

> That pale, that white-fac'd shore,—
> As a long-parted mother with her child.—
> So weeping, smiling, greet I thee, my earth!
> And do thee favour with my royal hands.—

---

of *Henry the Sixth* and *Henry the Eighth,* how little) of them may be really his: how far inferior hands have contributed to a result, true on the whole to the greater, that is to say, the Shakespearian, elements in them.

Then (of Bolingbroke)

> Ere the crown he looks for live in peace,
> Ten thousand bloody crowns of mothers' sons
> Shall ill become the flower of England's face;
> Change the complexion of her maid-pale peace
> To scarlet indignation, and bedew
> My pastures' grass with faithful English blood.—

> Why have they dared to march?—

asks York,

> So many miles upon her peaceful bosom,
> Frighting her pale-fac'd visages with war?—

waking, according to Richard,

> Our peace, which in our country's cradle,
> Draws the sweet infant breath of gentle sleep:

bedrenching "with crimson tempest"

> The fresh green lap of fair king Richard's land:—

frighting "fair peace" from "our quiet confines," laying

> The summer's dust with showers of blood,
> Rained from the wounds of slaughter'd Englishmen:

bruising

> Her flowerets with the armed hoofs
> Of hostile paces.

Perhaps it is not too fanciful to note in this play a peculiar recoil from the mere instruments of warfare, the contact of the "rude ribs," the "flint bosom," of Barkloughly Castle or Pomfret or

> Julius Caesar's ill-erected tower:

the

> Boisterous untun'd drums
> With harsh-resounding trumpets' dreadful bray
> And grating shock of wrathful iron arms.

It is as if the lax, soft beauty of the king took effect, at least by contrast, on everything beside.

One gracious prerogative, certainly, Shakespeare's English kings possess: they are a very eloquent company, and Richard is the most sweet-tongued of them all. In no other play perhaps is there such a flush of those gay, fresh, variegated flowers of speech—colour and figure, not lightly attached to, but fused into, the very phrase itself—which Shakespeare cannot help dispensing to his characters, as in this "play of the Deposing of King Richard the Second," an exquisite poet if he is nothing else, from first to last, in light and gloom alike, able to see all things poetically, to give a poetic turn to his conduct of them, and refreshing with his golden language the tritest aspects of that ironic contrast between the pretensions of a king and the actual necessities of his destiny. What a garden of words! With him, blank verse, infinitely graceful, deliberate, musical in inflexion, becomes indeed a true "verse royal," that rhyming lapse, which to the Shakespearian ear, at least in youth, came as the last touch of refinement on it, being here doubly appropriate. His eloquence blends with that fatal beauty, of which he was so frankly aware, so amiable to his friends, to his wife, of the effects of which on the people his enemies were so much afraid, on which Shakespeare himself dwells so attentively as the "royal blood" comes and goes in the face with his rapid changes of temper. As happens with sensitive natures, it attunes him to a congruous suavity of manners, by which anger itself became flattering: it blends with his merely youthful hopefulness and high spirits, his sympathetic love for gay people, things, apparel—"his cote of gold and stone, valued at thirty thousand marks," the novel Italian fashions he preferred, as also with those real amiabilities that made people forget the darker touches of his character, but never tire of the pathetic rehearsal of his fall, the meekness of which would have seemed merely abject in a less graceful performer.

Yet it is only fair to say that in the painstaking "revival" of *King Richard the Second,* by the late Charles Kean, those who were very young thirty years ago were afforded much more than Shakespeare's play could ever have been before—the very person of the king based on the stately old portrait in Westminster Abbey, "the earliest extant contemporary likeness of any English sovereign," the grace, the winning pathos, the sympathetic voice of the player, the tasteful archaeology confronting vulgar modern London with a scenic reproduction, for once really agreeable, of the London of Chaucer. In the hands of Kean the play became like an exquisite performance of the violin.

The long agony of one so gaily painted by nature's self, from his "tragic abdication" till the hour in which he

> Sluiced out his innocent soul thro' streams of blood,

was for playwrights a subject ready to hand, and became early the theme of a popular drama, of which some have fancied surviving favourite fragments in the rhymed parts of Shakespeare's work.

> The king Richard of Yngland
> Was in his flowris then regnand:
> But his flowris efter sone
> Fadyt, and ware all undone:—

says the old chronicle. Strangely enough, Shakespeare supposes him an over-confident believer in that divine right of kings, of which people in Shakespeare's time were coming to hear so much; a general right, sealed to him (so Richard is made to think) as an ineradicable personal gift by the touch—stream rather, over head and breast and shoulders—of the "holy oil" of his consecration at Westminster; not however, through some oversight, the genuine balm used at the coronation of his successor, given, according to legend, by the Blessed Virgin to Saint Thomas of Canterbury. Richard himself found that, it was said, among other forgotten treasures, at the crisis of his changing fortunes, and vainly sought reconsecration therewith—understood, wistfully, that it was reserved for his happier rival. And yet his coronation, by the pageantry, the amplitude, the learned care, of its order, so lengthy that the king, then only eleven years of age, and fasting, as a communicant at the ceremony, was carried away in a faint, fixed the type under which it has ever since continued. And nowhere is there so emphatic a reiteration as in *Richard the Second* of the sentiment which those singular rites were calculated to produce.

> Not all the water in the rough rude sea
> Can wash the balm from an anointed king,—

as supplementing another, almost supernatural, right.— "Edward's seven sons," of whom Richard's father was one,

> Were as seven phials of his sacred blood.

But this, too, in the hands of Shakespeare, becomes for him, like any other of those fantastic, ineffectual, easily discredited, personal graces, as capricious in its operation on men's wills as merely physical beauty, kindling himself to eloquence indeed, but only giving double pathos to insults which "barbarism itself" might have pitied—the dust in his face as he returns, through the streets of London, a prisoner in the train of his victorious enemy.

> How soon my sorrow hath destroyed my face!

he cries, in that most poetic invention of the mirror scene, which does but reinforce again that physical charm which all confessed. The sense of "divine right" in kings is found to act not so much as a secret of power over others, as of infatuation to themselves. And of all those personal gifts the one which alone never altogether fails him is just that royal utterance, his appreciation of the poetry of his own hapless lot, an eloquent self-pity, infecting others in spite of themselves, till they too become irresistibly eloquent about him.

In the Roman Pontifical, of which the order of Coronation is really a part, there is no form for the inverse process, no rite of "degradation," such as that by which an offending priest or bishop may be deprived, if not of the essential quality of "orders," yet, one by one, of its outward dignities. It is as if Shakespeare had had in mind some such inverted rite, like those old ecclesiastical or military ones, by which human hardness, or human justice, adds the last touch of unkindness to the execution of its sentences, in the scene where Richard "deposes" himself as in some long, agonising ceremony, reflectively drawn out, with an extraordinary refinement of intelligence and variety of piteous appeal, but also with a felicity of poetic invention, which puts these pages into a very select class, with the finest "vermeil and ivory" work of Chatterton or Keats.

> Fetch hither Richard that in common view
> He may surrender!—

And Richard more than concurs: he throws himself into the part, realises a type, falls gracefully as on the world's stage.—Why is he sent for?

> To do that office of thine own good will
> Which tired majesty did make thee offer.—

> Now mark me! how I will undo myself.

"Hath Bolingbroke deposed thine intellect?" the Queen asks him, on his way to the Tower:—

Hath Bolingbroke
Deposed thine intellect? hath he been in thy heart?

And in truth, but for that adventitious poetic gold, it would be only "plume-plucked Richard."—

I find myself a traitor with the rest,
For I have given here my soul's consent
To undeck the pompous body of a king.

He is duly reminded, indeed, how

That which in mean men we entitle patience
Is pale cold cowardice in noble breasts.

Yet at least within the poetic bounds of Shakespeare's play, through Shakespeare's bountiful gifts, his desire seems fulfilled.—

O! that I were as great
As is my grief.

And his grief becomes nothing less than a central expression of all that in the revolutions of Fortune's wheel goes *down* in the world.

No! Shakespeare's kings are not, nor are meant to be, great men: rather, little or quite ordinary humanity, thrust upon greatness, with those pathetic results, the natural self-pity of the weak heightened in them into irresistible appeal to others as the net result of their royal prerogative. One after another they seem to lie composed in Shakespeare's embalming pages, with just that touch of nature about them, making the whole world akin, which has infused into their tombs at Westminster a rare poetic grace. It is that irony of kingship, the sense that it is in its happiness child's play, in its sorrows, after all, but children's grief, which gives its finer accent to all the changeful feeling of these wonderful speeches:—the great meekness of the graceful, wild creature, tamed at last.—

> Give Richard leave to live till Richard die!

his somewhat abject fear of death, turning to acquiescence at moments of extreme weariness:—

> My large kingdom for a little grave!
> A little little grave, an obscure grave!—

his religious appeal in the last reserve, with its bold reference to the judgment of Pilate, as he thinks once more of his "anointing."

And as happens with children he attains contentment finally in the merely passive recognition of superior strength, in the naturalness of the result of the great battle as a matter of course, and experiences something of the royal prerogative of poetry to obscure, or at least to attune and soften men's griefs. As in some sweet anthem of Handel, the sufferer, who put finger to the organ under the utmost pressure of mental conflict, extracts a kind of peace at last from the mere skill with which he sets his distress to music.—

> Beshrew thee, Cousin, that didst lead me forth
> Of that sweet way I was in to despair!

"With Cain go wander through the shades of night!" —cries the new king to the gaoler Exton, dissimulating his share in the murder he is thought to have suggested; and in truth there is something of the murdered Abel about Shakespeare's Richard. The fact seems to be that he died of "waste and a broken heart": it was by way of proof that his end had been a natural one that, stifling a real fear of the face, the face of Richard, on men's minds, with

the added pleading now of all dead faces, Henry exposed
the corpse to general view; and Shakespeare, in bringing
it on the stage, in the last scene of his play, does but follow
out the motive with which he has emphasised Richard's
physical beauty all through it—that "most beauteous inn,"
as the Queen says quaintly, meeting him on the way to
death—residence, then soon to be deserted, of that way-
ward, frenzied, but withal so affectionate soul. Though the
body did not go to Westminster immediately, his tomb,

> That small model of the barren earth
> Which serves as paste and cover to our bones,*

the effigy clasping the hand of his youthful consort, was
already prepared there, with "rich gilding and ornaments,"
monument of poetic regret, for Queen Anne of Bohemia,
not of course the "Queen" of Shakespeare, who however
seems to have transferred to this second wife something of
Richard's wildly proclaimed affection for the first. In this
way, through the connecting link of that sacred spot, our
thoughts once more associate Richard's two fallacious pre-
rogatives, his personal beauty and his "anointing."

According to Johnson, *Richard the Second* is one of
those plays which Shakespeare has "apparently revised";
and how doubly delightful Shakespeare is where he seems
to have revised! "Would that he had blotted a thousand"
—a thousand hasty phrases, we may venture once more to
say with his earlier critic now that the tiresome German
superstition has passed away which challenged us to a
dogmatic faith in the plenary verbal inspiration of every
one of Shakespeare's clowns. Like some melodiously con-

* Perhaps a *double entendre:*—of any ordinary grave, as compris-
ing, in effect, the whole small earth now left to its occupant: or,
of such a tomb as Richard's in particular, with its actual model,
or effigy, of the clay of him. Both senses are so characteristic that
it would be a pity to lose either.

tending anthem of Handel's, I said, of Richard's meek
"undoing" of himself in the mirror-scene; and, in fact,
the play of *Richard the Second* does, like a musical composition, possess a certain concentration of all its parts, a
simple continuity, an evenness in execution, which are rare
in the great dramatist. With *Romeo and Juliet,* that perfect symphony (symphony of three independent poetic
forms set in a grander one * which it is the merit of
German criticism to have detected) it belongs to a small
group of plays, where, by happy birth and consistent evolution, dramatic form approaches to something like the
unity of a lyrical ballad, a lyric, a song, a single strain of
music. Which sort of poetry we are to account the highest,
is perhaps a barren question. Yet if, in art generally, unity
of impression is a note of what is perfect, then lyric poetry,
which in spite of complex structure often preserves the
unity of a single passionate ejaculation, would rank higher
than dramatic poetry, where, especially to the reader, as
distinguished from the spectator assisting at a theatrical
performance, there must always be a sense of the effort
necessary to keep the various parts from flying asunder, a
sense of imperfect continuity, such as the older criticism
vainly sought to obviate by the rule of the dramatic
"unities." It follows that a play attains artistic perfection
just in proportion as it approaches that unity of lyrical
effect, as if a song or ballad were still lying at the root of
it, all the various expression of the conflict of character
and circumstance falling at last into the compass of a
single melody, or musical theme. As, historically, the earliest classic drama arose out of the chorus, from which this
or that person, this or that episode, detached itself, so,
into the unity of a choric song the perfect drama ever
tends to return, its intellectual scope deepened, compli-

* The Sonnet: the Aubade: the Epithalamium.

cated, enlarged, but still with an unmistakable singleness, or identity, in its impression on the mind. Just there, in that vivid single impression left on the mind when all is over, not in any mechanical limitation of time and place, is the secret of the "unities"—the true imaginative unity— of the drama.

1889

Austin Dobson

"VADER CATS"

To an uninstructed reader the homely name that heads this paper does not, of itself, suggest any special distinction. When we are informed that Jacob Cats was a native of Holland, our first impression is of some typical Dutchman, squat-figured and stolid, preoccupied with tulips and a pipe. If it be added that he wrote verses, speculation goes no farther than to conceive a minstrel of the type of Longfellow's "Cobbler of Hagenau," chirruping his songs at his work bench, and having ever

> at his side,
> Among his leathers and his tools,
> Reynard the Fox, the Ship of Fools,
> Or Eulenspiegel, open wide.

Each of these forecasts, however, is equally at fault. As a Dutchman, Jacob Cats was one of the prominent men of his age. He had gained honour as a Greek Scholar at Leyden University; he had travelled in France and England, visiting both Oxford and Cambridge. He was an accomplished jurist; and though—as some authorities allege—he had but little success as a politician, he was, at all events, a great civic dignitary in the great days of the Netherlands, holding important office as a magistrate at

From *Sidewalk Studies* by Austin Dobson. Reprinted by permission of the publishers, the Oxford University Press.

Middleburgh and Dordrecht, and ultimately proceeding Grand Pensionary of Holland. He was twice Ambassador to England, being knighted on the first occasion by Charles I. When finally, at the age of seventy-two, he obtained the permission of the States to retire into private life at his country-seat of Sorgh-vliet—his "Sans-Souci" or "Castle-Careless"—on the Scheveningen Road, it was as a man who on the whole had deserved well of his generation, and might fairly be permitted to "cultivate his garden," and write his "Reminiscences."

But if he acquired a reputation as a citizen, he earned a still greater reputation as a poet. He was a contemporary of Hooft and Vondel, and that delightful Tesselschade Visscher, of whom Mr. Edmund Gosse has given us so pleasant a portrait; and he was probably the most popular of the four. By his readers he was affectionately styled "Vader Cats"; and his collected works in familiar moments were known as the "House-hold Bible." His big folio was to be found by poor men's hearths, and in the windows of the rich—even as Baker's "Chronicle" lay in the window of Sir Roger de Coverley. When now we open the vast volume (*i.e.,* Jan Jacobz Schipper's Amsterdam edition of 1655), its bulk appals us. It is a book to be approached only from the side of dimension. Like Shakespeare's fat knight, it measures so much about. Not to lay stress on the blackness of the type, which is in itself portentous, it is printed in two columns,—sometimes even in three. Turning the tall pages timidly, you become conscious, in addition to a Babel of proverbs and emblems in all languages, of a long didactic poem on "Marriage" (*Houwelik*), which traces that institution, with abundant illustration, from maidenhood to widowhood. Then of another, and a still longer effort, entitled "Nuptial Ring" (*Trou-ringh*), wherein it is treated, among other things, of Crates and Hipparchia, of Adam and Eve, of Masinissa and Sophonisba, of Eginhard and the daughter of Charlemagne, of Jacob and Rachel. (Jacob, it may be noted in parenthesis, has apparently been educated in France, for in the picture he has carved "la belle Rachell" upon a tree-trunk, and written under it "Vive l'Amour.") Then there is a "pastoral romance" of "Galatea"; a poem on "Country-Life" (*Buytenleven*), in the frontispiece of which is a view of Sorgh-vliet, and towards the end of the book, another series of poems called invitingly "Coffins for the Living" (*Doodt-Kiste voor de Levendige*). These are only part of the contents. Beside and between them are numerous other pieces, accompanied like the rest by prefaces and sub-prefaces, by appendices, excursuses, commentaries, head-notes, shoulder-notes, side-notes, foot-notes, postscripts, and addresses to the *Lector benignus* (*"goetgunstige Leser"*) which hedge them in on all sides. Poetry, with our Dutch poet, is not by any means a trickling rill from Helicon; it is an inundation *à la mode du pays*,—a flood in a flat land, covering everything far and near with its sluggish waters.

To this immoderate and incontinent effusiveness is probably to be attributed the fact that, notwithstanding their excellent precepts and praiseworthy morality, the verses of Jacob Cats do not seem to have largely attracted the translator. Report, indeed, affirms that his entire works have been "done into German"; but this would be of little service to the ordinary English reader. The French, on the other hand, have contented themselves with an imitation of the short piece entitled "Children's Games" (*Kinder-Spel*). In our own country, multifarious old Thomas Heywood, the dramatist, paraphrased the first part of *Houwelick* under the title of "An Emblematicall Dialogue, interpreted from the excellent and most learned *D. Fac. Catzius;* which showeth how Virgins in their chaste loves ought to bear themselves." And as late as 1860 many of the emblems and proverbs were translated by Richard Pigot to accompany the "freely-rendered" cuts of John

Leighton. But our concern here is less with the text than with the old copper-plates which originally accompanied it, and which, fortunately for us, speak a universal language.

These, printed in the body of the page, are generally uniform in size, and surrounded by a conventional border. Many of them bear the initials or names of such well-known engravers as Hondius, the two Mathams, and Crispin van Queborn. But the main interest centres in the chief designer, Adrian van der Venne, a painter of considerable ability, and noted especially for the prodigious canvases on which, like the Frenchman Lebrun, he depicted the battles of the seventeenth century. After drifting to and fro, he seems to have settled at Middleburgh, where Cats also resided from 1602 to 1620. His brother, Jan Pietersz van der Venne, was a bookseller and publisher of the town, and for him he executed numberless book-illustrations in addition to those now under consideration. He is said also to have possessed no mean literary talent, and to have tried his hand at satire. It is probably a natural consequence of his way of work that he should reproduce his environment; and many views and memories of the capital of Zeeland and the surrounding country are traceable in his compositions. Perhaps the most interesting of these is to be found in the large head-piece to the above-mentioned "Children's Games," the background of which exhibits the great square of Middleburgh, with its old Gothic houses and central clump of trees. This is, moreover, as delightful a picture as any in the gallery. Down the middle of the foreground, which is filled by a crowd of figures, advances a regiment of little Dutchmen, marching to drum and fife, and led by a fire-eating captain of fifteen. Around this central group are dispersed knots of children, playing leap-frog, flying kites, blowing bubbles, whipping tops, walking on stilts, skipping and the like. In one corner the boys are busy with blind man's buff;

in the other the girls, with their stiff-head-dresses and vandyked aprons, are occupied with their dolls. Under the pump some seventeenth century equivalent for chuck-farthing seems to be going on vigorously; and, not to be behindhand in the fun, two little fellows in the distance are standing upon their heads. The whole composition is full of life and movement, and—so conservative is child-hood—might, but for the costume and scene, represent a playground of today. No doubt it represented, with far closer fidelity, the playground of the artist's time.

It is this note of literalness—this truth to what lay near-est—that constitutes the chief charm of these illustrations. Many of those to the "Emblems" are quaint with that in-ventive strangeness and naïve ingenuity which have a fascination apart from technical merit. But, as a rule, the artist is strongest in what he has seen. His lions are more or less heraldic; his crocodiles are badly stuffed; his sala-manders of doubtful actuality. There is no such faltering when he shows us a hammer striking a flint on a cushion, or a pair of snuffers cropping a candle, or the interior of a blacksmith's shop. What applies to the still-life applies equally to the figures. When the subject is a tailor sitting cross-legged in his stall, or a woman warming her feet and gazing into the embers, there is no doubt of the reality of the studies. Some of them, indeed, are finished works in genre.

What would one not give for such an illustrated copy of Shakespeare! In these pages of Jacob Cats we have the authentic Holland of the seventeenth century:—its vanes and spires and steep-roofed houses; its gardens with their geometric tulip-beds, their formally-clipped alleys and arches, their shining parallelograms of water. Here are its old-fashioned interiors, with the deep fireplaces and queer andirons, the huge four-posters, the prim portraits on the wall, the great brass-clamped coffers and carved armoires for the ruffs and starched collars and stiff farthingales of the women. In one picture you may see the careful house-wife mournfully inspecting a moth-eaten garment which she has just taken from a chest that Wardour Street might envy; in another she is energetically cuffing the "foolish fat scullion," who has let the spotted Dalmatian coach-dog overturn the cauldron at the fire. Here an old crone, with her spectacles on, is cautiously probing the contents of the said cauldron with a fork; here the mistress of the house is peeling pears; here the plump and soft-hearted cheese-wife is entertaining an admirer. Outside there are pictures as vivid. Here are the clumsy leather-topped coach with its masked occupant and stumbling horses; the towed *trekschuit,* with its merry freight, sliding swiftly through the low-lying landscape; the windy mole, stretching sea-ward, with its blown and flaring beacon-fire. Here again in the street is the toy-shop with its open front and store of mimic drums and halberds for the martial little burghers; here are the fruiteress with her stall of grapes and melons, the ratcatcher with his string of trophies, the fowler with his clap-net, the furrier with his stock of skins. Many of the designs have also that additional interest which is uni-versal as well as local. Such is the one to the proverb, "Between two stools one comes to the ground," or, as Cats has it "Nemo potest Thetidem simul et Galatean amare." The luckless Philander of the story has been try-ing to solve the problem, but without success. He has been flirting among the sandhills with Thetis, who has her fish upon her head in "ocean-smelling osier"; and now Galatea the milkmaid has come suddenly upon them in a hat which looks like an inverted basin with a tuft: and he will probably experience what is high-Dutch for a *mauvais quart d'heure.* Another illustrates as pertinently the adage, "It is ill hunting with unwilling hounds," although the dogs are but a detail in the landscape, and the real moral is pointed by erring humanity. "Griet," pour soul, shame-faced and ill at ease, stands awkwardly by the door-settle, looking away from the other actors in the drama, apparently her suitor and his father. By the purse in her hand we must conclude she is rich; by a certain constraint in her carriage we may perhaps also infer that she is not so well-born as her intended. It is, in fact, a Batavian "marriage *à la mode*" that is in progress, if such a word may be employed where nothing is progressing. For if the lady is simply passive, the gentleman, whose name is Claes, is violently demonstrative. He resists all efforts of his senior to bring him to the point—gesticulates wildly, and digs his right heel doggedly in the ground. He will none of her, nor all her "brooches, pearls and owches,"—her gear and household stuff,—her rents and her comings-in.

The round cap and collar of the female figure in this picture, the short skirt with its rigid folds and dark border, the puffed shoulder-pieces and long chatelaine, remind us of one characteristic of these designs which might be anticipated in so observant an artist, but which not the less deserves especial mention. This is the excellence and variety of the costume. And it is not only the peasants and fish-women whose dress is faithfully reproduced, but that of the better classes is as scrupulously delineated. It would take a chapter to describe the wonderful swaggering cavaliers, with their long-plumed hats and slashed jerkins, their endless tags and aiglets and rosettes; or the sumptuous ladies with their broidered sleeves, and purfled stomachers, and monumental ruffs. The design inscribed "Amor, ut pila, vices exigit," which may be roughly Englished by "Love asks return," is an example of this, which is as good as any. In a trim garden, with symmetrically-clipped trees and hedges, a gentleman and a lady are playing at battledore and shuttlecock. The former, whose right foot is neatly turned out after the most approved fashion, so as to show the inside of his calf, has just delivered his blow; the latter leaps lightly to return it with as much agility as may be consistent with good manners and a buckramed state attire.

There is a certain grim side to these Batavian moralities which is not without its significance. Through the whole series it peeps out here and there; but it is more plainly manifest in the later works, when we must suppose old age to be stealing upon the writer, and busying his thoughts with sombre images of mortality and decay. The illustration to one of these—a full-page plate—is certainly a most gruesome allegory of life. A man is seen scaling an apple-tree which clings with snake-like roots to the side of a burning pit or well, inhabited by a fearsome and ravening dragon. About the brim of the pit a restless bear runs backwards and forwards, eager for its prey; but rats are gnawing busily at the tree-trunk, and by and by the tree, climber and all, will topple crashing in the flames. Another composition—the frontispiece to "Coffins for the Living"—takes up two pages and is even more impressive. The scene is a kind of cemetery with magnificent sepulchral monuments, wherefrom the covers have been lifted so as to exhibit their mouldering tenants. To the right a party of richly-clad Orientals are gazing curiously at a crowned skeleton:—"Where are the riches of Croesus?" On the opposite side of the picture, a personage resembling an Eastern Mage, and a beautiful and majestic woman— perhaps the Queen of Sheba—bend wonderingly over a second tomb:—"Where is the wisdom of Solomon?" Here it is a group of soldiers that is attracted; there a knot of heroes. But the main interest centres in front of a lofty canopy, the sable curtains of which are drawn aside by grinning anatomies, discovering a figure more pitiful than any in its forlorn and fleshless impotence:—"Where is the beauty of Helen?" "Was *this* the face that launch'd a thousand ships, And burnt the topless towers of Ilium?" Surely a frutiful theme for the gray-haired sage of Sorgh-vliet, when the blast whistled keener through his wind-

stripped espaliers, and the dead leaves gathered at the
garden borders!

And here we close the great folio. But what a picture-
book it must have been in the days when picture-books
were fewer! One can imagine the "clunch" Dutch children
poring over it, much as Charles Lamb pored over the
queer illustrations in Stackhouse's "History of the Bible."
One can even fancy that their minds took a certain haunting after-colour or savour from this early study, like the
jar which, as Horace says, remembers its first wine. That
the volume is a favourite with the distinguished Dutch
artist, now naturalised among us, Sir Lawrence Alma-
Tadema, is, perhaps, not remarkable; nor is it remarkable
that (as Mr. Wood Warter relates) it should have attracted the wandering and omnivorous appetite of Southey.
But it is surely of special interest that it was among the
first art-treasures of Reynolds, who loved it as a boy, and
many of whose sketches—"done by Joshua out of pure
idleness"—were copied from the gallery of "Vader Cats."

1902

Gilbert K. Chesterton

ON CERTAIN MODERN WRITERS AND THE INSTITUTION OF THE FAMILY

THE family may fairly be considered, one would think, an ultimate human institution. Every one would admit that it has been the main cell and central unit of almost all societies hitherto, except, indeed, such societies as that of Lacedaemon, which went in for "efficiency," and has, therefore, perished, and left not a trace behind. Christianity, even enormous as was its revolution, did not alter this ancient and savage sanctity, it merely reversed it. It did not deny the trinity of father, mother, and child. It merely read it backwards, making it run child, mother, father. This it called, not the family, but the Holy Family, for many things are made holy by being turned upside down. But some sages of our decadence have made a serious attack on the family. They have impugned it, as I think, wrongly; and its defenders have defended it, and defended it wrongly. The common defence of the family is that, amid the stress and fickleness of life, it is peaceful, pleasant, and at one. But there is another defence of the family which is possible, and to me evident; this defence is that the family is not peaceful and not pleasant and not at one.

From *Heretics* by G. K. Chesterton. Reprinted by permission of John Lane, The Bodley Head Limited.

It is not fashionable to say much nowadays of the advantages of the small community. We are told that we must go in for large empires and large ideas. There is one advantage, however, in the small state, the city, or the village, which only the wilfully blind can overlook. The man who lives in a small community lives in a much larger world. He knows much more of the fierce varieties and uncompromising divergences of men. The reason is obvious. In a large community we can choose our companions. In a small community our companions are chosen for us. Thus in all extensive and highly civilized societies groups come into existence founded upon what is called sympathy, and shut out the real world more sharply than the gates of a monastery. There is nothing really narrow about the clan; the thing which is really narrow is the clique. The men of the clan live together because they all wear the same tartan or are all descended from the same sacred cow; but in their souls, by the divine luck of things, there will always be more colours than in any tartan. But the men of the clique live together because they have the same kind of soul, and their narrowness is a narrowness of spiritual coherence and contentment, like that which exists in hell. A big society exists in order to form cliques. A big society is a society for the promotion of narrowness. It is a machinery for the purpose of guarding the solitary and sensitive individual from all experience of the bitter and bracing human compromises. It is, in the most literal sense of the words, a society for the prevention of Christian knowledge.

We can see this change, for instance, in the modern transformation of the thing called a club. When London was smaller, and the parts of London more self-contained and parochial, the club was what it still is in villages, the opposite of what it is now in great cities. Then the club was valued as a place where a man could be sociable. Now the club is valued as a place where a man can be unsociable. The more the enlargement and elaboration of

our civilization goes on the more the club ceases to be
a place where a man can have a noisy argument, and becomes more and more a place where a man can have what
is somewhat fantastically called a quiet chop. Its aim is to
make a man comfortable, and to make a man comfortable
is to make him the opposite of sociable. Sociability, like all
good things, is full of discomforts, dangers, and renunciations. The club tends to produce the most degraded of all
combinations—the luxurious anchorite, the man who combines the self-indulgence of Lucullus with the insane loneliness of St. Simeon Stylites.

If we were tomorrow morning snowed up in the street
in which we live, we should step suddenly into a much
larger and much wilder world than we have ever known.
And it is the whole effort of the typically modern person
to escape from the street in which he lives. First he invents modern hygiene and goes to Margate. Then he
invents modern culture and goes to Florence. Then he
invents modern imperialism and goes to Timbuctoo. He
goes to the fantastic borders of the earth. He pretends to
shoot tigers. He almost rides on a camel. And in all this
he is still essentially fleeing from the street in which he
was born; and of this flight he is always ready with his
own explanation. He says he is fleeing from his street because it is dull; he is lying. He is really fleeing from his
street because it is a great deal too exciting. It is exciting
because it is exacting; it is exacting because it is alive.
He can visit Venice because to him the Venetians are only
Venetians; the people in his own street are men. He can
stare at the Chinese because for him the Chinese are a
passive thing to be stared at; if he stares at the old lady
in the next garden, she becomes active. He is forced to
flee, in short, from the too stimulating society of his equals
—of free men, perverse, personal, deliberately different
from himself. The street in Brixton is too glowing and
overpowering. He has to soothe and quiet himself among

tigers and vultures, camels and crocodiles. These creatures are indeed very different from himself. But they do not put their shape or color or custom into a decisive intellectual competition with his own. They do not seek to destroy his principles and assert their own; the stranger monsters of the suburban street do seek to do this. The camel does not contort his features into a fine sneer because Mr. Robinson has not got a hump; the cultured gentleman at No. 5 does exhibit a sneer because Robinson has not got a dado. The vulture will not roar with laughter because a man does not fly; but the major at No. 9 will roar with laughter because a man does not smoke. The complaint we commonly have to make of our neighbours is that they will not, as we express it, mind their own business. We do not really mean that they will not mind their own business. If our neighbours did not mind their own business they would be asked abruptly for their rent, and would rapidly cease to be our neighbours. What we really mean when we say that they cannot mind their own business is something much deeper. We do not dislike them because they have so little force and fire that they cannot be interested in themselves. We dislike them because they have so much force and fire that they can be interested in us as well. What we dread about our neighbours, in short, is not the narrowness of their horizon, but their superb tendency to broaden it. And all aversions to ordinary humanity have this general character. They are not aversions to its feebleness (as is pretended), but to its energy. The misanthropes pretend that they despise humanity for its weakness. As a matter of fact, they hate it for its strength.

Of course, this shrinking from the brutal vivacity and brutal variety of common men is a perfectly reasonable and excusable thing as long as it does not pretend to any point of superiority. It is when it calls itself aristocracy or aestheticism or a superiority to the bourgeoisie that its inherent weakness has in justice to be pointed out. Fastidiousness is the most pardonable of vices; but it is the most unpardonable of virtues. Nietzsche, who represents most prominently this pretentious claim of the fastidious, has a description somewhere—a very powerful description in the purely literary sense—of the disgust and disdain which consume him at the sight of the common people with their common faces, their common voices, and their common minds. As I have said, this attitude is almost beautiful if we may regard it as pathetic. Nietzsche's aristocracy has about it all the sacredness that belongs to the weak. When he makes us feel that he cannot endure the innumerable faces, the incessant voices, the overpowering omnipresence which belongs to the mob, he will have the sympathy of anybody who has ever been sick on a steamer or tired in a crowded omnibus. Every man has hated mankind when he was less than a man. Every man has had humanity in his eyes like a blinding fog, humanity in his nostrils like a suffocating smell. But when Nietzsche has the incredible lack of humour and lack of imagination to ask us to believe that his aristocracy is an aristocracy of strong muscles or an aristocracy of strong wills, it is necessary to point out the truth. It is an aristocracy of weak nerves.

We make our friends; we make our enemies; but God makes our next-door neighbour. Hence he comes to us clad in all the careless terrors of nature; he is as strange as the stars, as reckless and indifferent as the rain. He is Man, the most terrible of the beasts. That is why the old religions and the old scriptural language showed so sharp a wisdom when they spoke, not of one's duty towards humanity, but one's duty towards one's neighbour. The duty towards humanity may often take the form of some choice which is personal or even pleasurable. That duty may be a hobby; it may even be a dissipation. We may work in the East End because we are peculiarly fitted to work in the East End, or because we think we are; we may fight for the cause of international peace because we are very fond of fighting. The most monstrous martyrdom, the most repulsive experience, may be the result of choice or a kind of taste. We may be so made as to be particularly fond of lunatics or specially interested in leprosy. We may love Negroes because they are black or German Socialists because they are pedantic. But we have to love our neighbour because he is there—a much more alarming reason for a much more serious operation. He is the sample of humanity which is actually given us. Precisely because he may be anybody he is everybody. He is a symbol because he is an accident.

Doubtless men flee from small environments into lands that are very deadly. But this is natural enough; for they are not fleeing from death. They are fleeing from life. And this principle applies to ring within ring of the social system of humanity. It is perfectly reasonable that men should seek for some particular variety of the human type, so long as they are seeking for that variety of the human type, and not for mere human variety. It is quite proper that a British diplomatist should seek the society of Japanese generals, if what he wants is Japanese generals. But if what he wants is people different from himself, he had much better stop at home and discuss religion with the housemaid. It is quite reasonable that the village genius should come up to conquer London if what he wants is to conquer London. But if he wants to conquer something fundamentally and symbolically hostile and also very strong, he had much better remain where he is and have a row with the rector. The man in the suburban street is quite right if he goes to Ramsgate for the sake of Ramsgate —a difficult thing to imagine. But if, as he expresses it, he goes to Ramsgate "for a change," then he would have a much more romantic and even melodramatic change if he jumped over the wall into his neighbour's garden. The consequences would be bracing in a sense far beyond the possibilities of Ramsgate hygiene.

Now, exactly as this principle applies to the empire, to the nation within the empire, to the city within the nation, to the street within the city, so it applies to the home within the street. The institution of the family is to be commended for precisely the same reasons that the institution of the nation, or the institution of the city, are in this matter to be commended. It is a good thing for a man to live in a family for the same reason that it is a good thing for a man to be besieged in a city. It is a good thing for a man to live in a family in the same sense that it is a beautiful and delightful thing for a man to be snowed up in a street. They all force him to realize that life is not a thing from outside but a thing from inside. Above all, they all insist upon the fact that life, if it be a truly stimulating and fascinating life, is a thing which, of its nature, exists in spite of ourselves. The modern writers who have suggested, in a more or less open manner, that the family is a bad institution, have generally confined themselves to suggesting, with much sharpness, bitterness, or pathos, that perhaps the family is not always very congenial. Of course the family is a good institution because it is uncongenial. It is wholesome precisely because it contains so many divergencies and varieties. It is, as the sentimentalists say, like a little kingdom, and, like most other little kingdoms, is generally in a state of something resembling anarchy. It is exactly because our brother George is not interested in our religious difficulties, but is interested in the Trocadero Restaurant, that the family has some of the bracing qualities of the commonwealth. It is precisely because our uncle Henry does not approve of the theatrical ambitions of our sister Sarah that the family is like humanity. The men and women who, for good reasons and bad, revolt against the family, are, for good reasons and bad, simply revolting against mankind. Aunt Elizabeth is unreasonable, like mankind. Papa is excitable, like mankind. Our youngest brother is mischievous, like mankind. Grandpapa is stupid, like the world; he is old, like the world.

Those who wish, rightly or wrongly, to step out of all this, do definitely wish to step into a narrower world. They are dismayed and terrified by the largeness and variety of the family. Sarah wishes to find a world wholly consisting of private theatricals; George wishes to think the Trocadero a cosmos. I do not say, for a moment, that the flight to this narrower life may not be the right thing for the individual, any more than I say the same thing about flight into a monastery. But I do say that anything is bad and artificial which tends to make these people succumb to the strange delusion that they are stepping into a world which is actually larger and more varied than their own. The best way that a man could test his readiness to encounter the common variety of mankind would be to climb down a chimney into any house at random, and get on as well as possible with the people inside. And that is essentially what each one of us did on the day that he was born.

This is, indeed, the sublime and special romance of the family. It is romantic because it is a toss-up. It is romantic because it is everything that its enemies call it. It is romantic because it is arbitrary. It is romantic because it is there. So long as you have groups of men chosen rationally, you have some special or sectarian atmosphere. It is when you have groups of men chosen irrationally that you have men. The element of adventure begins to exist; for an adventure is, by its nature, a thing that comes to us. It is a thing that chooses us, not a thing that we choose. Falling in love has been often regarded as the supreme adventure, the supreme romantic accident. In so much as there is in it something outside ourselves, something of a sort of merry fatalism, this is very true. Love does take us and transfigure and torture us. It does break our hearts with

an unbearable beauty, like the unbearable beauty of mu
sic. But in so far as we have certainly something to d
with the matter; in so far as we are in some sense pre
pared to fall in love and in some sense jump into it; in s
far as we do to some extent choose and to some exten
even judge—in all this falling in love is not truly romantic
is not truly adventurous at all. In this degree the suprem
adventure is not falling in love. The supreme adventur
is being born. There we do walk suddenly into a splendi
and startling trap. There we do see something of whic
we have not dreamed before. Our father and mother d
lie in wait for us and leap out on us, like brigands from
bush. Our uncle is a surprise. Our aunt is, in the beauti
ful common expression, a bolt from the blue. When w
step into the family, by the act of being born, we do ste
into a world which is incalculable, into a world which ha
its own strange laws, into a world which could do withou
us, into a world that we have not made. In other words
when we step into the family we step into a fairy-tale.

This colour as of a fantastic narrative ought to cling t
the family and to our relations with it throughout life
Romance is the deepest thing in life; romance is deepe
even than reality. For even if reality could be proved to b
misleading, it still could not be proved to be unimportan
or unimpressive. Even if the facts are false, they are sti
very strange. And this strangeness of life, this unexpecte
and even perverse element of things as they fall out, re
mains incurably interesting. The circumstances we ca
regulate may become tame or pessimistic; but the "circum
stances over which we have no control" remain god-like t
those who, like Mr. Micawber, can call on them an
renew their strength. People wonder why the novel is th
most popular form of literature; people wonder why it i
read more than books of science or books of metaphysics
The reason is very simple; it is merely that the novel i
more true than they are. Life may sometimes legitimate

appear as a book of science. Life may sometimes appear, and with a much greater legitimacy, as a book of metaphysics. But life is always a novel. Our existence may cease to be a song; it may cease even to be a beautiful lament. Our existence may not be an intelligible justice, or even a recognizable wrong. But our existence is still a story. In the fiery alphabet of every sunset is written "to be continued in our next." If we have sufficient intellect, we can finish a philosophical and exact deduction, and be certain that we are finishing it right. With the adequate brain-power we could finish any scientific discovery, and be certain that we were finishing it right. But not with the most gigantic intellect could we finish the simplest or silliest story, and be certain that we were finishing it right. That is because a story has behind it, not merely intellect which is partly mechanical, but will, which is in its essence divine. The narrative writer can send his hero to the gallows if he likes in the last chapter but one. He can do it by the same divine caprice whereby he, the author, can go to the gallows himself, and to hell afterwards if he chooses. And the same civilization, the chivalric European civilization which asserted freewill in the thirteenth century, produced the thing called "fiction" in the eighteenth. When Thomas Aquinas asserted the spiritual liberty of man, he created all the bad novels in the circulating libraries.

But in order that life should be a story or romance to us, it is necessary that a great part of it, at any rate, should be settled for us without our permission. If we wish life to be a system, this may be a nuisance; but if we wish it to be a drama, it is an essential. It may often happen, no doubt, that a drama may be written by somebody else which we like very little. But we should like it still less if the author came before the curtain every hour or so, and forced on us the whole trouble of inventing the next act. A man has control over many things in his life; he has control over enough things to be the hero of a novel. But if he had control over everything, there would be so much hero that there would be no novel. And the reason why the lives of the rich are at bottom so tame and uneventful is simply that they can choose the events. They are dull because they are omnipotent. They fail to feel adventures because they can make the adventures. The thing which keeps life romantic and full of fiery possibilities is the existence of these great plain limitations which force all of us to meet the things we do not like or do not expect. It is vain for the supercilious moderns to talk of being in uncongenial surroundings. To be in a romance is to be in uncongenial surroundings. To be born into this earth is to be born into uncongenial surroundings, hence to be born into a romance. Of all these great limitations and frameworks which fashion and create the poetry and variety of life, the family is the most definite and important. Hence it is misunderstood by the moderns, who imagine that romance would exist most perfectly in a complete state of what they call liberty. They think that if a man makes a gesture it would be a startling and romantic matter that the sun should fall from the sky. But the startling and romantic thing about the sun is that it does not fall from the sky. They are seeking under every shape and form a world where there are no limitations—that is, a world where there are no outlines; that is, a world where there are no shapes. There is nothing baser than that infinity. They say they wish to be as strong as the universe, but they really wish the whole universe as weak as themselves.

1905

William James

WHAT PRAGMATISM MEANS

SOME years ago, being with a camping party in the mountains, I returned from a solitary ramble to find everyone engaged in a ferocious metaphysical dispute. The *corpus* of the dispute was a squirrel—a live squirrel supposed to be clinging to one side of a tree-trunk; while over against the tree's opposite side a human being was imagined to stand. This human witness tries to get sight of the squirrel by moving rapidly round the tree, but no matter how fast he goes, the squirrel moves as fast in the opposite direction, and always keeps the tree between himself and the man, so that never a glimpse of him is caught. The resultant metaphysical problem now is this: *Does the man go round the squirrel or not?* He goes round the tree, sure enough, and the squirrel is on the tree; but does he go round the squirrel? In the unlimited leisure of the wilderness, discussion had been worn threadbare. Everyone had taken sides, and was obstinate; and the numbers on both sides were even. Each side, when I appeared therefore appealed to me to make it a majority. Mindful of the scholastic adage that whenever you meet a contradiction you must make a distinction, I immediately sought and found one, as follows: "Which party is right," I said, "depends on what you *practically mean* by 'going round' the

From *Pragmatism* by William James. Reprinted by permission of Longmans, Green & Co., Inc.

squirrel. If you mean passing from the north of him to the east, then to the south, then to the west, and then to the north of him again, obviously the man does go round him, for he occupies these successive positions. But if on the contrary you mean being first in front of him, then on the right of him, then behind him, then on his left, and finally in front again, it is quite as obvious that the man fails to go round him, for by the compensating movements the squirrel makes, he keeps his belly turned towards the man all the time, and his back turned away. Make the distinction, and there is no occasion for any farther dispute. You are both right and both wrong according as you conceive the verb 'to go round' in one practical fashion or the other."

Although one or two of the hotter disputants called my speech a shuffling evasion, saying they wanted no quibbling or scholastic hair-splitting, but meant just plain honest English "round," the majority seemed to think that the distinction had assuaged the dispute.

I tell this trivial anecdote because it is a peculiarly simple example of what I wish now to speak of as *the pragmatic method*. The pragmatic method is primarily a method of settling metaphysical disputes that otherwise might be interminable. Is the world one or many?—fated or free?—material or spiritual?—here are notions either of which may or may not hold good of the world; and disputes over such notions are unending. The pragmatic method in such cases is to try to interpret each notion by tracing its respective practical consequences. What difference would it practically make to any one if this notion rather than that notion were true? If no practical difference whatever can be traced, then the alternatives mean practically the same thing, and all dispute is idle. Whenever a dispute is serious, we ought to be able to show some practical difference that must follow from one side or the other's being right.

A glance at the history of the idea will show you still better what pragmatism means. The term is derived from the same Greek work πρᾶγμα, meaning action, from which our words "practice" and "practical" come. It was first introduced into philosophy by Mr. Charles Peirce in 1878. In an article entitled "How to Make Our Ideas Clear," in the *Popular Science Monthly* for January of that year Mr. Peirce, after pointing out that our beliefs are really rules for action, said that, to develop a thought's meaning, we need only determine what conduct it is fitted to produce: that conduct is for us its sole significance. And the tangible fact at the root of all our thought-distinctions, however subtle, is that there is no one of them so fine as to consist in anything but a possible difference of practice. To attain perfect clearness in our thoughts of an object, then, we need only consider what conceivable effects of a practical kind the object may involve—what sensations we are to expect from it, and what reactions we must prepare. Our conception of these effects, whether immediate or remote, is then for us the whole of our conception of the object, so far as that conception has positive significance at all.

This is the principle of Peirce, the principle of pragmatism. It lay entirely unnoticed by anyone for twenty years, until I, in an address before Professor Howison's philosophical union at the University of California, brought it forward again and made a special application of it to religion. By that date (1898) the times seemed ripe for its reception. The word "pragmatism" spread, and at present it fairly spots the pages of the philosophic journals. On all hands we find the "pragmatic movement" spoken of, sometimes with respect, sometimes with contumely, seldom with clear understanding. It is evident that the term applies itself conveniently to a number of tendencies that hitherto have lacked a collective name, and that it has "come to stay."

To take in the importance of Peirce's principle, one must get accustomed to applying it to concrete cases. I found a few years ago that Ostwald, the illustrous Leipzig chemist, had been making perfectly distinct use of the principle of pragmatism in his lectures on the philosophy of science, though he had not called it by that name.

"All realities influence our practice," he wrote me, "and that influence is their meaning for us. I am accustomed to put questions to my classes in this way: In what respects would the world be different if this alternative or that were true? If I can find nothing that would become different, then the alternative has no sense."

That is, the rival views mean practically the same thing, and meaning, other than practical, there is for us none. Ostwald in a published lecture gives this example of what he means. Chemists have long wrangled over the inner constitution of certain bodies called "tautomerous." Their properties seemed equally consistent with the notion that an instable hydrogen atom oscillates inside of them, or that they are instable mixtures of two bodies. Controversy raged, but never was decided. "It would never have begun," says Ostwald, "if the combatants had asked themselves what particular experimental fact could have been made different by one or the other view being correct. For it would then have appeared that no difference of fact could possibly ensue; and the quarrel was as unreal as if, theorizing in primitive times about the raising of dough by yeast, one party should have invoked a 'brownie,' while another insisted on an 'elf' as the true cause of the phenomenon." *

* I find a still more radical pragmatism than Ostwald's in an address by Professor W. S. Franklin: "I think that the sickliest notion of physics, even if a student gets it, is that it is 'the science of masses, molecules, and the ether.' And I think that the healthiest notion, even if a student does not wholly get it, is that physics is the science of the ways of taking hold of bodies and pushing them!"

It is astonishing to see how many philosophical disputes collapse into insignificance the moment you subject them to this simple test of tracing a concrete consequence. There can be no difference anywhere that doesn't *make* a difference elsewhere—no difference in abstract truth that doesn't express itself in a difference in concrete fact and in conduct consequent upon that fact, imposed on somebody, somehow, somewhere, and somewhen. The whole function of philosophy ought to be to find out what definite difference it will make to you and me, at definite instants of our life, if this world-formula or that world-formula be the true one.

There is absolutely nothing new in the pragamatic method. Socrates was an adept at it. Aristotle used it methodically. Locke, Berkeley, and Hume made momentous contributions to truth by its means. Shadworth Hodgson keeps insisting that realities are only what they are "known as." But these forerunners of pragmatism used it in fragments: they were preluders only. Not until in our time has it generalized itself, become conscious of a universal mission, pretended to a conquering destiny. I believe in that destiny, and I hope I may end by inspiring you with my belief.

Pragmatism represents a perfectly familiar attitude in philosophy, the empiricist attitude, but it represents it, as it seems to me, both in a more radical and in a less objectionable form than it has ever yet assumed. A pragmatist turns his back resolutely and once for all upon a lot of inveterate habits dear to professional philosophers. He turns away from abstraction and insufficiency, from verbal solutions, from bad *a priori* reasons, from fixed principles, closed systems, and pretended absolutes and origins. He turns towards concreteness and adequacy, towards facts, towards action and towards power. That means the empiricist temper regnant and the rationalist temper sincerely given up. It means the open air and possibilities of nature, as against dogma, artificiality, and the pretence of finality in truth.

At the same time it does not stand for any special results. It is a method only. But the general triumph of that method would mean an enormous change in what I called in my last lecture the "temperament" of philosophy. Teachers of the ultra-rationalistic type would be frozen out, much as the courtier type is frozen out in republics, as the ultramontane type of priest is frozen out in protestant lands. Science and metaphysics would come much nearer together, would in fact work absolutely hand in hand.

Metaphysics has usually followed a very primitive kind of quest. You know how men have always hankered after unlawful magic, and you know what a great part in magic *words* have always played. If you have his name, or the formula of incantation that binds him, you can control the spirit, genie, afrite, or whatever the power may be. Solomon knew the names of all the spirits, and having their names, he held them subject to his will. So the universe has always appeared to the natural mind as a kind of enigma, of which the key must be sought in the shape of some illuminating or power-bringing word or name. That word names the universe's *principle,* and to possess it is after a fashion to possess the universe itself. "God," "Matter," "Reason," "the Absolute," "Energy," are so many solving names. You can rest when you have them. You are at the end of your metaphysical quest.

But if you follow the pragmatic method, you cannot look on any such word as closing your quest. You must bring out of each word its practical cash-value, set it at work within the stream of your experience. It appears less as a solution, then, than as a program for more work, and more particularly as an indication of the ways in which existing realities may be *changed*.

Theories thus become instruments, not answers to enigmas, in which we can rest. We don't lie back upon them, we move forward, and, on occasion, make nature over again by their aid. Pragmatism unstiffens all our theories, limbers them up and sets each one at work. Being nothing essentially new, it harmonizes with many ancient philosophic tendencies. It agrees with nominalism, for instance, in always appealing to particulars; with utilitarianism in emphasizing practical aspects; with positivism in its disdain for verbal solutions, useless questions and metaphysical abstractions.

All these, you see, are *anti-intellectualist* tendencies. Against rationalism as a pretension and a method pragmatism is fully armed and militant. But, at the outset, at least, it stands for no particular results. It has no dogmas, and no doctrines save its method. As the young Italian pragmatist Papini has well said, it lies in the midst of our theories, like a corridor in a hotel. Innumerable chambers open out of it. In one you may find a man writing an atheistic volume; in the next some one on his knees praying for faith and strength; in a third a chemist investigating a body's properties. In a fourth a system of idealistic metaphysics is being excogitated; in a fifth the impossibility of metaphysics is being shown. But they all own the corridor, and all must pass through it if they want a practicable way of getting into or out of their respective rooms.

No particular results then, so far, but only an attitude of orientation, is what the pragmatic method means. *The attitude of looking away from first things, principles, "categories," supposed necessities; and of looking towards last things, fruits, consequences, facts.*

So much for the pragmatic method! You may say that I have been praising it rather than explaining it to you, but I shall presently explain it abundantly enough by showing how it works on some familiar problems. Meanwhile the word pragmatism has come to be used in a still wider sense, as meaning also a certain *theory of truth*. I mean to give a whole lecture to the statement of that theory, after first paving the way, so I can be very brief now. But brevity is hard to follow, so I ask for your redoubled attention for a quarter of an hour. If much remains obscure, I hope to make it clearer in the later lectures.

One of the most successfully cultivated branches of philosophy in our time is what is called inductive logic, the study of the conditions under which our sciences have evolved. Writers on this subject have begun to show a singular unanimity as to what the laws of nature and elements of fact mean, when formulated by mathematicians, physicists and chemists. When the first mathematical, logical, and natural uniformities, the first *laws,* were discovered, men were so carried away by the clearness, beauty and simplification that resulted, that they believed themselves to have deciphered authentically the eternal thoughts of the Almighty. His mind also thundered and reverberated in syllogisms. He also thought in conic sections, squares and roots and ratios and geometrized like Euclid. He made Kepler's laws for the planets to follow; he made velocity increase proportionally to the time in falling bodies; he made the law of the sines for light to obey when refracted; he established the classes, orders, families and genera of plants and animals, and fixed the distances between them. He thought the archetypes of all things, and devised their variations; and when we rediscover any one of these his wondrous institutions, we seize his mind in its very literal intention.

But as the sciences have developed farther, the notion has gained ground that most, perhaps all, of our laws are only approximations. The laws themselves, moreover, have grown so numerous that there is no counting them; and so many rival formulations are proposed in all the branches of science that investigators have become accus-

tomed to the notion that no theory is absolutely a tran-
script of reality, but that any one of them may from
some point of view be useful. Their great use is to summarize old facts and to lead to new ones. They are only
a man-made language, a conceptual short-hand, as some
one calls them, in which we write our reports of nature;
and languages, as is well known, tolerate much choice of
expression and many dialects.

Thus human arbitrariness has driven divine necessity
from scientific logic. If I mention the names of Sigwart,
Mach, Ostwald, Pearson, Milhaud, Poincaré, Duhem,
Ruyssen, those of you who are students will easily identify
the tendency I speak of, and will think of additional
names.

Riding now on the front of this wave of scientific logic
Messrs. Schiller and Dewey appear with their pragmatis-
tic account of what truth everywhere signifies. Everywhere, these teachers say, "truth" in our ideas and beliefs
means the same thing that it means in science. It means,
they say, nothing but this, *that ideas (which themselves
are but parts of our experience) become true just in so
far as they help us to get into satisfactory relation with
other parts of our experience,* to summarize them and get
about among them by conceptual short-cuts instead of
following the interminable succession of particular phenomena. Any idea upon which we can ride, so to speak;
any idea that will carry us prosperously from any one
part of our experience to any other part, linking things
satisfactorily, working securely, simplifying, saving labor;
is true for just so much, true in so far forth, true *instru-
mentally.* This is the "instrumental" view of truth taught
so successfully at Chicago, the view that truth in our ideas
means their power to "work," promulgated so brilliantly
at Oxford.

Messrs. Dewey, Schiller and their allies, in reaching
this general conception of all truth, have only followed the

example of geologists, biologists and philologists. In the
establishment of these other sciences, the successful stroke
was always to take some simple process actually observable
in operation—as denudation by weather, say, or variation
from parental type, or change of dialect by incorporation
of new words and pronunciations—and then to generalize
it, making it apply to all times, and produce great results
by summating its effects through the ages.

The observable process which Schiller and Dewey particularly singled out for generalization is the familiar one
by which any individual settles into *new opinions*. The
process here is always the same. The individual has a stock
of old opinions already, but he meets a new experience
that puts them to a strain. Somebody contradicts them;
or in a reflective moment he discovers that they contradict
each other; or he hears of facts with which they are incompatible; or desires arise in him which they cease to
satisfy. The result is an inward trouble to which his mind
till then had been a stranger, and from which he seeks
to escape by modifying his previous mass of opinions.
He saves as much of it as he can, for in this matter of
belief we are all extreme conservatives. So he tries to
change first this opinion, and then that (for they resist
change very variously), until at last some new idea comes
up which he can graft upon the ancient stock with a
minimum of disturbance of the latter, some idea that medi-
ates between the stock and the new experience and runs
them into one another most felicitously and expediently.

This new idea is then adopted as the true one. It preserves the older stock of truths with a minimum of modi-
fication, stretching them just enough to make them admit
the novelty, but conceiving that in ways as familiar as the
case leaves possible. An *outrée* explanation, violating all
our preconceptions, would never pass for a true account of
a novelty. We should scratch round industriously till we
found something less excentric. The most violent revolu-

tions in an individual's beliefs leave most of his old order
standing. Time and space, cause and effect, nature and
history, and one's own biography remain untouched. New
truth is always a go-between, a smoother-over of transi-
tions. It marries old opinion to new fact so as ever to
show a minimum of jolt, a maximum of continuity. We
hold a theory true just in proportion to its success in solving this "problem of maxima and minima." But success
in solving this problem is eminently a matter of approxi-
mation. We say this theory solves it on the whole more
satisfactorily than that theory; but that means more satisfactorily to ourselves, and individuals will emphasize their
points of satisfaction differently. To a certain degree,
therefore, everything here is plastic.

The point I now urge you to observe particularly is the
part played by the older truths. Failure to take account
of it is the source of much of the unjust criticism levelled
against pragmatism. Their influence is absolutely con-
trolling. Loyalty to them is the first principle—in most
cases it is the only principle; for by far the most usual way
of handling phenomena so novel that they would make
for a serious rearrangement of our preconception is to ignore them altogether, or to abuse those who bear witness
for them.

You doubtless wish examples of this process of truth's
growth, and the only trouble is their superabundance. The
simplest case of new truth is of course the mere numerical
addition of new kinds of facts, or of new single facts of
old kinds, to our experience—an addition that involves no
alteration in the old beliefs. Day follows day, and its contents are simply added. The new contents themselves are
not true, they simply *come* and *are*. Truth is *what we say
about* them, and when we say that they have come, truth
is satisfied by the plain additive formula.

But often the day's contents oblige a rearrangement. If I
should now utter piercing shrieks and act like a maniac

on this platform, it would make many of you revise your ideas as to the probable worth of my philosophy. "Radium" came the other day as part of the day's content, and seemed for a moment to contradict our ideas of the whole order of nature, that order having come to be identified with what is called the conservation of energy. The mere sight of radium paying heat away indefinitely out of its own pocket seemed to violate that conservation. What to think? If the radiations from it were nothing but an escape of unsuspected "potential" energy, pre-existent inside of the atoms, the principle of conservation would be saved. The discovery of "helium" as the radiation's outcome, opened a way to this belief. So Ramsay's view is generally held to be true, because, although it extends our old ideas of energy, it causes a minimum of alteration in their nature.

I need not multiply instances. A new opinion counts as "true" just in proportion as it gratifies the individual's desire to assimilate the novel in his experience to his beliefs in stock. It must both lean on old truth and grasp new fact; and its sucess (as I said a moment ago) in doing this, is a matter for the individual's appreciation. When old truth grows, then, by new truth's addition, it is for subjective reasons. We are in the process and obey the reasons. That new idea is truest which performs most felicitously its function of satisfying our double urgency. It makes itself true, gets itself classed as true, by the way it works; grafting itself then upon the ancient body of truth, which thus grows much as a tree grows by the activity of a new layer of cambium.

Now Dewey and Schiller proceed to generalize this observation and to apply it to the most ancient parts of truth. They also once were plastic. They also were called true for human reasons. They also mediated between still earlier truths and what in those days were novel observations. Purely objective truth, truth in whose establishment the function of giving human satisfaction in marrying previous parts of experience with newer parts played no rôle whatever, is nowhere to be found. The reasons why we call things true is the reason why they *are* true, for "to be true" *means* only to perform this marriage-function.

The trail of the human serpent is thus over everything. Truth independent; truth that we *find* merely; truth no longer malleable to human need; truth incorrigible, in a word; such truth exists indeed superabundantly—or is supposed to exist by rationalistically minded thinkers; but then it means only the dead heart of the living tree, and its being there means only that truth also has its paleontology, and its "prescription," and may grow stiff with years of veteran service and petrified in men's regard by sheer antiquity. But how plastic even the oldest truths nevertheless really are has been vividly shown in our day by the transformation of logical and mathematical ideas, a transformation which seems even to be invading physics. The ancient formulas are reinterpreted as special expressions of much wider principles, principles that our ancestors never got a glimpse of in their present shape and formulation.

Mr. Schiller still gives to all this view of truth the name of "Humanism," but, for this doctrine too, the name of pragmatism seems fairly to be in the ascendant, so I will treat it under the name of pragmatism in these lectures.

Such then would be the scope of pragmatism—first, a method; and second, a genetic theory of what is meant by truth. And these two things must be our future topics.

What I have said of the theory of truth will, I am sure, have appeared obscure and unsatisfactory to most of you, by reason of its brevity. I shall make amends for that hereafter. In a lecture on "common sense" I shall try to show what I mean by truths grown petrified by antiquity. In another lecture I shall expatiate on the idea that our thoughts become true in proportion as they successfully exert their go-between function. In a third I shall show how hard it is to discriminate subjective from objective factors in Truth's development. You may not follow me wholly in these lectures; and if you do, you may not wholly agree with me. But you will, I know, regard me at least as serious, and treat my effort with respectful consideration.

You will probably be surprised to learn, then, that Messrs. Schiller's and Dewey's theories have suffered a hailstorm of contempt and ridicule. All rationalism has risen against them. In influential quarters Mr. Schiller, in particular, has been treated like an impudent schoolboy who deserves a spanking. I should not mention this, but for the fact that it throws so much sidelight upon that rationalistic temper to which I have opposed the temper of pragmatism. Pragmatism is uncomfortable away from facts. Rationalism is comfortable only in the presence of abstractions. This pragmatist talk about truths in the plural, about their utility and satisfactoriness, about the success with which they "work," etc., suggests to the typical intellectualist mind a sort of coarse lame second-rate makeshift article of truth. Such truths are not real truth. Such tests are merely subjective. As against this, objective truth must be something non-utilitarian, haughty, refined, remote, august, exalted. It must be an absolute correspondence of our thoughts with an equally absolute reality. It must be what we *ought* to think unconditionally. The conditioned ways in which we *do* think are so much irrelevance and matter for psychology. Down with psychology, up with logic, in all this question!

See the exquisite contrast of the types of mind! The pragmatist clings to facts and concreteness, observes truth at its work in particular cases, and generalizes. Truth, for him, becomes a class-name for all sorts of definite working-values in experience. For the rationalist it remains a pure abstraction, to the bare name of which we must defer. When the pragmatist undertakes to show in detail just *why* we must defer, the rationalist is unable to recognize the concretes from which his own abstraction is taken. He accuses us of *denying* truth; whereas we have only sought to trace exactly why people follow it and always ought to follow it. Your typical ultra-abstractionist fairly shudders at concreteness: other things equal, he positively prefers the pale and spectral. If the two universes were offered, he would always choose the skinny outline rather than the rich thicket of reality. It is so much purer, clearer, nobler.

I hope that as these lectures go on, the concreteness and closeness to facts of the pragmatism which they advocate may be what approves itself to you as its most satisfactory peculiarity. It only follows here the example of the sister-sciences, interpreting the unobserved by the observed. It brings old and new harmoniously together. It converts the absolutely empty notion of a static relation of "correspondence" (what that may mean we must ask later) between our minds and reality, into that of a rich and active commerce (that anyone may follow in detail and understand) between particular thoughts of ours, and the great universe of other experiences in which they play their parts and have their uses.

But enough of this at present? The justification of what I say must be postponed. I wish now to add a word in further explanation of the claim I made at our last meeting, that pragmatism may be a happy harmonizer of empiricist ways of thinking with the more religious demands of human beings.

Men who are strongly of the fact-loving temperament, you may remember me to have said, are liable to be kept at a distance by the small sympathy with facts which that philosophy from the present-day fashion of idealism offers them. It is far too intellectualistic. Old fashioned theism was bad enough, with its notion of God as an exalted monarch, made up of a lot of unintelligible or preposterous "attributes"; but, so long as it held strongly by the argument from design, it kept some touch with concrete realities. Since, however, Darwinism has once for all displaced design from the minds of the "scientific," theism has lost that foothold; and some kind of an immanent or pantheistic deity working *in* things rather than above them is, if any, the kind recommended to our contemporary imagination. Aspirants to a philosophic religion turn, as a rule, more hopefully nowadays towards idealistic pantheism than towards the older dualistic theism, in spite of the fact that the latter still counts able defenders.

But, as I said in my first lecture, the brand of pantheism offered is hard for them to assimilate if they are lovers of facts, or empirically minded. It is the absolutistic brand, spurning the dust and reared upon pure logic. It keeps no connexion whatever with concreteness. Affirming the Absolute Mind, which is its substitute for God, to be the rational presupposition of all particulars of fact, whatever they may be, it remains supremely indifferent to what the particular facts in our world actually are. Be they what they may, the Absolute will father them. Like the sick lion in Esop's fable, all footprints lead into his den, but *nulla vestigia retrorsum*. You cannot redescend into the world of particulars by the Absolute's aid, or deduce any necessary consequences of detail important for your life from your idea of his nature. He gives you indeed the assurance that all is well with *Him,* and for his eternal way of thinking; but thereupon he leaves you to be finitely saved by your own temporal devices.

Far be it from me to deny the majesty of this conception, or its capacity to yield religious comfort to a most respectable class of minds. But from the human point of view, no one can pretend that it doesn't suffer from the faults of remoteness and abstractness. It is eminently a product of what I have ventured to call the rationalistic temper. It disdains empiricism's needs. It substitutes a pallid outline for the real world's richness. It is dapper, it is noble in the bad sense, in the sense in which to be noble is to be inapt for humble service. In this real world of sweat and dirt, it seems to me that when a view of things is "noble," that ought to count as a presumption against its truth, and as a philosophic disqualification. The prince of darkness may be a gentleman, as we are told he is, but whatever the God of earth and heaven is, he can surely be no gentleman. His menial services are needed in the dust of our human trials, even more than his dignity is needed in the empyrean.

Now pragmatism, devoted though she be to facts, has no such materialistic bias as ordinary empiricism labors under. Moreover, she has no objection whatever to the realizing of abstractions, so long as you get about among particulars with their aid and they actually carry you somewhere. Interested in no conclusions but those which our minds and our experiences work out together, she has no *a priori* prejudices against theology. *If theological ideas prove to have a value for concrete life, they will be true, for pragmatism, in the sense of being good for so much. For how much more they are true, will depend entirely on their relations to the other truths that also have to be acknowledged.*

What I said just now about the Absolute, of transcendental idealism, is a case in point. First, I called it majestic and said it yielded religious comfort to a class of minds, and then I accused it of remoteness and sterility. But so far as it affords such comfort, it surely is not sterile; it has that amount of value; it performs a concrete function. As a good pragmatist, I myself ought to call the Absolute true "in so far forth," then; and I unhesitatingly now do so.

But what does *true in so far forth* mean in this case? To answer, we need only apply the pragmatic method. What do believers in the Absolute mean by saying that their belief affords them comfort? They mean that since, in the Absolute finite evil is "overruled" already, we may, therefore, whenever we wish, treat the temporal as if it were potentially the eternal, be sure that we can trust its outcome, and, without sin, dismiss our fear and drop the worry of our finite responsibility. In short, they mean that we have a right ever and anon to take a moral holiday, to let the world wag in its own way, feeling that its issues are in better hands than ours and are none of our business.

The universe is a system of which the individual members may relax their anxieties occasionally, in which the don't-care mood is also right for men, and moral holidays in order,—that, if I mistake not, is part, at least, of what the Absolute is "known-as," that is the great difference in our particular experiences which his being true makes, for us, that is his cash-value when he is pragmatically interpreted. Farther than that the ordinary lay-reader in philosophy who thinks favorably of absolute idealism does not venture to sharpen his conceptions. He can use the Absolute for so much, and so much is very precious. He is pained at hearing you speak incredulously of the Absolute, therefore, and disregards your criticisms because they deal with aspects of the conception that he fails to follow.

If the Absolute means this, and means no more than this, who can possibly deny the truth of it? To deny it would be to insist that men should never relax, and that holidays are never in order.

I am well aware how odd it must seem to some of you to hear me say that an idea is "true" so long as to believe it is profitable to our lives. That it is *good,* for as much as it profits, you will gladly admit. If what we do by its aid is good, you will allow the idea itself to be good in so far forth, for we are the better for possessing it. But is it not a strange misuse of the word "truth," you will say, to call ideas also "true" for this reason?

To answer this difficulty fully is impossible at this stage of my account. You touch here upon the very central point of Messrs. Schiller's, Dewey's and my own doctrine of truth, which I can not discuss with detail until my sixth lecture. Let me now say only this, that truth is *one species of good,* and not, as is usually supposed, a category distinct from good, and co-ordinate with it. *The true is the name of whatever proves itself to be good in the way of belief, and good, too, for definite, assignable reasons.* Surely you must admit this, that if there were *no* good for life in true ideas, or if the knowledge of them were positively disadvantageous and false ideas the only useful ones, then the current notion that truth is divine and precious, and its pursuit a duty, could never have grown up or become a dogma. In a world like that, our duty would be to *shun* truth, rather. But in this world, just as certain foods are not only agreeable to our taste, but good for our teeth, our stomach, and our tissues; so certain ideas are not only agreeable to think about, or agreeable as supporting other ideas that we are fond of, but they are also helpful in life's practical struggles. If there be any life that it is really better we should lead, and if there be any idea which, if believed in, would help us to lead that life, then it would be really *better for us* to believe in that idea, *unless, indeed, belief in it incidentally clashed with other greater vital benefits.*

What would be better for us to believe! This sounds very like a definition of truth. It comes very near to saying "what we *ought* to believe": and in *that* definition none of you would find any oddity. Ought we ever not to believe what it is *better for us* to believe? And can we then keep the notion of what is better for us, and what is true for us, permanently apart?

Pragmatism says no, and I fully agree with her. Probably you also agree, so far as the abstract statement goes, but with a suspicion that if we practically did believe everything that made for good in our own personal lives, we should be found indulging all kinds of fancies about this world's affairs, and all kinds of sentimental superstitions about a world hereafter. Your suspicion here is undoubtedly well founded, and it is evident that something happens when you pass from the abstract to the concrete that complicates the situation.

I said just now that what is better for us to believe is true *unless the belief incidentally clashes with some other vital benefit.* Now in real life what vital benefits is any particular belief of ours most liable to clash with? What indeed except the vital benefits yielded by *other beliefs* when these prove incompatible with the first ones? In other words, the greatest enemy of any one of our truths may be the rest of our truths. Truths have once for all this desperate instinct of self-preservation and of desire to extinguish whatever contradicts them. My belief in the Absolute, based on the good it does me, must run the gauntlet of all my other beliefs. Grant that it may be true in giving me a moral holiday. Nevertheless, as I conceive it,—and let me speak now confidentally, as it were, and merely in my own private person,—it clashes with other truths of mine whose benefits I hate to give up on its account. It happens to be associated with a kind of logic of which I am the enemy, I find that it entangles me in metaphysical paradoxes that are inacceptable, etc., etc. But as I have enough trouble in life already without adding the trouble of carrying these intellectual inconsistencies, I personally just give up the Absolute. I just *take* my moral holidays; or else as a professional philosopher, I try to justify them by some other principle.

If I could restrict my notion of the Absolute to its bare holiday-giving value, it wouldn't clash with my other truths. But we can not easily thus restrict our hypotheses. They carry supernumerary features, and these it is that clash so. My disbelief in the Absolute means then disbelief in those other supernumerary features, for I fully believe in the legitimacy of taking moral holidays.

You see by this what I meant when I called pragmatism a mediator and reconciler and said, borrowing the word from Papini, that she "unstiffens" our theories. She has in fact no prejudices whatever, no obstructive dogmas, no rigid canons of what shall count as proof. She is completely genial. She will entertain any hypothesis, she will consider any evidence. It follows that in the religious field she is at a great advantage both over positivistic empiricism, with its anti-theological bias, and over religious rationalism, with its exclusive interest in the remote, the noble, the simple, and the abstract in the way of conception.

In short, she widens the field of search for God. Rationalism sticks to logic and the empyrean. Empiricism sticks to the external senses. Pragmatism is willing to take anything, to follow either logic or the senses and to count the humblest and most personal experiences. She will count mystical experiences if they have practical consequences. She will take a God who lives in the very dirt of private fact—if that should seem a likely place to find him.

Her only test of probable truth is what works best in the way of leading us, what fits every part of life best and combines with the collectivity of experience's demands, nothing being omitted. If theological ideas should do this, if the notion of God, in particular, should prove to do it, how could pragmatism possibly deny God's existence? She could see no meaning in treating as "not true" a notion that was pragmatically so successful. What other kind of truth could there be, for her, than all this agreement with concrete reality?

In my last lecture I shall return again to the relations of pragmatism with religion. But you see already how democratic she is. Her manners are as various and flexible, her resources as rich and endless, and her conclusions as friendly as those of mother nature.

1906

Hilaire Belloc

THE MOWING OF A FIELD

THERE is a valley in South England remote from ambition and from fear, where the passage of strangers is rare and unperceived, and where the scent of the grass in summer is breathed only by those who are native to that unvisited land. The roads to the Channel do not traverse it; they choose upon either side easier passes over the range. One track alone leads up through it to the hills, and this is changeable: now green where men have little occasion to go, now a good road where it nears the homesteads and the barns. The woods grow steep above the slopes; they reach sometimes the very summit of the heights, or, when they cannot attain them, fill in and clothe the combes. And, in between, along the floor of the valley, deep pastures and their silence are bordered by lawns of chalky grass and the small yew trees of the Downs.

The clouds that visit its sky reveal themselves beyond the one great rise, and sail, white and enormous, to the other, and sink beyond that other. But the plains above which they have travelled and the Weald to which they go, the people of the valley cannot see and hardly recall. The wind, when it reaches such fields, is no longer a gale from the salt, but fruitful and soft, an inland breeze; and

From *Hills and the Sea* by Hilaire Belloc. Reprinted by permission of Charles Scribner's Sons.

those whose blood was nourished here feel in that wind the fruitfulness of our orchards and all the life that all things draw from the air.

In this place, when I was a boy, I pushed through a fringe of beeches that made a complete screen between me and the world, and I came to a glade called No Man's Land. I climbed beyond it, and I was surprised and glad, because from the ridge of that glade I saw the sea. To this place very lately I returned.

The many things that I recovered as I came up the countryside were not less charming than when a distant memory had enshrined them, but much more. Whatever veil is thrown by a longing recollection had not intensified nor even made more mysterious the beauty of that happy ground; not in my very dreams of morning had I, in exile, seen it more beloved or more rare. Much also that I had forgotten now returned to me as I approached— a group of elms, a little turn of the parson's wall, a small paddock beyond the graveyard close, cherished by one man, with a low wall of very old stone guarding it all around. And all these things fulfilled and amplified my delight, till even the good vision of the place, which I had kept so many years, left me and was replaced by its better reality. "Here," I said to myself, "is a symbol of what some say is reserved for the soul: pleasure of a kind which cannot be imagined save in the moment when at last it is attained."

When I came to my own gate and my own field, and had before me the house I knew, I looked around a little (though it was already evening), and I saw that the grass was standing as it should stand when it is ready for the scythe. For in this, as in everything that a man can do—of those things at least which are very old—there is an exact moment when they are done best. And it has been remarked of whatever rules us that it works blunderingly, seeing that the good things given to man are not given at the precise moment when they would have filled him with delight. But, whether this be true or false, we can choose the just turn of the seasons in everything we do of our own will, and especially in the making of hay. Many think that hay is best made when the grass is thickest; and so they delay until it is rank and in flower, and has already heavily pulled the ground. And there is another false reason for delay, which is wet weather. For very few will understand (though it comes year after year) that we have rain always in South England between sickle and the scythe, or say just after the weeks of east wind are over. First we have a week of sudden warmth, as though the South had come to see us all; then we have the weeks of east and south-east wind; and then we have more or less of that rain of which I spoke, and which always astonishes the world. Now it is just before, or during, or at the very end of that rain—but not later—that grass should be cut for hay. True, upland grass, which is always thin, should be cut earlier than the grass in the bottoms and along the water meadows; but not even the latest, even in the wettest seasons, should be left (as it is) to flower and even to seed. For what we get when we store our grass is not a harvest of something ripe, but a thing just caught in its prime before maturity: as witness that our corn and straw are best yellow, but our hay is best green. So also Death should be represented with a scythe and Time with a sickle; for Time can take only what is ripe, but Death comes always too soon. In a word, then, it is always much easier to cut grass too late than too early; and I, under that evening and come back to these pleasant fields, looked at the grass and knew that it was time. June was in full advance: it was the beginning of that season when the night has already lost her foothold of the earth and hovers over it, never quite descending, but mixing sunset with the dawn.

Next morning, before it was yet broad day, I awoke,

and thought of the mowing. The birds were already chattering in the trees beside my window, all except the nightingale, which had left and flown away to the Weald, where he sings all summer by day as well as by night in the oaks and the hazel spinneys, and especially along the little river Adur, one of the rivers of the Weald. The birds and the thought of the mowing had awakened me, and I went down the stairs and along the stone floors to where I could find a scythe; and when I took it from its nail, I remembered how, fourteen years ago, I had last gone out with my scythe, just so, into the fields at morning. In between that day and this were many things, cities and armies, and a confusion of books, mountains and the desert, and horrible great breadths of sea.

When I got out into the long grass the sun was not yet risen, but there were already many colours in the eastern sky, and I made haste to sharpen my scythe, so that I might get to the cutting before the dew should dry. Some say that it is best to wait till all the dew has risen, so as to get the grass quite dry from the very first. But, though it is an advantage to get the grass quite dry, yet it is not worth while to wait till the dew has risen. For, in the first place, you lose many hours of work (and those the coolest), and next—which is more important—you lose that great ease and thickness in cutting which comes of the dew. So I at once began to sharpen my scythe.

There is an art also in the sharpening of a scythe, and it is worth describing carefully. Your blade must be dry, and that is why you will see men rubbing the scythe-blade with grass before they whet it. Then also your rubber must be quite dry, and on this account it is a good thing to lay it on your coat and keep it there during all your day's mowing. The scythe you stand upright, with the blade pointing away from you, and you put your left hand firmly on the back of the blade, grasping it: then you pass the rubber first down one side of the blade-edge and then down the other, beginning near the handle and going on to the point and working quickly and hard. When you first do this you will, perhaps, cut your hand; but it is only at first that such an accident will happen to you.

To tell when the scythe is sharp enough this is the rule. First the stone clangs and grinds against the iron harshly; then it rings musically to one note; then, at last, it purrs as though the iron and stone were exactly suited. When you hear this, your scythe is sharp enough; and I, when I heard it in that June dawn, with everything quite silent except the birds, let down the scythe and bent myself to mow.

When one does anything anew, after so many years, one fears very much for one's trick or habit. But all things once learnt are easily recoverable, and I very soon recovered the swing and power of the mower. Mowing well and mowing badly—or rather not mowing at all—are separated by very little; as is also true of writing verse, of playing the fiddle, and of dozens of other things, but of nothing more than of believing. For the bad or young or untaught mower without tradition, the mower Promethean, the mower original and contemptuous of the past, does all these things: He leaves great crescents of grass uncut. He digs the point of the scythe hard into the ground with a jerk. He loosens the handles and even the fastening of the blade. He twists the blade with his blunders, he blunts the blade, he chips it, dulls it, or breaks it clean off at the tip. If any one is standing by he cuts him in the ankle. He sweeps up into the air wildly, with nothing to resist his stroke. He drags up earth with the grass, which is like making the meadow bleed. But the good mower who does things just as they should be done and have been for a hundred thousand years, falls into none of these fooleries. He goes forward very steadily, his scythe-blade just barely missing the ground, every grass falling; the swish and rhythm of his mowing are always the same.

So great an art can only be learnt by continual practice; but this much is worth writing down, that, as in all good work, to know the thing with which you work is the core of the affair. Good verse is best written on good paper with an easy pen, not with a lump of coal on a whitewashed wall. The pen thinks for you; and so does the scythe mow for you if you treat it honourably and in a manner that makes it recognize its service. The manner is this. You must regard the scythe as a pendulum that swings, not as a knife that cuts. A good mower puts no more strength into his stroke than into his lifting. Again, stand up to your work. The bad mower, eager and full of pain, leans forward and tries to force the scythe through the grass. The good mower, serene and able, stands as nearly straight as the shape of the scythe will let him, and follows up every stroke closely, moving his left foot forward. Then also let every stroke get well away. Mowing is a thing of ample gestures, like drawing a cartoon. Then, again, get yourself into a mechanical and repetitive mood: be thinking of anything at all but your mowing, and be anxious only when there seems some interruption to the monotony of the sound. In this mowing should be like one's prayers— all of a sort and always the same, and so made that you can establish a monotony and work them, as it were, with half your mind: that happier half, the half that does not bother.

In this way, when I had recovered the art after so many years, I went forward over the field, cutting lane after lane through the grass, and bringing out its most secret essences with the sweep of the scythe until the air was full of odours. At the end of every lane I sharpened my scythe and looked back at the work done, and then carried my scythe down again upon my shoulder to begin another. So, long before the bell rang in the chapel above me—that is, long before six o'clock, which is the time for the *Angelus*—I had many swathes already lying in order parallel like soldiery; and the high grass yet standing, making a great contrast with the shaven part, looked dense and high. As it says in the *Ballad of Val-ès-Dunes*, where—

> The tall son of the Seven Winds
> Came riding out of Hither-hythe,

and his horse-hoofs (you will remember) trampled into the press and made a gap in it, and his sword (as you know)

> . . . was like a scythe
> In Arcus when the grass is high
> And all the swathes in order lie,
> And there's the bailiff standing by
> A-gathering of the tithe.

So I mowed all that morning, till the houses awoke in the valley, and from some of them rose a little fragrant smoke, and men began to be seen.

I stood still and rested on my scythe to watch the awakening of the village, when I saw coming up to my field a man whom I had known in older times, before I had left the Valley.

He was of that dark silent race upon which all the learned quarrel, but which, by whatever meaningless name it may be called—Iberian, or Celtic, or what you will—is the permanent root of all England, and makes England wealthy and preserves it everywhere, except perhaps in the Fens and in a part of Yorkshire. Everywhere else you will find it active and strong. These people are intensive; their thoughts and their labours turn inward. It is on account of their presence in these islands that our gardens are the richest in the world. They also love low rooms and ample fires and great warm slopes of thatch. They have, as I believe, an older acquaintance with the English air than any other of all the strains that make up England. They hunted in the Weald with stones, and camped in the pines of the green-sand. They lurked under the oaks of the upper rivers, and saw the legionaries go up, up the straight paved road from the sea. They helped the few pirates to destroy the towns, and mixed with those pirates and shared the spoils of the Roman villas, and were glad to see the captains and the priests destroyed. They remain; and no admixture of the Frisian pirates, or the Breton, or the Angevin and Norman conquerors, has very much affected their cunning eyes.

To this race, I say, belonged the man who now approached me. And he said to me, "Mowing?" And I answered, "Ar." Then he also said "Ar," as in duty bound; for so we speak to each other in the Stenes of the Downs.

Next he told me that, as he had nothing to do, he would lend me a hand; and I thanked him warmly, or, as we say, "kindly." For it is a good custom of ours always to treat bargaining as though it were a courteous pastime; and though what he was after was money, and what I wanted was his labour at the least pay, yet we both played the comedy that we were free men, the one granting a grace and the other accepting it. For the dry bones of commerce, avarice and method and need, are odious to the Valley; and we cover them up with a pretty body of fiction and observances. Thus, when it comes to buying pigs, the buyer does not begin to decry the pig and the vendor to praise it, as is the custom with lesser men; but tradition makes them do business in this fashion:—

First the buyer will go up to the seller when he sees him in his own steading, and, looking at the pig with admiration, the buyer will say that rain may or may not fall, or that we shall have snow or thunder, according to the time of year. Then the seller, looking critically at the pig, will agree that the weather is as his friend maintains. There is no haste at all; great leisure marks the dignity of their exchange. And the next step is, that the buyer says: "That's a fine pig you have there, Mr.—" (giving the seller's name). "Ar, powerful fine pig." Then the seller, saying also "Mr." (for twin brothers rocked in one cradle give each other ceremonious observance here), the seller, I say, admits, as though with reluctance, the strength and beauty of the pig, and falls into deep thought. Then the buyer says, as though moved by a great desire, that he is ready to give so much for the pig, naming half the proper price, or a little less. Then the seller remains in silence for some moments; and at last begins to shake his head slowly, till he says: "I don't be thinking of selling the pig, anyways." He will also add that a party only Wednesday offered him so much for the pig—and he names about double the proper price. Thus all ritual is duly accomplished; and the solemn act is entered upon with reverence and in a spirit of truth. For when the buyer uses this phrase: "I'll tell you what I *will* do," and offers within half a crown of the pig's value, the seller replies that he can refuse him nothing, and names half a crown above its value; the difference is split, the pig is sold, and in the quiet soul of each runs the peace of something accomplished.

Thus do we buy a pig or land or labourer or malt or lime, always with elaboration and set forms; and many a London man has paid double and more for his violence and his greedy haste and very unchivalrous higgling. As happened with the land at Underwaltham, which the mortgagees had begged and implored the estate to take at twelve hundred, and had privately offered to all the world at a thousand, but which a sharp direct man, of the kind that makes great fortunes, a man in a motor-car, a man in a fur coat, a man of few words, bought for two thousand three hundred before my very eyes, protesting that they might take his offer or leave it; and all because he did not begin by praising the land.

Well then, this man I spoke of offered to help me, and he went to get his scythe. But I went into the house and brought out a gallon jar of small ale for him and for me; for the sun was now very warm, and small ale goes well with mowing. When we had drunk some of this ale in mugs called "I see you," we took each a swathe, he a little behind me because he was the better mower; and so for many hours we swung, one before the other, mowing and mowing at the tall grass of the field. And the sun rose to noon and we were still at our mowing; and we ate food, but only for a little while, and we took again to our mowing. And at last there was nothing left but a small square of grass, standing like a square of linesmen who keep their formation, tall and unbroken, with all the dead lying around them when a battle is over and done.

Then for some little time I rested after all those hours; and the man and I talked together, and a long way off we heard in another field the musical sharpening of a scythe.

The sunlight slanted powdered and mellow over the breadth of the valley; for day was nearing its end. I went to fetch rakes from the steading; and when I had come back the last of the grass had fallen, and all the field lay flat and smooth, with the very green short grass in lanes between the dead and yellow swathes.

These swathes we raked into cocks to keep them from the dew against our return at daybreak; and we made the cocks as tall and steep as we could, for in that shape they best keep off the dew, and it is easier also to spread them after the sun has risen. Then we raked up every straggling blade, till the whole field was a clean floor for the tedding and the carrying of the hay next morning. The grass we had mown was but a little over two acres; for that is all the pasture on my little tiny farm.

When we had done all this, there fell upon us the

beneficent and deliberate evening; so that as we sat a little while together near the rakes, we saw the valley more solemn and dim around us, and all the trees and hedgerows quite still, and held by a complete silence. Then I paid my companion his wage, and bade him a good night, till we should meet in the same place before sunrise.

He went off with a slow and steady progress, as all our peasants do, making their walking a part of the easy but continual labour of their lives. But I sat on, watching the light creep around towards the north and change, and the waning moon coming up as though by stealth behind the woods of No Man's Land.

1906

Henry Adams

HARVARD COLLEGE
(1854-1858)

ONE day in June, 1854, young Adams walked for the last time down the steps of Mr. Dixwell's school in Boylston Place, and felt no sensation but one of unqualified joy that this experience was ended. Never before or afterwards in his life did he close a period so long as four years without some sensation of loss—some sentiment of habit—but school was what in after life he commonly heard his friends denounce as an intolerable bore. He was born too old for it. The same thing could be said of most New England boys. Mentally they never were boys. Their education as men should have begun at ten years old. They were fully five years more mature than the English or European boy for whom schools were made. For the purposes of future advancement, as afterwards appeared, these first six years of a possible education were wasted in doing imperfectly what might have been done perfectly in one, and in any case would have had small value. The next regular step was Harvard College. He was more than glad to go. For generation after generation, Adamses and Brookses and Boylstons and Gorhams had gone to Harvard College, and although none of them, as far as known, had ever done any good there, or thought himself the better for it, custom, social ties, convenience,

From *The Autobiography of Henry Adams*. Reprinted by permission of Houghton Mifflin Company.

and above all, economy, kept each generation in the track. Any other education would have required a serious effort, but no one took Harvard College seriously. All went there because their friends went there, and the College was their ideal of social self-respect.

Harvard College, as far as it educated at all, was a mild and liberal school, which sent young men into the world with all they needed to make respectable citizens, and something of what they wanted to make useful ones. Leaders of men it never tried to make. Its ideals were altogether different. The Unitarian clergy had given to the College a character of moderation, balance, judgment, restraint, what the French called *mesure;* excellent traits, which the College attained with singular success, so that its graduates could commonly be recognized by the stamp, but such a type of character rarely lent itself to autobiography. In effect, the school created a type but not a will. Four years of Harvard College, if successful, resulted in an autobiographical blank, a mind on which only a watermark had been stamped.

The stamp, as such things went, was a good one. The chief wonder of education is that it does not ruin everybody concerned in it, teachers and taught. Sometimes in after life, Adams debated whether in fact it had not ruined him and most of his companions, but, disappointment apart, Harvard College was probably less hurtful than any other university then in existence. It taught little, and that little ill, but it left the mind open, free from bias, ignorant of facts, but docile. The graduate had few strong prejudices. He knew little, but his mind remained supple, ready to receive knowledge.

What caused the boy most disappointment was the little he got from his mates. Speaking exactly, he got less than nothing, a result common enough in education. Yet the College Catalogue for the years 1854 to 1861 shows a list of names rather distinguished in their time. Alexander

Agassiz and Phillips Brooks led it; H. H. Richardson and O. W. Holmes helped to close it. As a rule the most promising of all die early, and never get their names into a Dictionary of Contemporaries, which seems to be the only popular standard of success. Many died in the war. Adams knew them all, more or less; he felt as much regard, and quite as much respect for them then, as he did after they won great names and were objects of a vastly wider respect; but, as help towards education, he got nothing whatever from them or they from him until long after they had left college. Possibly the fault was his, but one would like to know how many others shared it. Accident counts for much in companionship as in marriage. Life offers perhaps only a score of possible companions, and it is mere chance whether they meet as early as school or college, but it is more than a chance that boys brought up together under like conditions have nothing to give each other. The Class of 1858, to which Henry Adams belonged, was a typical collection of young New Englanders, quietly penetrating and aggressively commonplace; free from meannesses, jealousies, intrigues, enthusiasms, and passions; not exceptionally quick; not consciously sceptical; singularly indifferent to display, artifice, florid expression, but not hostile to it when it amused them; distrustful of themselves, but little disposed to trust any one else; with not much humor of their own, but full of readiness to enjoy the humor of others; negative to a degree that in the long run became positive and triumphant. Not harsh in manners or judgment, rather liberal and open-minded, they were still as a body the most formidable critics one would care to meet, in a long life exposed to criticism. They never flattered, seldom praised; free from vanity, they were not intolerant of it; but they were objectiveness itself; their attitude was a law of nature; their judgment beyond appeal, not an act either of intellect or emotion or of will, but a sort of gravitation.

This was Harvard College incarnate, but even for Harvard College, the Class of 1858 was somewhat extreme. Of unity this band of nearly one hundred young men had no keen sense, but they had equally little energy of repulsion. They were pleasant to live with, and above the average of students—German, French, English, or what not—but chiefly because each individual appeared satisfied to stand alone. It seemed a sign of force; yet to stand alone is quite natural when one has no passions; still easier when one has no pains.

Into this unusually dissolvent medium, chance insisted on enlarging Henry Adams's education by tossing a trio of Virginians as little fitted for it as Sioux Indians to a treadmill. By some further affinity, these three outsiders fell into relation with the Bostonians among whom Adams as a schoolboy belonged, and in the end with Adams himself, although they and he knew well how thin an edge of friendship separated them in 1856 from mortal enmity. One of the Virginians was the son of Colonel Robert E. Lee, of the Second United States Cavalry; the two others who seemed instinctively to form a staff for Lee, were town-Virginians from Petersburg. A fourth outsider came from Cincinnati and was half Kentuckian, N. L. Anderson, Longworth on the mother's side. For the first time Adams's education brought him in contact with new types and taught him their values. He saw the New England type measure itself with another, and he was part of the process.

Lee, known through life as "Roony," was a Virginian of the eighteenth century, much as Henry Adams was a Bostonian of the same age. Roony Lee had changed little from the type of his grandfather, Light Horse Harry. Tall, largely built, handsome, genial, with liberal Virginian openness towards all he liked, he had also the Virginian habit of command and took leadership as his natural habit. No one cared to contest it. None of the New Englanders

wanted command. For a year, at least, Lee was the most
popular and prominent young man in his class, but then
seemed slowly to drop into the background. The habit of
command was not enough, and the Virginian had little
else. He was simple beyond analysis; so simple that even
the simple New England student could not realize him.
No one knew enough to know how ignorant he was; how
childlike; how helpless before the relative complexity of a
school. As an animal, the Southerner seemed to have every
advantage, but even as an animal he steadily lost ground.

The lesson in education was vital to these young men,
who, within ten years, killed each other by scores in the
act of testing their college conclusions. Strictly, the Southerner had no mind; he had temperament. He was not a
scholar; he had no intellectual training; he could not analyze an idea, and he could not even conceive of admitting
two, but in life one could get along very well without
ideas, if one had only the social instinct. Dozens of eminent statesmen were men of Lee's type, and maintained
themselves well enough in the legislature, but college was
a sharper test. The Virginian was weak in vice itself,
though the Bostonian was hardly a master of crime. The
habits of neither were good; both were apt to drink hard
and to live low lives; but the Bostonian suffered less than
the Virginian. Commonly the Bostonian would take some
care of himself even in his worst stages, while the Virginian became quarrelsome and dangerous. When a Virginian had brooded a few days over an imaginary grief
and substantial whiskey, none of his Northern friends
could be sure that he might not be waiting, round the
corner, with a knife or pistol, to revenge insult by the dry
light of *delirium tremens;* and when things reached this
condition, Lee had to exhaust his authority over his own
staff. Lee was a gentleman of the old school, and, as every
one knows, gentlemen of the old school drank almost as
much as gentlemen of the new school; but this was not

his trouble. He was sober even in the excessive violence of political feeling in those years; he kept his temper and his friends under control.

Adams liked the Virginians. No one was more obnoxious to them, by name and prejudice; yet their friendship was unbroken and even warm. At a moment when the immediate future posed no problem in education so vital as the relative energy and endurance of North and South, this momentary contact with Southern character was a sort of education for its own sake; but this was not all. No doubt the self-esteem of the Yankee, which tended naturally to self-distrust, was flattered by gaining the slow conviction that the Southerner, with his slave-owning limitations, was as little fit to succeed in the struggle of modern life as though he were still a maker of stone axes, living in caves, and hunting the *bos primigenius,* and that every quality in which he was strong, made him weaker; but Adams had begun to fear that even in this respect one eighteenth-century type might not differ deeply from another. Roony Lee had changed little from the Virginian of a century before; but Adams was himself a good deal nearer the type of his great-grandfather than to that of a railway superintendent. He was little more fit than the Virginians to deal with a future America which showed no fancy for the past. Already Northern society betrayed a preference for economists over diplomats or soldiers— one might even call it a jealousy—against which two eighteenth-century types had little chance to live, and which they had in common to fear.

Nothing short of this curious sympathy could have brought into close relations two young men so hostile as Roony Lee and Henry Adams, but the chief difference between them as collegians consisted only in their difference of scholarship: Lee was a total failure, Adams a partial one. Both failed, but Lee felt his failure more sensibly, so that he gladly seized the chance of escape by accepting a commission offered him by General Winfield Scott in the force then being organized against the Mormons. He asked Adams to write his letter of acceptance, which flattered Adams's vanity more than any Northern compliment could do, because, in the days of violent political bitterness, it showed a certain amount of good temper. The diplomat felt his profession.

If the student got little from his mates, he got little more from his masters. The four years passed at college were, for his purposes, wasted. Harvard College was a good school, but at bottom what the boy disliked most was any school at all. He did not want to be one in a hundred—one per cent of an education. He regarded himself as the only person for whom his education had value, and he wanted the whole of it. He got barely half of an average. Long afterwards, when the devious path of life led him back to teach in his turn what no student naturally cared or needed to know, he diverted some dreary hours of faculty-meetings by looking up his record in the class-lists, and found himself graded precisely in the middle. In the one branch he most needed—mathematics—barring the few first scholars, failure was so nearly universal that no attempt at grading could have had value, and whether he stood fortieth or ninetieth must have been an accident or the personal favor of the professor. Here his education failed lamentably. At best he could never have been a mathematician; at worst he would never have cared to be one; but he needed to read mathematics, like any other universal language, and he never reached the alphabet.

Beyond two or three Greek plays, the student got nothing from the ancient languages. Beyond some incoherent theories of free-trade and protection, he got little from Political Economy. He could not afterwards remember to have heard the name of Karl Marx mentioned, or the title of "Capital." He was equally ignorant of Auguste Comte. These were the two writers of his time who most influ-

enced its thought. The bit of practical teaching he afterwards reviewed with most curiosity was the course in
Chemistry, which taught him a number of theories that
befogged his mind for a lifetime. The only teaching that
appealed to his imagination was a course of lectures by
Louis Agassiz on the Glacial period and Palaeontology,
which had more influence on his curiosity than the rest
of the college instruction altogether. The entire work of
the four years could have been easily put into the work
of any four months in after life.

Harvard College was a negative force, and negative
forces have value. Slowly it weakened the violent political
bias of childhood, not by putting interests in its place, but
by mental habits which had no bias at all. It would also
have weakened the literary bias, if Adams had been capable of finding other amusement, but the climate kept
him steady to desultory and useless reading, till he had
run through libraries of volumes which he forgot even to
their title-pages. Rather by instinct than by guidance, he
turned to writing, and his professors or tutors occasionally
gave his English composition a hesitating approval; but in
that branch, as in all the rest, even when he made a long
struggle for recognition, he never convinced his teachers
that his abilities, at their best, warranted placing him on
the rank-list, among the first third of his class. Instructors
generally reach a fairly accurate gauge of their scholars'
powers. Henry Adams himself held the opinion that his
instructors were very nearly right, and when he became a
professor in his turn, and made mortifying mistakes in
ranking his scholars, he still obstinately insisted that on
the whole, he was not far wrong. Student or professor, he
accepted the negative standard because it was the standard
of the school.

He never knew what other students thought of it, or
what they thought they gained from it; nor would their
opinion have much affected his. From the first, he wanted

to be done with it, and stood watching vaguely for a path and a direction. The world outside seemed large, but the paths that led into it were not many and lay mostly through Boston, where he did not want to go. As it happened, by pure chance, the first door of escape that seemed to offer a hope led into Germany, and James Russell Lowell opened it.

Lowell, on succeeding Longfellow as Professor of Belles-Lettres, had duly gone to Germany, and had brought back whatever he found to bring. The literary world then agreed that truth survived in Germany alone, and Carlyle, Matthew Arnold, Renan, Emerson, with scores of popular followers, taught the German faith. The literary world had revolted against the yoke of coming capitalism—its money-lenders, its bank directors, and its railway magnates. Thackeray and Dickens followed Balzac in scratching and biting the unfortunate middle class with savage ill-temper, much as the middle class had scratched and bitten the Church and Court for a hundred years before. The middle class had the power, and held its coal and iron well in hand, but the satirists and idealists seized the press, and as they were agreed that the Second Empire was a disgrace to France and a danger to England, they turned to Germany because at that moment Germany was neither economical nor military, and a hundred years behind western Europe in the simplicity of its standard. German thought, method, honesty, and even taste, became the standards of scholarship. Goethe was raised to the rank of Shakespeare—Kant ranked as a law-giver above Plato. All serious scholars were obliged to become German, for German thought was revolutionizing criticism. Lowell had followed the rest, not very enthusiastically, but with sufficient conviction, and invited his scholars to join him. Adams was glad to accept the invitation, rather for the sake of cultivating Lowell than Germany, but still in perfect good faith. It was the first serious attempt he had made to direct his own education, and he was sure of getting some education out of it; not perhaps anything that he expected, but at least a path.

Singularly circuitous and excessively wasteful of energy the path proved to be, but the student could never see what other was open to him. He could have done no better had he foreseen every stage of his coming life, and he would probably have done worse. The preliminary step was pure gain. James Russell Lowell had brought back from Germany the only new and valuable part of its universities, the habit of allowing students to read with him privately in his study. Adams asked the privilege, and used it to read a little, and to talk a great deal, for the personal contact pleased and flattered him, as that of older men ought to flatter and please the young even when they altogether exaggerate its value. Lowell was a new element in the boy's life. As practical a New Englander as any, he leaned towards the Concord faith rather than towards Boston where he properly belonged; for Concord, in the dark days of 1856, glowed with pure light. Adams approached it in much the same spirit as he would have entered a Gothic Cathedral, for he well knew that the priests regarded him as only a worm. To the Concord Church all Adamses were minds of dust and emptiness, devoid of feeling, poetry or imagination; little higher than the common scourings of State Street; politicians of doubtful honesty; natures of narrow scope; and already, at eighteen years old, Henry had begun to feel uncertainty about so many matters more important than Adamses that his mind rebelled against no discipline merely personal, and he was ready to admit his unworthiness if only he might penetrate the shrine. The influence of Harvard College was beginning to have its effect. He was slipping away from fixed principles; from Mount Vernon Street; from Quincy; from the eighteenth century; and his first steps led toward Concord.

He never reached Concord, and to Concord Church he, like the rest of mankind who accepted a material universe, remained always an insect, or something much lower—a man. It was surely no fault of his that the universe seemed to him real; perhaps—as Mr. Emerson justly said—it was so; in spite of the long-continued effort of a lifetime, he perpetually fell back into the heresy that if anything universal was unreal, it was himself and not the appearances; it was the poet and not the banker; it was his own thought, not the thing that moved it. He did not lack the wish to be transcendental. Concord seemed to him, at one time, more real than Quincy; yet in truth Russell Lowell was as little transcendental as Beacon Street. From him the boy got no revolutionary thought whatever—objective or subjective as they used to call it—but he got good-humored encouragement to do what amused him, which consisted in passing two years in Europe after finishing the four years of Cambridge.

The result seemed small in proportion to the effort, but it was the only positive result he could ever trace to the influence of Harvard College, and he had grave doubts whether Harvard College influenced even that. Negative results in plenty he could trace, but he tended towards negation on his own account, as one side of the New England mind had always done, and even there he could never feel sure that Harvard College had more than reflected a weakness. In his opinion the education was not serious, but in truth hardly any Boston student took it seriously, and none of them seemed sure that President Walker himself, or President Felton after him, took it more seriously than the students. For them all, the college offered chiefly advantages vulgarly called social, rather than mental.

Unluckily for this particular boy, social advantages were his only capital in life. Of money he had not much, of mind not more, but he could be quite certain that, barring his own faults, his social position would never be questioned. What he needed was a career in which social position had value. Never in his life would he have to explain who he was; never would he have need of acquaintance to strengthen his social standing; but he needed greatly some one to show him how to use the acquaintance he cared to make. He made no acquaintance in college which proved to have the smallest use in after life. All his Boston friends he knew before, or would have known in any case, and contact of Bostonian with Bostonian was the last education these young men needed. Cordial and intimate as their college relations were, they all flew off in different directions the moment they took their degrees. Harvard College remained a tie, indeed, but a tie little stronger than Beacon Street and not so strong as State Street. Strangers might perhaps gain something from the college if they were hard pressed for social connections. A student like H. H. Richardson, who came from far away New Orleans, and had his career before him to chase rather than to guide, might make valuable friendships at college. Certainly Adams made no acquaintance there that he valued in after life so much as Richardson, but still more certainly the college relation had little to do with the later friendship. Life is a narrow valley, and the roads run close together. Adams would have attached himself to Richardson in any case, as he attached himself to John La Farge or Augustus St. Gaudens or Clarence King or John Hay, none of whom were at Harvard College. The valley of life grew more and more narrow with years, and certain men with common tastes were bound to come together. Adams knew only that he would have felt himself on a more equal footing with them had he been less ignorant, and had he not thrown away ten years of early life in acquiring what he might have acquired in one.

Socially or intellectually, the college was for him negative and in some ways mischievous. The most tolerant man of the world could not see good in the lower habits of the students, but the vices were less harmful than the virtues. The habit of drinking—though the mere recollection of it made him doubt his own veracity, so fantastic it seemed in later life—may have done no great or permanent harm; but the habit of looking at life as a social relation—an affair of society—did no good. It cultivated a weakness which needed no cultivation. If it had helped to make men of the world, or give the manners and instincts of any profession—such as temper, patience, courtesy, or a faculty of profiting by the social defects of opponents— it would have been education better worth having than mathematics or languages; but so far as it helped to make anything it helped only to make the college standard permanent through life. The Bostonian educated at Harvard College remained a collegian, if he stuck only to what the college gave him. If parents went on, generation after generation, sending their children to Harvard College for the sake of its social advantages, they perpetuated an inferior social type, quite as ill-fitted as the Oxford type for success in the next generation.

Luckily the old social standard of the college, as President Walker or James Russell Lowell still showed it, was admirable, and if it had little practical value or personal influence on the mass of students, at least it preserved the tradition for those who liked it. The Harvard graduate was neither American nor European, nor even wholly Yankee; his admirers were few, and his critics many; perhaps his worst weakness was his self-criticism and self-consciousness; but his ambitions, social or intellectual, were not necessarily cheap even though they might be negative. Afraid of serious risks, and still more afraid of personal ridicule, he seldom made a great failure of life, and nearly always led a life more or less worth living. So Henry Adams, well aware that he could not succeed as a scholar, and finding his social position beyond improvement or need of effort, betook himself to the single ambition which otherwise would scarcely have seemed a true outcome of the college, though it was the last remnant of the old Unitarian supremacy. He took to the pen. He wrote.

The College Magazine printed his work, and the College Societies listened to his addresses. Lavish of praise the readers were not; the audiences, too, listened in silence; but this was all the encouragement any Harvard collegian had a reasonable hope to receive; grave silence was a form of patience that meant possible future acceptance; and Henry Adams went on writing. No one cared enough to criticise, except himself who soon began to suffer from reaching his own limits. He found that he could not be this—or that—or the other; always precisely the things he wanted to be. He had not wit or scope or force. Judges always ranked him beneath a rival, if he had any; and he believed the judges were right. His work seemed to him thin, commonplace, feeble. At times he felt his own weakness so fatally that he could not go on; when he had nothing to say, he could not say it, and he found that he had very little to say at best. Much that he then wrote must be still in existence in print or manuscript, though he never cared to see it again, for he felt no doubt that it was in reality just what he thought it. At best it showed only a feeling for form; an instinct of exclusion. Nothing shocked—not even its weakness.

Inevitably an effort leads to an ambition—creates it— and at that time the ambition of the literary student, which almost took place of the regular prizes of scholarship, was that of being chosen as the representative of his class—the Class Orator—at the close of their course. This was political as well as literary success, and precisely the sort of eighteenth-century combination that fascinated an eighteenth-century boy. The idea lurked in his mind, at first as a dream, in no way serious or even possible for he stood outside the number of what were known as popular men. Year by year, his position seemed to improve, or perhaps his rivals disappeared, until at last, to his own great astonishment, he found himself a candidate. The habits of the college permitted no active candidacy; he and his rivals had not a word to say for or against themselves, and he was never even consulted on the subject; he was not present at any of the proceedings, and how it happened he never could quite divine, but it did happen that one evening on returning from Boston he received notice of his election, after a very close contest, as Class Orator over the head of the first scholar, who was undoubtedly a better orator and a more popular man. In politics the success of the poorer candidate is common enough, and Henry Adams was a fairly trained politician, but he never understood how he managed to defeat not only a more capable but a more popular rival.

To him the election seemed a miracle. This was no mock-modesty; his head was as clear as ever it was in an indifferent canvass, and he knew his rivals and their following as well as he knew himself. What he did not know, even after four years of education, was Harvard College. What he could never measure was the bewildering impersonality of the men, who, at twenty years old, seemed to set no value either on official or personal standards. Here were nearly a hundred young men who had lived together intimately during four of the most impressionable years of life, and who, not only once but again and again, in different ways, deliberately, seriously, dispassionately, chose as their representatives precisely those of their companions who seemed least to represent them. As far as these Orators and Marshals had any position at all in a collegiate sense, it was that of indifference to the college. Henry Adams never professed the smallest faith in universities of any kind, either as boy or man, nor had he the faintest admiration for the university graduate, either in Europe or in America; as a collegian he was only known apart from his fellows by his habit of standing outside the college; and yet the singular fact remained that this commonplace body of young men chose him repeatedly to express his and their commonplaces. Secretly, of course, the successful candidate flattered himself—and them—with the hope that they might perhaps not be so commonplace as they thought themselves; but this was only another proof that all were identical. They saw in him a representative—the kind of representative they wanted—and he saw in them the most formidable array of judges he could ever meet, like so many mirrors of himself, an infinite reflection of his own shortcomings.

All the same, the choice was flattering; so flattering that it actually shocked his vanity; and would have shocked it more, if possible, had he known that it was to be the only flattery of the sort he was ever to receive. The function of Class Day was, in the eyes of nine-tenths of the students, altogether the most important of the college, and the figure of the Orator was the most conspicuous in the function. Unlike the Orators at regular Commencements, the Class Day Orator stood alone, or had only the Poet for rival. Crowded into the large church, the students, their families, friends, aunts, uncles, and chaperones, attended all the girls of sixteen or twenty who wanted to show their summer dresses or fresh complexions, and there, for an hour or two, in a heat that might have melted bronze, they listened to an Orator and a Poet in clergyman's gowns, reciting such platitudes as their own experience and their mild censors permitted them to utter. What Henry Adams said in his Class Oration of 1858 he soon forgot to the last word, nor had it the least value for education; but he naturally remembered what was said of it. He remembered especially one of his eminent uncles or relations remarking that, as the work of so young a man, the oration was singularly wanting in enthusiasm. The

young man—always in search of education—asked himself
whether, setting rhetoric aside, this absence of enthusiasm
was a defect or a merit, since, in either case, it was all that
Harvard College taught, and all that the hundred young
men, whom he was trying to represent, expressed. Another
comment threw more light on the effect of the college
education. One of the elderly gentlemen noticed the
orator's "perfect self-possession." Self-possession indeed!
If Harvard College gave nothing else, it gave calm. For
four years each student had been obliged to figure daily
before dozens of young men who knew each other to the
last fibre. One had done little but read papers to Societies,
or act comedy in the Hasty Pudding, not to speak of all
sorts of regular exercises, and no audience in future life
would ever be so intimately and terribly intelligent as
these. Three-fourths of the graduates would rather have
addressed the Council of Trent or the British Parliament
than have acted Sir Anthony Absolute or Dr. Ollapod
before a gala audience of the Hasty Pudding. Self-possession was the strongest part of Harvard College, which
certainly taught men to stand alone, so that nothing
seemed stranger to its graduates than the paroxysms of
terror before the public which often overcame the graduates of European universities. Whether this was, or was
not, education, Henry Adams never knew. He was ready
to stand up before any audience in America or Europe,
with nerves rather steadier for the excitement, but whether
he should ever have anything to say, remained to be
proved. As yet he knew nothing. Education had not
begun.

First printed, 1907;
first published, 1918.

Bertrand Russell

A FREE MAN'S WORSHIP

To Dr. Faustus in his study Mephistopheles told the history of the Creation saying:

"The endless praises of the choirs of angels had begun to grow wearisome; for, after all, did he not deserve their praise? Had he not given them endless joy? Would it not be more amusing to obtain undeserved praise, to be worshipped by beings whom he tortured? He smiled inwardly, and resolved that the great drama should be performed.

"For countless ages the hot nebula whirled aimlessly through space. At length it began to take shape, the central mass threw off planets, the planets cooled, boiling seas and burning mountains heaved and tossed, from black masses of cloud hot sheets of rain deluged the barely solid crust. And now the first germ of life grew in the depths of the ocean, and developed rapidly in the fructifying warmth into vast forest trees, huge ferns springing from the damp mould, sea monsters breeding, fighting, devouring, and passing away. And from the monsters, as the play unfolded itself, Man was born, with the power of thought, the knowledge of good and evil, and the cruel thirst for worship. And Man saw that all is passing in this mad, monstrous world, that all is struggling to snatch,

From *Mysticism and Logic, and other essays* by Bertrand Russell. Reprinted by permission of George Allen & Unwin Ltd.

at any cost, a few brief moments of life before Death's inexorable decree. And Man said: 'There is a hidden purpose, could we but fathom it, and the purpose is good; for we must reverence something, and in the visible world there is nothing worthy of reverence.' And Man stood aside from the struggle, resolving that God intended harmony to come out of chaos by human efforts. And when he followed the instincts which God had transmitted to him from his ancestry of beasts of prey, he called it Sin, and asked God to forgive him. But he doubted whether he could be justly forgiven, until he invented a divine Plan by which God's wrath was to have been appeased. And seeing the present was bad, he made it yet worse, that thereby the future might be better. And he gave God thanks for the strength that enabled him to forego even the joys that were possible. And God smiled; and when he saw that Man had become perfect in renunciation and worship, he sent another sun through the sky, which crashed into Man's sun; and all returned again to nebula.

" 'Yes,' he murmured, 'it was a good play; I will have it performed again.' "

Such, in outline, but even more purposeless, more void of meaning, is the world which Science presents for our belief. Amid such a world, if anywhere, our ideals henceforward must find a home. That Man is the product of causes which had no prevision of the end they were achieving; that his origin, his growth, his hopes and fears, his loves and his beliefs, are but the outcome of accidental collocations of atoms; that no fire, no heroism, no intensity of thought and feeling, can preserve an individual life beyond the grave; that all the labours of the ages, all the devotion, all the inspiration, all the noonday brightness of human genius, are destined to extinction in the vast death of the solar system, and that the whole temple of Man's achievement must inevitably be buried beneath the debris of a universe in ruins—all these things, if not quite beyond dispute, are yet so nearly certain, that no philosophy which rejects them can hope to stand. Only within the scaffolding of these truths, only on the firm foundation of unyielding despair, can the soul's habitation henceforth be safely built.

How, in such an alien and inhuman world, can so powerless a creature as Man preserve his aspirations untarnished? A strange mystery it is that Nature, omnipotent but blind, in the revolutions of her secular hurryings through the abysses of space, has brought forth at last a child, subject still to her power, but gifted with sight, with knowledge of good and evil, with the capacity of judging all the works of his unthinking Mother. In spite of Death, the mark and seal of the parental control, Man is yet free, during his brief years, to examine, to criticise, to know, and in imagination to create. To him alone, in the world with which he is acquainted, this freedom belongs; and in this lies his superiority to the resistless forces that control his outward life.

The savage, like ourselves, feels the oppression of his impotence before the powers of Nature; but having in himself nothing that he respects more than Power, he is willing to prostrate himself before his gods, without inquiring whether they are worthy of his worship. Pathetic and very terrible is the long history of cruelty and torture, of degradation and human sacrifice, endured in the hope of placating the jealous gods: surely, the trembling believer thinks, when what is most precious has been freely given, their lust for blood must be appeased, and more will not be required. The religion of Moloch—as such creeds may be generically called—is in essence the cringing submission of the slave, who dare not, even in his heart, allow the thought that his master deserves no adulation. Since the independence of ideals is not yet acknowledged, Power

may be freely worshipped, and receive an unlimited respect, despite its wanton infliction of pain.

But gradually, as morality grows bolder, the claim of
the ideal world begins to be felt; and worship, if it is not
to cease, must be given to gods of another kind than those
created by the savage. Some, though they feel the demands of the ideal, will still consciously reject them, still
urging that naked Power is worthy of worship. Such is the
attitude inculcated in God's answer to Job out of the
whirlwind: the divine power and knowledge are paraded,
but of the divine goodness there is no hint. Such also is
the attitude of those who, in our own day, base their
morality upon the struggle for survival, maintaining that
the survivors are necessarily the fittest. But others, not
content with an answer so repugnant to the moral sense,
will adopt the position which we have become accustomed
to regard as specially religious, maintaining that, in some
hidden manner, the world of fact is really harmonious with
the world of ideals. Thus Man creates God, all-powerful
and all-good, the mystic unity of what is and what
should be.

But the world of fact, after all, is not good; and, in
submitting our judgment to it, there is an element of
slavishness from which our thoughts must be purged.
For in all things it is well to exalt the dignity of Man,
by freeing him, as far as possible, from the tyranny of
non-human Power. When we have realised that Power is
largely bad, that man, with his knowledge of good and
evil, is but a helpless atom in a world which has no such
knowledge, the choice is again presented to us: Shall we
worship Force, or shall we worship Goodness? Shall our
God exist and be evil, or shall he be recognised as the
creation of our own conscience?

The answer to this question is very momentous, and
affects profoundly our whole morality. The worship of
Force, to which Carlyle and Nietzsche and the creed of

Militarism have accustomed us, is the result of failure to maintain our own ideals against a hostile universe: it is itself a prostrate submission to evil, a sacrifice of our best to Moloch. If strength indeed is to be respected, let us respect rather the strength of those who refuse that false "recognition of facts" which fails to recognise that facts are often bad. Let us admit that, in the world we know, there are many things that would be better otherwise, and that the ideals to which we do and must adhere are not realised in the realm of matter. Let us preserve our respect for truth, for beauty, for the ideal of perfection which life does not permit us to attain, though none of these things meet with the approval of the unconscious universe. If Power is bad, as it seems to be, let us reject it from our hearts. In this lies Man's true freedom: in determination to worship only the God created by our own love of the good, to respect only the heaven which inspires the insight of our best moments. In action, in desire, we must submit perpetually to the tyranny of outside forces; but in thought, in aspiration, we are free, free from our fellow-men, free from the petty planet on which our bodies impotently crawl, free even, while we live, from the tyranny of death. Let us learn, then, that energy of faith which enables us to live constantly in the vision of the good; and let us descend, in action, into the world of fact, with that vision always before us.

When first the opposition of fact and ideal grows fully visible, a spirit of fiery revolt, of fierce hatred of the gods, seems necessary to the assertion of freedom. To defy with Promethean constancy a hostile universe, to keep its evil always in view, always actively hated, to refuse no pain that the malice of Power can invent, appears to be the duty of all who will not bow before the inevitable. But indignation is still a bondage, for it compels our thoughts to be occupied with an evil world; and in the fierceness of desire from which rebellion springs there is a kind of self-assertion which it is necessary for the wise to overcome. Indignation is a submission of our thoughts, but not of our desires; the Stoic freedom in which wisdom consists is found in the submission of our desires, but not of our thoughts. From the submission of our desires springs the virtue of resignation; from the freedom of our thoughts springs the whole world of art and philosophy, and the vision of beauty by which, at last, we half reconquer the reluctant world. But the vision of beauty is possible only to unfettered contemplation, to thoughts not weighted by the load of eager wishes; and thus Freedom comes only to those who no longer ask of life that it shall yield them any of those personal goods that are subject to the mutations of Time. Although the necessity of renunciation is evidence of the existence of evil, yet Christianity, in preaching it, has shown a wisdom exceeding that of the Promethean philosophy of rebellion. It must be admitted that, of the things we desire, some, though they prove impossible, are yet real goods; others, however, as ardently longed for, do not form part of a fully purified ideal. The belief that what must be renounced is bad, though sometimes false, is far less often false than untamed passion supposes; and the creed of religion, by providing a reason for proving that it is never false, has been the means of purifying our hopes by the discovery of many austere truths.

But there is in resignation a further good element: even real goods, when they are unattainable, ought not to be fretfully desired. To every man comes, sooner or later, the great renunciation. For the young, there is nothing unattainable; a good thing desired with the whole force of a passionate will, and yet impossible, is to them not credible. Yet, by death, by illness, by poverty, or by the voice of duty, we must learn, each one of us, that the world was not made for us, and that, however beautiful may be the things we crave, Fate may nevertheless forbid them. It is the part of courage, when misfortune comes, to bear without repining the ruin of our hopes, to turn away our thoughts from vain regrets. This degree of submission to Power is not only just and right: it is the very gate of wisdom.

But passive renunciation is not the whole of wisdom; for not by renunciation alone can we build a temple for the worship of our own ideals. Haunting foreshadowings of the temple appear in the realm of imagination, in music, in architecture, in the untroubled kingdom of reason, and in the golden sunset magic of lyrics, where beauty shines and glows, remote from the touch of sorrow, remote from the fear of change, remote from the failures and disenchantments of the world of fact. In the contemplation of these things the vision of heaven will shape itself in our hearts, giving at once a touchstone to judge the world about us, and an inspiration by which to fashion to our needs whatever is not incapable of serving as a stone in the sacred temple.

Except for those rare spirits that are born without sin, there is a cavern of darkness to be traversed before that temple can be entered. The gate of the cavern is despair, and its floor is paved with the gravestones of abandoned hopes. There Self must die; there the eagerness, the greed of untamed desire must be slain, for only so can the soul be freed from the empire of Fate. But out of the cavern the Gate of Renunciation leads again to the daylight of wisdom, by whose radiance a new insight, a new joy, a new tenderness, shine forth to gladden the pilgrim's heart.

When, without the bitterness of impotent rebellion, we have learnt both to resign ourselves to the outward rule of Fate and to recognise that the non-human world is unworthy of our worship, it becomes possible at last so to transform and refashion the unconscious universe, so to transmute it in the crucible of imagination, that a new image of shining gold replaces the old idol of clay. In all the multiform facts of the world—in the visual shapes of trees and mountains and clouds, in the events of the life of man, even in the very omnipotence of Death—the insight of creative idealism can find the reflection of a beauty which its own thoughts first made. In this way mind asserts its subtle mastery over the thoughtless forces of Nature. The more evil the material with which it deals, the more thwarting to untrained desire, the greater is its achievement in inducing the reluctant rock to yield up its hidden treasures, the prouder its victory in compelling the opposing forces to swell the pageant of its triumph. Of all the arts, Tragedy is the proudest, the most triumphant; for it builds its shining citadel in the very centre of the enemy's country, on the very summit of his highest mountain; from its impregnable watch-towers, his camps and arsenals, his columns and forts, are all revealed; within its walls the free life continues, while the legions of Death and Pain and Despair, and all the servile captains of tyrant Fate, afford the burghers of that dauntless city new spectacles of beauty. Happy those sacred ramparts, thrice happy the dwellers on that all-seeing eminence. Honour to those brave warriors who, through countless ages of warfare, have preserved for us the priceless heritage of liberty, and have kept undefiled by sacrilegious invaders the home of the unsubdued.

But the beauty of Tragedy does but make visible a quality which, in more or less obvious shapes, is present always and everywhere in life. In the spectacle of Death, in the endurance of intolerable pain, and in the irrevocableness of a vanished past, there is a sacredness, an overpowering awe, a feeling of the vastness, the depth, the inexhaustible mystery of existence, in which, as by some strange marriage of pain, the sufferer is bound to the world by bonds of sorrow. In these moments of insight, we lose all eagerness of temporary desire, all struggling and striving for petty ends, all care for the little trivial things that, to a superficial view, make up the common life of day by day; we see, surrounding the narrow raft illumined by the flickering light of human comradeship, the dark ocean on whose rolling waves we toss for a brief hour; from the great night without, a chill blast breaks in upon our refuge; all the loneliness of humanity amid hostile forces is concentrated upon the individual soul, which must struggle alone, with what courage it can command, against the whole weight of a universe that cares nothing for its hopes and fears. Victory, in this struggle with the powers of darkness, is the true baptism into the glorious company of heroes, the true initiation into the overmastering beauty of human existence. From that awful encounter of the soul with the outer world, renunciation, wisdom, and charity are born; and with their birth a new life begins. To take into the inmost shrine of the soul the irresistible forces whose puppets we seem to be—Death and change, the irrevocableness of the past, and the powerlessness of man before the blind hurry of the universe from vanity to vanity—to feel these things and know them is to conquer them.

This is the reason why the Past has much magical power. The beauty of its motionless and silent pictures is like the enchanted purity of last autumn, when the leaves, though one breath would make them fall, still glow against the sky in golden glory. The Past does not change or strive; like Duncan, after life's fitful fever it sleeps well; what was eager and grasping, what was petty and transitory, has faded away, the things that were beautiful and eternal shine out like stars in the night. Its beauty, to a soul not worthy of it, is unendurable; but to a soul which has conquered Fate it is the key of religion.

The life of Man, viewed outwardly, is but a small thing in comparison with the forces of Nature. The slave is doomed to worship Time and Fate and Death, because they are greater than anything he finds in himself, and because all his thoughts are of things which they devour. But, great as they are, to think of them greatly, to feel their passionless splendour, is greater still. And such thought makes us free men; we no longer bow before the inevitable in oriental subjection, but we absorb it, and make it a part of ourselves. To abandon the struggle for private happiness, to expel all eagerness of temporary desire, to burn with passion for eternal things—this is emancipation, and this is the free man's worship. And this liberation is effected by a contemplation of Fate; for Fate itself is subdued by the mind which leaves nothing to be purged by the purifying fire of Time.

United with his fellow-men by the strongest of all ties, the tie of a common doom, the free man finds that a new vision is with him always, shedding over every daily task the light of love. The life of Man is a long march through the night, surrounded by invisible foes, tortured by weariness and pain, towards a goal that few can hope to reach, and where none may tarry long. One by one, as they march, our comrades vanish from our sight, seized by the silent orders of omnipotent Death. Very brief is the time in which we can help them, in which their happiness or misery is decided. Be it ours to shed sunshine on their path, to lighten their sorrows by the balm of sympathy, to give them the pure joy of a never-tiring affection, to strengthen failing courage, to instil faith in hours of despair. Let us not weigh in grudging scales their merits and demerits, but let us think only of their need—of the sorrows, the difficulties, perhaps the blindnesses, that make the misery of their lives; let us remember that they are fellow-sufferers in the same darkness, actors in the same tragedy with ourselves. And so, when their day is over, when their good and their evil have become eternal by the immortality of the past, be it ours to feel that, where they suffered, where they failed, no deed of ours was the cause; but wherever a spark of the divine fire kindled in their hearts, we were ready with encouragement, with sympathy, with brave words in which high courage glowed.

Brief and powerless is Man's life; on him and all his race the slow, sure doom falls pitiless and dark. Blind to good and evil, reckless of destruction, omnipotent matter rolls on its relentless way; for Man, condemned today to lose his dearest, tomorrow himself to pass through the gate of darkness, it remains only to cherish, ere yet the blow falls, the lofty thoughts that ennoble his little day; disdaining the coward terrors of the slave to Fate, to worship at the shrine that his own hands have built; undismayed by the empire of chance, to preserve a mind free from the wanton tyranny that rules his outward life; proudly defiant of the irresistible forces that tolerate, for a moment, his knowledge and his condemnation, to sustain alone, a weary but unyielding Atlas, the world that his own ideals have fashioned despite the trampling march of unconscious power.

1910

John Jay Chapman

THE COMIC

IN the caverns of our nature lie hid various emotions like beasts in a lair. They are shy to the voice of question or of curiosity, and they slink and crouch all the more, if we try to lure them out for inspection. But they come gambolling and roaring forth at the call of ingenuous human utterance. Any utterance that has in it no afterthought, but is mere speech that has grown out of a need to speak, lays a spell upon the wild things within us. Before the echo of it has died away they are rampant in the open, ignorant of how they came forth. Let no one then wonder at the difficulties that surround all study of the human emotions,—blushing giants, vanishing Genii that they are.

It is easy for us today to see that comedy is in its nature the same sort of thing as tragedy. They arise out of the same need, convey the same truth, depend upon the same talent. The English drama interwove comedy and tragedy in the same play, and Shakespeare's greatness in one is of a piece with his greatness in the other. Indeed there are scenes in Lear, Shylock, and Henry IV where tragedy and comedy are overlaid—where the same scene is both tragic and comic and we laugh and cry at the same time. But for a Greek to have seen this identity is very remarkable; because Greek tragedy and Greek comedy represented distinct professions and were totally different in their methods of appeal. A Greek tragedy was a drama of fate, based on a familiar bit of religious folk-lore. The plot was known, the interest lay in the treatment. A Greek comedy, however, was a farrago of licentious nonsense, developed in the course of a fantastic narrative-play: it was what we should call a musical extravaganza. Greek comedy is gigantesque buffoonery, interspersed with lyric and choral passages of divine beauty—the whole, following a traditional model as to its arrangement.

With this machinery Aristophanes proceeds to shake the stones of the Greek theatre with inextinguishable laughter. He will do anything to raise a laugh. He introduces Socrates hung up in a basket and declaring that he is flying in the air and speculating about the sun. He makes the god Dionysus—the very god in whose honour the theatre and festival exist—to leap from the stage in a moment of comic terror, and hide himself under the long cloak of his own high-priest, whose chair of state was in the front row of the pit. Is it possible to imagine what sort of a scene in the theatre this climax must have aroused? There has been no laughter since Aristophanes. There is something of the same humor in Rabelais; but Rabelais is a book, and there each man laughs alone over his book, not in company with his whole city or tribe, as in the Greek theatre.

Now what is it they are laughing at? It is sallies of wit, personal hits, local allusions, indecencies, philosophical cracks, everything from refined satire to the bludgeons of abuse—and the whole thing is proceeding in an atmosphere of fun, of wild spirits, of irrepressible devilry. Compared to Aristophanes, Shakespeare is not funny; he lacks size. He is a great and thoughtful person, of superabundant genius and charm, who makes Dutch interiors, drenched in light. But Aristophanes splits the heavens with a jest, and the rays of truth stream down from inaccessible solitudes of speculation. He has no epigram, no cleverness, no derivative humor. He is bald foolery. And yet he conveys mysticism: he conveys divinity. He alone stands still while the whole empyrean of Greek life circles about him.

From what height of suddenly assumed superiority does the race of birds commiserate mankind:

"Come now, ye men, in nature darkling, like to the race of leaves, of little might, figures of clay, shadowy feeble tribes, wingless creatures of a day, miserable mortals, dream-like men, give your attention to us the immortals, the ever-existing, the ethereal, the ageless, who meditate eternal counsels, in order that when you have heard everything from us accurately about sublime things, the nature of birds, and the origin of gods and rivers, of Erebus and Chaos, you may henceforth bid Prodicus from me go weep, when you know them accurately." *

Into what depth of independent thought did the man dream himself, that such fancies could take hold of him? When Aristophanes has had his say, there is nothing left over: There is no frame nor shell: there is no theatre nor world. Everything is exploded and scattered into sifting, oscillating, shimmering, slowly-sinking fragments of meaning and allusion. If anyone should think that I am going to analyze the intellect of Aristophanes, he is in error. I wish only to make a remark about it; namely, that his power is somehow rooted in personal detachment, in philosophical independence.

It was the genius of Aristophanes which must have suggested to Plato the idea which he throws out in the last paragraph of the Symposium. That great artist, Plato, has left many luminous half-thoughts behind him. He sets each one in a limbo—in a cocoon of its own light—and leaves it in careless-careful fashion, as if it were hardly worth investigation. The rascal! The setting has cost him sleepness nights and much parchment. He has redrawn and

* Hickie's translation.

arranged it a hundred times. He is unable to fathom the idea, and yet it fascinates him. The setting in which Plato has placed his suggestion about the genius of tragedy and comedy is so very wonderful—both as a picture and as his apology for not carrying the idea further—that I must quote it, if only as an act of piety, and for my own pleasure.

"Agathon arose in order that he might take his place on the couch by Socrates, when suddenly a band of revellers entered, and spoiled the order of the banquet. Someone who was going out having left the door open, they had found their way in, and made themselves at home; great confusion ensued, and everyone was compelled to drink large quantities of wine. Aristodemus said that Eryximachus, Phaedrus and others went away—he himself fell asleep, and as the nights were long, took a good rest: he was awakened toward daybreak by a crowing of cocks, and when he awoke, the others were either asleep or had gone away; there remained only Socrates, Aristophanes, and Agathon, who were drinking out of a large goblet which they passed round, and Socrates was discoursing to them. Aristodemus was only half awake, and he did not hear the beginning of the discourse; the chief thing which he remembered was Socrates compelling the other two to acknowledge that the genius of comedy was the same with that of tragedy, and that the true artist in tragedy was an artist in comedy also. To this they were constrained to assent, being drowsy and not quite following the argument. And first of all Aristophanes dropped off; then, when the day was already dawning, Agathon. Socrates, having laid them to sleep, rose to depart, Aristodemus, as his manner was, following him. At the Lyceum he took a bath, and passed the day as usual. In the evening he retired to rest at his own home." *

What can Plato have had in mind, that glimmers to us

* Jowett's translation.

in the dawn as a sort of dim, divine intimation, and is almost immediately drowned by daylight and the market-place? I suppose that Plato may have had in mind certain moments in comedy where the self-deluded isolation of some character is so perfectly given as to be almost sublime, and thus to suggest tragedy; or Plato may have had the opposite experience, and may have found himself almost ready to laugh at the fate of Ajax, whose weaknesses of character work out so inevitably, so logically, so beautifully in the tragedy of Sophocles. Perhaps the thought passed through Plato's mind: "If this were not tragedy, what wonderful comedy it would be! If only the climax were less painful, if the mad Ajax, instead of killing himself, should merely be driven to eat grass like an ox for a season, or put on his clothes hind-side-before—in fact, if Ajax's faults could only be punished quite mildly in the outcome, here would be a comedy indeed!"

The stuff of which tragedy and comedy are made is the same stuff. The foibles of mankind work up more easily into comedy than into tragedy; and this is the chief difference between the two. We readily understand the Nemesis of temperament, the fatality of character, when it is exposed upon a small scale. This is the business of comedy; and we do not here require the labored artifice of gods, mechanical plot, and pointed allegory to make us realize the moral.

But in tragedy we have the large scale to deal with. A tragedy is always the same thing. It is a world of complicated and traditional stage devices for making us realize the helplessness of mankind before destiny. We are told from the start to expect the worst: there is going to be suffering, and the suffering is going to be logical, inevitable, necessary. There is also an implication to be conveyed that this suffering is somehow in accord with the moral constitution of the universe. The aim of the whole thing is to teach us to submit—to fit us for life.

There is profound truth at the bottom of these ideas; for whether you accept this truth in the form of the Christian doctrine of humility, or in the form of the Pagan doctrine of reverence for the gods, there is no question that a human being who is in the state of mind of Lear or of Ajax is in a dangerous state. He is going to be punished: he is going to punish himself. The complexities of human life, however, make this truth very difficult to convey upon the grand scale. It is, in daily existence, obscured by other and more obvious truths. In order to dig it out and present it and make it seem at all probable, every historical device and trapping and sign-post of suggestion—every stage tradition must be used. The aim is so exalted and sombre and the machinery is so ponderous that laughter is out of the question: it is forbidden. The magnitude of the issues oppress us; and we are told that it would be cruel to the hero and to the actor and to the author for us to laugh. And yet we are always on the verge of laughter, and any inattention to the rubric may bring on a fit of it. If a windlass breaks we really laugh harder than the occasion warrants.

In reading the Book of Job, where the remoteness of the scene and certain absurdities in the plot relieve the strain of tragedy, we laugh inevitably; and the thing that makes us laugh is the very thing that ought to fill us with awe—the rigor of the logic.

Thus much for the sunny side of tragedy. But let us recur to the night side of comedy. Falstaff is a comic figure, is he not? And yet what thoughtful man is there who has not enough of the Puritan in him to see the tragedy of such a character as Falstaff? How must Falstaff have appeared to Bunyan!—every stroke of genius which to us makes for the comic, adding a phosphor-gleam of hell-fire. And Bunyan is right: Falstaff is an awful picture; and had Shakespeare punished him adequately he would appear awful. Let us imagine that Shakespeare had written a play about the old age of Falstaff, picturing his decay of intellect, his destitution, his flickering return to humor which is no longer funny—what could have been more tragic?

Was it with such arguments as these that Socrates put Aristophanes and Agathon to sleep on the famous morning which Plato chronicles? We cannot tell. Plato has cast the magic of a falling star over the matter and thus leaves it: his humor, his knack, his destiny compelled him to treat subjects in this way. Something passes, and after a light has fallen off into the sea, we ask, "What was it?" Enough for Plato's purpose that he has placed Comedy where, perhaps, no philosopher before or after him ever had the vision to place it—in the heaven of man's highest endeavour.

2

The divine affinities of comedy have thus been established, and we may make some few stray observations on the nature of the comic, not hoping to explain laughter, which must remain forever a spontaneous mystery, but only to point out places where this mystery crosses the other mysteries and refuses to be merged in them, keeping its own course and intensifying the darkness of our ignorance by its coruscations. In the first place the comic is about the most durable vehicle that truth has ever found. It pretends to deal with momentary interest in terms of farce and exaggeration; and yet it leaves an image that strikes deeper and lasts longer than philosophy.

In our search for truth we are continually getting into vehicles that break down or turn into something else, even during our transit. Let us take, for example, the case of Plato's dialogues. How much we have enjoyed them, how much trusted them! And yet there comes a time when we feel about Plato's work that it is almost too well lighted and managed, too filled with parlor elegance. He seems more interested in the effects that can be got by manipulating philosophy than in any serious truth. There is something superficial about the pictures of Greek life that you get from Plato. The marble is too white, the philosophers are too considerate of each other's feelings, Socrates is too clever, everything is a little arranged. Greek life was not quite like that, and the way to convince yourself of this is to read Aristophanes.

In Aristophanes you have the convincing hurly-burly, the sweating, mean, talented, scrambling, laughing life of the Mediterranean—that same life of which you find records in the recent Cretan discoveries, dating from 2500 B.C., or which you may observe in the market-places of Naples today. Plato's dialogues do not give this life. They give a picture of something that never existed, something that sounds like an enchanted picture, a picture of life as it ought to be for the leisure classes, but as it never has been and never can be while the world lasts, even for them.

The ideas which we carry in our minds criticize each other, despite all we can do to keep them apart. They attack and mutilate each other, like the monsters in a drop of muddy water, or the soldiers of Cadmus when the stone of controversy was thrown among them. It is as hard to preserve the *entente cordiale* between hostile thoughts as between hostile bulldogs. We have no sooner patted the head of the courtly and affable Socrates given to us by Plato—the perfect scholar and sweet gentleman—than the vulgarian Socrates given us by Aristophanes—the frowzy all-nighter, the notorious enemy to bathing—flies at the throat of Plato's darling and leaves him rumpled. So far as manners and customs go, nothing can rival good comic description: it supersedes everything else. You can neither write nor preach it down, nor put it down by law. Hogarth had depicted the England of the early Georges in such a way as to convince us. No mortal vehicle of expression can upset Hogarth.

When we come to pictures of life which belong to a

more serious species—to poetry, to history, to religion—we find the same conflicts going on in our minds: one source criticizes another. One belief eats up the next belief as the acid eats the plate. It is not merely the outside of Socrates that Aristophanes has demolished. He has a little damaged the philosophy of Socrates. He undermines Greek thought: he helps and urges us not to take it seriously. He thus becomes an ally of the whole world of later Christian thought. If I were to go to Athens tomorrow, the first man I would seek out would be Aristophanes. He is a modern: he is a man.

We have been speaking of Greek thought and Greek life; yet between that life and ourselves there have intervened some centuries of Christianity, including the Middle Ages, during which Jewish influence pervaded and absorbed other thought. The Hebrew ruled and subdued in philosophy, poetry, and religion. The Hebrew influence is the most powerful influence ever let loose upon the world. Every book written since this Hebrew domination is saturated with Hebrew. It has thus become impossible to see the classics as they were. Between them and us is an atmosphere of mordant, powerful, Hebraic thought, which transmutes and fantastically recolors them. How the classics would have laughed over our conception of them! Virgil was a witch during the Middle Ages and now he is an acolyte, a person over whom the modern sentimental school maunders in tears. The classics would feel toward our notions of them somewhat as a Parisian feels toward a French vaudeville after it has been prepared for the American stage. Christianity is to blame.

I have perhaps spoken as if Christianity has blown over with the Middle Ages; but it has not. The Middle Ages have blown over; but Christianity seems, in some ways, never to have been understood before the nineteenth century. It is upon us, sevenfold strong. Its mysteries supersede the other mysteries; its rod threatens to eat up the rods of the other magicians. These tigers of Christian criticism within us attack the classics. The half-formed objections to Plato which I have mentioned are seriously reinforced by the Hebrew dispensation, which somehow reduces the philosophic speculations of Greece to the status of favors at a cotillion. It is senseless to contrast Christ with Socrates; it is unfair and even absurd to review Greek life and thought by the light of Hebrew life and thought. But to do so is inevitable. We are three parts Hebrew in our nature and we see the Mediterranean culture with Hebrew eyes. The attempts of such persons as Swinburne and Pater to writhe themselves free from the Hebrew domination always betray that profound seriousness which comes from the Jew. These men make a break for freedom—they will be joyous, antique, and irresponsible. Alas, they are sadder than the Puritans and shallower than Columbine.

It has become forever and perpetually impossible for any-one to treat Greek thought on a Greek basis: the basis is gone. As I wrote the words a page or two back about "Comedy having been placed by Plato in the heavens of man's highest endeavour," I thought to myself, "Perhaps I ought to say highest *artistic* endeavour." There spoke the Jew monitor which dogs our classical studies, sniffing at them and hinting that they are trivial. In the eye of that monitor there is no room for the comic in the whole uni-verse: there is no such thing as the comic. The comic is something outside the Jewish dispensation, a kind of irre-ducible unreason, a skeptical or satanic element.

One would conclude from their records that the Jews were people who never laughed except ironically. To be sure, Michal laughed at David's dancing, and Sara laughed at the idea of having a child, and various people in the New Testament laughed others "to scorn." But nobody seems to have laughed heartily and innocently. One gets the impression of a race devoid of humor. This is partly because it is not the province of religious writings to record humor; but it is mainly because Jewish thought condemns humor. Wherever humor arises in a Christian civilization— as in the popular Gothic humor—it is a local race-element, an unsubdued bit of something foreign to Judah. Where the Bible triumphs utterly, as in Dante and Calvin, there is no humor.

And yet the comic survives in us. It eludes the criticism of Christianity as the sunlight eludes the net. Yes, not only our own laughter survives, but the old classic comedy still seems comic—and more truly comic than the old lyric poetry seems poetic or the drama dramatic. Ancient poesy must always be humored and nursed a little; but when the comic strikes home, it is our own comic; no allowances need be made for it.

There is a kind of laughter that makes the whole universe throb. It has in it the immediate flash of the power of God. We can no more understand it than we can understand other religious truth. It reminds us that we are not wholly Jew. There is light in the world that does not come from Israel; nevertheless, that this is a part of the same light that shines through Israel we surely know.

I have not tried to analyze laughter; but only to show the mystery that surrounds its origin. Now a certain mystery surrounds all human expression. The profoundest truths can only be expressed through the mystery of paradox—as philosophers, poets, prophets, and moralists have agreed since the dawn of time. This saying sounds hard; but its meaning is easy. The meaning is that Truth can never be exactly stated; every statement is a misfit. But truth can be alluded to. A paradox says frankly, "What I say here is not a statement of the truth, but is a mere allusion to the truth." The comic vehicle does the same. It pretends only to allude to the truth, and by this method makes a directer appeal to experience than any attempted statement of truth can make.

There is, no doubt, some reason at the back of this

strange fact, that our most expressive language is a mere series of hints and gestures—that we can only hope, whether by word or chisel, to give, as it were, a side reference to truth. To fathom this reason would be to understand the nature of life and mind.

I have often thought that the fact that life does not originate in us, but is a thing supplied to us from moment to moment—as the power of the electric current is supplied to the light—accounts for the paradoxical nature of our minds and souls. It is commonplace that the poet is inspired—that Orpheus was carried away by the god. So also it is a commonplace that the religious person is absorbed in the will of God—as St. Paul said, his own strength was due to his weakness. So also it is a commonplace of modern scientific psychology that unconsciousness accompanies high intellectual activity. Sir Isaac Newton solved his problems by the art he had of putting them off his mind—of committing them to the unconscious.

All these are but different aspects of the same truth, and we must regard consciousness as resistance to the current of life. If this be true, it is clear that any wilful attempt to tell the truth must be *pro tanto* defeat itself, for it is only by the surrender of our will that truth becomes effective. This idea, being a universal idea, is illustrated by everything; and the less you try to understand it, the more fully will you understand it. In fact one great difficulty that a child or a man has in learning anything, comes from his trying too hard to understand.

Once imagine that our understanding of a thing comes from our ceasing to prevent ourselves from understanding it, and we have the problem in its true form. Accept once for all that all will is illusion, and that the expressive power is something that acts most fully when least impeded by will, and there remains no paradox anywhere. The things we called paradoxes become deductions. Of course St. Paul's weakness was the foundation of his strength; of course Orpheus was irresponsible; of course the maximum of intellectual power will be the maximum of unimpeded, unconscious activity. And as for our Comic, of course—whatever laughter may be in itself—laughter merely calls and vanishes. Such things are jokes, burlesques, humor. They state nothing; they assume inaccuracy; they cry aloud and vanish, leaving the hearer to become awakened to his own thoughts. They are mere stimuli—mere gesture and motion, and hence the very truest, very strongest form of human appeal.

1910

Max Beerbohm

SEEING PEOPLE OFF

I AM not good at it. To do it well seems to me
one of the most difficult things in the world, and probably
seems so to you, too.

To see a friend off from Waterloo to Vauxhall were easy
enough. But we are never called on to perform that small
feat. It is only when a friend is going on a longish journey,
and will be absent for a longish time, that we turn up at
the railway station. The dearer the friend, and the longer
the journey, and the longer the likely absence, the earlier
do we turn up, and the more lamentably do we fail. Our
failure is in exact ratio to the seriousness of the occasion,
and to the depth of our feeling.

In a room, or even on a door-step, we can make the
farewell quite worthily. We can express in our faces the
genuine sorrow we feel. Nor do words fail us. There is no
awkwardness, no restraint, on either side. The thread of
our intimacy has not been snapped. The leave-taking is
an ideal one. Why not, then, leave the leave-taking at
that? Always, departing friends implore us not to bother
to come to the railway station next morning. Always, we
are deaf to these entreaties, knowing them to be not quite
sincere. The departing friends would think it very odd of

From *Yet Again* by Max Beerbohm. Reprinted by permission of
William Heinemann, Ltd.

us if we took them at their word. Besides, they really do want to see us again. And that wish is heartily reciprocated. We duly turn up. And then, oh then, what a gulf yawns! We stretch our arms vainly across it. We have utterly lost touch. We have nothing at all to say. We gaze at each other as dumb animals gaze at human beings. We "make conversation"—and *such* conversation! We know that these are the friends from whom we parted overnight. They know that we have not altered. Yet, on the surface everything is different; and the tension is such that we only long for the guard to blow his whistle and put an end to the farce.

On a cold grey morning of last week I duly turned up at Euston, to see off an old friend who was starting for America.

Overnight, we had given him a farewell dinner, in which sadness was well mingled with festivity. Years probably would elapse before his return. Some of us might never see him again. Not ignoring the shadow of the future, we gaily celebrated the past. We were as thankful to have known our guest as we were grieved to lose him; and both these emotions were made evident. It was a perfect farewell.

And now, here we were, stiff and self-conscious on the platform; and, framed in the window of the railway-carriage, was the face of our friend; but it was as the face of a stranger—a stranger anxious to please, an appealing stranger, an awkward stranger. "Have you got everything?" asked one of us, breaking a silence. "Yes, everything," said our friend, with a pleasant nod. "Everything," he repeated, with the emphasis of an empty brain. "You'll be able to lunch on the train," said I, though this prophecy had already been made more than once. "Oh yes," he said with conviction. He added that the train went straight through to Liverpool. This fact seemed to strike us as rather odd. We exchanged glances. "Doesn't it stop at

Crewe?" asked one of us. "No," said our friend, briefly. He seemed almost disagreeable. There was a long pause. One of us, with a nod and a forced smile at the traveller, said "Well!" The nod, the smile, the unmeaning mono-syllable, were returned conscientiously. Another pause was broken by one of us with a fit of coughing. It was an obviously assumed fit, but it served to pass the time. The bustle of the platform was unabated. There was no sign of the train's departure. Release—ours, and our friend's— was not yet.

My wandering eye alighted on a rather portly middle-aged man who was talking earnestly from the platform to a young lady at the next window but one to ours. His fine profile was vaguely familiar to me. The young lady was evidently American, and he was evidently English; other-wise I should have guessed from his impressive air that he was her father. I wished I could hear what he was say-ing. I was sure he was giving the very best advice; and the strong tenderness of his gaze was really beautiful. He seemed magnetic, as he poured out his final injunctions. I could feel something of his magnetism even where I stood. And the magnetism, like the profile, was vaguely familiar to me. Where had I experienced it?

In a flash I remembered. The man was Hubert le Ros. But how changed since last I saw him! That was seven or eight years ago, in the Strand. He was then (as usual) out of an engagement, and borrowed half-a-crown. It seemed a privilege to lend anything to him. He was always magnetic. And why his magnetism had never made him successful on the London stage was always a mystery to me. He was an excellent actor, and a man of sober habit. But, like many others of his kind, Hubert le Ros (I do not, of course, give the actual name by which he was known) drifted seedily away into the provinces; and I, like every one else, ceased to remember him.

It was strange to see him, after all these years, here on

the platform of Euston, looking so prosperous and solid. It was not only the flesh that he had put on, but also the clothes, that made him hard to recognise. In the old days, an imitation fur coat had seemed to be as integral a part of him as were his ill-shorn lantern jaws. But now his costume was a model of rich and sombre moderation, drawing, not calling, attention to itself. He looked like a banker. Anyone would have been proud to be seen off by him.

"Stand back, please." The train was about to start, and I waved farewell to my friend. Le Ros did not stand back. He stood clasping in both hands the hands of the young American. "Stand back, sir, please!" He obeyed, but quickly darted forward again to whisper some final word. I think there were tears in her eyes. There certainly were tears in his when, at length, having watched the train out of sight, he turned round. He seemed, nevertheless, delighted to see me. He asked me where I had been hiding all these years; and simultaneously repaid me the half-crown as though it had been borrowed yesterday. He linked his arm in mine, and walked me slowly along the platform, saying with what pleasure he read my dramatic criticisms every Saturday.

I told him, in return, how much he was missed on the stage. "Ah, yes," he said, "I never act on the stage nowadays." He laid some emphasis on the word "stage," and I asked him where, then, he did act. "On the platform," he answered. "You mean," said I, "that you recite at concerts?" He smiled. "This," he whispered, striking his stick on the ground, "is the platform I mean." Had his mysterious prosperity unhinged him? He looked quite sane. I begged him to be more explicit.

"I suppose," he said presently, giving me a light for the cigar which he had offered me, "you have been seeing a friend off?" I assented. He asked me what I supposed he had been doing. I said that I had watched him doing the same thing. "No," he said gravely. "That lady was not a friend of mine. I met her for the first time this morning, less than half an hour ago, *here*," and again he struck the platform with his stick.

I confessed that I was bewildered. He smiled. "You may," he said, "have heard of the Anglo-American Social Bureau?" I had not. He explained to me that of the thousands of Americans who annually pass through England there are many hundreds who have no English friends. In the old days they used to bring letters of introduction. But the English are so inhospitable that these letters are hardly worth the paper they are written on. "Thus," said Le Ros, "the A.A.S.B. supplies a long-felt want. Americans are a sociable people, and most of them have plenty of money to spend. The A.A.S.B. supplies them with English friends. Fifty per cent of the fees is paid over to the friends. The other fifty is retained by the A.A.S.B. I am not, alas, a director. If I were, I should be a very rich man indeed. I am only an employé. But even so I do very well. I am one of the seers-off."

Again I asked for enlightenment. "Many Americans," he said, "cannot afford to keep friends in England. But they can all afford to be seen off. The fee is only five pounds (twenty-five dollars) for a single traveller; and eight pounds (forty dollars) for a party of two or more. They send that in to the Bureau, giving the date of their departure, and a description by which the seer-off can identify them on the platform. And then—well, then they are seen off."

"But is it worth it?" I exclaimed. "Of course it is worth it," said Le Ros. "It prevents them from feeling 'out of it.' It earns them the respect of the guard. It saves them from being despised by their fellow-passengers—the people who are going to be on the boat. It gives them a footing for the whole voyage. Besides, it is a great pleasure in itself. You saw me seeing that young lady off.

Didn't you think I did it beautifully?" "Beautifully," I
admitted. "I envied you. There was I—" "Yes, I can
imagine. There were you, shuffling from foot to foot,
staring blankly at your friend, trying to make conversation. I know. That's how I used to be myself, before I
studied, and went in to the thing professionally. I don't
say I'm perfect yet. I'm still a martyr to platform fright.
A railway station is the most difficult of all places to act
in, as you have discovered for yourself." "But," I said
with resentment, "I wasn't trying to act. I really *felt*."
"So did I, my boy," said Le Ros. "You can't act without
feeling. What's his name, the Frenchman—Diderot, yes—
said you could; but what did *he* know about it? Didn't
you see those tears in my eyes when the train started? I
hadn't forced them. I tell you I was *moved*. So were you, I
dare say. But you couldn't have pumped up a tear to prove
it. You can't act. At any rate," he added kindly, "not
in a railway station." "Teach me!" I cried. He looked
thoughtfully at me. "Well," he said at length, "the seeing-
off season is practically over. Yes, I'll give you a course. I
have a good many pupils on hand already; but yes," he
said, consulting an ornate note-book, "I could give you an
hour on Tuesdays and Fridays."

   His terms, I confess, are rather high. But I don't grudge
the investment.

                                              1910

George Santayana

PATRIOTISM

PATRIOTISM is a form of piety. It is right to prefer our own country to all others because we are children and citizens before we can be travellers or philosophers. Specific character is a necessary point of origin for universal relations: a pure nothing can have no radiation and no scope. It is no accident for the soul to be embodied: her very essence is to express and bring to fruition the functions and resources of the body. Its instincts sustain her ideals and its relations her world. A native country is a sort of second body, another enveloping organism to give the will definition. A specific inheritance strengthens the soul. Cosmopolitanism has doubtless its place, because a man may well cultivate in himself, and represent in his nation, affinities to other peoples, and such assimilation to them as is compatible with personal integrity and clearness of purpose. Plasticity to things foreign need not be inconsistent with happiness and utility at home. But happiness and utility are possible nowhere to a man who represents nothing and who looks out on the world without a plot of his own to stand on, either on earth or in heaven. He wanders from place to place, a voluntary exile, always querulous, always uneasy, always

Reprinted from *Little Essays* by George Santayana; used by permission of the publishers, Charles Scribner's Sons and Constable & Company Limited.

alone. His very criticisms express no ideal. His experience is without sweetness, without cumulative fruits, and his children, if he has them, are without morality. For reason and happiness are like other flowers—they wither when plucked. On the other hand, to be always harping on nationality is to convert what should be a recognition of natural conditions into a ridiculous pride in one's own oddities. Nature has hidden the roots of things, and though botany must now and then dig them up for the sake of comprehension, their place is still under ground. A man's feet must be planted in his country, but his eyes should survey the world.

Where parties and governments are bad, as they are in most ages and countries, it makes practically no difference to a community, apart from local ravages, whether its own army or the enemy's is victorious in war, nor does it really affect any man's welfare whether the party he happens to belong to is in office or not. These issues concern, in such cases, only the army itself, whose lives and fortunes are at stake, or the official classes, who lose their places when their leaders fall from power. The private citizen in any event continues in such countries to pay a maximum of taxes and to suffer, in all his private interests, a maximum of vexation and neglect. Nevertheless, because he has some son at the front, some cousin in the government, or some historical sentiment for the flag and the nominal essence of his country, the oppressed subject will glow like the rest with patriotic ardour, and will decry as dead to duty and honour anyone who points out how perverse is this helpless allegiance to a government representing no public interest.

In proportion as governments become good and begin to operate for the general welfare, patriotism itself becomes representative and an expression of reason; but just in the same measure does hostility to that government on the part of foreigners become groundless and perverse. A competitive patriotism involves ill-will toward all other states and a secret and constant desire to see them thrashed and subordinated. It follows that a good government, while it justifies this governmental patriotism in its subjects, disallows it in all other men. For a good government is an international benefit, and the prosperity and true greatness of any country is a boon sooner or later to the whole world; it may eclipse alien governments and draw away local populations or industries, but it necessarily benefits alien individuals in so far as it is allowed to affect them at all.

Animosity against a well-governed country is therefore madness. A rational patriotism would rather take the form of imitating and supporting that so-called foreign country, and even, if practicable, of fusing with it. The invidious and aggressive form of patriotism, though inspired generally only by local conceit, would nevertheless be really justified if such conceit happened to be well grounded. A dream of universal predominance visiting a truly virtuous and intelligent people would be an aspiration toward universal beneficence. For every man who is governed at all must be governed by others; the point is, that the others, in ruling him, shall help him to be himself and give scope to his congenial activities. When coerced in that direction he obeys a force which, in the best sense of the word, *represents* him, and consequently he is truly free; nor could he be ruled by a more native and rightful authority than by one that divines and satisfies his true necessities.

A man's nature is not, however, a quantity or quality fixed unalterably and *a priori*. As breeding and selection improve a race, so every experience modifies the individual and offers a changed basis for future experience. The language, religion, education, and prejudices acquired in youth bias character and predetermine the directions in which development may go on. A child might possibly change his country; a man can only wish that he might change it. Therefore, among the true interests which a government should represent, nationality itself must be included.]

Mechanical forces, we must not weary of repeating, do not come merely to vitiate the ideal; they come to create it. The historical background of life is a part of its substance, and the ideal can never grow independently of its spreading roots. A sanctity hangs about the sources of our being, whether physical, social, or imaginary. The ancients who kissed the earth on returning to their native country expressed nobly and passionately what every man feels for those regions and those traditions whence the sap of his own life has been sucked in. There is a profound friendliness in whatever revives primordial habits, however they may have been overlaid with later sophistications. For this reason the homelier words of a mother tongue, the more familiar assurances of an ancestral religion, and the very savour of childhood's dishes, remain always a potent means to awaken emotion. Such ingrained influences, in their vague totality, make a man's true nationality. A government, in order to represent the general interests of its subjects, must move in sympathy with their habits and memories; it must respect their idiosyncrasy for the same reason that it protects their lives. If parting from a single object of love be, as it is, true dying, how much more would a shifting of all the affections be death to the soul.

Man is certainly an animal that, when he lives at all, lives for ideals. Something must be found to occupy his imagination, to raise pleasure and pain into love and hatred, and change the prosaic alternative between comfort and discomfort into the tragic one between happiness and sorrow. Now that the hue of daily adventure is so dull, when religion for the most part is so vague and accommodating, when even war is a vast impersonal business, nationality seems to have slipped into the place of honour.

It has become the one eloquent, public, intrepid illusion. Illusion, I mean, when it is taken for an ultimate good or a mystical essence, for of course nationality is a fact. People speak some particular language and are very uncomfortable where another is spoken or where their own is spoken differently. They have habits, judgments, assumptions to which they are wedded, and a society where all this is unheard of shocks them and puts them at a galling disadvantage. To ignorant people the foreigner as such is ridiculous, unless he is superior to them in numbers or prestige, when he becomes hateful. It is natural for a man to like to live at home, and to live long elsewhere without a sense of exile is not good for his moral integrity. It is right to feel a greater kinship and affection for what lies nearest to oneself. But this necessary fact and even duty of nationality is accidental; like age or sex it is a physical fatality which can be made the basis of specific and comely virtues; but it is not an end to pursue, or a flag to flaunt, or a privilege not balanced by a thousand incapacities. Yet of this distinction our contemporaries tend to make an idol, perhaps because it is the only distinction they feel they have left.

1905, 1913

Stephen Leacock

A, B, AND C

THE HUMAN ELEMENT IN MATHEMATICS

THE student of arithmetic who has mastered the first four rules of his art, and successfully striven with money sums and fractions, finds himself confronted by an unbroken expanse of questions known as problems. These are short stories of adventure and industry with the end omitted, and though betraying a strong family resemblance, are not without a certain element of romance.

The characters in the plot of a problem are three people called A, B, and C. The form of the question is generally of this sort:

"A, B, and C do a certain piece of work. A can do as much work in one hour as B in two, or C in four. Find how long they work at it."

Or thus:

"A, B, and C are employed to dig a ditch. A can dig as much in one hour as B can dig in two, and B can dig twice as fact as C. Find how long, etc., etc."

Or after this wise:

"A lays a wager that he can walk faster than B or C. A can walk half as fast again as B, and C is only an indifferent walker. Find how far, and so forth."

The occupations of A, B, and C are many and varied.

Reprinted by permission of Dodd, Mead & Company and McClelland & Stewart Limited from *Literary Lapses* by Stephen Leacock.

In the older arithmetics they contented themselves with doing "a certain piece of work." This statement of the case, however, was found too sly and mysterious, or possibly lacking in romantic charm. It became the fashion to define the job more clearly and to set them at walking matches, ditch-digging, regattas, and piling cord wood. At times, they became commercial and entered into partnership, having with their old mystery a "certain" capital. Above all they revel in motion. When they tire of walking-matches—A rides on horseback or borrows a bicycle and competes with his weaker-minded associates on foot. Now they race on locomotives; now they row; or again they become historical and engage stage-coaches; or at times they are aquatic and swim. If their occupation is actual work they prefer to pump water into cisterns, two of which leak through holes in the bottom and one of which is water-tight. A, of course, has the good one; he also takes the bicycle, and the best locomotive, and the right of swimming with the current. Whatever they do they put money on it, being all three sports. A always wins.

In the early chapters of the arithmetic, their identity is concealed under the names John, William, and Henry, and they wrangle over the division of marbles. In algebra they are often called X, Y, Z. But these are only their Christian names, and they are really the same people.

Now to one who has followed the history of these men through countless pages of problems, watched them in their leisure hours dallying with cord wood, and seen their panting sides heave in the full frenzy of filling a cistern with a leak in it, they become something more than mere symbols. They appear as creatures of flesh and blood, living men with their own passions, ambitions, and aspirations like the rest of us. Let us view them in turn. A is a full-blooded blustering fellow, of energetic temperament, hot-headed and strong-willed. It is he who proposes everything, challenges B to work, makes the bets, and bends the others to his will. He is a man of great physical strength and phenomenal endurance. He has been known to walk forty-eight hours at a stretch, and to pump ninety-six. His life is arduous and full of peril. A mistake in the working of a sum may keep him digging a fortnight without sleep. A repeating decimal in the answer might kill him.

B is a quiet, easy-going fellow, afraid of A and bullied by him, but very gentle and brotherly to little C, the weakling. He is quite in A's power, having lost all his money in bets.

Poor C is an undersized, frail man, with a plaintive face. Constant walking, digging, and pumping has broken his health and ruined his nervous system. His joyless life has driven him to drink and smoke more than is good for him, and his hand often shakes as he digs ditches. He has not the strength to work as the others can, in fact, as Hamlin Smith has said, "A can do more work in one hour than C in four."

The first time that ever I saw these men was one evening after a regatta. They had all been rowing in it, and it had transpired that A could row as much in one hour as B in two, or C in four. B and C had come in dead fagged and C was coughing badly. "Never mind, old fellow," I heard B say, "I'll fix you up on the sofa and get you some hot tea." Just then A came blustering in and shouted, "I say, you fellows, Hamlin Smith has shown me three cisterns in his garden and he says we can pump them until tomorrow night. I bet I can beat you both. Come on. You can pump in your rowing things, you know. Your cistern leaks a little, I think, C." I heard B growl that it was a dirty shame and that C was used up now, but they went, and presently I could tell from the sound of the water that A was pumping four times as fast as C.

For years after that I used to see them constantly about town and always busy. I never heard of any of them eating or sleeping. Then owing to a long absence from home, I lost sight of them. On my return I was surprised to no longer find A, B, and C at their accustomed tasks; on inquiry I heard that work in this line was now done by N, M, and O, and that some people were employing for algebraical jobs four foreigners called Alpha, Beta, Gamma, and Delta.

Now it chanced one day that I stumbled upon old D, in the little garden in front of his cottage, hoeing in the sun. D is an aged labouring man who used occasionally to be called in to help A, B, and C. "Did I know 'em, sir?" he answered, "why, I knowed 'em ever since they was little fellows in brackets. Master A, he were a fine lad, sir, though I always said, give me Master B for kind-heartedness-like. Many's the job as we've been on together, sir, though I never did no racing nor aught of that, but just the plain labour, as you might say. I'm getting a bit too old and stiff for it nowadays, sir—just scratch about in the garden here and grow a bit of a logarithm, or raise a common denominator or two. But Mr. Euclid he use me still for them propositions, he do."

From the garrulous old man I learned the melancholy end of my former acquaintances. Soon after I left town, he told me, C had been taken ill. It seems that A and B had been rowing on the river for a wager, and C had been running on the bank and then sat in a draught. Of course the bank had refused the draught and C was taken ill. A and B came home and found C lying helpless in bed. A shook him roughly and said, "Get up, C, we're going to pile wood." C looked so worn and pitiful that B said, "Look here, A, I won't stand this, he isn't fit to pile wood tonight." C smiled feebly and said, "Perhaps I might pile a little if I sat up in bed." Then B, thoroughly alarmed, said, "See here, A, I'm going to fetch a doctor; he's dying." A flared up and answered, "You've no money to fetch a doctor." "I'll reduce him to his lowest terms," B said firmly, "that'll fetch him." C's life might even then have been saved but they made a mistake about the medicine. It stood at the head of the bed on a bracket, and the nurse accidentally removed it from the bracket without changing the sign. After the fatal blunder C seems to have sunk rapidly. On the evening of the next day, as the shadows deepened in the little room, it was clear to all that the end was near. I think that even A was affected at the last as he stood with bowed head, aimlessly offering to bet with the doctor on C's laboured breathing. "A," whispered C, "I think I'm going fast." "How fast do you think you'll go, old man?" murmured A. "I don't know," said C, "but I'm going at any rate."—The end came soon after that. C rallied for a moment and asked for a certain piece of work that he had left downstairs. A put it in his arms and he expired. As his soul sped heavenward A watched its flight with melancholy admiration. B burst into a passionate flood of tears and sobbed, "Put away his little cistern and the rowing clothes he used to wear, I feel as if I could hardly ever dig again."—The funeral was plain and un-ostentatious. It differed in nothing from the ordinary, ex-cept that out of deference to sporting men and mathema-ticians, A engaged two hearses. Both vehicles started at the same time, B driving the one which bore the sable parallelopiped containing the last remains of his ill-fated friend. A on the box of the empty hearse generously con-sented to a handicap of a hundred yards, but arrived first at the cemetery by driving four times as fast as B. (Find the distance to the cemetery.) As the sarcophagus was low-ered, the grave was surrounded by the broken figures of the first book of Euclid.—It was noticed that after the death of C, A became a changed man. He lost interest in racing with B, and dug but languidly. He finally gave up his work and settled down to live on the interest of his bets.—B never recovered from the shock of C's death; his grief preyed upon his intellect and it became deranged. He grew moody and spoke only in monosyllables. His disease became rapidly aggravated, and he presently spoke only in words whose spelling was regular and which presented no difficulty to the beginner. Realizing his precarious condition he voluntarily submitted to be incarcerated in an asylum, where he abjured mathematics and devoted himself to writing the History of the Swiss Family Robinson in words of one syllable.

1918

H. L. Mencken

THE GENEALOGY
OF ETIQUETTE

Barring sociology (which is yet, of course, scarcely a science at all, but rather a monkey-shine which happens to pay, like play-acting or theology), psychology is the youngest of the sciences, and hence chiefly guess-work, empiricism, hocus-pocus, poppycock. On the one hand, there are still enormous gaps in its data, so that the determination of its simplest principles remains difficult, not to say impossible; and, on the other hand, the very hallowness and nebulosity of it, particularly around its edges, encourages a horde of quacks to invade it, sophisticate it and make nonsense of it. Worse, this state of affairs tends to such confusion of effort and direction that the quack and the honest inquirer are often found in the same man. It is, indeed, a commonplace to encounter a professor who spend his days in the laborious accumulation of psychological statistics, sticking pins into babies and plotting upon a chart the ebb and flow of their yells, and his nights chasing poltergeists and other such celestial fauna over the hurdles of a spiritualist's atelier, or gazing into a crystal in the privacy of his own chamber. The Binét test and the buncombe of mesmerism are alike the children of what we roughly denominate psychology, and perhaps of equal legitimacy. Even so ingenious and competent an investigator as Prof. Dr. Sigmund Freud, who has told us a lot that is of the first importance about the materials and machinery of thought, has also told us a lot that is trivial and dubious. The essential doctrines of Freudism, no doubt, come close to the truth, but many of Freud's remoter deductions are far more scandalous than sound, and many of the professed Freudians, both American and European, have grease-paint on their noses and bladders in their hands and are otherwise quite indistinguishable from evangelists and circus clowns.

In this condition of the science it is no wonder that we find it wasting its chief force upon problems that are petty and idle when they are not downright and palpably insoluble, and passing over problems that are of immediate concern to all of us, and that might be quite readily solved, or, at any rate, considerably illuminated, by an intelligent study of the data already available. After all, not many of us care a hoot whether Sir Oliver Lodge and the Indian chief Wok-a-wok-a-mok are happy in heaven, for not many of us have any hope or desire to meet them there. Nor are we greatly excited by the discovery that, of twenty-five freshmen who are hit with clubs, $17\frac{3}{4}$ will say "Ouch!" and $22\frac{1}{5}$ will say "Damn!"; nor by a table showing that 38.2 per centum of all men accused of homicide confess when locked up with the carcasses of their victims, including 23.4 per centum who are innocent; nor by plans and specifications, by Cagliostro out of Lucrezia Borgia, for teaching poor, God-forsaken school children to write before they can read and to multiply before they can add; nor by endless disputes between half-witted pundits as to the precise difference between perception and cognition; nor by even longer feuds, between pundits even crazier, over free will, the subconscious, the endoneurium, the functions of the corpora quadrigemina, and the meaning of dreams in which one is pursued by hyenas, process-servers or grass-widows.

Nay; we do not bubble with rejoicing when such fruits of psychological deep-down-diving and much-mud-up-bringing researches are laid before us, for after all they do not offer us any nourishment, there is nothing in them to engage our teeth, they fail to make life more comprehensible, and hence more bearable. What we yearn to know something about is the process whereby the ideas of everyday are engendered in the skulls of those about us, to the end that we may pursue a straighter and a safer course through the muddle that is life. Why do the great majority of Presbyterians (and, for that matter, of Baptists, Episcopalians, and Swedenborgians as well) regard it as unlucky to meet a black cat and lucky to find a pin? What are the logical steps behind the theory that it is indecent to eat peas with a knife? By what process does an otherwise sane man arrive at the conclusion that he will go to hell unless he is baptized by total immersion in water? What causes men to be faithful to their wives: habit, fear, poverty, lack of imagination, lack of enterprise, stupidity, religion? What is the psychological basis of commercial morality? What is the true nature of the vague pooling of desires that Rousseau called the social contract? Why does an American regard it as scandalous to wear dress clothes at a funeral, and a Frenchman regard it as equally scandalous *not* to wear them? Why is it that men trust one another so readily, and women trust one another so seldom? Why are we all so greatly affected by statements that we know are not true?—e.g., in Lincoln's Gettysburg speech, the Declaration of Independence and the CIII Psalm. What is the origin of the so-called double standard of morality? Why are women forbidden to take off their hats in church? What is happiness? Intelligence? Sin? Courage? Virtue? Beauty?

All these are questions of interest and importance to all

of us, for their solution would materially improve the accuracy of our outlook upon the world, and with it our mastery of our environment, but the psychologists, busily engaged in chasing their tails, leave them unanswered and, in most cases, even unasked. The late William James, more acute than the general, saw how precious little was known about the psychological inwardness of religion, and to the illumination of this darkness he addressed himself in his book, "The Varieties of Religious Experience." But life being short and science long, he got little beyond the statement of the problem and the marshaling of the grosser evidence—and even at this business he allowed himself to be constantly interrupted by spooks, hobgoblins, seventh sons of seventh sons and other such characteristic pets of psychologists. In the same way one Gustav le Bon, a Frenchman, undertook a psychological study of the crowd mind—and then blew up. Add the investigations of Freud and his school, chiefly into abnormal states of mind, and those of Lombroso and his school, chiefly quackish and for the yellow journals, and the idle romancing of such inquirers as Prof. Dr. Thorstein Veblen, and you have exhausted the list of contributions to what may be called practical and everyday psychology. The rev. professors, I daresay, have been doing some useful plowing and planting. All of their meticulous pinsticking and measuring and chart-making, in the course of time, will enable their successors to approach the real problems of mind with more assurance than is now possible, and perhaps help to their solution. But in the meantime the public and social utility of psychology remains very small, for it is still unable to differentiate accurately between the true and the false, or to give us any effective protection against the fallacies, superstitions, crazes and hysterias which rage in the world.

In this emergency it is not only permissible but even laudable for the amateur to sniff inquiringly through the psychological pasture, essaying modestly to uproot things that the myopic (or, perhaps more accurately, hyper-metropic) professionals have overlooked. The late Friedrich Wilhelm Nietzsche did it often, and the usufructs were many curious and daring guesses, some of them probably close to accuracy, as to the genesis of this, that or the other common delusion of man—i.e., the delusion that the law of the survival of the fittest may be repealed by an act of Congress. Into the same field several very inter-esting expeditions have been made by Dr. Elsie Clews Parsons, a lady once celebrated by Park Row for her in-vention of trial marriage—an invention, by the way, in which the Nietzsche aforesaid preceded her by at least a dozen years. The records of her researches are to be found in a brief series of books: "The Family," "The Old-Fash-ioned Woman" and "Fear and Conventionality." Ap-parently they have wrung relatively little esteem from the learned, for I seldom encounter a reference to them, and Dr. Parsons herself is denied the very modest reward of mention in "Who's Who in America." Nevertheless, they are extremely instructive books, particularly "Fear and Conventionality." I know of no other work, indeed, which offers a better array of observations upon that powerful complex of assumptions, prejudices, instinctive reactions, racial emotions and unbreakable vices of mind which enters so massively into the daily thinking of all of us. The author does not concern herself, as so many psycholo-gists fall into the habit of doing, with thinking as a purely laboratory phenomenon, a process *in vacuo*. What she deals with is thinking as it is done by men and women in the real world—thinking that is only half intellectual, the other half being as automatic and unintelligent as swal-lowing, blinking the eye or falling in love.

The power of the complex that I have mentioned is usually very much underestimated, not only by psycholo-gists, but also by all other persons who pretend to culture. We take pride in the fact that we are thinking animals, and like to believe that our thoughts are free, but the truth is that nine-tenths of them are rigidly conditioned by the babbling that goes on around us from birth, and that the business of considering this babbling objectively, separating the true in it from the false, is an intellectual feat of such stupendous difficulty that very few men are ever able to achieve it. The amazing slanging which went on between the English professors and the German professors in the early days of the late war showed how little even cold and academic men are really moved by the bald truth and how much by hot and unintelligible likes and dislikes. The patriotic hysteria of the war simply allowed these eminent pedagogues to say of one another openly and to loud applause what they would have been ashamed to say in times of greater amenity, and what most of them would have denied stoutly that they believed. Nevertheless, it is probably a fact that before there was a sign of war the average English professor, deep down in his heart, thought that any man who ate sauerkraut, and went to the opera in a sackcoat, and intrigued for the appellation of *Geheimrat,* and preferred German music to English poetry, and venerated Bismarck, and called his wife "Mutter," was a scoundrel. He did not say so aloud, and no doubt it would have offended him had you accused him of believing it, but he believed it all the same, and his belief in it gave a muddy, bilious color to his view of German metaphysics, German electrochemistry and the German chronology of Babylonian kings. And by the same token the average German professor, far down in the ghostly recesses of his hulk, held that any man who read the London *Times,* and ate salt fish at first breakfast, and drank tea of an afternoon, and spoke of Oxford as a university was a *Schafskopf,* a *Schuft* and possibly even a *Schweinehund.*

Nay, not one of us is a free agent. Not one of us actually thinks for himself, or in any orderly and scientific manner. The pressure of environment, of mass ideas, of the socialized intelligence, improperly so called, is too enormous to be withstood. No American, no matter how sharp his critical sense, can ever get away from the notion that democracy is, in some subtle and mysterious way, more conducive to human progress and more pleasing to a just God than any of the systems of government which stand opposed to it. In the privacy of his study he may observe very clearly that it exalts the facile and specious man above the really competent man, and from this observation he may draw the conclusion that its abandonment would be desirable, but once he emerges from his academic seclusion and resumes the rubbing of noses with his fellow-men, he will begin to be tortured by a sneaking feeling that such ideas are heretical and unmanly, and the next time the band begins to play he will thrill with the best of them—or the worst. The actual phenomenon, in truth, was copiously on display during the war. Having myself the character among my acquaintances of one holding the democratic theory in some doubt, I was often approached by gentlemen who told me, in great confidence, that they had been seized by the same tremors. Among them were journalists employed daily in demanding that democracy be forced upon the whole world, and army officers engaged, at least theoretically, in forcing it. All these men, in reflective moments, struggled with ifs and buts. But every one of them, in his public capacity as a good citizen, quickly went back to *thinking* as a good citizen was then expected to think, and even to a certain inflammatory ranting for what, behind the door, he gravely questioned. . . .

It is the business of Dr. Parsons, in "Fear and Conventionality," to prod into certain of the ideas which thus pour into every man's mind from the circumambient air, sweeping away, like some huge cataract, the feeble resistance that his own powers of ratiocination can offer. In particular, she devotes herself to an examination of those

general ideas which condition the thought and action of
man as a social being—those general ideas which govern
his everyday attitude toward his fellow-men and his pre-
vailing view of himself. In one direction they lay upon us
the bonds of what we call etiquette, i.e., the duty of considering the habits and feelings of those around us—and
in another direction they throttle us with what we call
morality—i.e., the rules which protect the life and property
of those around us. But, as Dr. Parsons shows, the boundary
between etiquette and morality is very dimly drawn, and
it is often impossible to say of a given action whether it is
downright immoral or merely a breach of the punctilio.
Even when the moral law is plainly running, considerations of mere amenity and politeness may still make themselves felt. Thus, as Dr. Parsons points out, there is even
an etiquette of adultery. "The *ami de la famille* vows not
to kiss his mistress in her husband's house"—not in fear,
but "as an expression of conjugal consideration," as a sign
that he has not forgotten the thoughtfulness expected of a
gentleman. And in this delicate field, as might be expected, the differences in racial attitudes are almost dia-
metrical. The Englishman, surprising his wife with a lover,
sues the rogue for damages and has public opinion behind
him, but for an American to do it would be for him to
lose caste at once and forever. The plain and only duty
of the American is to open upon the fellow with artillery,
hitting him if the scene is south of the Potomac and missing
him if it is above.

I confess to an endless interest in such puzzling niceties,
and to much curiosity as to their origins and meaning.
Why do we Americans take off our hats when we meet a
flapper on the street, and yet stand covered before a male
of the highest eminence? A Continental would regard this
last as boorish to the last degree; in greeting any equal
or superior, male or female, actual or merely conventional,
he lifts his head-piece. Why does it strike us as ludicrous

to see a man in dress clothes before 6 P.M.? The Continental puts them on whenever he has a solemn visit to make, whether the hour be six or noon. Why do we regard it as indecent to tuck the napkin between the waistcoat buttons—or into the neck!—at meals? The Frenchman does it without thought of crime. So does the Italian. So does the German. All three are punctilious men—far more so, indeed, than we are. Why do we snicker at the man who wears a wedding ring? Most Continentals would stare askance at the husband who didn't. Why is it bad manners in Europe and America to ask a stranger his or her age, and a friendly attention in China? Why do we regard it as absurd to distinguish a woman by her husband's title—e.g., Mrs. Judge Jones, Mrs. Professor Smith? In Teutonic and Scandinavian Europe the omission of the title would be looked upon as an affront.

Such fine distinctions, so ardently supported, raise many interesting questions, but the attempt to answer them quickly gets one bogged. Several years ago I ventured to lift a sad voice against a custom common in America: that of married men, in speaking of their wives, employing the full panoply of "Mrs. Brown." It was my contention—supported, I thought, by logical considerations of the loftiest order—that a husband, in speaking of his wife to his equals, should say "my wife"—that the more formal mode of designation should be reserved for inferiors and for strangers of undetermined position. This contention, somewhat to my surprise, was vigorously combated by various volunteer experts. At first they rested their case upon the mere authority of custom, forgetting that this custom was by no means universal. But finally one of them came forward with a more analytical and cogent defense— the defense, to wit, that "my wife" connoted proprietorship and was thus offensive to a wife's *amour propre*. But what of "my sister" and "my mother"? Surely it is nowhere the custom for a man, addressing an equal, to speak of his sister as "Miss Smith." . . . The discussion, however, came to nothing. It was impossible to carry it on logically. The essence of all such inquiries lies in the discovery that there is a force within the liver and lights of man that is infinitely more potent than logic. His reflections, perhaps, may take on intellectually recognizable forms, but they seldom lead to intellectually recognizable conclusions.

Nevertheless, Dr. Parsons offers something in her book that may conceivably help to a better understanding of them, and that is the doctrine that the strange persistence of these rubber-stamp ideas, often unintelligible and sometimes plainly absurd, is due to fear, and that this fear is the product of a very real danger. The safety of human society lies in the assumption that every individual composing it, in a given situation, will act in a manner hitherto approved as seemly. That is to say, he is expected to react to his environment according to a fixed pattern, not necessarily because that pattern is the best imaginable, but simply because it is determined and understood. If he fails to do so, if he reacts in a novel manner—conducive, perhaps, to his better advantage or to what he thinks is his better advantage—then he disappoints the expectation of those around him, and forces them to meet the new situation he has created by the exercise of independent thought. Such independent thought, to a good many men, is quite impossible, and to the overwhelming majority of men, extremely painful. "To all of us," says Dr. Parsons, "to the animal, to the savage and to the civilized being, few demands are as uncomfortable, . . . disquieting or fearful as the call to innovate . . . Adaptations we all of us dislike or hate. We dodge or shirk them as best we may." And the man who compels us to make them against our wills we punish by withdrawing from him that understanding and friendliness which he, in turn, looks for and counts upon. In other words, we set him apart as one who is anti-social and not to be dealt with, and according as his rebellion has been small or great, we call him a boor or a criminal.

This distrust of the unknown, this fear of doing something unusual, is probably at the bottom of many ideas and institutions that are commonly credited to other motives. For example, monogamy. The orthodox explanation of monogamy is that it is a manifestation of the desire to have and to hold property—that the husband defends his solitary right to his wife, even at the cost of his own freedom, because she is the pearl among his chattels. But Dr. Parsons argues, and with a good deal of plausibility, that the real moving force, both in the husband and the wife, may be merely the force of habit, the antipathy to experiment and innovation. It is easier and safer to stick to the one wife than to risk adventures with another wife—and the immense social pressure that I have just described is all on the side of sticking. Moreover, the indulgence of a habit automatically strengthens its bonds. What we have done once or thought once, we are more apt than we were before to do and think again. Or, as the late Prof. William James put it, "the selection of a particular hole to live in, of a particular mate, . . . a particular anything, in short, out of a possible multitude . . . carries with it an insensibility to *other* opportunities and occasions—an insensibility which can only be described physiologically as an inhibition of new impulses by the habit of old ones already formed. The possession of homes and wives of our own makes us strangely insensible to the charms of other people. . . . The original impulse which got us homes, wives, . . . seems to exhaust itself in its first achievements and to leave no surplus energy for reacting on new cases." Thus the benedict looks no more on women (at least for a while), and the post-honeymoon bride, as the late David Graham Phillips once told us, neglects the bedizenments which got her a man.

In view of the popular or general character of most of the taboos which put a brake upon personal liberty in thought and action—that is to say, in view of their enforcement by people in the mass, and not by definite specialists in conduct—it is quite natural to find that they are of extra force in democratic societies, for it is the distinguishing mark of democratic societies that they exalt the powers of the majority almost infinitely, and tend to deny the minority any rights whatever. Under a society dominated by a small caste the revolutionist in custom, despite the axiom to the contrary, has a relatively easy time of it, for the persons whose approval he seeks for his innovation are relatively few in number, and most of them are already habituated to more or less intelligible and independent thinking. But under a democracy he is opposed by a horde so vast that it is a practical impossibility for him, without complex and expensive machinery, to reach and convince all of its members, and even if he could reach them he would find most of them quite incapable of rising out of their accustomed grooves. They cannot understand innovations that are genuinely novel and they don't want to understand them; their one desire is to put them down. Even at this late day, with enlightenment raging through the republic like a pestilence, it would cost the average Southern or Middle Western Congressman his seat if he appeared among his constituents in spats, or wearing a wrist-watch. And if a Justice of the Supreme Court of the United States, however gigantic his learning and his juridic rectitude, were taken in crim. con. with the wife of a Senator, he would be destroyed instanter. And if, suddenly revolting against the democratic idea, he were to propose, however gingerly, its abandonment, he would be destroyed with the same dispatch.

But how, then, explain the fact that the populace is constantly ravished and set aflame by fresh brigades of moral, political and sociological revolutionists—that it is forever playing the eager victim to new mountebanks? The explanation lies in the simple circumstance that these performers upon the public midriff are always careful to ladle out nothing actually new, and hence nothing incomprehensible, alarming and accursed. What they offer is always the same old panacea with an extra-gaudy label—the tried, tasted and much-loved dose, the colic cure that mother used to make. Superficially, the United States seems to suffer from an endless and astounding neophilism; actually all its thinking is done within the boundaries of a very small group of political, economic and religious ideas, most of them unsound. For example, there is the fundamental idea of democracy—the idea that all political power should remain in the hands of the populace, that its exercise by superior men is intrinsically immoral. Out of this idea spring innumerable notions and crazes that are no more, at bottom, than restatements of it in sentimental terms: rotation in office, direct elections, the initiative and referendum, the recall, the popular primary, and so on. Again, there is the primary doctrine that the possession of great wealth is a crime—a doctrine half a religious heritage and half the product of mere mob envy. Out of it have come free silver, trust-busting, government ownership, muck-racking, Populism, Bleaseism, Progressivism, the milder forms of Socialism, the whole gasconade of "reform" politics. Yet again, there is the ineradicable peasant suspicion of the man who is having a better time in the world—a suspicion grounded, like the foregoing, partly upon undisguised envy and partly upon archaic and barbaric religious taboos. Out of it have come all the glittering pearls of the uplift, from Abolition to Prohibition, and from the crusade against horseracing to the Mann Act. The whole political history of the United States is a history of these three ideas. There has never been an issue before the people that could not be translated into one or another of them. What is more, they have also colored the fundamental philosophical (and particularly epistemological) doctrines of the American people, and their moral theory, and even their foreign relations. The late war, very unpopular at the start, was "sold" to them, as the advertising phrase has it, by representing it as a campaign for the salvation of democracy, half religious and wholly altruistic. So represented to them, they embraced it; represented as the highly obscure and complex thing it actually was, it would have been beyond their comprehension, and hence abhorrent to them.

Outside this circle of their elemental convictions they are quite incapable of rational thought. One is not surprised to hear of Bismarck, a thorough royalist, discussing democracy with calm and fairness, but it would be unimaginable for the American people, or for any other democratic people, to discuss royalism in the same manner: it would take a cataclysm to bring them to any such violation of their mental habits. When such a cataclysm occurs, they embrace the new ideas that are its fruits with the same adamantine firmness. One year before the French Revolution, disobedience to the king was unthinkable to the average Frenchman; only a few daringly immoral men cherished the notion. But one year *after* the fall of the Bastile, obedience to the king was equally unthinkable. The Russian Bolsheviki, whose doings have furnished a great deal of immensely interesting material to the student of popular psychology, put the principle into plain words. Once they were in the saddle, they decreed the abolition of the old imperial censorship and announced that speech would be free henceforth—but only so long as it kept within the bounds of the Bolshevist revelation! In other words, any citizen was free to think and speak whatever he pleased—but only so long as it did not violate certain fundamental ideas. This is precisely the sort of freedom that has prevailed in the United States since the first days. It is the only sort of freedom comprehensible to the average man. It accurately reveals his constitutional inability to shake himself free from the illogical and often quite unintelligible prejudices, instincts and mental vices that condition ninety per cent of all his thinking. . . .

But here I wander into political speculation and no doubt stand in contumacy of some statute of Congress. Dr. Parsons avoids politics in her very interesting book. She confines herself to the purely social relations, e.g., between man and woman, parent and child, host and guest, master and servant. The facts she offers are vastly interesting, and their discovery and coordination reveal a tremendous industry, but of even greater interest are the facts that lie over the margin of her inquiry. Here is a golden opportunity for other investigators: I often wonder that the field is so little explored. Perhaps the Freudians, once they get rid of their sexual obsession, will enter it and chart it. No doubt the inferiority complex described by Prof. Dr. Alfred Adler will one day provide an intelligible explanation of many of the puzzling phenomena of mob thinking. In the work of Prof. Dr. Freud himself there is, perhaps, a clew to the origin and anatomy of Puritanism, that worst of intellectual nephritises. I live in hope that the Freudians will fall upon the business without much further delay. Why do otherwise sane men believe in spirits? What is the genesis of the American axiom that the fine arts are unmanly? What is the precise machinery of the process called falling in love? Why do people believe newspapers? Let there be light!

1919

T. S. Eliot

ANDREW MARVELL

THE tercentenary of the former member for Hull deserves not only the celebration proposed by that favoured borough, but a little serious reflection upon his writing. That is an act of piety, which is very different from the resurrection of a deceased reputation. Marvell has stood high for some years; his best poems are not very many, and not only must be well known, from the *Golden Treasury* and the *Oxford Book of English Verse,* but must also have been enjoyed by numerous readers. His grave needs neither rose nor rue nor laurel; there is no imaginary justice to be done; we may think about him, if there be need for thinking, for our own benefit, not his. To bring the poet back to life—the great, the perennial, task of criticism—is in this case to squeeze the drops of the essence of two or three poems; even confining ourselves to these, we may find some precious liquor unknown to the present age. Not to determine rank, but to isolate this quality, is the critical labour. The fact that of all Marvell's verse, which is itself not a great quantity, the really valuable part consists of a very few poems indicates that the un-known quality of which we speak is probably a literary rather than a personal quality; or, more truly, that it is

a quality of a civilization, of a traditional habit of life.
A poet like Donne, or like Baudelaire or Laforgue, may
almost be considered the inventory of an attitude, a system
of feeling or of morals. Donne is difficult to analyse: what
appears at one time a curious personal point of view may
at another time appear rather the precise concentration of a
kind of feeling diffused in the air about him. Donne and
his shroud, the shroud and his motive for wearing it, are
inseparable, but they are not the same thing. The seventeenth century sometimes seems for more than a moment
to gather up and to digest into its art all the experience of
the human mind which (from the same point of view)
the later centuries seem to have been partly engaged in
repudiating. But Donne would have been an individual at
any time and place; Marvell's best verse is the product of
European, that is to say Latin, culture.

Out of that high style developed from Marlowe through
Jonson (for Shakespeare does not lend himself to these
genealogies) the seventeenth century separated two qualities: wit and magniloquence. Neither is as simple or as
apprehensible as its name seems to imply, and the two
are not in practice antithetical; both are conscious and cultivated, and the mind which cultivates one may cultivate
the other. The actual poetry, of Marvell, of Cowley, of
Milton, and of others, is a blend in varying proportions.
And we must be on guard not to employ the terms with
too wide a comprehension; for like the other fluid terms
with which literary criticism deals, the meaning alters with
the age, and for precision we must rely to some degree
upon the literacy and good taste of the reader. The wit of
the Caroline poets is not the wit of Shakespeare, and it
is not the wit of Dryden, the great master of contempt, or
of Pope, the great master of hatred, or of Swift, the great
master of disgust. What is meant is some quality which is
common to the songs in *Comus* and Cowley's *Anacreon-
tics* and Marvell's *Horatian Ode*. It is more than a tech-

nical accomplishment, or the vocabulary and syntax of an epoch; it is, what we have designated tentatively as wit, a tough reasonableness beneath the slight lyric grace. You cannot find it in Shelley or Keats or Wordsworth; you cannot find more than an echo of it in Landor; still less in Tennyson or Browning; and among contemporaries Mr. Yeats is a Irishman and Mr. Hardy is a modern Englishman—that is to say, Mr. Hardy is without it and Mr. Yeats is outside of the tradition altogether. On the other hand, as it certainly exists in Lafontaine, there is a large part of it in Gautier. And of the magniloquence, the deliberate exploitation of the possibilities of magnificence in language which Milton used and abused, there is also use and even abuse in the poetry of Baudelaire.

Wit is not a quality that we are accustomed to associate with "Puritan" literature, with Milton or with Marvell. But if so, we are at fault partly in our conception of wit and partly in our generalizations about the Puritans. And if the wit of Dryden or of Pope is not the only kind of wit in the language, the rest is not merely a little merriment or a little levity or a little impropriety or a little epigram. And, on the other hand, the sense in which a man like Marvell is a "Puritan" is restricted. The persons who opposed Charles I and the persons who supported the Commonwealth were not all of the flock of Zeal-of-the-land Busy or the United Grand Junction Ebenezer Temperance Association. Many of them were gentlemen of the time who merely believed, with considerable show of reason, that government by a Parliament of gentlemen was better than government by a Stuart; though they were, to that extent, Liberal Practitioners, they could hardly foresee the tea-meeting and the Dissidence of Dissent. Being men of education and culture, even of travel, some of them were exposed to that spirit of the age which was coming to be the French spirit of the age. This spirit, curiously enough, was quite opposed to the tendencies latent or the forces active in Puritanism; the content does great damage to the poetry of Milton; Marvell, an active servant of the public, but a lukewarm partisan, and a poet on a smaller scale, is far less injured by it. His line on the statue of Charles II, "It is such a King as no chisel can mend," may be set off against his criticism of the Great Rebellion: "Men . . . ought and might have trusted the King." Marvell, therefore, more a man of the century than a Puritan, speaks more clearly and unequivocally with the voice of his literary age than does Milton.

This voice speaks out uncommonly strong in the *Coy Mistress*. The theme is one of the great traditional commonplaces of European literature. It is the theme of *O mistress mine,* of *Gather ye rosebuds,* of *Go, lovely rose;* it is in the savage austerity of Lucretius and the intense levity of Catullus. Where the wit of Marvell renews the theme is in the variety and order of the images. In the first of the three paragraphs Marvell plays with a fancy which begins by pleasing and leads to astonishment.

> Had we but world enough and time,
> This coyness, lady, were no crime,
> . . . I would
> Love you ten years before the Flood,
> And you should, if you please, refuse
> Till the conversion of the Jews;
> My vegetable love should grow
> Vaster than empires and more slow. . . .

We notice the high speed, the succession of concentrated images, each magnifying the original fancy. When this process has been carried to the end and summed up, the poem turns suddenly with that surprise which has been one of the most important means of poetic effect since Homer:

But at my back I always hear
Time's wingèd chariot hurrying near,
And yonder all before us lie
Deserts of vast eternity.

A whole civilization resides in these lines:

Pallida Mors aequo pulsat pede pauperum tabernas,
Regumque turris. . . .

And not only Horace but Catullus himself:

Nobis, cum semel occidit brevis lux,
Nox est perpetua una dormienda.

The verse of Marvell has not the grand reverberation of
Catullus's Latin; but the image of Marvell is certainly
more comprehensive and penetrates greater depths than
Horace's.

A modern poet, had he reached the height, would very
likely have closed on this moral reflection. But the three
strophes of Marvell's poem have something like a syllo-
gistic relation to each other. After a close approach to the
mood of Donne,

then worms shall try
That long-preserved virginity. . . .
The grave's a fine and private place,
But none, I think, do there embrace,

the conclusion,

Let us roll all our strength and all
Our sweetness up into one ball,
And tear our pleasures with rough strife,
Thorough the iron gates of life.

It will hardly be denied that this poem contains wit;
but it may not be evident that this wit forms the crescendo
and diminuendo of a scale of great imaginative power.
The wit is not only combined with, but fused into, the

imagination. We can easily recognize a witty fancy in the successive images ("my *vegetable* love," "till the conversion of the Jews"), but this fancy is not indulged, as it sometimes is by Cowley or Cleveland, for its own sake. It is structural decoration of a serious idea. In this it is superior to the fancy of L'Allegro, Il Penseroso, or the lighter and less successful poems of Keats. In fact, this alliance of levity and seriousness (by which the seriousness is intensified) is a characteristic of the sort of wit we are trying to identify. It is found in

> Le squelette était invisible
> Au temps heureux de l'art païen!

of Gautier, and in the *dandysme* of Baudelaire and Laforgue. It is in the poem of Catullus which has been quoted, and in the variation of Ben Jonson:

> Cannot we deceive the eyes
> Of a few poor household spies?
> 'Tis no sin love's fruits to steal,
> But that sweet sin to reveal,
> To be taken, to be seen,
> These have sins accounted been.

It is in Propertius and Ovid. It is a quality of a sophisticated literature; a quality which expands in English literature just at the moment before the English mind altered; it is not a quality which we should expect Puritanism to encourage. When we come to Gray and Collins, the sophistication remains only in the language, and has disappeared from the feeling. Gray and Collins were masters, but they had lost that hold on human values, that firm grasp of human experience, which is a formidable achievement of the Elizabethan and Jacobean poets. This wisdom, cynical perhaps but untired (in Shakespeare, a terrifying clairvoyance), leads toward, and is only completed by, the religious comprehension; it leads to the point of the *Ainsi tout leur a craqué dans la main* of Bouvard and Pécuchet.

The difference between imagination and fancy, in view of this poetry of wit, is a very narrow one. Obviously, an image which is immediately and unintentionally ridiculous is merely a fancy. In the poem *Upon Appleton House,* Marvell falls in with one of these undesirable images, describing the attitude of the house toward its master:

> Yet thus the leaden house does sweat,
> And scarce endures the master great;
> But, where he comes, the swelling hall
> Stirs, and the square grows spherical;

which, whatever its intention, is more absurd than it was intended to be. Marvell also falls into the even commoner error of images which are overdeveloped or distracting; which support nothing but their own misshapen bodies:

> And now the salmon-fishers moist
> Their leathern boats begin to hoist;
> And, like Antipodes in shoes,
> Have shod their heads in their canoes.

Of this sort of image a choice collection may be found in Johnson's *Life of Cowley.* But the images in the *Coy Mistress* are not only witty, but satisfy the elucidation of Imagination given by Coleridge:

"This power . . . reveals itself in the balance or reconcilement of opposite or discordant qualities: of sameness, with difference; of the general, with the concrete; the idea with the image; the individual with the representative; the sense of novelty and freshness with old and familiar objects; a more than usual state of emotion with more than usual order; judgment ever awake and steady self-possession with enthusiasm and feeling profound or vehement. . . ."

Coleridge's statement applies also to the following verses, which are selected because of their similarity, and because they illustrate the marked caesura which Marvell often introduces in a short line:

> The tawny mowers enter next,
> Who seem like Israelites to be
> Walking on foot through a green sea . . .
>
> And now the meadows fresher dyed,
> Whose grass, with moister colour dashed,
> Seems as green silks but newly washed . . .
>
> He hangs in shades the orange bright,
> Like golden lamps in a green night . . .
>
> Annihilating all that's made
> To a green thought in a green shade . . .
>
> Had it lived long, it would have been
> Lilies without, roses within.

The whole poem, from which the last of these quotations is drawn (*The Nymph and the Fawn*), is built upon a very slight foundation, and we can imagine what some of our modern practitioners of slight themes would have made of it. But we need not descend to an invidious contemporaneity to point the difference. Here are six lines from *The Nymph and the Fawn*:

> I have a garden of my own,
> But so with roses overgrown
> And lilies, that you would it guess
> To be a little wilderness;
> And all the spring-time of the year
> It only lovèd to be there.

And here are five lines from *The Nymph's Song to Hylas* in the *Life and Death of Jason,* by William Morris:

> I know a little garden close
> Set thick with lily and red rose.
> Where I would wander if I might
> From dewy dawn to dewy night,
> And have one with me wandering.

So far the resemblance is more striking than the difference, although we might just notice the vagueness of allusion in the last line to some indefinite person, form, or phantom, compared with the more explicit reference of emotion to object which we should expect from Marvell. But in the latter part of the poem Morris divaricates widely:

> Yet tottering as I am, and weak,
> Still have I left a little breath
> To seek within the jaws of death
> An entrance to that happy place;
> To seek the unforgotten face
> Once seen, once kissed, once reft from me
> Anigh the murmuring of the sea.

Here the resemblance, if there is any, is to the latter part of the *Coy Mistress*. As for the difference, it could not be more pronounced. The effect of Morris's charming poem depends upon the mistiness of the feeling and the vagueness of its object; the effect of Marvell's upon its bright, hard precision. And this precision is not due to the fact that Marvell is concerned with cruder or simpler or more carnal emotions. The emotion of Morris is not more refined or more spiritual; it is merely more vague: if any one doubts whether the more refined or spiritual emotion can be precise, he should study the treatment of the varieties of discarnate emotion in the *Paradiso*. A curious result of the comparison of Morris's poem with Marvell's is that the former, though it appears to be more serious, is found to be the slighter; and Marvell's *Nymph and the Fawn,* appearing more slight, is the more serious.

> So weeps the wounded balsam; so
> The holy frankincense doth flow;
> The brotherless Heliades
> Melt in such amber tears as these.

These verses have the suggestiveness of true poetry; and the verses of Morris, which are nothing if not an attempt to suggest, really suggest nothing; and we are inclined to infer that the suggestiveness is the aura around a bright clear centre, that you cannot have the aura alone. The day-dreamy feeling of Morris is essentially a slight thing; Marvell takes a slight affair, the feeling of a girl for her pet, and gives it a connexion with the inexhaustible and terrible nebula of emotion which surrounds all our exact and practical passions and mingles with them. Again, Marvell does this in a poem which, because of its formal pastoral machinery, may appear a trifling object:

> *Clorinda.* Near this, a fountain's liquid bell
> Tinkles within the concave shell.

> *Damon.*   Might a soul bathe there and be clean,
> Or slake its drought?

where we find that a metaphor has suddenly rapt us to the image of spiritual purgation. There is here the element of *surprise,* as when Villon says:

> Necessité faict gens mesprendre
> Et faim saillir le loup des boys,

the surprise which Poe considered of the highest importance, and also the restraint and quietness of tone which make the surprise possible. And in the verses of Marvell which have been quoted there is the making the familiar strange, and the strange familiar, which Coleridge attributed to good poetry.

The effort to construct a dream-world, which alters English poetry so greatly in the nineteenth century, a dream-world utterly different from the visionary realities of the *Vita Nuova* or of the poetry of Dante's contemporaries, is a problem of which various explanations may no doubt be found; in any case, the result makes a poet of the nineteenth century, of the same size as Marvell, a more trivial and less serious figure. Marvell is no greater personality than William Morris, but he had something much more solid behind him: he had the vast and penetrating influence of Ben Jonson. Jonson never wrote anything purer than Marvell's *Horatian Ode;* this ode has that same quality of wit which was diffused over the whole Elizabethan product and concentrated in the work of Jonson. And, as was said before, this wit which pervades the poetry of Marvell is more Latin, more refined, than anything that succeeded it. The great danger, as well as the great interest and excitement, of English prose and verse, compared with French, is that it permits and justifies an exaggeration of particular qualities to the exclusion of others. Dryden was great in wit, as Milton in magniloquence; but the former, by isolating this quality and making it by itself into great poetry, and the latter, by coming to dispense with it altogether, may perhaps have injured the language. In Dryden wit becomes almost fun, and thereby loses some contact with reality; becomes pure fun, which French wit almost never is.

> The midwife placed her hand on his thick skull,
> With this prophetic blessing: Be thou dull . . .

> A numerous host of dreaming saints succeed,
> Of the true old enthusiastic breed.

This is audacious and splendid; it belongs to satire besides which Marvell's Satires are random babbling, but it is perhaps as exaggerated as:

> Oft he seems to hide his face,
> But unexpectedly returns,

And to his faithful champion hath in place
Bore witness gloriously; whence Gaza mourns
And all that band them to resist
His uncontrollable intent.

How oddly the sharp Dantesque phrase "whence Gaza mourns" springs out from the brilliant contortions of Milton's sentence!

Who from his private gardens, where
He lived reservèd and austere,
    (As if his highest plot
    To plant the bergamot)

Could by industrious valour climb
To ruin the great work of Time,
    And cast the kingdoms old
    Into another mold;

  .   .   .   .

The Pict no shelter now shall find
Within his parti-coloured mind,
    But, from this valour sad,
    Shrink underneath the plaid:

There is here an equipoise, a balance and proportion of tones, which, while it cannot raise Marvell to the level of Dryden or Milton, extorts an approval which these poets do not receive from us, and bestows a pleasure at least different in kind from any they can often give. It is what makes Marvell a classic; or classic in a sense in which Gray and Collins are not; for the latter, with all their accredited purity, are comparatively poor in shades of feeling to contrast and unite.

We are baffled in the attempt to translate the quality indicated by the dim and antiquated term wit into the equally unsatisfactory nomenclature of our own time. Even Cowley is only able to define it by negatives:

Comely in thousand shapes appears;
   Yonder we saw it plain; and here 'tis now,
   Like spirits in a place, we know not how.

It has passed out of our critical coinage altogether, and no
new term has been struck to replace it; the quality seldom
exists, and is never recognized.

In a true piece of Wit all things must be
   Yet all things there agree;
As in the Ark, join'd without force or strife,
All creatures dwelt, all creatures that had life.
   Or as the primitive forms of all
   (If we compare great things with small)
Which, without discord or confusion, lie
In that strange mirror of the Deity.

So far Cowley has spoken well. But if we are to attempt
even no more than Cowley, we, placed in a retrospective
attitude, must risk much more than anxious generalizations. With our eye still on Marvell, we can say that wit
is not erudition; it is sometimes stifled by erudition, as in
much of Milton. It is not cynicism, though it has a kind
of toughness which may be confused with cynicism by the
tender-minded. It is confused with erudition because it
belongs to an educated mind, rich in generations of experience; and it is confused with cynicism because it implies a constant inspection and criticism of experience. It
involves, probably, a recognition, implicit in the expression
of every experience, of other kinds of experience which
are possible, which we find as clearly in the greatest as in
poets like Marvell. Such a general statement may seem to
take us a long way from *The Nymph and the Fawn,* or
even from the *Horatian Ode;* but it is perhaps justified by
the desire to account for that precise taste of Marvell's
which finds for him the proper degree of seriousness for
every subject which he treats. His errors of taste, when he

trespasses, are not sins against this virtue; they are conceits, distended metaphors and similes, but they never consist in taking a subject too seriously or too lightly. This virtue of wit is not a peculiar quality of minor poets, or of the minor poets of one age or of one school; it is an intellectual quality which perhaps only becomes noticeable by itself, in the work of lesser poets. Furthermore, it is absent from the work of Wordsworth, Shelley, and Keats, on whose poetry nineteenth-century criticism has unconsciously been based. To the best of their poetry wit is irrelevant:

> Art thou pale for weariness
> Of climbing heaven and gazing on the earth,
> Wandering companionless
> Among the stars that have a different birth,
> And ever changing, like a joyless eye,
> That finds no object worth its constancy?

We should find it difficult to draw any useful comparison between these lines of Shelley and anything by Marvell. But later poets, who would have been the better for Marvell's quality, were without it; even Browning seems oddly immature, in some way, beside Marvell. And nowadays we find occasionally good irony, or satire, which lack wit's internal equilibrium, because their voices are essentially protests against some outside sentimentality or stupidity; or we find serious poets who are afraid of acquiring wit, lest they lose intensity. The quality which Marvell had, this modest and certainly impersonal virtue—whether we call it wit or reason, or even urbanity—we have patently failed to define. By whatever name we call it, and however we define that name, it is something precious and needed and apparently extinct; it is what should preserve the reputation of Marvell. *C'était une belle âme, comme on ne fait plus à Londres.*

1921

Frank Moore Colby

CONFESSIONS
OF A GALLOMANIAC

Down to the outbreak of the war I had no more desire to converse with a Frenchman in his own language than with a modern Greek. I thought I understood French well enough for my own purposes, because I had read it off and on for twenty years, but when the war aroused sympathies and sharpened curiosities that I had not felt before, I realized the width of the chasm that cut me off from what I wished to feel. Nor could it be bridged by any of the academic, natural, or commercial methods that I knew of. They were either too slow or they led in directions that I did not wish to go. I tried a phonograph, and after many bouts with it I acquired part of a sermon by Bossuet and real fluency in discussing a quinsy sore throat with a Paris physician, in case I ever went there and had one. I then took fourteen conversation lessons from a Mme. Carnet, and being rather well on in years at the start, I should, if I had kept on diligently, have been able at the age of eighty-five to inquire faultlessly my way to the post-office. I could already ask for butter and sing a song written by Henry IV—when my teacher went to France to take care of her half-brother's children. I will say this for Mme. Carnet. I came to understand perfectly the

French for all her personal and family affairs. No human being has ever confided in me so abundantly as she did. No human being has so sternly repressed any answering confidences of my own. Her method of instruction, if it was one, was that of jealous, relentless, unbridled soliloquy.

Thrown on the world with no power of sustaining a conversation on any other subject than the members of the Carnet family, I nevertheless resolved to take no more lessons but to hunt down French people and make them talk. What I really needed was a governess to take me to and from my office and into the park at noon, but at my age that was out of the question. Then began a career of hypocritical benevolence. I scraped acquaintance with every Frenchman whom I heard talking English very badly, and I became immensely interested in his welfare. I formed the habit of introducing visiting Frenchmen to French-speaking Americans, and sitting, with open mouth, in the flow of their conversation. Then I fell in with M. Bernou, the commissioner who was over here buying guns, and whose English and my French were so much alike that we agreed to interchange them. We met daily for two weeks and walked for an hour in the park, each tearing at the other's language. Our conversations, as I look back on them, must have run about like this:

"It calls to walk," said he, smiling brilliantly.

"It is good morning," said I, "better than I had extended."

"I was at you yestairday ze morning, but I did not find."

"I was obliged to leap early," said I, "and I was busy standing up straight all around the forenoon."

"The book I prayed you send, he came, and I thank, but positively are you not deranged?"

"Don't talk," said I. "Never talk again. It was really nothing anywhere. I had been very happy, I reassure."

"Pardon, I glide, I glode. There was the hide of a banane. Did I crash you?"

"I notice no insults," I replied. "You merely gnawed my arm."

Gestures and smiles of perfect understanding.

I do not know whether Bernou, who like myself was middle-aged, felt as I did on these occasions, but by the suppression of every thought that I could not express in my childish vocabulary, I came to feel exactly like a child. They said I ought to think in French and I tried to do so, but thinking in French when there is so little French to think with, divests the mind of its acquisitions of forty years. Experience slips away for there are not words enough to lay hold of it. Knowledge of good and evil does not exist; the sins have no names, and the mind under its linguistic limitations is like a rather defective toy Noah's ark. From the point of view of Bernou's and my vocabulary, Central Park was as the Garden of Eden after six months—new and unnamed things everywhere. A dog, a tree, a statue taxed all our powers of description, and on a complex matter like a policeman our minds could not meet at all. We could only totter together a few steps in any mental direction. Yet there was a real pleasure in this earnest interchange of insipidities and they were highly valued on each side. For my part I shall always like Bernou, and feel toward him as my childhood's friend. I wonder if he noticed that I was an old, battered man, bothered with a tiresome profession. I certainly never suspected that he was. His language utterly failed to give me that impression.

After I lost Bernou I fastened upon an unfrocked priest who had come over here and gone into the shoe trade—a small, foxy man, who regarded me, I think, in the light of an aggressor. He wanted to become completely American and forget France, and as I was trying to reverse the process, I rather got in his way. He could talk of mediaeval liturgies and his present occupation, but nothing in between, and as he spoke English very well, his practical mind revolted at the use of a medium of communication in which one of us almost strangled when there was another available in which we both were at ease. I could not pump much French out of him. He would burst into English rather resentfully. Then I took to the streets at lunch-time and tried newsdealers, book-shops, restaurants, invented imaginary errands, bought things that I did not want, and exchanged them for objects even less desirable. That kept a little conversation going day by day, but on the whole it was a dry season. It is a strange thing. There are more than thirty thousand of them in the city of New York, and I had always heard that the French are a clannish folk and hate to learn another language, but most of my overtures in French brought only English upon me. The more pains I took the more desirable it seemed to them that I should be spared the trouble of continuing. I was always diving into French and they were always pulling me out again. They thought they were humane.

French people hate broken French worse than most of us hate broken English. But when dragged out into the light of English I tried to talk just as foolishly in order that they might think it was not really my French that was the matter with me. Sometimes that worked quite well. Finding me just as idiotic in my own language they went back to theirs. It certainly worked well with my friend M. Bartet, a paralytic tobacconist in the West Thirties near the river, to whom my relation was for several months that of a grandchild, though I believe we were of the same age. He tried to form my character by bringing me up on such praiseworthy episodes of his early life as he thought I was able to grasp.

Now at the end of a long year of these persistent puerilities I am able to report two definite results: In the first place a sense of my incapacity and ignorance infinitely vaster than when I began, and in the second a profound distrust, possibly vindictive in its origin, of all Americans in the city of New York, who profess an acquaintance with French culture, including teachers, critics, theater audiences, lecture audiences, and patronesses of visiting Frenchmen.

It was perhaps true, as people said at the time, that a certain French theatrical experiment in New York could not continue for the simple reason that it was too good a thing for the theater-going public to support. It may be that the precise equivalent of the enterprise, even if not hampered by a foreign language, could not have permanently endured. Yet from what I saw of its audiences, critics, enthusiasts, and from what I know of the American Gallophile generally, including myself, I believe the linguistic obstacle to have been more serious than they would have us suppose—serious enough to account for the situation without dragging in our aesthetic incapacity. It was certainly an obstacle that less than one-half of any audience ever succeeded in surmounting.

I do not mean that the rest of the audience got nothing out of it, for so expressive were the players by other means than words, that they often sketched the play out in pantomime. The physical activities of the troupe did not arise, as some of the critics declared, from the vivacity of the Gallic temperament; nor were they assumed, as others believed, because in the seventeenth century French actors had been acrobats. These somewhat exaggerated gestures were occasioned by the perception that the majority of the spectators were beginners in French. They were supplied by these ever-tactful people as a running translation for a large body of self-improving Americans.

I do not blame other Americans for dabbling in French, since I myself am the worst of dabblers, but I see no reason why any of us should pretend that it is anything more than dabbling. The usual way of reading French does not lead even to an acquaintance with French literature. Everybody knows that words in a living language in order to be understood have to be lived with. They are not felt as a part of living literature when you see them pressed out and labeled in a glossary, but only when you hear them fly about. A word is not a definite thing susceptible of dictionary explanation. It is a cluster of associations, reminiscent of the sort of men that used it, suggestive of social class, occupation, mood, dignity or the lack of it, primness, violences, pedantries, or platitudes. It hardly seems necessary to say that words in a living literature ought to ring in the ear with the sounds that really belong to them, or that poetry without an echo cannot be felt.

It may be that there is no way out of it. Perhaps it is inevitable that the colleges which had so long taught the dead languages as if they were buried should now teach the living ones as if they were dead. But there is no need of pretending that this formal acquaintance with books results in an appreciation of literature. No sense of the intimate quality of a writer can be founded on a verbal vacuum. His plots, his place in literature, his central motives, and the opinion of his critics could all be just as adequately conveyed, if his books were studied in the language of the deaf and dumb. Of course, one may be drawn to an author by that process but it would hardly be the artistic attraction of literature; it is as if one felt drawn to a woman by an interest exclusively in her bones.

Elementary as these remarks may seem I offer them to Gallophiles without apology. On the contrary I rather fear that I am writing over their heads.

1921

Lytton Strachey

THE LAST ELIZABETHAN

THE shrine of Poetry is a secret one; and it is
fortunate that this should be the case; for it gives a sense
of security. The cult is too mysterious and intimate to
figure upon census papers; there are no turnstiles at the
temple gates; and so, as all inquiries must be fruitless,
the obvious plan is to take for granted a good attendance
of worshippers, and to pass on. Yet, if Apollo were to
come down (after the manner of deities) and put questions—must we suppose to the Laureate?—as to the number of the elect, would we be quite sure of escaping wrath
and destruction? Let us hope for the best; and perhaps,
if we were bent upon finding out the truth, the simplest
way would be to watch the sales of the new edition of the
poems of Beddoes, which Messrs. Routledge have lately
added to the "Muses' Library." How many among Apollo's pew-renters, one wonders, have ever read Beddoes,
or, indeed, have ever heard of him? For some reason or
another, this extraordinary poet has not only never received the recognition which is his due, but has failed
almost entirely to receive any recognition whatever. If his
name is known at all, it is known in virtue of the one or
two of his lyrics which have crept into some of the current
anthologies. But Beddoes' highest claim to distinction does

From *Literary Essays* by Lytton Strachey. Reprinted by permission of Harcourt, Brace and Company, Inc.

not rest upon his lyrical achievements, consummate as those achievements are; it rests upon his extraordinary eminence as a master of dramatic blank verse. Perhaps his greatest misfortune was that he was born at the beginning of the nineteenth century, and not at the end of the sixteenth. His proper place was among that noble band of Elizabethans, whose strong and splendid spirit gave to England, in one miraculous generation, the most glorious heritage of drama that the world has known. If Charles Lamb had discovered his tragedies among the folios of the British Museum, and had given extracts from them in the *Specimens of Dramatic Poets,* Beddoes' name would doubtless be as familiar to us now as those of Marlowe and Webster, Fletcher and Ford. As it happened, however, he came as a strange and isolated phenomenon, a star which had wandered from its constellation, and was lost among alien lights. It is to very little purpose that Mr. Ramsay Colles, his latest editor, assures us that "Beddoes is interesting as marking the transition from Shelley to Browning"; it is to still less purpose that he points out to us a passage in *Death's Jest Book* which anticipates the doctrines of *The Descent of Man.* For Beddoes cannot be hoisted into line with his contemporaries by such methods as these; nor is it in the light of such after-considerations that the value of his work must be judged. We must take him on his own merits, "unmixed with seconds": we must discover and appraise his peculiar quality for its own sake.

> He hath skill in language;
> And knowledge is in him, root, flower, and fruit,
> A palm with winged imagination in it,
> Whose roots stretch even underneath the grave;
> And on them hangs a lamp of magic science
> In his soul's deepest mine, where folded thoughts
> Lie sleeping on the tombs of magi dead.

If the neglect suffered by Beddoes' poetry may be accounted for in more ways than one, it is not so easy to understand why more curiosity has never been aroused by the circumstances of his life. For one reader who cares to concern himself with the intrinsic merit of a piece of writing there are a thousand who are ready to explore with eager sympathy the history of the writer; and all that we know both of the life and the character of Beddoes possesses those very qualities of peculiarity, mystery, and adventure, which are so dear to the hearts of subscribers to circulating libraries. Yet only one account of his career has ever been given to the public; and that account, fragmentary and incorrect as it is, has long been out of print. It was supplemented some years ago by Mr. Gosse, who was able to throw additional light upon one important circumstance, and who has also published a small collection of Beddoes' letters. The main biographical facts, gathered from these sources, have been put together by Mr. Ramsay Colles, in his introduction to the new edition; but he has added nothing fresh; and we are still in almost complete ignorance as to the details of the last twenty years of Beddoes' existence—full as those years certainly were of interest and even excitement. Nor has the veil been altogether withdrawn from that strange tragedy which, for the strange tragedian, was the last of all.

Readers of Miss Edgeworth's letters may remember that her younger sister Anne married a distinguished Clifton physician, Dr. Thomas Beddoes. Their eldest son, born in 1803, was named Thomas Lovell, after his father and grandfather, and grew up to be the author of *The Brides' Tragedy* and *Death's Jest Book*. Dr. Beddoes was a remarkable man, endowed with high and varied intellectual capacities and a rare independence of character. His scientific attainments were recognised by the University of Oxford, where he held the post of Lecturer in Chemistry, until the time of the French Revolution, when he was obliged to resign it, owing to the scandal caused by the unconcealed intensity of his liberal opinions. He then settled at Clifton as a physician, established a flourishing practice, and devoted his leisure to politics and scientific research. Sir Humphry Davy, who was his pupil, and whose merit he was the first to bring to light, declared that "he had talents which would have exalted him to the pinnacle of philosophical eminence, if they had been applied with discretion." The words are curiously suggestive of the history of his son; and indeed the poet affords a striking instance of the hereditary transmission of mental qualities. Not only did Beddoes inherit his father's talents and his father's inability to make the best use of them; he possessed in a no less remarkable degree his father's independence of mind. In both cases, this quality was coupled with a corresponding eccentricity of conduct, which occasionally, to puzzled onlookers, wore the appearance of something very near insanity. Many stories are related of the queer behaviour of Dr. Beddoes. One day he astonished the ladies of Clifton by appearing at a tea-party with a packet of sugar in his hand; he explained that it was East Indian sugar, and that nothing would induce him to eat the usual kind, which came from Jamaica and was made by slaves. More extraordinary were his medical prescriptions; for he was in the habit of ordering cows to be conveyed into his patients' bedrooms, in order, as he said, that they might "inhale the animals' breath." It is easy to imagine the delight which the singular spectacle of a cow climbing upstairs into an invalid's bedroom must have given to the future author of *Harpagus* and *The Oviparous Tailor*. But "little Tom," as Miss Edgeworth calls him, was not destined to enjoy for long the benefit of parental example; for Dr. Beddoes died in the prime of life, when the child was not yet six years old.

The genius at school is usually a disappointing figure, for, as a rule, one must be commonplace to be a successful boy. In that preposterous world, to be remarkable is to be overlooked; and nothing less vivid than the white-hot blaze of a Shelley will bring with it even a distinguished martyrdom. But Beddoes was an exception, though he was not a martyr. On the contrary, he dominated his fellows as absolutely as if he had been a dullard and a dunce. He was at Charterhouse; and an entertaining account of his existence there has been preserved to us in a paper of school reminiscences, written by Mr. C. D. Bevan, who had been his fag. Though his place in the school was high, Beddoes' interests were devoted not so much to classical scholarship as to the literature of his own tongue. Cowley, he afterwards told a friend, had been the first poet he had understood; but no doubt he had begun to understand poetry many years before he went to Charterhouse; and while he was there, the reading which he chiefly delighted in was the Elizabethan drama. "He liked acting," says Mr. Bevan, "and was a good judge of it, and used to give apt though burlesque imitations of the popular actors, particularly Kean and Macready. Though his voice was harsh and his enunciation offensively conceited, he read with so much propriety of expression and manner, that I was always glad to listen: even when I was pressed into the service as his accomplice, his enemy, or his love, with a due accompaniment of curses, caresses, or kicks, as the course of his declamation required. One play in particular, Marlowe's *Tragedy of Dr. Faustus,* excited my admiration in this way; and a liking for the old English drama, which I still retain, was created and strengthened by such recitations." But Beddoes' dramatic performances were not limited to the works of others; when the occasion arose he was able to supply the necessary material himself. A locksmith had incurred his displeasure by putting a bad lock on his bookcase; Beddoes vowed vengeance; and when next the man appeared he was received by a dramatic interlude, representing his last moments, his horror and remorse, his death, and the funeral procession, which was interrupted by fiends, who carried off body and soul to eternal torments. Such was the realistic vigour of the performance that the locksmith, according to Mr. Bevan, "departed in a storm of wrath and execrations, and could not be persuaded, for some time, to resume his work."

Besides the interlude of the wicked locksmith, Beddoes' school compositions included a novel in the style of Fielding (which has unfortunately disappeared), the beginnings of an Elizabethan tragedy, and much miscellaneous verse. In 1820 he left Charterhouse, and went to Pembroke College, Oxford, where, in the following year, while still a freshman, he published his first volume, *The Improvisatore,* a series of short narratives in verse. The book had been written in part while he was at school; and its immaturity is obvious. It contains no trace of the nervous vigour of his later style; the verse is weak, and the sentiment, to use his own expression, "Moorish." Indeed, the only interest of the little work lies in the evidence which it affords that the singular pre-occupation which eventually dominated Beddoes' mind had, even in these early days, made its appearance. The book is full of death. The poems begin on battle-fields and end in charnel-houses; old men are slaughtered in cold blood, and lovers are struck by lightning into mouldering heaps of corruption. The boy, with his elaborate exhibitions of physical horror, was doing his best to make his readers' flesh creep. But the attempt was far too crude; and in after years, when Beddoes had become a past-master of that difficult art, he was very much ashamed of his first publication. So eager was he to destroy every trace of its existence, that he did not spare even the finely bound copies of his friends. The story goes that he amused himself by visiting their libraries with a penknife, so that, when next they took out the precious volume, they found the pages gone.

Beddoes, however, had no reason to be ashamed of his

next publication, *The Brides' Tragedy,* which appeared in 1822. In a single bound, he had reached the threshold of poetry, and was knocking at the door. The line which divides the best and most accomplished verse from poetry itself—that subtle and momentous line which every one can draw, and no one can explain—Beddoes had not yet crossed. But he had gone as far as it was possible to go by the aid of mere skill in the art of writing, and he was still in his twentieth year. Many passages in *The Brides' Tragedy* seem only to be waiting for the breath of inspiration which will bring them into life; and indeed, here and there, the breath has come, the warm, the true, the vital breath of Apollo. No one, surely, whose lips had not tasted of the waters of Helicon, could have uttered such words as these:

> Here's the blue violet, like Pandora's eye,
> When first it darkened with immortal life

or a line of such intense imaginative force as this:

> I've huddled her into the wormy earth;

or this splendid description of a stormy sunrise:

> The day is in its shroud while yet an infant;
> And night with giant strides stalks o'er the world,
> Like a swart Cyclops, on its hideous front
> One round, red, thunder-swollen eye ablaze.

The play was written on the Elizabethan model, and, as a play, it is disfigured by Beddoes' most characteristic faults: the construction is weak, the interest fluctuates from character to character, and the motives and actions of the characters themselves are for the most part curiously remote from the realities of life. Yet, though the merit of the tragedy depends almost entirely upon the verse, there are signs in it that, while Beddoes lacked the gift of construction, he nevertheless possessed one important dramatic faculty—the power of creating detached scenes of interest and beauty. The scene in which the half-crazed Leonora imagines to herself, beside the couch on which her dead daughter lies, that the child is really living after all, is dramatic in the highest sense of the word; the situation, with all its capabilities of pathetic irony, is conceived and developed with consummate art and absolute restraint. Leonora's speech ends thus:

> . . . Speak, I pray thee, Floribel,
> Speak to thy mother; do but whisper "aye";
> Well, well, I will not press her; I am sure
> She has the welcome news of some good fortune,
> And hoards the telling till her father comes;
> . . . Ah! She half laughed. I've guessed it then;
> Come tell me, I'll be secret. Nay, if you mock me,
> I must be very angry till you speak.
> Now this is silly; some of these young boys
> Have dressed the cushions with her clothes in sport.
> 'Tis very like her. I could make this image
> Act all her greetings; she shall bow her head:
> "Good-morrow, mother"; and her smiling face
> Falls on my neck.—Oh, heaven, 'tis she indeed!
> I know it all—don't tell me.

The last seven words are a summary of anguish, horror, and despair, such as Webster himself might have been proud to write.

The Brides' Tragedy was well received by critics; and a laudatory notice of Beddoes in the *Edinburgh*, written by Bryan Waller Procter—better known then than now under his pseudonym of Barry Cornwall—led to a lasting friendship between the two poets. The connection had an important result, for it was through Procter that Beddoes became acquainted with the most intimate of all his friends—Thomas Forbes Kelsall, then a young lawyer at Southampton. In the summer of 1823 Beddoes stayed at

Southampton for several months, and, while ostensibly studying for his Oxford degree, gave up most of his time to conversations with Kelsall and to dramatic composition. It was a culminating point in his life: one of those moments which come, even to the most fortunate, once and once only—when youth, and hope, and the high exuberance of genius combine with circumstance and opportunity to crown the marvellous hour. The spadework of *The Brides' Tragedy* had been accomplished; the seed had been sown; and now the harvest was beginning. Beddoes, "with the delicious sense," as Kelsall wrote long afterwards, "of the laurel freshly twined around his head," poured out, in these Southampton evenings, an eager stream of song. "His poetic composition," says his friend, "was then exceedingly facile: more than once or twice has he taken home with him at night some unfinished act of a drama, in which the editor [Kelsall] had found much to admire, and, at the next meeting, has produced a new one, similar in design, but filled with other thoughts and fancies, which his teeming imagination had projected, in its sheer abundance, and not from any feeling, right or fastidious, of unworthiness in its predecessor. Of several of these very striking fragments, large and grand in their aspect as they each started into form,

Like the red outline of beginning Adam,

. . . the only trace remaining is literally the impression thus deeply cut into their one observer's mind. The fine verse just quoted is the sole remnant, indelibly stamped on the editor's memory, of one of these extinct creations." Fragments survive of at least four dramas, projected, and brought to various stages of completion, at about this time. Beddoes was impatient of the common restraints; he was dashing forward in the spirit of his own advice to another poet:

Creep not nor climb,
As they who place their topmost of sublime
On some peak of this planet, pitifully.
Dart eaglewise with open wings, and fly
Until you meet the gods!

Eighteen months after his Southampton visit, Beddoes took his degree at Oxford, and, almost immediately, made up his mind to a course of action which had the profoundest effect upon his future life. He determined to take up the study of medicine; and with that end in view established himself, in 1825, at the University at Göttingen. It is very clear, however, that he had no intention of giving up his poetical work. He took with him to Germany the beginnings of a new play—"a very Gothic-styled tragedy," he calls it, "for which I have a jewel of a name—*Death's Jest Book;* of course," he adds, "no one will ever read it"; and, during his four years at Göttingen, he devoted most of his leisure to the completion of this work. He was young; he was rich; he was interested in medical science; and no doubt it seemed to him that he could well afford to amuse himself for half-a-dozen years, before he settled down to the poetical work which was to be the serious occupation of his life. But, as time passed, he became more and more engrossed in the study of medicine, for which he gradually discovered he had not only a taste but a gift; so that at last he came to doubt whether it might not be his true vocation to be a physician, and not a poet after all. Engulfed among the students of Göttingen, England and English ways of life, and even English poetry, became dim to him; "dir, dem Anbeter der seligen Gottheiten der Musen, u.s.w.," he wrote to Kelsall, "was Unterhaltendes kann der Liebhaber von Knochen, der fleissige Botaniker und Phisiolog mittheilen?" In 1830 he was still hesitating between the two alternatives. "I sometimes wish," he told the same friend, "to devote myself exclusively to the study of anatomy and physiology in science, of languages, and dramatic poetry"; his pen had run away with him; and his "exclusive devotion" turned out to be a double one, directed towards widely different ends. While he was still in this state of mind, a new interest took possession of him —an interest which worked havoc with his dreams of dramatic authorship and scientific research: he became involved in the revolutionary movement which was at that time beginning to agitate Europe. The details of his adventures are unhappily lost to us, for we know nothing more of them than can be learnt from a few scanty references in his rare letters to English friends; but it is certain that the part he played was an active, and even a dangerous one. He was turned out of Würzburg by "that ingenious Jackanapes," the King of Bavaria; he was an intimate friend of Hegetschweiler, one of the leaders of liberalism in Switzerland; and he was present in Zurich when a body of six thousand peasants, "half unarmed, and the other half armed with scythes, dungforks and poles, entered the town and overturned the liberal government." In the tumult Hegetschweiler was killed, and Beddoes was soon afterwards forced to fly the canton. During the following years we catch glimpses of him, flitting mysteriously over Germany and Switzerland, at Berlin, at Baden, at Giessen, a strange solitary figure, with tangled hair and meerschaum pipe, scribbling lampoons upon the King of Prussia, translating Grainger's *Spinal Cord* into German, and Schoenlein's *Diseases of Europeans* into English, exploring Pilatus and the Titlis, evolving now and then some ghostly lyric or some rabelaisian tale, or brooding over the scenes of his "Gothic-styled tragedy," wondering if it were worthless or inspired, and giving it— as had been his wont for the last twenty years—just one more touch before he sent it to the press. He appeared in England once or twice, and in 1846 made a stay of several months, visiting the Procters in London, and going down to Southampton to be with Kelsall once again. Eccentricity had grown on him; he would shut himself for days in his bedroom, smoking furiously; he would fall into fits of long and deep depression. He shocked some of his relatives by arriving at their country house astride a donkey; and he amazed the Procters by starting out one evening to set fire to Drury Lane Theatre with a lighted five-pound note. After this last visit to England, his history becomes even more obscure than before. It is known that in 1847 he was in Frankfort, where he lived for six months in close companionship with a young baker called Degen—"a nice-looking young man, nineteen years of age," we are told, "dressed in a blue blouse, fine in expression, and of a natural dignity of manner"; and that, in the spring of the following year, the two friends went off to Zurich, where Beddoes hired the theatre for a night in order that Degen might appear on the stage in the part of Hotspur. At Basel, however, for some unexplained reason, the friends parted, and Beddoes fell immediately into the profoundest gloom. "Il a été misérable," said the waiter at the Cigogne Hotel, where he was staying, "il a voulu se tuer." It was true. He inflicted a deep wound in his leg with a razor, in the hope, apparently, of bleeding to death. He was taken to the hospital, where he constantly tore off the bandages, until at last it was necessary to amputate the leg below the knee. The operation was successful. Beddoes began to recover, and, in the autumn, Degen came back to Basel. It seemed as if all were going well; for the poet, with his books around him, and the blue-bloused Degen by his bedside, talked happily of politics and literature, and of an Italian journey in the spring. He walked out twice; was he still happy? Who can tell? Was it happiness, or misery, or what strange impulse, that drove him, on his third walk, to go to a chemist's shop in the town, and to obtain there a phial of deadly poison? On the evening of that day—the 26th of January,

1849—Dr. Ecklin, his physician, was hastily summoned, to find Beddoes lying insensible upon the bed. He never recovered consciousness, and died that night. Upon his breast was found a pencil note, addressed to one of his English friends. "My dear Philips," it began, "I am food for what I am good for—worms." A few testamentary wishes followed. Kelsall was to have the manuscripts; and —"W. Beddoes must have a case (50 bottles) of Champagne Moet, 1847 growth, to drink my death in . . . I ought to have been, among other things," the gruesome document concluded, "a good poet. Life was too great a bore on one peg, and that a bad one. Buy for Dr. Ecklin one of Reade's best stomach-pumps." It was the last of his additions to *Death's Jest Book,* and the most *macabre* of all.

Kelsall discharged his duties as literary executor with exemplary care. The manuscripts were fragmentary and confused. There were three distinct drafts of *Death's Jest Book,* each with variations of its own; and from these Kelsall compiled his first edition of the drama, which appeared in 1850. In the following year he brought out the two volumes of poetical works, which remained for forty years the only record of the full scope and power of Beddoes' genius. They contain reprints of *The Brides' Tragedy* and *Death's Jest Book,* together with two unfinished tragedies, and a great number of dramatic fragments and lyrics; and the poems are preceded by Kelsall's memoir of his friend. Of these rare and valuable volumes the Muses' Library edition is almost an exact reprint, except that it omits the memoir and revives *The Improvisatore.* Only one other edition of Beddoes exists—the limited one brought out by Mr. Gosse in 1890, and based upon a fresh examination of the manuscripts. Mr. Gosse was able to add ten lyrics and one dramatic fragment to those already published by Kelsall; he made public for the first time the true story of Beddoes' suicide, which Kelsall had concealed; and, in 1893, he followed up his edition of the poems by a volume of Beddoes' letters. It is clear, therefore, that there is no one living to whom lovers of Beddoes owe so much as to Mr. Gosse. He has supplied most important materials for the elucidation of the poet's history: and, among the lyrics which he has printed for the first time, are to be found one of the most perfect specimens of Beddoes' command of unearthly pathos—*The Old Ghost*—and one of the most singular examples of his vein of grotesque and ominous humour—*The Oviparous Tailor.* Yet it may be doubted whether even Mr. Gosse's edition is the final one. There are traces in Beddoes' letters of unpublished compositions which may still come to light. What has happened, one would like to know, to *The Ivory Gate,* that "volume of prosaic poetry and poetical prose," which Beddoes talked of publishing in 1837? Only a few fine stanzas from it have ever appeared. And, as Mr. Gosse himself tells us, the variations in *Death's Jest Book* alone would warrant the publication of a variorum edition of that work—"if," he wisely adds, for the proviso contains the gist of the matter—"if the interest in Beddoes should continue to grow."

"Say what you will, I am convinced the man who is to awaken the drama must be a bold, trampling fellow—no creeper into worm-holes—no reviver even—however good. These reanimations are vampire-cold." The words occur in one of Beddoes' letters, and they are usually quoted by critics, on the rare occasions on which his poetry is discussed, as an instance of the curious incapacity of artists to practice what they preach. But the truth is that Beddoes was not a "creeper into worm-holes," he was not even a "reviver"; he was a reincarnation. Everything that we know of him goes to show that the laborious and elaborate effort of literary reconstruction was quite alien to his spirit. We have Kelsall's evidence as to the ease and abundance of his composition; we have the character

of the man, as it shines forth in his letters and in the
history of his life—records of a "bold, trampling fellow,"
if ever there was one; and we have the evidence of his
poetry itself. For the impress of a fresh and vital intelligence is stamped unmistakably upon all that is best in
his work. His mature blank verse is perfect. It is not an
artificial concoction galvanized into the semblance of life;
it simply lives. And, with Beddoes, maturity was pre-
cocious, for he obtained complete mastery over the most
difficult and dangerous of metres at a wonderfully early
age. Blank verse is like the Djin in the Arabian Nights;
it is either the most terrible of masters, or the most powerful of slaves. If you have not the magic secret, it will take
your best thoughts, your bravest imaginations, and change
them into toads and fishes; but, if the spell be yours, it
will turn into a flying carpet and lift your simplest utterance into the highest heaven. Beddoes had mastered the
"Open, Sesame" at an age when most poets are still
mouthing ineffectual wheats and barleys. In his twenty-
second year, his thoughts filled and moved and animated
his blank verse as easily and familiarly as a hand in a glove.
He wishes to compare, for instance, the human mind,
with its knowledge of the past, to a single eye receiving
the light of the stars; and the object of the comparison
is to lay stress upon the concentration on one point of a
vast multiplicity of objects. There could be no better exercise for a young verse-writer than to attempt his own
expression of this idea, and then to examine these lines
by Beddoes—lines where simplicity and splendour have
been woven together with the ease of accomplished art.

How glorious to live! Even in one thought
The wisdom of past times to fit together,
And from the luminous minds of many men
Catch a reflected truth; as, in one eye,

Light, from unnumbered worlds and farthest planets
Of the star-crowded universe, is gathered
Into one ray.

The effect is, of course, partly produced by the diction;
but the diction, fine as it is, would be useless without the
phrasing—that art by which the two forces of the metre
and the sense are made at once to combat, to combine
with, and to heighten each other. It is, however, impossible to do more than touch upon this side—the technical
side—of Beddoes' genius. But it may be noticed that in
his mastery of phrasing—as in so much besides—he was a
true Elizabethan. The great artists of that age knew that
without phrasing dramatic verse was a dead thing; and it
is only necessary to turn from their pages to those of an
eighteenth-century dramatist—Addison, for instance—to
understand how right they were.

Beddoes' power of creating scenes of intense dramatic
force, which had already begun to show itself in *The
Brides' Tragedy*, reached its full development in his subsequent work. The opening act of *The Second Brother*—
the most nearly complete of his unfinished tragedies—is a
striking example of a powerful and original theme treated
in such a way that, while the whole of it is steeped in
imaginative poetry, yet not one ounce of its dramatic
effectiveness is lost. The duke's next brother, the heir to
the dukedom of Ferrara, returns to the city, after years of
wandering, a miserable and sordid beggar—to find his
younger brother, rich, beautiful, and reckless, leading a
life of gay debauchery, with the assurance of succeeding
to the dukedom when the duke dies. The situation presents possibilities for just those bold and extraordinary
contrasts which were so dear to Beddoes' heart. While
Marcello, the second brother, is meditating over his
wretched fate, Orazio, the third, comes upon the stage,
crowned and glorious, attended by a train of singing

revellers, and with a courtesan upon either hand. "Wine in a ruby!" he exclaims, gazing into his mistress's eyes:

> I'll solemnize their beauty in a draught
> Pressed from the summer of an hundred vines.

Meanwhile Marcello pushes himself forward, and attempts to salute his brother.

ORAZIO

Insolent beggar!

MARCELLO

Prince! But we must shake hands.
Look you, the round earth's like a sleeping serpent,
Who drops her dusky tail upon her crown
Just here. Oh, we are like two mountain peaks
Of two close planets, catching in the air:
You, King Olympus, a great pile of summer,
Wearing a crown of gods; I, the vast top
Of the ghosts' deadly world, naked and dark,
With nothing reigning on my desolate head
But an old spirit of a murdered god,
Palaced within the corpse of Saturn's father.

They begin to dispute, and at last Marcello exclaims—

ORAZIO

Aye, Prince, you have a brother—
The Duke—he'll scourge you.

MARCELLO

Nay, *the second,* sir,
Who, like an envious river, flows between
Your footsteps and Ferrara's throne. . . .

ORAZIO

Stood he before me there,
By you, in you, as like as you're unlike,
Straight as you're bowed, young as you are old,

And many years nearer than him to Death,
The falling brilliancy of whose white sword
Your ancient locks so silvery reflect,
I would deny, outswear, and overreach,
And pass him with contempt, as I do you.
Jove! How we waste the stars: set on, my friends.

And so the revelling band pass onward, singing still, as
they vanish down the darkened street:

Strike, you myrtle-crownèd boys,
Ivied maidens, strike together! . . .

And Marcello is left alone:

I went forth
Joyfully, as the soul of one who closes
His pillowed eyes beside an unseen murderer,
And like its horrible return was mine,
To find the heart, wherein I breathed and beat,
Cold, gashed, and dead. Let me forget to love,
And take a heart of venom: let me make
A staircase of the frightened breasts of men,
And climb into a lonely happiness!
And thou, who only art alone as I,
Great solitary god of that one sun,
I charge thee, by the likeness of our state,
Undo these human veins that tie me close
To other men, and let your servant griefs
Unmilk me of my mother, and pour in
Salt scorn and steaming hate!

A moment later he learnt that the duke has suddenly
died, and that the dukedom is his. The rest of the play
affords an instance of Beddoes' inability to trace out a
story, clearly and forcibly, to an appointed end. The
succeeding acts are crowded with beautiful passages, with
vivid situations, with surprising developments, but the

central plot vanishes away into nothing, like a great river dissipating itself among a thousand streams. It is, indeed, clear enough that Beddoes was embarrassed with his riches, that his fertile mind conceived too easily, and that he could never resist the temptation of giving life to his imaginations, even at the cost of killing his play. His conception of Orazio, for instance, began by being that of a young Bacchus, as he appears in the opening scene. But Beddoes could not leave him there; he must have a romantic wife, whom he has deserted; and the wife, once brought into being, must have an interview with her husband. The interview is an exquisitely beautiful one, but it shatters Orazio's character, for, in the course of it, he falls desperately in love with his wife; and meanwhile the wife herself has become so important and interesting a figure that she must be given a father, who in his turn becomes the central character in more than one exciting scene. But, by this time, what has happened to the second brother? It is easy to believe that Beddoes was always ready to begin a new play rather than finish an old one. But it is not so certain that his method was quite as inexcusable as his critics assert. To the reader, doubtless, his faulty construction is glaring enough; but Beddoes wrote his plays to be acted, as a passage in one of his letters very clearly shows. "You are, I think," he writes to Kelsall, "disinclined to the stage: now I confess that I think this is the highest aim of the dramatist, and should be very desirous to get on it. To look down on it is a piece of impertinence, as long as one chooses to write in the form of a play, and is generally the result of one's own ability to produce anything striking and affecting in that way." And it is precisely upon the stage that such faults of construction as those which disfigure Beddoes' tragedies matter least. An audience, whose attention is held and delighted by a succession of striking incidents clothed in splendid speech, neither cares nor knows whether the effect of the whole, as a whole, is worthy of the separate parts. It would be foolish, in the present melancholy condition of the art of dramatic declamation, to wish for the public performance of *Death's Jest Book;* but it is impossible not to hope that the time may come when an adequate representation of that strange and great work may be something more than "a possibility more thin than air." Then, and then only, shall we be able to take the true measure of Beddoes' genius.

Perhaps, however, the ordinary reader finds Beddoes' lack of construction a less distasteful quality than his disregard of the common realities of existence. Not only is the subject-matter of the greater part of his poetry remote and dubious; his very characters themselves seem to be infected by their creator's delight in the mysterious, the strange, and the unreal. They have no healthy activity; or, if they have, they invariably lose it in the second act; in the end, they are all hypochondriac philosophers, puzzling over eternity and dissecting the attributes of Death. The central idea of *Death's Jest Book*—the resurrection of a ghost—fails to be truly effective, because it is difficult to see any clear distinction between the phantom and the rest of the characters. The duke, saved from death by the timely arrival of Wolfram, exclaims "Blest hour!" and then, in a moment, begins to ponder, and agonise, and dream:

> And yet how palely, with what faded lips
> Do we salute this unhoped change of fortune!
> Thou art so silent, lady; and I utter
> Shadows of words, like to an ancient ghost,
> Arisen out of hoary centuries
> Where none can speak his language.

Orazio, in his brilliant palace, is overcome with the same feelings:

Methinks, these fellows, with their ready jests,
Are like to tedious bells, that ring alike
Marriage and death.

And his description of his own revels applies no less to
the whole atmosphere of Beddoes' tragedies:

Voices were heard, most loud, which no man owned:
There were more shadows too than there were men;
And all the air more dark and thick than night
Was heavy, as 'twere made of something more
Than living breaths.

It would be vain to look, among such spectral imagin-
ings as these, for guidance in practical affairs, or for
illuminating views on men and things, or for a philosophy,
or, in short, for anything which may be called a "criticism
of life." If a poet must be a critic of life, Beddoes was
certainly no poet. He belongs to the class of writers of
which, in English literature, Spenser, Keats, and Milton
are the dominant figures—the writers who are great
merely because of their art. Sir James Stephen was only
telling the truth when he remarked that Milton might
have put all that he had to say in *Paradise Lost* into a
prose pamphlet of two or three pages. But who cares
about what Milton had to say? It is his way of saying it
that matters; it is his expression. Take away the expression from the *Satires* of Pope, or from *The Excursion,* and,
though you will destroy the poems, you will leave behind
a great mass of thought. Take away the expression from
Hyperion, and you will leave nothing at all. To ask which
is the better of the two styles is like asking whether a
peach is better than a rose, because, both being beautiful,
you can eat the one and not the other. At any rate, Beddoes is among the roses: it is in his expression that his
greatness lies. His verse is an instrument of many modula-
tions, of exquisite delicacy, of strange suggestiveness, of

amazing power. Playing on it, he can give utterance to the subtlest visions, such as this:

> Just now a beam of joy hung on his eyelash;
> But, as I looked, it sunk into his eye,
> Like a bruised worm writhing its form of rings
> Into a darkening hole.

Or to the most marvellous of vague and vast conceptions, such as this:

> I begin to hear
> Strange but sweet sounds, and the loud rocky dashing
> Of waves, where time into Eternity
> Falls over ruined worlds.

Or he can evoke sensations of pure loveliness, such as these:

> So fair a creature! of such charms compact
> As nature stints elsewhere: which you may find
> Under the tender eyelid of a serpent,
> Or in the gurge of a kiss-coloured rose,
> By drops and sparks: but when she moves, you see,
> Like water from a crystal overfilled,
> Fresh beauty tremble out of her and lave
> Her fair sides to the ground.

Or he can put into a single line all the long memories of adoration:

> My love was much;
> My life but an inhabitant of his.

Or he can pass in a moment from tiny sweetness to colossal turmoil:

> I should not say
> How thou art like the daisy in Noah's meadow,
> On which the foremost drop of rain fell warm
> And soft at evening: so the little flower

Wrapped up its leaves, and shut the treacherous water
Close to the golden welcome of its breast,
Delighting in the touch of that which led
The shower of oceans, in whose billowy drops
Tritons and lions of the sea were warring,
And sometimes ships on fire sunk in the blood
Of their own inmates; others were of ice,
And some had islands rooted in their waves,
Beasts on their rocks, and forest-powdering winds,
And showers tumbling on their tumbling self,
And every sea of every ruined star
Was but a drop in the world-melting flood.

He can express alike the beautiful tenderness of love, and
the hectic, dizzy, and appalling frenzy of extreme rage:—

. . . What shall I do? I speak all wrong,
And lose a soul-full of delicious thought
By talking. Hush! Let's drink each other up
By silent eyes. Who lives, but thou and I,
My heavenly wife? . . .
I'll watch thee thus, till I can tell a second
By thy cheek's change.

In that, one can almost feel the kisses; and, in this, one
can almost hear the gnashing of the teeth. "Never!" exclaims the duke to his son Torrismond:

There lies no grain of sand between
My loved and my detested! Wing thee hence,
Or thou dost stand tomorrow on a cobweb
Spun o'er the well of clotted Acheron,
Whose hydrophobic entrails stream with fire!
And may this intervening earth be snow,
And my step burn like the mid coal of Ætna,
Plunging me, through it all, into the core,
Where in their graves the dead are shut like seeds,
If I do not—O, but he is my son!

Is not that tremendous? But, to find Beddoes in his most characteristic mood, one must watch him weaving his mysterious imagination upon the woof of mortality. One must wander with him through the pages of *Death's Jest Book*, one must grow accustomed to the dissolution of reality, and the opening of the nettled lips of graves; one must learn that "the dead are most and merriest," one must ask—"Are the ghosts eaves-dropping?"—one must realise that "murder is full of holes." Among the ruins of his Gothic cathedral, on whose cloister walls the Dance of Death is painted, one may speculate at ease over the fragility of existence, and, within the sound of that dark ocean,

> Whose tumultuous waves
> Are heaped, contending ghosts,

one may understand how it is that

> Death is mightier, stronger, and more faithful
> To man than Life.

Lingering there, one may watch the Deaths come down from their cloister, and dance and sing amid the moonlight; one may laugh over the grotesque contortions of skeletons; one may crack jokes upon corruption; one may sit down with phantoms, and drink to the health of Death.

In private intercourse Beddoes was the least morbid of human beings. His mind was like one of those Gothic cathedrals of which he was so fond—mysterious within, and filled with a light at once richer and less real than the light of day; on the outside, firm, and towering, and immediately impressive; and embellished, both inside and out, with grinning gargoyles. His conversation, Kelsall tells us, was full of humour and vitality, and untouched by any trace of egoism or affectation. He loved discussion, plunging into it with fire, and carrying it onward with high dexterity and good-humoured force. His letters are excellent: simple, spirited, spicy, and as original as his verse; flavoured with that vein of rattling open-air humour which had produced his school-boy novel in the style of Fielding. He was a man whom it would have been a rare delight to know. His character, so eminently English, compact of courage, of originality, of imagination, and with something coarse in it as well, puts one in mind of Hamlet: not the melodramatic sentimentalist of the stage; but the real Hamlet, Horatio's Hamlet, who called his father's ghost old truepenny, who forged his uncle's signature, who fought Laertes, and ranted in a grave, and lugged the guts into the neighbour room. His tragedy, like Hamlet's, was the tragedy of an over-powerful will— a will so strong as to recoil upon itself, and fall into indecision. It is easy for a weak man to be decided—there is so much to make him so; but a strong man, who can do anything, sometimes leaves everything undone. Fortunately Beddoes, though he did far less than he might have done, possessed so rich a genius that what he did, though small in quantity, is in quality beyond price. "I might have been, among other things, a good poet," were his last words. "Among other things"! Aye, there's the rub. But, in spite of his own "might have been," a good poet he was. Perhaps for him, after all, there was very little to regret; his life was full of high nobility; and what other way of death would have befitted the poet of death? There is a thought constantly recurring throughout his writings—in his childish as in his most mature work— the thought of the beauty and the supernal happiness of soft and quiet death. He had visions of "rosily dying," of "turning to daisies gently in the grave," of a "pink reclining death," of death coming like a summer cloud over the soul. "Let her deathly life pass into death," says one of his earliest characters, "like music on the night wind." And, in *Death's Jest Book,* Sibylla has the same thoughts:

> O Death! I am thy friend,
> I struggle not with thee, I love thy state:
> Thou canst be sweet and gentle, be so now;
> And let me pass praying away into thee,
> As twilight still does into starry night.

Did his mind, obsessed and overwhelmed by images of death, crave at last for the one thing stranger than all these—the experience of it? It is easy to believe so, and that, ill, wretched, and abandoned by Degen at the miserable Cigogne Hotel, he should seek relief in the gradual dissolution which attends upon loss of blood. And then, when he had recovered, when he was almost happy once again, the old thoughts, perhaps, came crowding back upon him—thoughts of the futility of life, and the supremacy of death and the mystical whirlpool of the unknown, and the long quietude of the grave. In the end, Death had grown to be something more than Death to him—it was, mysteriously and transcendentally, Love as well.

> Death's darts are sometimes Love's. So Nature tells,
> When laughing waters close o'er drowning men;
> When in flowers' honied corners poison dwells;
> When Beauty dies: and the unwearied ken
> Of those who seek a cure for long despair
> Will learn . . .

What learning was it that rewarded him? What ghostly knowledge of eternal love?

> If there are ghosts to raise,
> What shall I call,

Out of hell's murky haze,
    Heaven's blue pall?
—Raise my loved long-lost boy
To lead me to his joy.—
    There are no ghosts to raise;
    Out of death lead no ways;
        Vain is the call.

    —Know'st thou not ghosts to sue?
        No love thou hast.
    Else lie, as I will do,
        And breathe thy last.
So out of Life's fresh crown
Fall like a rose-leaf down.
    Thus are the ghosts to woo;
    Thus are all dreams made true,
        Ever to last!

1922

(*written 1907*)

Robert Lynd

THE LIFE OF SENSATIONS

THERE is nothing that destroys the excitement
of motoring more surely than good roads and careful driving. Luckily in France—at least, in the part of France in
which I have been studying the rainfall during a typical
twentieth-century summer—good roads are few and careful drivers would be warned by the police as obstructors of
the traffic. The main roads are in a good many places
much as they were when Julius Caesar divided Gaul into
three parts. They do not merely contain ruts and hollows
as large as a baby's bath. They are also full of deep pits—
pits so deep that you dare scarcely look over the edge for
fear of feeling giddy. If you did look into one of them,
you would need a telescope to see to the bottom, and
probably you would then descry the tiny figure of a man
who, having fallen in, had been vainly calling for help for
days. If you drive over this kind of road even at thirty
miles an hour, you enjoy all the ups and downs of the
roughest kind of Channel crossing. The very swish of a
wheel through one of the flooded pits produces a wave that
washes right over the rocking car. As the French chauffeur
plunges ahead, his eyes are alight with a fierce excitement,
and he keeps calling to you through the roar and rattle
of the storm: "C'est très dangereux, monsieur—très dangereux." You shout back, "Oui," and hope that, now that

From *The Money Box* by Robert Lynd. Reprinted by permission
of Methuen and Co., Ltd.

he has noticed it, he will slow down a little. But he goes
swiftly ahead, shouting things about "les grands trous"
and "les bosses" and, as the car is swung sideways by one
of them, excitedly screams: "Voilà," and puts on the
accelerator. He goes on repeating that these are "très mauvaises routes" and shouting "très dangereux" in a crescendo till you begin to see the words in capital letters.
You flash past a signpost warning you that a crossing is
coming. The sign looks horribly like the crossbones in a
letter threatening death. Again you hope that he has
noticed, but you don't know the French for "crossroads"
and so cannot ask him. He puts on speed in the evident
determination not to let any car coming in a sideways
direction pass the crossing before him. You rise a little in
your seat to try to see over the hedges that hide the side-
roads from your view. You prick your ears for the sound
of approaching wheels or the honk of a horn. You try to
make up your mind whether in the event of a collision the
car that is going faster is the one that is likely to do the
more damage or to suffer it. To do it, you hope. You are
now past the crossing in safety, and you sink back in your
seat in a luxury of reaction. You begin to take an interest
in the needle of the speedometer which swings and sways
between 70 and 80. It certainly seems very fast, and, as you
turn the kilometres into miles in your head, you realize
that it is even faster than you feared. You wish the chauffeur would not be quite so reckless. Suppose a tyre should
burst. As you fly past, an elderly peasant skips out of the
way and falls back against a ditch, waving a stick and
cursing. You agree with the elderly peasant. Just then,
miles ahead of you along the sand-coloured road, you see
a speck no bigger than a midge. The chauffeur sees it too,
and puts on the accelerator. Gradually, it becomes about
the size of a fly. The chauffeur becomes excited and puts
on the accelerator again. You dash forward, at such a pace
that you scarcely know whether you are passing dry land
or sea, and the speck in the distance increases to the large-

ness of a man's hand. You now know that it is another
motor-car and that you are chasing it. You begin somehow
to long to overtake it. The motor-car ahead of you must
be going at about sixty miles an hour. You wonder
whether your own man couldn't do seventy. Joy, you are
catching up. The car takes a flying leap into the air, and
you do not know for a moment whether it will fall on its
feet or its side or upside down. "Un grand trou," shouts
the chauffeur when you have reached. the earth again.
"Très dangereux," you shout back with enthusiasm,
holding on your hat. "Très dangereux," he replies in the
same spirit, accelerating the accelerator. "Chassez," you
shout to him encouragingly. "Oui, monsieur," he replies,
kicking something to see if he can make the car go faster.
Happily, he can, and the other car becomes larger and
larger as the road becomes hilly, and you pursue it, making
a noise like a fleet of battleplanes shaving the roofs of a
town. It disappears round a curve and over the crest of a
hill. You follow, and perceive it flying down the hill at a
pace that has never yet been achieved outside the pages of
fiction. You give chase, the four wheels off the ground,
reaching the bottom of the hill in a whirl of resolve
either to overtake the enemy or to perish in the attempt,
and in another kilometre you are on its heels, the stones
flying against your mud-guards as though it were re-
cording the beatings of an exhausted heart. Neck and
neck, you pass a crossroad together with its sign of men's
bones. And, after that, with another access of speed, you
honk your horn victoriously, and sweep past, like a Rolls-
Royce overtaking a taxi-cab. Your car seems just to kiss
the mudguard of the other as it flies past. "Très dangereux," you call out breathlessly. "Très dangereux," the
chauffeur agrees with a happy smile. "Très mauvaises
routes," you say to him ecstatically. "Oui, oui, très mauvaises routes," he replies, and puts on the accelerator.
"Des grands trous," you shout. "Voilà," he cries, as the
car, having just escaped from one, rears and bucks.

But, alas, it is impossible in English prose to convey the excitement of motoring in France. It is at once extraordinarily terrifying and extraordinarily pleasant. You keep thinking "If I live through this, it will be great fun." But you never feel quite certain that you will live through it. And, when you come to one of those steep, narrow, corkscrew roads, that go downhill for miles and miles—roads that are marked with a "Z" on the signposts—you are prepared for the worst at every turn of the road. You also wish that the chauffeur did not think it necessary to take both hands off the wheel and gesticulate every time he speaks. You say to him, "Beaucoup de tournes—très brusques." Immediately, he is waving both hands in the air to express his opinion of the turns, and only takes the wheel again in time to twist round the next bend. "Très dangereux," you cry to him, when your heart has recovered from its dropped beat. He again takes both hands from the wheel, waves them above his head, repeating, "Très—très dangereux!" and seizes the wheel just in time to duck under the bow of a suddenly-appearing charabanc. In the end you decide that it is safer not to address him at all, and you do not until he goes bumping over a railway crossing after a sharp turn, while three women in black fly screaming from under the wheels. The chauffeur is indignant, and calls out: "Je ne l'ai pas vu." You call back, "Très dangereux." "Très dangereux," he yells frantically, and speeds on towards the next crossroads. Luckily, there are comparatively few people who use motor-cars in France, and most of the crossroads are bare of hedges, so that one has a good chance of seeing an approaching vehicle before the collision has occurred. Still, so far as I could see, every motorist takes it for granted that the other motorist will take all the steps necessary to avoid the collision. Our chauffeur certainly drove as though there were not another vehicle on the roads of France, and, if we had not an accident, it was only because there was nothing to run into at the really dangerous places. The worst of it was that the chauffeur kept giving me statistics of the various accidents that had taken place at various "dangereux" corners and that my French is so bad that I could not be sure whether five people were killed at such and such a spot every day or only every year. I shall really have to learn French before I risk another motor-ride along the French roads. Disciples of M. Coué will realize how unnerving it is to carry on a prolonged conversation consisting of little more than a repetition of the words, "Très dangereux."

But how safe it felt to be back at dinner in the hotel! How delicious the soup tasted! How mellow the vin ordinaire! After dinner, somebody proposed to tell fortunes by cards, but I firmly refused to be led back out of my sense of sweet security into a life of sensations with aces of spades and dark women casting a cloud over the future. "Then what about planchette?" I was asked. I shrink from dealings with spirits, but I hate being a spoil-sport, so consented, and in a few minutes an alphabet had been placed in a ring round the table and we were all pressing a finger lightly on an inverted wine glass in the centre. The glass began to stir uneasily, and, on being spoken to and asked who it was, it slowly spelt out the name, "Clemence Dane." It said that it wanted to talk about books, and, on being asked what it thought of Mr. Forster's "Passage to India," replied: "Good, but have not read it." It then became frivolous, and, to every question that was addressed to it, replied with the one word, "Cabbage." If you asked its opinion of anybody, it immediately spelt out either "Cabbage" or "A bad cabbage," as though it were determined on mocking us. As all present had given their words of honour not to push or pull the glass, it may be assumed that none of them was deliberately trifling, but the nonsense became so monotonous in the end that we bade the spirit farewell and called up another in its stead. We asked the new spirit who it was, and it replied: "A fay." We asked it what it wished to talk to us about, and to our horror the glass immediately spelt out the words, "A bad cabbage." One lady went pale and said: "This may be a warning." Another declared that cabbage was a vegetable never served at the hotel, and that the whole thing was absurd. We pursued our investigations, however, and were told that the cabbage was to appear during dinner on the following evening, and that none of us must on any account touch it. Being of a humane disposition, we asked: "But what about the other people in the hotel? Won't they be in danger, too?" The glass spelt "yes." "And, if a cabbage appears, must we tell them not to eat it?" The glass spelt: "You must warn." "But surely," we protested, "Madame P."—the hotel-keeper's wife—"will be very much annoyed with us?" The glass replied: "You must vex." It is all very well to mock at human credulity, but I am convinced that every one of us was apprehensive during all that night and all the next day lest a cabbage should appear at the evening meal, and one of us should have to rise and denounce it in public. I certainly was feeling ill at ease during the first two courses of the dinner, though I knew very well that, if a cabbage did appear, the task of denouncing it would be deputed to a woman. Then, as the vegetables were being brought in, a girl who had a good view of the door suddenly cried: "Look, it *is* cabbage after all." Everyone at the table started and stared at everybody else with a wild surmise, till someone had the courage to look round and in a moment uttered a cry of joy: "No, it's only runner beans." Once again, as during the motor-ride, we enjoyed the blessed relief of those who have escaped disaster by the skin of their teeth. We called for a *vieille cure,* and another one, that evening with a good conscience. And after that we went to another room and had a lone and interesting conversation with the spirit of Alcibiades.

1925

C. E. Montague

MATTHEW ARNOLD

WALKING with an elder brother in the streets of Oxford in my youth, I was struck by the looks of a tall oldish man with the shapeliest features, the stoop of a scholarly Jove, and an air of the most distinguished melancholy. "That's Matthew Arnold," my brother said when we had passed him. My heart had already told me that it was someone illustrious.

It was wet at the time; I could not kneel down on the Merton Street cobbles. Still, I turned round at the name and adored the Olympian back with all my eyes till it vanished round the corner of Oriel. For no italics, no capitals, not all the massed resources of typographical emphasis could tell you the fervour with which we swore by Arnold in those remote 'eighties, unless we were such as swore by the rival and comparatively sulphurous godhead of Swinburne. Was it not Arnold who in one famous and beautiful sentence of prose had doubled, to our sense, the beauty of our own Oxford, "whispering from her towers the last enchantments of the Middle Age"? And was it not he who had taught us the delicate fascination of doubt and the tremors, the thrills, the delicious venturings and flutterings of spiritual trouble?

Remember, Arnold flourished at a time when people of

From *A Writer's Notes on his Trade* by C. E. Montague. Reprinted by permission of Chatto and Windus.

education had pretty well lived down the original shock and distress that were caused by the first serious work of scholars on the Bible. The process, as someone had called it, of robbing millions of pious souls of their hope of eternal damnation had already entered on its second stage. It had almost ceased to be seismic or cyclonic. It was becoming more tranquilly detergent, erosive or decompository. And now, as promoted by Arnold, it had a sensuous beauty that charmed the young mind. Lit with the softened light of an imagination more tender and brooding than fiery, lustrous with the burnished older scholarship, twinkling with quiet ironies that seemed to take you ever so flatteringly into the confidence of a spirit august beyond words, the scepticism of Arnold had beautiful manners and entrancing tones. We are told that Ophelia could turn "Hell itself" to "favour and to prettiness." Arnold went one better and extracted those delights from the tragic decline of that institution.

The late George Russell, the last of great Whig wits, and himself a devoted High Churchman, told a friend that "Arnold's wish to believe, coupled with his inability to do so, was one of the most pathetic things I have ever known." The good Russell need not have grieved. Many men and women derive enjoyment from ill-health; but to the proper temperament a congenial complaint in the body is, as a source of agreeable emotions, nothing to a gentle malady of the soul. "Let us sit upon the ground," says the most human Richard the Second of Shakespeare, "and tell sad stories of the death of kings." Let us sit, says Matthew Arnold to himself, upon the window-seat of our hotel at Dover, and tell sad stories of the death of faith. And so he does, and writes the lovely lines of "Dover Beach":

> Listen! you hear the grating roar
> Of pebbles which the waves draw back, and fling,

At their return, up the high strand,
Begin, and cease, and then again begin,
With tremulous cadence slow, and bring
The eternal note of sadness in. . . .

The sea of faith
Was once, too, at the full, and round earth's shore
Lay like the folds of a bright girdle furl'd.
But now I only hear
Its melancholy, long, withdrawing roar.

And he enjoys himself immensely, as anybody would
who was writing such good lines. And if anything had interrupted him while doing it, even the first trump of a
new and completely reassuring revelation, he would have
murmured, like Richard, "Beshrew thee, . . . which didst
lead me forth From that sweet way I was in to despair."
For no one is unhappy in the act of writing delightful
things. Nature makes no mistake about that. She wants
to have everything good and takes care that man, at any
rate, shall have more pleasure than pain in carrying out
this admirable purpose.

A writer will often tell you that this or that meritori-
ous production of his has been written in agony. A classical case is Tennyson's saying in "In Memoriam" that
the composing of it was a mere

                              mechanic exercise,
            Like dull narcotics, numbing pain.

Don't believe him. Nothing so good as the good parts
of "In Memoriam" was ever done like that. To say that
it was is like Boswell's saying that he would suffer vexation if he were in Parliament and saw things going wrong.
"That's cant, sir," said Johnson. "Clear your *mind* of
cant. You may *talk* as other people do: you may say to a
man, 'Sir, I am your most humble servant.' You are *not*
his most humble servant. You may say, 'These are bad

times; it is a melancholy thing to be reserved to such times.' You don't mind the times. You tell a man 'I am sorry you had such bad weather the last day of your journey, and were so much wet.' You don't care sixpence whether he is wet or dry. You may *talk* in this manner; it is a mode of talking in society: but don't *think* foolishly." In Tennyson's and Arnold's age, and in the company they kept, there was a mode of talking as if artists of every sort ought to go about studded with visible and audible tokens that their heart was in their work and that every emotion to which they offered an expression was genuinely gnawing at their souls. In this way poor Irving, the great tragic actor, had to go about, all his life, with a manner and look that almost amounted to a suit of sables; Tennyson had to be always the mourner for Hallam, Browning the optimist, virilist sage, and Arnold the heartbroken outcast from the snug household of faith, wearying in spiritual wastes of sand and thorns. They all kept it up very well, and none better than Arnold. But it must have been, at bottom, just what Johnson called a mode of talking. When any one of them was working at his craft, at the top of his form, he must have been in ecstasy, as every other artist is, as Fra Angelico was when he painted a picture of Heaven and as Orcagna was when he painted a picture of Hell.

It was this ecstasy, too, and not merely certain charges of new theological explosives, made in Germany, that Arnold, in prose and in verse, could communicate to our minds. That was how he gave us medicines, as Falstaff says, to make us love him. Under his winning conductorship there was intellectual luxury to be got out of tottering creeds and melting rigidities. Walter Pater, though his mind was travelling at the time in the direction opposite to Arnold's, had lately ventured to diagnose an exquisite fascination in states of decay—a faint and fine aroma as of immemorial oak panelling and fading tapestries. Arnold

taught our adolescent senses to snuff up some such delectable fragrance among the fragments of the orthodoxy
which he shattered for us with a grace and courtesy so
remarkable. It is important, says Bacon, to have in your
garden some plants of the sort that smell sweetest when
trodden upon; Arnold filled our garden with a scent of
nice crushed Fundamentalism in an age when that re-
doubtable word was yet unborn.

There was another suave chain that bound us to Arnold.
I mention it with some diffidence in a much-altered world.
We were notably serious, and Arnold's seriousness kept
us in countenance. You may say there are always some
serious young men. Yes, there are, even now. Some men
are born to be serious, others achieve it, and others have it
thrust upon them by economic and other forces. But seriousness was "the done thing" at the English universities
in the 'eighties. It was the mode of the day. Carlyle had
sown the seed; Browning had watered it; Ruskin had
helped to give it increase. T. H. Green was dominating
Oxford with a philosophy that escorted you straight to
the life of good works and honest endeavour. Arnold
Toynbee was founding a whole school of new social
service. Rossetti, Watts, Burne-Jones, diverse in other
ways, seemed to be wholly at one on the point that the
cult of beauty was a most serious, if not an anxious and
mournful affair. So seriousness became the only wear. If
you were of the kind that conforms, you soon decided
that life was real, life was earnest, you took horse to hunt
the Beautiful and Good with your young friends—just as
persons of similar temperament are deciding today, with
the Jolly Beggars of Burns, that "life is all a variorum: we
regard not how it goes." Even the reprobated disciples of
Swinburne practised their loyal little dissipations with
some gravity. So Arnold was the very man for us—
Arnold, with his "stream of tendency making for right-
eousness"; Arnold, who called all the world's poets up

to be judged by their measure of "excellent seriousness"
and ordered off the muse of Burns himself to the house of
correction because of her shortage of this solid quality.

2

I never saw Arnold again. He died a year or two after.
And presently I had to turn to and work—a novel experience—and found that work was a heavenly game and that
everything was remarkably well with the world, so far
as it dealt with me, though some of its other arrangements
seemed to admit of improvement. In this Elysian condition I somehow lost the habit of reading my Arnold and
gazing with a luscious melancholy at

> this strange disease of modern life,
> With its sick hurry, its divided aims,
> Its heads o'ertaxed, its palsied hearts.

I could not tell why. I could only suppose that, as Bene-
dick said of his failure of relish for bachelorhood, a man
loves the meat in his youth, that he cannot endure in his
age. But after a time I knew better, or thought so. For
something was said which, as soon as I read it, I felt to be
just the truth that I had been missing.

It was said by William Watson, the poet. Arnold had
been buried close to the Thames, and Watson was praising the choice of that bland and composed country-side
for the site of the grave in preference to the stern Cumber-
land hills, which the dead had loved too.

> 'Tis fittest thus! for though with skill
> He sang of beck and tarn and ghyll,
> The deep, authentic mountain-thrill
>   Ne'er shook his page.
> Somewhat of worldling mingled still
>   With bard and sage.

Yes, I said to myself; that was it. And perhaps it was just what had most charmed one's uncritical youth. For youth itself is apt to be worldly, unsure of its own presentableness, timid lest it be out of the swim and remote from the centre, wherever the centre may be. And Arnold had never failed, in one's youth, to give one that peace which the world *can* give—the restful sense of snuggling up close to a centre, of being taken right into a perfectly irreproachable "set." Oh of course, a most unmaterialist set; a set cultured up to the nines; a set as grandly free from mere gross common snobbishness as it had been from the raucous uncouthness of any poor "Philistines"— "outside our happy ground." But always a true set, elatingly exclusive, heart-warmingly superior. You felt, while you read, as if the right people had taken you up. In your glee at his majestic chaffing of spiritual boors and intellectual guys, of the young lions of popular journalism and the grim ways of Black Countries and of crude reformers, you melted agreeably into a set which you felt to be supremely eligible. Of course you were no common intellectual climber, but still you had sensations distinctly allied to those of Thackeray and his Arthur Pendennis on coming to town and finding themselves securely elected to Brooks or to the Megatherium Club. You too were enormously "in it."

"Why not?" you may very well ask. "Has not the art of every considerable writer a core to be reached? And must not the joint quest of this heart of the rose become a conscious fellowship of souls in some sense or other elect? And what else is a set?"

And yet there is something more in it. I fancy it arises from a certain special tinting of Arnold's own consciousness while he wrote—a delicate suffusion of his genius with charity towards what is dominant in the polite lettered caste, the caste which has mastered the secret of making the things of the mind—a favourite phrase of its own—

live at peace with what Burke calls the pomps and plausibilities of this world.

"But," you may object again, "was not Arnold the tireless critic of his country and his age, the lifelong arraigner of British limitedness and complacency, the crier of woe upon the darling mental vices of the principalities and powers of his world?"

Yes, he was quite a sincere and quite a good-sized Isaiah. And yet he wore the prophet's robe with a difference. He never let it look outlandish, as so many prophets have done, in the extravagance of their absorption in the primary business of saving mankind. Arnold's camel-hair raiment was always extremely well cut and he ate his locusts and wild honey with conspicuous refinement. It seems to have been necessary that Moses should kill an Egyptian before he could lead Israel out of Egypt with adequate authority. But Arnold would never have killed an Egyptian—nor even a Philistine. He would have dined out with all the best people in Egypt or Philistia, appraised their flesh-pots with intelligence and delighted them with his vivacious conversation. As the adroit William Penn described—and possibly invented—by Macaulay found means to stand well at the court of the persecuting James the Second, so did Arnold keep in with the world he chid. It liked entertaining him and he must have given, in these polite exchanges, as good as he got, for he could be charming.

3

Long after I had first read that revelatory stanza of Sir William Watson's, Arnold's letters were published. And they, too, threw a light. For I found an unexpected resemblance between their effect on my mind and the effect of the extremely different letters of Dickens. You may remember the all but religious ecstasy that fired the pen of Dickens whenever he touched upon the remarkable

satisfactoriness of the box-office receipts at his lectures. We
all like money, unless we are fools, but greater love hath
no man for money than glowed in those artless cries of the
great heart of Dickens. In some of these letters of Arnold's,
I seemed to feel glowing—not indeed that ingenuous gusto
of Dickens, but something distantly akin to it—a pure
white gem-like flame of delight in knowing all that was
nicest in the great world of his days. No arrant tuft-hunt-
ing, of course; no downright stalking of lions, as lions;
only something remotely related thereto, as the practice
of Shakespeare's Old Gobbo was to actual rapine—"indeed,
my father did something smack, something grow to, he
had a kind of taste." Arnold was always a rather poor man,
as things went at that time in England, though among
French civil servants and poets he would have counted as
rich. And "depend upon it, my boy," as Major Pendennis said to his nephew, "for a poor man there is nothing
like having good acquaintances." Like many other men of
high intellectual gifts, Arnold was ballasted with a just
proportion of Major Pendennis's practical wisdom.

No shame to him, either. At any rate, he that has in
him no grain of the staple alloys of this world, let him
throw the first stone, for I am not throwing. I touch on the
matter only by way of exploring the origin of a just per-
ceptible flatness afflicting at times the fine bell-like voice
which was engaged in crying "Woe!" here and "Woe!"
there so engagingly and so often. People, especially very
young ones, warn us today to keep out of the error of
thinking that a man's life and his art have much to do
with each other. And yet—so obstinate is nature, so careless of current critical fashions—there does somehow creep
into R. L. Stevenson's elegant family prayers and handsome harangues on practice and on morals a very slight
queerness of *timbre*. It may not amount to a positive
crack in the soul-animating trumpet. It only goes far
enough to commute the last thrill, the supreme dose of

awe in our minds, for a sup of savoursome amusement as we think what manner of man this moralist was in his life—how equally prone with us all to walk in the ways of his heart and in the sight of his eyes. Those who knew Thackeray in the flesh had consumed with the same piquant sauce the full meals of domestic virtue served up in his novels. And even those who had not known him, but still were sensitive readers, had been either ticked or put off, according to their several natures, by a certain still, small falsity of intonation that infests his celebrated commination services against the pomps and vanities of the great world. For the waters of moral elevation refuse, as flatly as do other waters, to rise higher than their source. No Stevenson can, by any elocutionary skill whatever, produce the authentic thunders of a Knox. And Arnold, too, had his appointed or acquired limits. He could never be tremendous. If he tried, you felt something was wrong, though you might not be able to say what it was till you read, long afterwards, one of his letters and thought to yourself that his were not the social valuations of the major prophets.

4

Within these limits set, perhaps, by a natural vein of timidity and by the best English upperclass education, what power he had! What beauty he commanded! And, in the main, how thoroughly he was on the right side! It is easy work to poke fun at his habit of crying up "sweetness and light"; but, after all, is there much to be said, on Europe's post-war experience, for the alternative cult of sourness and gloom? And if Arnold were not a distinguished Victorian, but a young author just rising above the horizon, what a refreshing spice of originality we should find in his frank preoccupation with matters of conduct and in his unconventional preference for conduct that is reputable.

Our literary criticism now is passing through a lively little epidemic of inverted priggishness. In fiction the rather lecherous hero, the gallant young fellow who forges a cheque, the charming woman with several young children who commits adultery for some tenuous reason, are very much in the mode. And the critic who wants to be in the mode lays it down that on no excuse is an imaginative author to betray a warmer liking for straight livers than for scrubs or polecats. Now, "this sort of thing," as the attitudinising critic and poet says in the comic opera, "takes a deal of training." It is like pirouetting on tiptoe. It is not natural to man. The natural man quite simply and frankly prefers those bus-conductors who do not steal people's change to those who do. He has an unreasoned general liking for monogamic women and for the man who can keep a hold on himself. Scold him as you may, he feels an unaffectedly greater enjoyment in the company of people whom nobody would want to blackball at a club. He finds such company more interesting. When he tries to acquiesce in the fashionable theory that the words "good" and "bad," in the moral sense, are obsolete solecisms, he feels as if he were trying on an extremely tight boot. What a thrill he would get from any unconventional pioneer who let fashion go hang and said that conduct was three-fourths of life, that most of us spend the greater part of our time in thinking out what we ought to do in this or that case, and that literature is only losing the way and going off to dawdle in blind alleys when it ceases to take count of the fact! Let him come to Arnold with a fresh mind, and that thrill will be his.

His, too, will be a liberal measure of poetry's most characteristic delight. What the great genius of Scott did for the Lowlands of his country, and that of Hardy for Wessex, that Arnold did, as De Wint did it in paint, for the southern English landscape of meadow, river, down and beach, with its contained and friendly amenity and the mild melancholy that becomes an heirloom of a countryside long settled and intensely humanised. His poems not only give this landscape reality; they give it a share of the trans-figured, enchanted reality attained by the river gardens of Bagdad when a boy first sees them in the *Arabian Nights*. We are all heirs to the loveliness of the visible world, but only by process of art can we be inducted into possession of this large estate. Some authentic poet or artist has to intervene and give the property its rights and empower it to attain perfection in our sight. Whatever his limitations, Arnold was poet enough to do that to the country he knew. From the Cotswolds to Dover, England shines with an increase of beauty that is of his giving.

1928

Rebecca West

TRIBUTE TO SOME
MINOR ARTISTS

THIS summer I am living on the French Riviera, which does not mean what you might think it must. One alights at a station at which only the slowest trains ever stop, and walks through a little village which has the disorder of a studio, whose inhabitants move about with the slouching and dishevelled aspect of artists at work, and have a right to look so, since they are practising an art in merely living; for they eat better meals than equivalent people anywhere else in the world, they sleep in softer beds with better linen, they design their days like pictures, balancing as in a skilful composition the human need for leisure against the human power and necessity to pay for leisure by work. Leaving behind its rubbish heaps that are like the twisted paint-tubes by the easel, one takes a coast road which winds among rocks that are rose-red, and red with the discretion of the rose, so that they do not quarrel with the blue sea at their base any more than the rose quarrels with the green leaf lower on the stem. Landwards there are hills, low but emphatic as mountains in form, covered with healthy growths which under grey northern skies would be a patchwork of warm colour, but is like pale tweed under this intense white light, which beats down colour as if it were conscious that itself is a syn-

From *The Strange Necessity* by Rebecca West. Reprinted by permission of A. D. Peters, Literary Agent.

thesis of all colours and is proud of it. Here and there are pinewoods, growing more sparsely than they do in Germany and in Scotland, as if this most rationalist of countries was going to stand no nonsense of the Erl-King or the Lady of the Lake type. And here and there are tiered and galleried quarries of porphyry, grey-blue like old-fashioned blotting-paper.

Presently one comes on a fold in the countryside where the land does not stand up in forms immutable and un-cultivated as cast-iron mouldings, where it assumes the softness of a cloak dropped from the shoulders. Here the water, such as there is here in the south in summer, seeps down from the hard hills. Here it is possible to grow trees, to have a garden. The road begins to run between villas. Over the first wall on the landward side looks an oleander, bending forth in the pose of a wife who has run to the end of the garden to see if her dear husband is nearing home; but the quality of its bright pink handsomeness is such that one is surprised by its domesticity, imagines a prelude to it of a different sort, and finds oneself remark-ing with a sage air that marriages of that kind often turn out well enough. There is a prodigious gate in this wall, a complication of trelliswork which must have been made by a man who thought a cutlet-frill was beautiful; but pushing it back one finds oneself under the strong, sober guardianship of palm-trees. Six stand on either side of the path. By night the trunks of them look like the naked bodies of Nubian slaves.

By day they look like armoured pillars in some Eastern palace; an arrow might fly through the interstices between the bronze-coloured plates, and some brown agility step forth from a sliding panel to work some subtle mutilation on the kill. Their long sharp-edged leaves remind one of swords, of fans; they imply a land too hot for man to live in unless he can make other people wait on him, where for that favourable position there is a ding-dong battle waged with weapons twice the height of a man and tortures leading the imagination of man twice as far as it is wise to go, where one may train great black slaves to noiseless waiting on one's wants by any means, by scaring them with wounds and setting red ants to people those wounds, but where they learn their lesson so well that at the last they come quite noiselessly between one and the door into the secret passage which one had had dug against the risk of overthrowal.

I never open that gate and step into the blackness which they maintain beneath them like a trust, letting through only slivers of sunlight or moonlight shaped like scimitars and glittering like metal, because of the profundity of the surrounding shadow, without being glad that they made the initial error which makes me not need to fear them, at the dawn of creation when all life had to choose whether to be animal and mobile or vegetable and immobile. There was some trouble saved us then by certain renunciations. If the synthesis of forces which is the red rose had chosen to be animal, if it had pushed its way along the strains into humanity, to what powerful a compulsion of love would our poor hearts have been exposed! And if the synthesis of forces which is the palm-tree had expressed itself in terms of the animal, had it stayed beast there would have been so much of the wild less easily conquerable, had it become man, there would have been a considerable increase of occasions when the weak found argument useless. It would not have qualified itself by melting into the common flood of humanity. The rose would have done that, one is certain; there would have been those in whom the strain was nearly pure, whose lives would have consisted of romances exquisite and numerous as petals, and as easily detachable from the parent stem; but there would also have been those not beautiful, not gifted, but fortunate in their hearts, in whom a slight trace of it had the wistful but powerful fragrance of the last drop in the scent-bottle.

But the palm-soul would have kept itself apart, would have made itself a separate people, a race. Followers of the Prophet, without a doubt. Islam might not have been so politically impotent, so merely a rattling of lances across the map, had this choice been made.

Behind them one sees, as one walks up to the house, the dusty shadow, pierced only by lean tree-trunks, which is a southern garden. These palm-mercenaries charge for the shade they cast by drinking the earth dry for yards around, so that there can be no flowers or grass. But these are not wanted here. One requires flowers in northern climates because one wants to set colour against the prevalent greyness, green grass to contrast with neutral mould, but here darkness alone can balance the prevalent light, and since the characteristic of the soil in these parts is that it is broken by heat into gritty particles, the impalpability of shadow is the most pleasing contrast to it. The aridity is quite by design. There is indeed nothing at all accidental about this place. There are no palm-trees, there is a clearing which permits the fullest pouring of sunshine down on the preposterous flight of concrete steps which rises from the avenue to the house, taking forms which no steps can lawfully assume, exhibiting bevelled edges which belong properly only to dressing-table sets and whirls inappropriate to any substance except whipped cream.

That staircase is not only illuminated, it is illuminating. For immediately on seeing it one perceives in that un-numbered dimension which is the imagination the figure of the architect who designed it and who chose the incredible gate. So solid does it appear that almost it obscures some of the trails of bougainvillea that surround the glass doors with snippets of pale magenta paper: a tall and slender personage carrying himself with a deliberate stoop because the early nineteenth century Romantics' convention of a connection between phthisis and the arts has never been repudiated in provincial France, wearing a moustache which trails like a delicate fern, a flowing tie which says he is an artist, a wildness of the pupil of the eye which says the same thing as the tie, and is as purely an arranged external device. There is just a suggestion of repressed but dominant horse-sense about him—say, in the retracted but abundant paunch which shows that he loves good food—to distinguish him from the handsome shabby goose who recites his lame verses in the cafés; there is just that to account for his being employed as an architect, to account for his building fantastic and comfortable houses.

According to the laws of this most mysterious dimension, one perceives at one and the same time this solid figure which is not there, and the main events of his fatuous but not contemptible life. He discovered himself an artist because of his mother's and grandmother's fond exclamations on his sensitivity. He studied his art in the nineties and was immensely excited by *l'Art Nouveau,* that curious movement towards distortion of form which tried to give all objects of common use from house down to hairpins aspects of the totally irrelevant, piercing a turret with gaping ellipses like the mouths of marine animals, giving a staircase a balustrade as strange as the skeleton of a dinosaur, going down to the sea to find decorations for objects peculiarly of the land, back to the past to find shapes for objects peculiarly of the present. He and his wife ventured on the long journey to Paris which at that time must have lasted the full twenty-four hours for those who could not afford seats in the *rapide,* because they wanted to see the Exposition of 1900. When the train was sliding into the Gare de Lyons he sharply bade his wife wipe her face with her handkerchief, which in those days was the only way a good woman could deal with shininess of the skin, since powder was still an unholy thing. And he was a little forgetful of her, walked sometimes rather too fast for her short step, as he moved dazed and speechless with emotion about this extraordinary Exposition, which in its exhibits and the buildings that housed them must have been like a fantasy created by the gentleman whose genius for the vigorous use of inappropriate material led him, in the Victorian comic song, to cut his throat with a lump of cheese. He turned his head away from her when in the mornings he lay in bed and day-dreamed of what might have happened if his talent had not been hampered by obscure parentage and lack of fortune and an early marriage, of how he might have worn a red ribbon in his button-hole and been kissed on both cheeks by great men with immense beards before a public that rose in applauding tiers to the furthest back seat conceivable by even such a mind when dreaming of an applauding public, of how duchesses bearing a close personal resemblance to greyhounds would have begged him to design houses for them, and more than that.

But quite often he was very glad that his wife was with him, particularly when they went into restaurants, and people seemed to be looking at his suit, which was being reflected in far too many mirrors at once. It was misery to be a provincial. But after all it was in the provinces that the true distinction of France was to be found. She agreed with him about that when he woke her about two in the morning to tell her; she consented to go home a day earlier than they had intended, although they had never had that afternoon he had promised her of just sitting in the Bois and watching the people drive by. And she stood by him always in the succeeding years when with the air of being a martyr to his art he engaged in ceaseless struggles with such of his clients as were gifted with some sense of the decorum of form and wanted things to look as if they were used for the purposes for which in fact they are. He was not without recognition of her goodness. If anything troubles him while he lies dying, which will happen in about ten years from now, after he has had a

marvellous time being a beautiful old man and a genius
who was too elevated to be accepted by his age, it will be
that he was not thinking entirely of his wife when he
designed the bedrooms of this villa where when one
wakens one sees the tossing of green branches in the
Empire mirrors over the mantelpieces, the high balconies
where one drinks the morning coffee with the mimosa
shaking fragrance at one with the golden feather-dusters
of its bloom. The commissioning client in this case was a
well-known playwright, and while designing it the architect had been much visited by dreams inspired by the
classic view of the playwright's opportunities and privileges, of wasp-waisted tragediennes slowly closing immense ostrich fans and relaxing into a slow-motion
surrender, of comediennes approaching the same considerations in a blither spirit, of taking the low road where
the tragediennes take the high road and getting to heaven
before them. This will probably have been his only in-
fidelity.

Each of these romantically conceived bedrooms has its
romantically conceived balcony; and there each of us lives
till lunch-time. At eight o'clock in the morning one crawls
out from under the white veil of the mosquito netting, on
which infatuated flying beetles have hung all night; one
puts on a dressing-gown and slippers and goes on to the
balcony for one's coffee. There is never enough milk with
it. That, oddly enough, is because the cook's father was
a stone-mason. He came from Carrara to work in the
porphyry quarries here and was killed a few days after his
arrival. Jasmine, who was then four years old, had to go
with her mother begging from door to door in a country
where doors open not too easily to either aliens or beggars
and hardly at all to those who combine these characters.
The consequence is that of the foods with which she was
acquainted at this time she is more than parsimonious.
Waste of them is associated in her mind with such calami-

ties that an enduring fear has been established. I have to
be firm to get a saucer of milk for the cat, she short-rations
us on bread, on macaroni, on cabbage. But I can have all
the langoustes I care to pay for, profusions of red mullet,
of chicken, of caviare, of Montrachet and Mersault of the
best years. Her fear has another grotesque and piteous
effect on my household economy, for when there are only
the five of us who live here at a meal there is ample of
the permitted food provided, but when there are guests
I have to go into the kitchen to make sure there is enough.
In those early days when the crust had to be shared it was
terrible, terrible. When I am ordering the meal her mouth
smiles widely, showing teeth that seem white as almonds
in her brown face; voluptuously because she is imagining
the taste of the food she is going to cook; gaily because
she likes the excitement of new people coming, of going
out into the lane and looking at the make of their auto-
mobiles and calculating their cost, peering round the
corner of the door at the women's dresses and enjoying
the pleasures of just judgment; proudly because she knows
the end of it will be deserved praise for her. But her hot,
black, brave eyes pucker up as if she were frightened.

Over this little matter of milk for the morning coffee
she has her way, for nobody complains, because of the
sense of well-being we have on these high shelves. Here
the particular dead rat which this puppy-like architect
brings in in his mouth, expecting to be patted and called
a good dog, is Pompeian classicism. There are white and
terra-cotta stucco pillars, and stone seats, to sit on which
one should wear a toga and must have a cushion, and balus-
trades of wrought iron, on which there climbs wisteria.
That, however, is not so pleasing, since at this late season
of the year it too powerfully suggests the standard design
on which is laid down the life of the woman artist. In the
spring it gave all its energy to the making of as much
blossom as the trunk would carry, pendants of pale mauve

flowers which look like an assemblage of butterflies as if
they had been attracted by their fragrance instead of creating it, lovely, abundant, narcissistic. As the year drew on
the flowers fell and it began to make leaves instead, the
leaves which are the real business of trees. Now there are
enough of these, they run everywhere, the extended growth
of the plant is guaranteed, and as if it felt it again had
leisure it puts out a second crop of flowers. They are a
deeper and more beautiful purple, they have as exquisite
and less volatile a scent; but half the buds never open,
they are as different in texture from the early blossom as
potpourri is from rose-leaves. There is above all an air
of effort, for which no enrichment of quality could ever
compensate. One thinks of the later work of Alice Meynell
in its contrast to the first poems of her youth. But one
does not see so much of the wisteria, one sets one's knees
against it as one leans over the balustrade during the
contemplative space after breakfast and before work, which
here is prolonged to the furthest limits of conscience, and
looks down on this garden that we keep entirely to ourselves, that we do not share with strangers any more than
Orientals do, who lock their pleasances in the central
courtyards of their homes.

For this garden which below seemed arid and to grow
no crop but shadow, has its parterres and its verdancies as
much as any garden, but on a different plane. It wears
them not on its soil, but in its upper air. Here as down
below the palm-trees are masters. Before all else one sees
the orange date-clusters at the base of the hard-edged
leaves; it might be that dark arms ringed with bracelets
of red gold, sign of a tribe, raise their swords with hilts
touching, sign of an oath. Round them and in among them
are the mimosas, that are in all ways delicate, that have
fluttering leaves like long fingers of narrow hands on little wrists explaining some fine meaning, that have small,
trembling, sunshine-coloured flowers that look as if they

would melt in the mouth if one should eat them, that shake with the bobbing movement which the dancing girl makes from the waist when her male partner lifts her high in the air. When the wind blows, and the palm-trees brandish themselves, and the mimosas dip and rise, it is as when the Negroes and the queens dance together in the ballet of Scheherazade. There are dark bushes set here and there to make one think of rest. There are acacias, a graceful species amusingly devitalized by sentimentality, this kind drooping its leaves with the grace of a young widow bowed in controllable grief, this one obscuring them with a smooth silver as of placid tears. They please, like the minor French novelists of the eighteenth century, by suggesting a universe in which nothing cuts deep. And round the garden as a palisade are the larches and firs, not shapely in form but offering many sorts of this blessed colour green, which is to the eye what water is to the mouth. White roses clamber out of the too absolute darkness beneath and hang in the more reasonable shadow on their arms in mats of flowers like the banners of an innocent army. Morning-glories climb the fence and try to hypnotize the house with their blue stars, common as dirt they are, with their albino-eye pink centres, with their form as vulgar as a gramophone horn, with their nought-and-cross system of veining, but blue, bluer than the Mediterranean which runs like a second wall behind the tree-trunks, a further boundary to our delight; low-bred, imbecile, irresistible beauties.

All these things, and the scent which swings on the breeze from the mimosa-tree to the balcony like a slim young trapeze acrobat, are one's own. This garden cannot be seen from any other villa; and no other villa has one like it. People can come to the house and can walk through the base of it without knowing that it is there. They need never know of it unless one likes them and takes them up on to the balconies to see it. Because of the secret garden in the architect's heart one has at last a secret garden. There is possibly nothing more necessary. To have a place full of delights and nothing but delights, which one does not have to explain and defend to people who have ideas unsympathetic to one, it is to economize the forces which keep one from ending like the wisteria, from committing the unpardonable sin of doing things with difficulty.

Not till lunch-time does one go downstairs; and there the spirit of the architect leaves one. He was not interested in the dining-room. He could not dream about it, because he really would have felt very strange sitting down to meals with anybody but his wife. But in the large high room to which in the end his collapsed fantasy declined, one's interest is taken over by the spirit of the dramatist whose house this is, who lets it furnished. The room is always dark. One opens the windows to let in the air, to admit the scent, so amusingly too sweet, so positively affable, which accumulates in a formless mass like a sand-heap round the oleanders; and one closes the shutters, all but one little slat which shows the cool blue-green fingers of the unsunned lower branches of the mimosas. As one's eyes get accustomed to the gloom there emerges the most amazing surrounding incongruity of furniture. Upstairs in the bedrooms all the furniture is good: old Provençal beds and cupboards and chests of drawers, cut in chestnut-wood warmly coloured as autumn, with sound workmanship though with a lack of appreciation of grace in form that is natural enough in a nation which does not set sufficient store on youth, which takes no notice of women under thirty, which with an insane logic gives them as much time to build up reputations of beauties as it gives men to build up their businesses. There are some of these noble solidities down here, but there are also horrors so dreadful that the architect would have adored them. There is a chaise-longue with a back shaped like a couch, painted with aluminum paint; there are chintzes on which crawl the many-coloured fruits of marriages between flowers and centipedes, and statuettes everywhere, of terra-cotta ladies wriggling bare shoulders and saying they cannot do a thing with their hair the day after they have washed it, of Joan of Arc sitting listening with that exasperated air of a young French woman in charge of an office, as if she did wish the voices wouldn't shout, and would speak at more regular hours; and of children giving each other flowers with such an insincere yet unctuous air that one suspects a mutual agreement to go out and torture the cat the minute the sitting is over.

It is an inconsistency which was completely explained when one found in a reference book that the dramatist had married twice. What was not so easily explained was the finding in one of those old wooden wall-cupboards in which the Provençals kept their salt and their matches, things no bigger than holy-water stoups and naïvely carved, of a finely worked female garment, of a kind that is well to wear but which it is possible to go home without. But of course there was widowerhood. When the servant found it on the morning after the party she did not like to take it to her master; she did not take it for herself, because she was honest and left alone what belonged to other people, also because she was virtuous and did not like touching anything to do with a girl of that sort, also because she was robust and it would not have fitted her. One wonders when the loser noticed the loss, and if she was sufficiently economist to put it down in her little note-book under the proper head of dilapidations. He should have married her. The pattern of the lace is very discreet, she would have been loyal to the first, the correct furniture. The second wife's clothes may always have come home to roost, but for all that she was no comfort to a man; she loved things, and the wrong things at that. It is probably she who will not let the old man sell the house, although he needs the money, for his pieces no longer hold the stage.

One perceives, on the evidence of this furniture, the marriages, the garment, why that would be so. His was the converse of the architect's case. That other, whom almost anybody would call a donkey, who was totally unable to learn what nearly all the rest of mankind masters easily, had yet the prime necessity of the artist, for he had idiosyncrasy; that is to say, there was the nucleus of a creative vortex in his mind, a spot where his individual vision of reality had become dynamic, was swirling around the general matter of his mental being so that it was precipitating in significant forms. But this dramatist, whom nobody in the world could call a donkey, was unable to do anything except learn what the rest of mankind has mastered. He has no idiosyncrasy, because he had no individual vision of reality to become dynamic, being one of those abject souls who do not aspire to one, who are agitated by the lower problem of giving the right reflexes to reality, who are all the time looking round nervously to see if they are giving the same ones as other people whom they modestly conceive to be their betters. It was his ambition to write plays because in the happy laughter of a theatre audience one can get the most immediate and numerically impressive guarantee that there is nothing in one's mind which is not familiar to the mass of persons living at the time.

His passion for the average showed in his wives. When he was a young man he had not the hardihood to marry a young girl, in case they should make the mistakes of youth together, for youth and its folly are in the nature of special cases, since the majority of human beings alive at any one time are middle-aged and sensible. So he married a woman older than himself. To make quite sure that his vitality, in which he took no pride since it was not the common lot, was counterbalanced, he chose one whose light was dimmed by temperament as well as years. Her desire to furnish her house with pedantically chosen furniture not so suitable to a modern home as to evoke visions of ancient Provence, with these old salt and taper cupboards, the wooden bird-cages in which they used to keep the bread, the tables on which they kneaded it, showed her to be of the same type which gratifies an instinctive recession by reading only quiet memoirs, diaries whose sole interest is that they are dated long ago. He was thereby laying up for himself a bereavement that came too early, which was sad. And it was sad too that in his second marriage also he had to placate his respect for the average. For he married this young and coarse woman because he was getting old, and because he feared that his age was giving him an involuntary etherealism; and still it remained true that the majority of human beings are middle-aged and sensible. This respect brought him no compensating rewards in his work. For it takes such enormous energy to master the innumerable superficial reactions of the crowd in any particular decade that one has none left to adapt oneself to the changes which take place in the next. So his pieces are no longer played; it is we who are living in his villa.

For all its implications it is a good room to sit in, to smell the oleander, to look at the mimosa, to eat *bœuf à la mode* embedded in a jelly which is a mixture of magnificences like a sunset; and to call Jasmine into later, to congratulate her and ask for the recipe. Her face is at once animated and heavy with undischarged genius as she says, "It's nothing, it's quite easy to make, the only thing is that it takes about five hours and it has to be watched very carefully." Then her eye wanders past one, her hand darts out like a sting, and she cries out, "The forest fire! Look, it has started again!" One turns about in one's chair and sees that the pool of sunshine between the two doors is the colour of a ginger cat. True enough, that means that somewhere some sublime valley is being laid waste as by war, and that for the rest of the day the sunward side of the sky will be a half-sphere of tortoise-shell, and the sea bruise green. Jasmine goes on, "It must be the same fire that started last night. It's burned all the village where we get our honey." She says it with an accent of terrible joy, of simultaneous consummation of fear and desire. One perceives that again and again she has destroyed her life when it was forming into shapes of happiness because of her loyalty to her early misery, her conviction that that has the sanction of ultimate reality, and that beside it all other things are trivial. "It must be spreading, it must be spreading fast. What shall we do? We will have to get the fishermen to row us out to sea." Her eyes shine. So Turner wanted the world to go up in fire. She continues to look out into the discoloured sunlight with a smiling fixity, until her fingers begin to work. In the meantime she must do something perfect. She says, "Don't go out to tea. I'm going to make you a cake. With potato flour, that's lightest."

1928

J. B. Priestley

THE PORT

THIS morning I went down to the docks with
my friend, the marine surveyor. He had a ship, now in
dry dock, to look over, the first for many weeks. There
have been very few ships, whole or damaged, in this
port these many months, and as we walked down towards
the docks, my friend talked of old days that would never
return with any tide. A vast fleet had sailed away from
this port for ever. My friend is not young and, like all his
kind, an admirable kind, he turns no rosy spectacles on
the future. He is not sentimental about the past and, like
all the men I have ever met who have had to do with the
sea, he cannot be sentimental about the future. He has
the usual close conservative grain of his type, and possibly
he exaggerates the evils of today and the peril of tomorrow, but it was impossible, keeping step with him and
following his pointing finger, not to feel that something
was passing from these seas. He kept lightly and realistically to the facts, the actual substance of the scene
around us, and it was left for me, romantic, sentimental,
literary, to make what I would of it. Perhaps the morning
artfully evoked the mood. It was bright enough, a good
day for late November, with a sun to see and feel, faintly

From *Apes and Angels* by J. B. Priestley. Reprinted by permission of Harold Matson, Literary Agent.

caressing your shoulders. But it was all so quiet, so dim. There was mist trailing through the town, and a white fog down the Channel. Beneath the bright upper air, the distant things were the merest wraiths and everything close at hand was hushed and faintly shining, a place in a dream. Now and then, but so rarely as to be startling, a siren would suddenly shatter the silence, coming from nowhere and leaving behind only a deeper quiet in which there was a faint irony, an irony of ghosts. Some one was calling the roll of ships, it seemed, and only these were answering.

We passed through the notorious quarter where the seamen's lodgings are, and as we walked along my friend told me stories about the place. He told them with that unconscious air of pride which very respectable citizens cannot escape if they describe to you the depravity of their city. This morning, however, the quarter looked innocent enough, merely so many streets of dingy little houses, with an outlandish name, an Ahmed or Chung Soo, here and there, an occasional vague Lascar or heavily muffled Negro standing at a corner, and some half-caste women cleaning their doorsteps. It seemed curiously vacant, lifeless. Perhaps most of them were asleep, though the morning was wearing away. Perhaps there were only a handful of sailors in all these lodging-houses, and Ahmed and the rest were still waiting for company. It looked as if some of them would have to wait for ever. Yet when we came out, passed the chandlers' and gaudy tobacconists' shops, and arrived at the dingy Board of Trade offices, there seemed to be people enough. The square there, muddy and raw, was filled with idlers, standing about in little groups and hardly making a movement. They were listless, drab, silent. They watched the heavy groaning tram creep jerkily up to the square. I had a feeling that they were all waiting for something to happen and yet knew that nothing would happen. What vile places these ports would

be if it were not for the fact that they are on the very
border of magic! Somewhere beyond this dreary tangle of
railway lines and little bridges and sheds is radiant fantasy,
emerald water and great scarlet birds, a glimpse of Per-
nambuco or Yucatan. You go this way, where our grime
seems thickest, cross your last plank, and when next you
tread on land, the cockatoos are screaming round you and
a black man is slashing at a green coco-nut so that you
may slake your thirst. As exits these ports are endurable,
but what foul entrances they must make! Who, coming
from the sea to England, would imagine that they too
lead back to a fantasy, lovelier and more subtle, the witch-
ery of meadow and hawthorn that is ours?

We made our way to the dry dock where my companion
had to inspect his ship. She was from Ireland and had
ripped some of her plates on the way over. There she was,
high and dry, with a little army of pygmies tinkering at
her. Here indeed was a most heartening noise and bustle.
We had collected one or two marine superintendents and
other persons of importance in the dock world, big solid
men, much given to shaking hands and addressing people
by name: "What d'you think, Cap'n Brown?" "That's so,
isn't it, Mr. Smith?" In third-rate stories about the sea,
the personages are always rather wild and picturesque, like
bad artists, but I have frequently noticed that in real life,
as in really good fiction, the men of the sea, skippers and
engineers and pilots and the like, are always very solid
and punctilious and respectable men, typical members of
what some fools are always calling the "bourgeoisie," who
may have done many wild and desperate things but whose
dream of life is a spell with the missis in a little suburban
villa, a tiny greenhouse, and a walk down the main street,
dressed in a good dark suit and a bowler hat, exchanging
greetings here and there: "Morning, Cap'n Brown!"
"Morning, Mr. Smith!"

It was odd to tread the decks of a ship and look down

to see no water but a dry floor and a host of men at work there, to smell the carbide from the acetylene welders below and to hear such a clanging and hammering that it seemed as if the whole ship were being knocked to pieces. It was odd, too, to go down there and watch the goggled men directing their awful flames and turning iron rivets into so many showers of sparks and liquid golden drops of metal, to look up at the vast curving hull of the ship and at the vast bronze propeller, now forlorn in mid-air. What a good solid job of work this mending of ships is, making most of our tasks seem mere hocus-pocus! I had left my companion with the chief officer (who looked exactly like Little Tich—taller certainly, but with the same face and figure—so that I expected him at any moment to break into song and dance), but after I had wandered round the ship and descended to the floor of the dock, their conference and tour ended. My friend joined me again, and told me all about plates being ripped, wood being spired into mere pulp by the sea-worm, ships that were down thirty fathom just off Lundy, all plain facts —for he is crammed with facts about everything—but to me as romantic as an Arabian Night. By this time we had left the dry dock behind; the noise of hammering had utterly vanished; and again there was silence.

Here and there a ship showed itself through the light mist that covered the docks, but the great basins, faintly shining, dream-like, seemed sadly vacant. Not long ago, I was told, all those docks were crowded with shipping, were a maze of derricks and smoke-stacks, but now not only was there room enough and to spare, but there was desolating vacancy. The rails were empty of trains, and we could stroll at ease over all the bridges, their "Keep to the Left" notices being now simply farcical. There was no traffic over them. No lorries came clattering through, no crowds of men rushed over them towards the town or the waiting boats. The great cranes or chutes were all motionless, as if they forlornly sniffed the raw, empty air, monsters awaiting a prey that never came. We left the docks, passed once more through the little square where the Board of Trade and the idlers stared at one another, and came at last to a great block of shipping offices, the tallest building in the neighbourhood. "I'll take you up to the roof," my companion said, pointing the way to the lift. "You get a good view up there." It was a flat roof, high above the surrounding chimney-pots, boasting of nothing but a tiny greenhouse, where the caretaker had his aerial garden. But beyond the immediate tangle of roofs and gloom of narrow-streets, there was nothing to be seen. The hills were completely lost in the thickening mist. Not a glimmer of the Channel came through the fog. The docks were fading out, and the nearest were only the faintest shadow. "You've been unlucky," I was told, "for any kind of clear day would have shown us everything." I promised that I would return and see it all. I hope I shall see it all: the Channel shining and brave with shipping; the docks alive with moving derricks; the air resounding with sirens and locomotive whistles and the shouts of busy men. But I could not help wondering whether I ever should, whether something had not gone for ever. I remember a solitary hooting, like a knell, as we quitted the roof, and how cheerful the smoking café seemed, with its smell of hot coffee, its tobacco smoke, its clatter of tongues and dominoes. There we had a good talk about the East India Company.

1928

Virginia Woolf

STREET HAUNTING

A LONDON ADVENTURE

NO ONE perhaps has ever felt passionately towards a lead pencil. But there are circumstances in which it can become supremely desirable to possess one; moments when we are set upon having an object, an excuse for walking half across London between tea and dinner. As the foxhunter hunts in order to preserve the breed of foxes, and the golfer plays in order that open spaces may be preserved from the builders, so when the desire comes upon us to go street rambling a pencil does for a pretext, and getting up we say: "Really I must buy a pencil," as if under cover of this excuse we could indulge safely in the greatest pleasure of town life in winter—rambling the streets of London.

The hour should be the evening and the season winter, for in winter the champagne brightness of the air and the sociability of the streets are grateful. We are not then taunted as in the summer by the longing for shade and solitude and sweet airs from the hayfields. The evening hour, too, gives us the irresponsibility which darkness and lamplight bestow. We are no longer quite ourselves. As we step out of the house on a fine evening between four and six, we shed the self our friends know us by and become part of that vast republican army of anonymous trampers, whose society is so agreeable after the solitude of one's own room. For there we sit surrounded by objects which perpetually express the oddity of our own temperaments and enforce the memories of our own experience. That bowl on the mantelpiece, for instance, was bought at Mantua on a windy day. We were leaving the shop when the sinister old woman plucked at our skirts and said she would find herself starving one of these days, but, "Take it!" she cried, and thrust the blue and white china bowl into our hands as if she never wanted to be reminded of her quixotic generosity. So, guiltily, but suspecting nevertheless how badly we had been fleeced, we carried it back to the little hotel where, in the middle of the night, the innkeeper quarrelled so violently with his wife that we all leant out into the courtyard to look, and saw the vines laced among the pillars and the stars white in the sky. The moment was stabilized, stamped like a coin indelibly among a million that slipped by imperceptibly. There, too, was the melancholy Englishman, who rose among the coffee cups and the little iron tables and revealed the secrets of his soul—as travellers do. All this—Italy, the windy morning, the vines laced about the pillars, the Englishman and the secrets of his soul—rise up in a cloud from the china bowl on the mantelpiece. And there, as our eyes fall to the floor, is that brown stain on the carpet. Mr. Lloyd George made that. "The man's a devil!" said Mr. Cummings, putting the kettle down with which he was about to fill the teapot so that it burnt a brown ring on the carpet.

But when the door shuts on us, all that vanishes. The shell-like covering which our souls have excreted to house themselves, to make for themselves a shape distinct from others, is broken, and there is left of all these wrinkles and roughness a central oyster of perceptiveness, an enormous eye. How beautiful a street is in winter! It is at once revealed and obscured. Here vaguely one can trace symmetrical straight avenues of doors and windows; here under the lamps are floating islands of pale light through which pass quickly bright men and women, who, for all their poverty and shabbiness, wear a certain look of unreality, an air of triumph, as if they had given life the slip, so that life, deceived of her prey, blunders on without them. But, after all, we are only gliding smoothly on the surface. The eye is not a miner, not a diver, not a seeker after buried treasure. It floats us smoothly down a stream; resting, pausing, the brain sleeps perhaps as it looks.

How beautiful a London street is then, with its islands of light, and its long groves of darkness, and on one side of it perhaps some tree-sprinkled, grass-grown space where night is folding herself to sleep naturally and, as one passes the iron railing, one hears those little cracklings and stirrings of leaf and twig which seem to suppose the silence of fields all round them, an owl hooting, and far away the rattle of a train in the valley. But this is London, we are reminded; high among the bare trees are hung oblong frames of reddish yellow light—windows; there are points of brilliance burning steadily like low stars—lamps; this empty ground, which holds the country in it and its peace, is only a London square, set about by offices and houses where at this hour fierce lights burn over maps, over documents, over desks where clerks sit turning with wetted forefinger the files of endless correspondence; or more suffusedly the firelight wavers and the lamplight falls upon the privacy of some drawing-room, its easy chairs, its papers, its china, its inlaid table, and the figure of a woman, accurately measuring out the precise number of spoons of tea which— She looks at the door as if she heard a ring downstairs and somebody asking, is she in?

But here we must stop peremptorily. We are in danger of digging deeper than the eye approves; we are impeding our passage down the smooth stream by catching at some branch or root. At any moment, the sleeping army may stir itself and wake in us a thousand violins and trumpets in response; the army of human beings may rouse itself and assert all its oddities and sufferings and sordidities. Let us dally a little longer, be content still with surfaces only—the glossy brilliance of the motor omnibuses; the carnal splendour of the butchers' shops with their yellow flanks and purple steaks; the blue and red bunches of flowers burning so bravely through the plate glass of the florist's windows.

For the eye has this strange property: it rests only in beauty; like a butterfly it seeks colour and basks in warmth. On a winter's night like this, when nature has been at pains to polish and preen herself, it brings back the prettiest trophies, breaks off little lumps of emerald and coral as if the whole earth were made of precious stone. The thing it cannot do (one is speaking of the average unprofessional eye) is to compose these trophies in such a way as to bring out the more obscure angles and relationships. Hence after a prolonged diet of this simple, sugary fare, of beauty pure and uncomposed, we become conscious of satiety. We halt at the door of the boot shop and make some little excuse, which has nothing to do with the real reason, for folding up the bright paraphernalia of the streets and withdrawing to some duskier chamber of the being where we may ask, as we raise our left foot obediently upon the stand: "What, then, is it like to be a dwarf?"

She came in escorted by two women who, being of normal size, looked like benevolent giants beside her. Smiling at the shop girls, they seemed to be disclaiming any lot in her deformity and assuring her of their protection. She wore the peevish yet apologetic expression usual on the faces of the deformed. She needed their kindness, yet she resented it. But when the shop girl had been summoned and the giantesses, smiling indulgently, had asked for shoes for "this lady" and the girl had pushed the little stand in front of her, the dwarf stuck her foot out with an impetuosity which seemed to claim all our attention. Look at that! Look at that! she seemed to demand of us all, as she thrust her foot out, for behold it was the shapely, perfectly proportioned foot of a well-grown woman. It was arched; it was aristocratic. Her whole manner changed as she looked at it resting on the stand. She looked soothed and satisfied. Her manner became full of self-confidence. She sent for shoe after shoe; she tried on pair after pair. She got up and pirouetted before a glass which reflected the foot only in yellow shoes, in fawn shoes, in shoes of lizard skin. She raised her little skirts and displayed her little legs. She was thinking that, after all, feet are the most important part of the whole person; women, she said to herself, have been loved for their feet alone. Seeing nothing but her feet, she imagined perhaps that the rest of her body was a piece with those beautiful feet. She was shabbily dressed, but she was ready to lavish any money upon her shoes. And as this was the only occasion upon which she was not afraid of being looked at but positively craved attention, she was ready to use any device to prolong the choosing and fitting. Look at my feet, she seemed to be saying, as she took a step this way and then a step that way. The shop girl good-humouredly must have said something flattering, for suddenly her face lit up in ecstasy. But, after all, the giantesses, benevolent though they were, had their own affairs to see to; she must make up her mind; she must decide which to choose. At length, the pair was chosen and, as she walked out between her guardians, with the parcel swinging from her finger, the ecstasy faded, knowledge returned, the old peevishness, the old apology came back, and by the time she had reached the street again she had become a dwarf only.

But she had changed the mood; she had called into being an atmosphere which, as we followed her out into the street, seemed actually to create the humped, the twisted, the deformed. Two bearded men, brothers, apparently, stone-blind, supporting themselves by resting a hand on the head of a small boy between them, marched down the street. On they came with the unyielding yet tremulous tread of the blind, which seems to lend to their approach something of the terror and inevitability of the fate that has overtaken them. As they passed, holding straight on, the little convoy seemed to cleave asunder the passers-by with the momentum of its silence, its directness, its disaster. Indeed, the dwarf had started a hobbling grotesque dance to which everybody in the street now conformed: the stout lady tightly swathed in shiny sealskin; the feeble-minded boy sucking the silver knob of his stick; the old man squatted on a doorstep as if, suddenly overcome by the absurdity of the human spectacle, he had sat down to look at it—all joined in the hobble and tap of the dwarf's dance.

In what crevices and crannies, one might ask, did they lodge, this maimed company of the halt and the blind? Here, perhaps, in the top rooms of these narrow old houses between Holborn and Soho, where people have such queer names, and pursue so many curious trades, are gold beaters, accordion pleaters, cover buttons, or support life, with even great fantasticality, upon a traffic in cups without saucers, china umbrella handles, and highly-coloured pictures of martyred saints. There they lodge, and it seems as if the lady in the sealskin jacket must find life tolerable, passing the time of day with the accordion pleater, or the man who covers buttons; life which is so fantastic cannot be altogether tragic. They do not grudge us, we are musing, our prosperity; when suddenly, turning the corner, we come upon a bearded Jew, wild, hunger-bitten, glaring out of his misery; or pass the humped body of an old woman flung abandoned on the step of a public building with a cloak over her like the hasty covering thrown over a dead horse or donkey. At such sights the nerves of the spine seem to stand erect; a sudden flare is brandished in our eyes; a question is asked which is never answered. Often enough these derelicts choose to lie not a stone's throw from theatres, within hearing of barrel organs, almost, as night draws on, within touch of the sequined cloaks and bright legs of diners and dancers. They lie close to those shop windows where commerce offers to a world of old women laid on doorsteps, of blind men, of hobbling dwarfs, sofas which are supported by the gilt necks of proud swans; tables inlaid with baskets of many coloured fruit; sideboards paved with green marble the better to support the weight of boars' heads; and carpets so softened with age that their carnations have almost vanished in a pale green sea.

Passing, glimpsing, everything seems accidentally but miraculously sprinkled with beauty, as if the tide of trade which deposits its burden so punctually and prosaically upon the shores of Oxford Street had this night cast up nothing but treasure. With no thought of buying, the eye is sportive and generous; it creates; it adorns; it enhances. Standing out in the street, one may build up all the chambers of an imaginary house and furnish them at one's will with sofa, table, carpet. That rug will do for the hall. That alabaster bowl shall stand on a carved table in the window. Our merrymaking shall be reflected in that thick round mirror. But, having built and furnished the house, one is happily under no obligation to possess it; one can dismantle it in the twinkling of an eye, and build and furnish another house with other chairs and other glasses. Or let us indulge ourselves at the antique jewellers, among the trays of rings and the hanging necklaces. Let us choose those pearls, for example, and then imagine how, if we put them on, life would be changed. It becomes instantly between two and three in the morning; the lamps are burning very white in the deserted streets of Mayfair. Only motor-cars are abroad at this hour, and one has a sense of emptiness, of airiness, of secluded gaiety. Wearing pearls, wearing silk, one steps out on to a balcony which overlooks the gardens of sleeping Mayfair. There are a few lights in the bedrooms of great peers returned from Court, of silk-stockinged footmen, of dowagers who have passed the hands of statesmen. A cat creeps along the garden wall. Love making is going on sibilantly, seductively in the darker places of the room behind thick green curtains. Strolling sedately as if he were promenading a terrace beneath which the shires and counties of England lie sunbathed, the aged Prime Minister recounts to Lady So-and-So with the curls and the emeralds the true history of some great crisis in the affairs of the land. We seem to be riding on the top of the highest mast of the tallest ship; and yet at the same time we know that nothing of this sort matters; love is not proved thus, nor great achievements completed thus: so that we sport with the moment and preen our feathers in it lightly, as we stand on the balcony watching the moonlit cat creep along Princess Mary's garden wall.

But what could be more absurd? It is, in fact, on the stroke of six; it is a winter's evening; we are walking to the Strand to buy a pencil. How, then, are we also on a balcony, wearing pearls in June? What could be more absurd? Yet it is nature's folly, not ours. When she set about her chief masterpiece, the making of man, she should have thought of one thing only. Instead, turning her head, looking over her shoulder, into each one of us she let creep instincts and desires which are utterly at variance with his main being, so that we are streaked, variegated, all of a mixture; the colours have run. Is the true self this which stands on the pavement in January, or that which bends over the balcony in June? Am I here, or am I there? Or is the true self neither this nor that, neither here nor there, but something so varied and wandering that it is only when we give the rein to its wishes and let it take its way unimpeded that we are indeed ourselves? Circumstances compel unity; for convenience' sake a man must be a whole. The good citizen when he opens his door in the evening must be banker, golfer, husband, father; not a nomad wandering the desert, a mystic staring at the sky, a debauchee in the slums of San Francisco, a soldier heading a revolution, a pariah howling with scepticism and solitude. When he opens his door, he must run his fingers through his hair and put his umbrella in the stand like the rest.

But here, none too soon, are the second-hand bookshops. Here we find anchorage in these thwarting currents of being; here we balance ourselves after the splendours and miseries of the streets. The very sight of the bookseller's wife with her foot on the fender, sitting beside a good coal fire, screened from the door, is sobering and cheerful. She is never reading, or only the newspaper; her talk, when it leaves bookselling, which it does so gladly, is about hats; she likes a hat to be practical, she says, as well as pretty. O no, they don't live at the shop; they live in Brixton; she must have a bit of green to look at. In summer a jar of flowers grown in her own garden is stood on the top of some dusty pile to enliven the shop. Books are everywhere; and always the same sense of adventure fills us. Second-hand books are wild books, homeless books; they have come together in vast flocks of variegated feather, and have a charm which the domesticated volumes of the library lack. Besides, in this random miscellaneous company we may rub against some complete stranger who will, with luck, turn into the best friend we have in the world. There is always a hope, as we reach down some greyish-white book from an upper shelf, directed by its air of shabbiness and desertion, of meeting here with a man who set out on horseback over a hundred years ago to explore the woollen market in the Midlands and Wales;

an unknown traveller, who stayed at inns, drank his pint, noted pretty girls and serious customs, wrote it all down stiffly, laboriously for sheer love of it (the book was published at his own expense); was infinitely prosy, busy, and matter-of-fact, and so let flow in without his knowing it the very scent of hollyhocks and the hay together with such a portrait of himself as gives him forever a seat in the warm corner of the mind's inglenook. One may buy him for eighteenpence now. He is marked three and sixpence, but the bookseller's wife, seeing how shabby the covers are and how long the book has stood there since it was bought at some sale of a gentleman's library in Suffolk, will let it go at that.

Thus, glancing round the bookshop, we make other such capricious friendships with the unknown and the vanished whose only record is, for example, this little book of poems, so fairly printed, so finely engraved, too, with a portrait of the author. For he was a poet and drowned untimely, and his verse, mild as it is and formal and sententious, sends forth still a frail fluty sound like that of a piano organ played in some back street resignedly by an old Italian organ-grinder in a corduroy jacket. There are travellers, too, row upon row of them, still testifying, indomitable spinsters that they were, to the discomforts that they endured and the sunsets they admired in Greece when Queen Victoria was a girl. A tour of Cornwall with a visit to the tin mines was thought worthy of voluminous record. People went slowly up the Rhine and did portraits of each other in Indian ink, sitting reading on deck beside a coil of rope; they measured the pyramids; were lost to civilization for years; converted Negroes in pestilential swamps. This packing up and going off, exploring deserts and catching fevers, settling in India for a lifetime, penetrating even to China and then returning to lead a parochial life at Edmonton, tumbles and tosses upon the dusty floor like an uneasy sea, so restless the English are, with the waves at their very door. The waters of travel and adventure seem to break upon little islands of serious effort and lifelong industry stood in jagged column upon the floor. In these piles of puce-bound volumes with gilt monograms on the back, thoughtful clergymen expound the gospels; scholars are to be heard with their hammers and their chisels chipping clear the ancient texts of Euripides and Aeschylus. Thinking, annotating, expounding goes on at a prodigious rate all around us and over everything, like a punctual, everlasting tide, washes the ancient sea of fiction. Innumerable volumes tell how Arthur loved Laura and they were separated and they were unhappy and then they met and they were happy ever after, as was the way when Victoria ruled these islands.

The number of books in the world is infinite, and one is forced to glimpse and nod and move on after a moment of talk, a flash of understanding, as, in the street outside, one catches a word in passing and from a chance phrase fabricates a lifetime. It is about a woman called Kate that they are talking, how "I said to her quite straight last night . . . if you don't think I'm worth a penny stamp, I said . . ." But who Kate is, and to what crisis in their friendship that penny stamp refers, we shall never know; for Kate sinks under the warmth of their volubility; and here, at the street corner, another page of the volume of life is laid open by the sight of two men consulting under the lamp-post. They are spelling out the latest wire from Newmarket in the stop press news. Do they think, then, that fortune will ever convert their rags into fur and broadcloth, sling them with watch-chains, and plant diamond pins where there is now a ragged open shirt? But the main stream of walkers at this hour sweeps too fast to let us ask such questions. They are wrapt, in this short passage from work to home, in some narcotic dream, now that they are free from the desk, and have the fresh air on their cheeks. They put on those bright clothes which they must hang up and lock the key upon all the rest of the day, and are great cricketers, famous actresses, soldiers who have saved their country at the hour of need. Dreaming, gesticulating, often muttering a few words aloud, they sweep over the Strand and across Waterloo Bridge whence they will be slung in long rattling trains, to some prim little villa in Barnes or Surbiton where the sight of the clock in the hall and the smell of the supper in the basement puncture the dream.

But we are come to the Strand now, and as we hesitate on the curb, a little rod about the length of one's finger begins to lay its bar across the velocity and abundance of life. "Really I must—really I must"—that is it. Without investigating the demand, the mind cringes to the accustomed tyrant. One must, one always must, do something or other; it is not allowed one simply to enjoy oneself. Was it not for this reason that, some time ago, we fabricated the excuse, and invented the necessity of buying something? But what was it? Ah, we remember, it was a pencil. Let us go then and buy this pencil. But just as we are turning to obey the command, another self disputes the right of the tyrant to insist. The usual conflict comes about. Spread out behind the rod of duty we see the whole breadth of the river Thames—wide, mournful, peaceful. And we see it through the eyes of somebody who is leaning over the Embankment on a summer evening, without a care in the world. Let us put off buying the pencil; let us go in search of this person—and soon it becomes apparent that this person is ourselves. For if we could stand there where we stood six months ago, should we not be again as we were then—calm, aloof, content? Let us try then. But the river is rougher and greyer than we remembered. The tide is running out to sea. It brings down with it a tug and two barges, whose load of straw is tightly bound down beneath tarpaulin covers. There is, too, close by us, a couple leaning over the balustrade with the curious lack of self-consciousness lovers have, as if the importance of the affair they are engaged on claims without question the indulgence of the human race. The sights we see and the sounds we hear now have none of the quality of the past; nor have we any share in the serenity of the person who, six months ago, stood precisely where we stand now. His is the happiness of death; ours the insecurity of life. He has no future; the future is even now invading our peace. It is only when we look at the past and take from it the element of uncertainty that we can enjoy perfect peace. As it is, we must turn, we must cross the Strand again, we must find a shop where, even at this hour, they will be ready to sell us a pencil. It is always an adventure to enter a new room; for the lives and characters of its owners have distilled their atmosphere into it, and directly we enter it we breast some new wave of emotion. Here, without a doubt, in the stationer's shop people had been quarrelling. Their anger shot through the air. They both stopped; the old woman—they were husband and wife evidently—retired to a back room; the old man whose rounded forehead and globular eyes would have looked well on the frontispiece of some Elizabethan folio, stayed to serve us. "A pencil, a pencil," he repeated, "certainly, certainly." He spoke with the distraction yet effusiveness of one whose emotions have been roused and checked in full flood. He began opening box after box and shutting them again. He said that it was very difficult to find things when they kept so many different articles. He launched into a story about some legal gentleman who had got into deep water owing to the conduct of his wife. He had known him for years; he had been connected with the Temple for half a century, he said, as if he wished his wife in the back room to overhear him. He upset a box of rubber bands. At last, exasperated by his incompetence, he pushed the swing door open and called out roughly: "Where d'you keep the pencils?" as if his wife had hidden them. The old lady came in. Looking at nobody, she put her hand with a fine air of righteous severity upon the right box. There were pencils. How then could he do without her? Was she not indispensable to him? In order to keep them there, standing side by side in forced neutrality, one had to be particular in one's choice of pencils; this was too soft, that too hard. They stood silently looking on. The longer they stood there, the calmer they grew; their heat was going down, their anger disappearing. Now, without a word said on either side, the quarrel was made up. The old man, who would not have disgraced Ben Jonson's title-page, reached the box back to its proper place, bowed profoundly his goodnight to us, and they disappeared. She would get out her sewing; he would read his newspaper; the canary would scatter them impartially with seed. The quarrel was over.

In these minutes in which a ghost has been sought for, a quarrel composed, and a pencil bought, the streets had become completely empty. Life had withdrawn to the top floor, and lamps were lit. The pavement was dry and hard; the road was of hammered silver. Walking home through the desolation one could tell oneself the story of the dwarf, of the blind men, of the party in the Mayfair mansion, of the quarrel in the stationer's shop. Into each of these lives one could penetrate a little way, far enough to give oneself the illusion that one is not entitled to a single mind, but can put on briefly for a few minutes the bodies and minds of others. One could become a washerwoman, a publican, a street singer. And what greater delight and wonder can there be than to leave the straight lines of personality and deviate into those footpaths that lead beneath brambles and thick tree trunks into the heart of the forest where live those wild beasts, our fellow men?

That is true: to escape is the greatest of pleasures; street haunting in winter the greatest of adventures. Still as we approach our own doorstep again, it is comforting to feel the old possessions, the old prejudices, fold us round; and the self, which has been blown about at so many street corners, which has battered like a moth at the flame of so many inaccessible lanterns, sheltered and enclosed. Here again is the usual door; here the chair turned as we left it and the china bowl and the brown ring on the carpet. And here—let us examine it tenderly, let us touch it with reverence—is the only spoil we have retrieved from all the treasures of the city, a lead pencil.

1930

Aldous Huxley

MEDITATION ON EL GRECO

THE pleasures of ignorance are as great, in their way, as the pleasures of knowledge. For though the light is good, though it is satisfying to be able to place the things that surround one in the categories of an ordered and comprehensible system, it is also good to find oneself sometimes in the dark, it is pleasant now and then to have to speculate with vague bewilderment about a world which ignorance has reduced to a quantity of mutually irrelevant happenings dotted, like so many unexplored and fantastic islands, on the face of a vast ocean of incomprehension. For me, one of the greatest charms of travel consists in the fact that it offers unique opportunities for indulging in the luxury of ignorance. I am not one of those conscientious travellers who, before they visit a new country, spend weeks mugging up its geology, its economics, its art history, its literature. I prefer, at any rate during my first few visits, to be a thoroughly unintelligent tourist. It is only later, when my ignorance has lost its virgin freshness, that I begin to read what the intelligent tourist would have known by heart before he bought his tickets. I read—and forthwith, in a series of apocalypses, my isolated and mysteriously odd impressions begin to assume significance, my jumbled memories fall harmoniously into patterns. The pleasures of ignorance have given place to the pleasures of knowledge.

I have only twice visited Spain—not often enough, that is to say, to have grown tired of ignorance. I still enjoy bewilderedly knowing as little as possible about all I see between the Pyrenees and Cape Trafalgar. Another two or three visits, and the time will be ripe for me to go to the London Library and look up "Spain" in the subject index. In one of the numerous, the all too numerous, books there catalogued I shall find, no doubt, the explanation of a little mystery that has mildly and intermittently puzzled me for quite a number of years—ever since, at one of those admirable Loan Exhibitions in Burlington House, I saw for the first time a version of El Greco's *Dream of Philip II.*

This curious composition, familiar to every visitor to the Escorial, represents the king, dressed and gloved like an undertaker in inky black, kneeling on a well-stuffed cushion in the centre foreground; beyond him, on the left, a crowd of pious kneelers, some lay, some clerical, but all manifestly saintly, are looking upwards into a heaven full of waltzing angels, cardinal virtues and biblical person-ages, grouped in a circle round the Cross and the luminous monogram of the Saviour. On the right a very large whale gigantically yawns, and a vast concourse, presumably of the damned, is hurrying (in spite of all that we learned in childhood about the anatomy of whales) down its crim-son throat. A curious picture, I repeat, and, as a work of art, not remarkably good; there are many much better Grecos belonging even to the same youthful period. Never-theless, in spite of its mediocrity, it is a picture for which I have a special weakness. I like it for the now sadly un-orthodox reason that the subject interests me. And the subject interests me because I do not know what the sub-ject is. For this dream of King Philip—what was it? Was it a visionary anticipation of the Last Judgment? A mystical peep into Heaven? An encouraging glimpse of the Almighty's short way with heretics? I do not know—do not at present even desire to know. In the face of so extravagant a phantasy as this of Greco's, the pleasures of ignorance are peculiarly intense. Confronted by the mysterious whale, the undertaker king, the swarming aerial saints and scurrying sinners, I give my fancy licence and fairly wallow in the pleasure of bewilderedly not knowing.

The fancy I like best of all that have occurred to me is the one which affirms that this queer picture was painted as a prophetic and symbolic autobiography, that it was meant to summarize hieroglyphically the whole of Greco's future development. For that whale in the right foreground—that great-grandfather of Moby Dick, with his huge yawn, his crimson gullet and the crowd of the damned descending, like bank clerks at six o'clock into the Underground—that whale, I say, is the most significantly autobiographical object in all El Greco's early pictures. For whither are they bound, those hastening damned? "Down the red lane," as our nurses used to say when they were encouraging us to swallow the uneatable viands of childhood. Down the red lane into a dim inferno of tripes. Down, in a word, into that strange and rather frightful universe which Greco's spirit seems to have come more and more exclusively, as he grew older, to inhabit. For in the Cretan's later painting every personage is a Jonah. Yes, *every* personage. Which is where *The Dream of Philip II* reveals itself as being imperfectly prophetic, a mutilated symbol. It is for the damned alone that the whale opens his mouth. If El Greco had wanted to tell the whole truth about his future development, he would have sent the blessed to join them, or at least have provided his saints and angels with another monster of their own, a supernal whale floating head downwards among the clouds, with a second red lane ascending, strait and narrow, towards a swallowed Heaven.

Paradise and Purgatory, Hell, and even the common Earth—for El Greco in his artistic maturity, every department of the universe was situated in the belly of a whale. His Annunciations and Assumptions, his Agonies and Transfigurations and Crucifixions, his Martyrdoms and Stigmatizations are all, without exception, visceral events. Heaven is no larger than the Black Hole of Calcutta, and God Himself is whale-engulfed.

Critics have tried to explain El Greco's pictorial agoraphobia in terms of his early, Cretan education. There is no space in his pictures, they assure us, because the typical art of that Byzantium, which was El Greco's spiritual home, was the mosaic, and the mosaic is innocent of depth. A specious explanation, whose only defect is that it happens to be almost entirely beside the point. To begin with, the Byzantine mosaic was not invariably without depth. Those extraordinary eight-century mosaics in the Omeyyid mosque at Damascus, for example, are as spacious and airy as impressionist landscapes. They are, it is true, somewhat exceptional specimens of the art. But even the commoner shut-in mosaics have really nothing to do with El Greco's painting, for the Byzantine saints and kings are enclosed, or, to be more accurate, are flatly inlaid in a kind of two-dimensional abstraction—in a pure Euclidean, plane-geometrical heaven of gold or blue. Their universe never bears the smallest resemblance to that whale's belly in which every one of El Greco's personages has his or her mysterious and appalling being. El Greco's world is no Flatland; there is depth in it—just a little depth. It is precisely this that makes it seem such a disquieting world. In their two-dimensional abstraction the personages of the Byzantine mosaists are perfectly at home; they are adapted to their environment. But, solid and three-dimensional, made to be the inhabitants of a spacious universe, El Greco's people are shut up in a world where there is perhaps just room enough to swing a cat, but no more. They are in prison and, which makes it worse, in a visceral prison. For all that surrounds them is organic, animal. Clouds, rock, drapery have all been mysteriously transformed into mucus and skinned muscle and peritoneum. The Heaven into which Count Orgaz ascends is like some cosmic operation for appendicitis. The Madrid *Resurrection* is a resurrection in a digestive tube. And from the later pictures we receive the gruesome impression that all the personages, both human and divine, have begun to suffer a process of digestion, are being gradually assimilated to their visceral surroundings. Even in the Madrid *Resurrection* the forms and texture of the naked flesh have assumed a strangely tripe-like aspect. In the case of the nudes in *Laocoon* and *The Opening of the Seventh Seal* (both of them works of El Greco's last years) this process of assimilation has been carried a good deal further. After seeing their draperies and the surrounding landscape gradually peptonized and transformed, the unhappy Jonahs of Toledo discover, to their horror, that they themselves are being digested. Their bodies, their arms and legs, their faces, fingers, toes are ceasing to be humanly their own; they are becoming—the process is slow but inexorably sure—part of the universal Whale's internal workings. It is lucky for them that El Greco died when he did. Twenty years more, and the Trinity, the Communion of Saints and all the human race would have found themselves reduced to hardly distinguishable excrescences on the surface of a cosmic gut. The most favoured might perhaps have aspired to be taenias and trematodes.

For myself, I am very sorry that El Greco did not live to be as old as Titian. At eighty or ninety he would have been producing an almost abstract art—a cubism without cubes, organic, purely visceral. What pictures he would then have painted! Beautiful, thrilling, profoundly appalling. For appalling are even the pictures he painted in middle age, dreadful in spite of their extraordinary power

and beauty. This swallowed universe into which he introduces us is one of the most disquieting creations of the
human mind. One of the most puzzling too. For what were
El Greco's reasons for driving mankind down the red lane?
What induced him to take God out of His boundless
Heaven and shut Him up in a fish's gut? One can only
obscurely speculate. All that I am quite certain of is that
there were profounder and more important reasons for the
whale than the memory of the mosaics—the wholly un-
visceral mosaics—which he may have seen in the course
of a Cretan childhood, a Venetian and Roman youth. Nor
will a disease of the eye account, as some have claimed, for
his strange artistic development. Diseases must be very
grave indeed before they become completely co-extensive
with their victims. That men are affected by their illnesses
is obvious; but it is no less obvious that, except when they
are almost *in extremis,* they are something more than the
sum of their morbid symptoms. Dostoevsky was not merely
personified epilepsy, Keats was other things besides a
simple lump of pulmonary tuberculosis. Men make use
of their illnesses at least as much as they are made use of
by them. It is likely enough that El Greco had something
wrong with his eyes. But other people have had the same
disease without for that reason painting pictures like the
Laocoon and *The Opening of the Seventh Seal.* To say
that El Greco was just a defective eyesight is absurd; he
was a man who used a defective eyesight.

Used it for what purpose? to express what strange
feeling about the world, what mysterious philosophy? It is
hard indeed to answer. For El Greco belongs as a metaphysician (every significant artist is a metaphysician, a
propounder of beauty-truths and form-theories) to no
known school. The most one can say, by way of classifica-
tion, is that, like most of the great artists of the Baroque,
he believed in the validity of ecstasy, of the non-rational,
"numinous" experiences out of which, as a raw material, the

reason fashions the gods or the various attributes of God. But the kind of ecstatic experience artistically rendered and meditated on by El Greco was quite different from the kind of experience which is described and symbolically "rationalized" in the painting, sculpture and architecture of the great Baroque artists of the *seicento*. Those mass-producers of spirituality, the Jesuits, had perfected a simple technique for the fabrication of orthodox ecstasies. They had cheapened an experience, hitherto accessible only to the spiritually wealthy, and so placed it within the reach of all. What the Italian *seicento* artists so brilliantly and copiously rendered was this cheapened experience and the metaphysic in terms of which it could be rationalized. "St. Teresa for All." "A John of the Cross in every Home." Such were, or might have been, their slogans. Was it to be wondered at if their sublimities were a trifle theatrical, their tendernesses treacly, their spiritual intuitions rather commonplace and vulgar? Even the greatest of the Baroque artists were not remarkable for subtlety and spiritual refinement.

With these rather facile ecstasies and the orthodox Counter-Reformation theology in terms of which they could be interpreted, El Greco has nothing to do. The bright reassuring Heaven, the smiling or lachrymose, but always all too human divinities, the stage immensities and stage mysteries, all the stock-in-trade of the *seicentisti*, are absent from his pictures. There is ecstasy and flamy aspiration; but always ecstasy and aspiration, as we have seen, within the belly of a whale. El Greco seems to be talking all the time about the physiological root of ecstasy, not the spiritual flower; about the primary corporeal facts of numinous experience, not the mental derivatives from them. However vulgarly, the artists of the Baroque were concerned with the flower, not the root, with the derivatives and theological interpretations, not the brute facts of immediate physical experience. Not that they were ignorant of the physiological nature of these primary facts. Bernini's astonishing *St. Teresa* proclaims it in the most unequivocal fashion; and it is interesting to note that in this statue (as well as in the very similar and equally astonishing *Ludovica Albertoni* in San Francesco a Ripa) he gives to the draperies a kind of organic and, I might say, intestinal lusciousness of form. A little softened, smoothed and simplified, the robe of the great mystic would be indistinguishable from the rest of the swallowed landscape inside El Greco's whale. Bernini saves the situation (from the Counter-Reformer's point of view) by introducing into his composition the figure of the dart-brandishing angel. This aerial young creature is the inhabitant of an unswallowed Heaven. He carries with him the implication of infinite spaces. Charmingly and a little preposterously (the hand which holds the fiery dart has a delicately crook'd little finger, like the hand of some too refined young person in the act of raising her tea-cup), the angel symbolizes the spiritual flower of ecstasy, whose physiological root is the swooning Teresa in her peritoneal robe. Bernini is, spiritually speaking, a *plein-airiste*.

Not so El Greco. So far as he is concerned, there is nothing outside the whale. The primary physiological fact of religious experience is also, for him, the final fact. He remains consistently on the plane of that visceral consciousness which we so largely ignore, but with which our ancestors (as their language proves) did so much of their feeling and thinking. "Where is thy zeal and thy strength, the sounding of the bowels and of thy mercies towards me?" "My heart is turned within me, my repentings are kindled together." "I will bless the Lord who hath given me counsel; my reins also instruct me in the night season." "For God is my record, how greatly I long after you all in the bowels of Jesus Christ." "For Thou hast possessed my reins." "Is Ephraim my dear son? . . . Therefore my bowels are troubled for him." The Bible abounds in such phrases—phrases which strike the modern reader as queer, a bit indelicate, even repellent. We are accustomed to thinking of ourselves as thinking entirely with our heads. Wrongly, as the physiologists have shown. For what we think and feel and are is to a great extent determined by the state of our ductless glands and viscera. The Psalmist drawing instruction from his reins, the Apostle with his yearning bowels, are thoroughly in the modern physiological movement.

El Greco lived at a time when the reality of the primary visceral consciousness was still recognized—when the heart and the liver, the spleen and reins did all a man's feeling for him, and the four humours of blood, phlegm, choler and melancholy determined his character and imposed his passing moods. Even the loftiest experiences were admitted to be primarily physiological. Teresa knew God in terms of an exquisite pain in her heart, her side, her bowels. But while Teresa, and along with her the generality of human beings, found it natural to pass from the realm of physiology into that of the spirit—from the belly of the whale out into the wide open sky—El Greco obstinately insisted on remaining swallowed. His meditations were all of religious experience and ecstasy—but always of religious experience in its raw physiological state, always of primary, immediate, visceral ecstasy. He expressed these meditations in terms of Christian symbols—of symbols, that is to say, habitually employed to describe experiences quite different from the primary physiological states on which he was accustomed to dwell. It is the contrast between these symbols, with their currently accepted significance, and the special private use to which El Greco puts them—it is this strange contrast which gives to El Greco's pictures their peculiarly disquieting quality. For the Christian symbols remind us of all the spiritual open spaces—the open spaces of altruistic feeling, the open spaces of abstract thought, the open spaces of free-floating spiritual ecstasy. El Greco imprisons them, claps them up in a fish's gut. The symbols of the spiritual open spaces are compelled by him to serve as a language in terms of which he talks about the close immediacies of visceral awareness, about the ecstasy that annihilates the personal soul, not by dissolving it out into universal infinity, but by drawing it down and drowning it in the warm, pulsating, tremulous darkness of the body.

Well, I have wandered far and fancifully from the undertaker king and his enigmatic nightmare of whales and Jonahs. But imaginative wandering is the privilege of the ignorant. When one doesn't know one is free to invent. I have seized the opportunity while it presented itself. One of these days I may discover what the picture is about, and when that has happened I shall no longer be at liberty to impose my own interpretations. Imaginative criticism is essentially an art of ignorance. It is only because we don't know what a writer or artist meant to say that we are free to concoct meanings of our own. If El Greco had somewhere specifically told us what he meant to convey by painting in terms of Black Holes and mucus, I should not now be in a position to speculate. But luckily he never told us; I am justified in letting my fancy loose to wander.

1931

George Orwell

SHOOTING AN ELEPHANT

IN Moulmein, in Lower Burma, I was hated by large numbers of people—the only time in my life that I have been important enough for this to happen to me. I was sub-divisional police officer of the town, and in an aimless, petty kind of way anti-European feeling was very bitter. No one had the guts to raise a riot, but if a European woman went through the bazaars alone somebody would probably spit betel juice over her dress. As a police officer I was an obvious target and was baited whenever it seemed safe to do so. When a nimble Burman tripped me up on the football field and the referee (another Burman) looked the other way, the crowd yelled with hideous laughter. This happened more than once. In the end the sneering yellow faces of young men that met me everywhere, the insults hooted after me when I was at a safe distance, got badly on my nerves. The young Buddhist priests were the worst of all. There were several thousands of them in the town and none of them seemed to have anything to do except stand on street corners and jeer at Europeans.

All this was perplexing and upsetting. For at that time

I had already made up my mind that imperialism was an evil thing and the sooner I chucked up my job and got out of it the better. Theoretically—and secretly, of course —I was all for the Burmese and all against their oppressors, the British. As for the job I was doing, I hated it more bitterly than I can perhaps make clear. In a job like that you see the dirty work of Empire at close quarters. The wretched prisoners huddling in the stinking cages of the lock-ups, the grey, cowed faces of the long-term convicts, the scarred buttocks of the men who had been flogged with bamboos—all these oppressed me with an intolerable sense of guilt. But I could get nothing into perspective. I was young and ill-educated and I had had to think out my problems in the utter silence that is imposed on every Englishman in the East. I did not even know that the British Empire is dying, still less did I know that it is a great deal better than the younger empires that are going to supplant it. All I knew was that I was stuck between my hatred of the empire I served and my rage against the evil-spirited little beasts who tried to make my job impossible. With one part of my mind I thought of the British Raj as an unbreakable tyranny, as something clamped down, in *saecula saeculorum,* upon the will of prostrate peoples; with another part I thought that the greatest joy in the world would be to drive a bayonet into a Buddhist priest's guts. Feelings like these are the normal by-products of imperialism; ask any Anglo-Indian official, if you can catch him off duty.

One day something happened which in a roundabout way was enlightening. It was a tiny incident in itself, but it gave me a better glimpse than I had had before of the real nature of imperialism—the real motives for which despotic governments act. Early one morning the sub-inspector at a police station the other end of the town rang me up on the 'phone and said that an elephant was ravaging the bazaar. Would I please come and do something

about it? I did not know what I could do, but I wanted
to see what was happening and I got on to a pony and
started out. I took my rifle, an old .44 Winchester and
much too small to kill an elephant, but I thought the
noise might be useful *in terrorem*. Various Burmans
stopped me on the way and told me about the elephant's
doings. It was not, of course, a wild elephant, but a tame
one which had gone "must." It had been chained up, as
tame elephants always are when their attack of "must"
is due, but on the previous night it had broken its chain
and escaped. Its mahout, the only person who could manage it when it was in that state, had set out in pursuit,
but had taken the wrong direction and was now twelve
hours' journey away, and in the morning the elephant
had suddenly reappeared in the town. The Burmese population had no weapons and were quite helpless against it.
It had already destroyed somebody's bamboo hut, killed a
cow and raided some fruit-stalls and devoured the stock;
also it had met the municipal rubbish van and, when the
driver jumped out and took to his heels, had turned the
van over and inflicted violences upon it.

The Burmese sub-inspector and some Indian constables
were waiting for me in the quarter where the elephant
had been seen. It was a very poor quarter, a labyrinth of
squalid bamboo huts, thatched with palm-leaf, winding
all over a steep hillside. I remember that it was a cloudy,
stuffy morning at the beginning of the rains. We began
questioning the people as to where the elephant had gone
and, as usual, failed to get any definite information. That
is invariably the case in the East; a story always sounds
clear enough at a distance, but the nearer you get to the
scene of events the vaguer it becomes. Some of the people
said that the elephant had gone in one direction, some said
that he had gone in another, some professed not even to
have heard of any elephant. I had almost made up my
mind that the whole story was a pack of lies, when we

heard yells a little distance away. There was a loud, scandalized cry of "Go away, child! Go away this instant!" and an old woman with a switch in her hand came round the corner of a hut, violently shooing away a crowd of naked children. Some more women followed, clicking their tongues and exclaiming; evidently there was something that the children ought not to have seen. I rounded the hut and saw a man's dead body sprawling in the mud. He was an Indian, a black Dravidian coolie, almost naked, and he could not have been dead many minutes. The people said that the elephant had come suddenly upon him round the corner of the hut, caught him with its trunk, put its foot on his back and ground him into the earth. This was the rainy season and the ground was soft, and his face had scored a trench a foot deep and a couple of yards long. He was lying on his belly with arms crucified and head sharply twisted to one side. His face was coated with mud, the eyes wide open, the teeth bared and grinning with an expression of unendurable agony. (Never tell me, by the way, that the dead look peaceful. Most of the corpses I have seen looked devilish.) The friction of the great beast's foot had stripped the skin from his back as neatly as one skins a rabbit. As soon as I saw the dead man I sent an orderly to a friend's house nearby to borrow an elephant rifle. I had already sent back the pony, not wanting it to go mad with fright and throw me if it smelt the elephant.

The orderly came back in a few minutes with a rifle and five cartridges, and meanwhile some Burmans had arrived and told us that the elephant was in the paddy fields below, only a few hundred yards away. As I started forward practically the whole population of the quarter flocked out of the houses and followed me. They had seen the rifle and were all shouting excitedly that I was going to shoot the elephant. They had not shown much interest in the elephant when he was merely ravaging their homes, but it was different now that he was going to be shot. It was a bit of fun to them, as it would be to an English crowd; besides they wanted the meat. It made me vaguely uneasy. I had no intention of shooting the elephant—I had merely sent for the rifle to defend myself if necessary —and it is always unnerving to have a crowd following you. I marched down the hill, looking and feeling a fool, with the rifle over my shoulder and an ever-growing army of people jostling at my heels. At the bottom, when you got away from the huts, there was a metalled road and beyond that a miry waste of paddy fields a thousand yards across, not yet ploughed but soggy from the first rains and dotted with coarse grass. The elephant was standing eight yards from the road, his left side towards us. He took not the slightest notice of the crowd's approach. He was tearing up bunches of grass, beating them against his knees to clean them and stuffing them into his mouth.

I had halted on the road. As soon as I saw the elephant I knew with perfect certainty that I ought not to shoot him. It is a serious matter to shoot a working elephant— it is comparable to destroying a huge and costly piece of machinery—and obviously one ought not to do it if it can possibly be avoided. And at that distance, peacefully eating, the elephant looked no more dangerous than a cow. I thought then and I think now that his attack of "must" was already passing off; in which case he would merely wander harmlessly about until the mahout came back and caught him. Moreover, I did not in the least want to shoot him. I decided that I would watch him for a little while to make sure that he did not turn savage again, and then go home.

But at that moment I glanced round at the crowd that had followed me. It was an immense crowd, two thousand at the least and growing every minute. It blocked the road for a long distance on either side. I looked at the sea of yellow faces above the garish clothes—faces all happy and excited over this bit of fun, all certain that the elephant was going to be shot. They were watching me as they would watch a conjurer about to perform a trick. They did not like me, but with the magical rifle in my hands I was momentarily worth watching. And suddenly I realized that I should have to shoot the elephant after all. The people expected it of me and I had got to do it; I could feel their two thousand wills pressing me forward, irresistibly. And it was at this moment, as I stood there with the rifle in my hands, that I first grasped the hollowness, the futility of the white man's dominion in the East. Here was I, the white man with his gun, standing in front of the unarmed native crowd—seemingly the leading actor of the piece; but in reality I was only an absurd puppet pushed to and fro by the will of those yellow faces behind. I perceived in this moment that when the white man turns tyrant it is his own freedom that he destroys. He becomes a sort of hollow, posing dummy, the conventionalized figure of a sahib. For it is the condition of his rule that he shall spend his life in trying to impress the "natives," and so in every crisis he has got to do what the "natives" expect of him. He wears a mask, and his face grows to fit it. I had got to shoot the elephant. I had committed myself to doing it when I sent for the rifle. A sahib has got to act like a sahib; he has got to appear resolute, to know his own mind and do definite things. To come all that way, rifle in hand, with two thousand people marching at my heels, and then to trail feebly away, having done nothing—no, that was impossible. The crowd would laugh at me. And my whole life, every white man's life in the East, was one long struggle not to be laughed at.

But I did not want to shoot the elephant. I watched him beating his bunch of grass against his knees, with that preoccupied grandmotherly air that elephants have. It seemed to me that it would be murder to shoot him. At that age I was not squeamish about killing animals, but

I had never shot an elephant and never wanted to. (Somehow it always seems worse to kill a *large* animal.) Besides, there was the beast's owner to be considered. Alive, the elephant was worth at least a hundred pounds; dead, he would only be worth the value of his tusks, five pounds, possibly. But I had got to act quickly. I turned to some experienced-looking Burmans who had been there when we arrived, and asked them how the elephant had been behaving. They all said the same thing: he took no notice of you if you left him alone, but he might charge if you went too close to him.

It was perfectly clear to me what I ought to do. I ought to walk up to within, say, twenty-five yards of the elephant and test his behavior. If he charged, I could shoot; if he took no notice of me, it would be safe to leave him until the mahout came back. But also I knew that I was going to do no such thing. I was a poor shot with a rifle and the ground was soft mud into which one would sink at every step. If the elephant charged and I missed him, I should have about as much chance as a toad under a steam-roller. But even then I was not thinking particularly of my own skin, only of the watchful yellow faces behind. For at that moment, with the crowd watching me, I was not afraid in the ordinary sense, as I would have been if I had been alone. A white man mustn't be frightened in front of "natives"; and so, in general, he isn't frightened. The sole thought in my mind was that if anything went wrong those two thousand Burmans would see me pursued, caught, trampled on and reduced to a grinning corpse like that Indian up the hill. And if that happened it was quite probable that some of them would laugh. That would never do. There was only one alternative. I shoved the cartridges into the magazine and lay down on the road to get a better aim.

The crowd grew very still, and a deep, low, happy sigh,

as of people who see the theatre curtain go up at last, breathed from innumerable throats. They were going to have their bit of fun after all. The rifle was a beautiful German thing with cross-hair sights. I did not then know that in shooting an elephant one would shoot to cut an imaginary bar running from ear-hole to ear-hole. I ought, therefore, as the elephant was sideways on, to have aimed straight at his ear-hole; actually I aimed several inches in front of this, thinking the brain would be further forward.

When I pulled the trigger I did not hear the bang or feel the kick—one never does when a shot goes home— but I heard the devilish roar of glee that went up from the crowd. In that instant, in too short a time, one would have thought, even for the bullet to get there, a mysterious, terrible change had come over the elephant. He neither stirred nor fell, but every line of his body had altered. He looked suddenly stricken, shrunken, immensely old, as though the frightful impact of the bullet had paralysed him without knocking him down. At last, after what seemed a long time—it might have been five seconds, I dare say—he sagged flabbily to his knees. His mouth slobbered. An enormous senility seemed to have settled upon him. One could have imagined him thousands of years old. I fired again into the same spot. At the second shot he did not collapse but climbed with desperate slowness to his feet and stood weakly upright, with legs sagging and head drooping. I fired a third time. That was the shot that did for him. You could see the agony of it jolt his whole body and knock the last remnant of strength from his legs. But in falling he seemed for a moment to rise, for as his hind legs collapsed beneath him he seemed to tower upward like a huge rock toppling, his trunk reaching skywards like a tree. He trumpeted, for the first and only time. And then down he came, his belly towards me, with a crash that seemed to shake the ground even where I lay.

I got up. The Burmans were already racing past me across the mud. It was obvious that the elephant would never rise again, but he was not dead. He was breathing very rhythmically with long rattling gasps, his great mound of a side painfully rising and falling. His mouth was wide open—I could see far down into caverns of pale pink throat. I waited a long time for him to die, but his breathing did not weaken. Finally I fired my two remaining shots into the spot where I thought his heart must be. The thick blood welled out of him like red velvet, but still he did not die. His body did not even jerk when the shots hit him, the tortured breathing continued without a pause. He was dying, very slowly and in great agony, but in some world remote from me where not even a bullet could damage him further. I felt that I had got to put an end to that dreadful noise. It seemed dreadful to see the great beast lying there, powerless to move and yet powerless to die, and not even to be able to finish him. I sent back for my small rifle and poured shot after shot into his heart and down his throat. They seemed to make no impression. The tortured gasps continued as steadily as the ticking of a clock.

In the end I could not stand it any longer and went away. I heard later that it took him half an hour to die. Burmans were bringing dahs and baskets even before I left, and I was told they had stripped his body almost to the bones by the afternoon.

Afterwards, of course, there were endless discussions about the shooting of the elephant. The owner was furious, but he was only an Indian and could do nothing. Besides, legally I had done the right thing, for a mad elephant has to be killed, like a mad dog, if its owner fails to control it. Among the Europeans opinion was divided. The older men said I was right, the younger men said it was a damn shame to shoot an elephant for killing a coolie, because an elephant was worth more than any damn Coringhee coolie. And afterwards I was very glad that the coolie had been killed; it put me legally in the right and it gave me a sufficient pretext for shooting the elephant. I often wondered whether any of the others grasped that I had done it solely to avoid looking a fool.

1931

Van Wyck Brooks

THE UNACKNOWLEDGED LEGISLATORS

I MUST confess I believe," said Mr. H. G. Wells, in one of his early essays, "that if, by some juggling with space and time, Julius Caesar, Napoleon, Edward IV, William the Conqueror, Lord Rosebery and Robert Burns had all been changed at birth it would not have produced any serious dislocation of the course of destiny." There we have the Marxist view of the great man, the logic of the economic interpretation of history, the antipole of Carlyle's view which prevailed throughout the world in the nineteenth century. Any other view of the individual and his powers is, to the Marxist, and as Mr. Wells himself puts it, "melodramatic." The world in general has come round to this way of thinking; for the war seemed to confirm it. Where were the soldiers, the statesmen, the individuals of any kind who were sufficiently evil to have caused the war, sufficiently wise to have stopped it, or strong enough to have compassed either of these actions? The world, people say, has become so "big" that the human will cannot control the forces that sweep it like the tides. And the hope of the liberals in the power of an organized intelligence that knows only an intelligent leadership, a leadership that has no spiritual sanction, is all

Taken from *Sketches in Criticism* by Van Wyck Brooks, published and copyrighted, 1932, by E. P. Dutton and Co., Inc., New York.

that stands between the popular mind and an almost Oriental fatalism.

And yet this universal modern view is one which the student of literature cannot accept. "Great writers and artists," said Tolstoy once, in conversation with an American friend, "are to me the high priests and leaders of evolution, the real sovereigns, who rule, not by force of guns and armies, but by moral authority." Was Tolstoy the victim of a delusion, intoxicated with the conceit of his own power, a power over words? The history of culture plainly bears him out. No doubt the creative spirit has always fought in its day on the losing side: the great men are always despised and rejected and speak in all appearance to the wind. But the great men are not time's laughing-stocks: even in the economic sphere it is they who rule. The Marxists reject great men and are themselves the creatures of Karl Marx; and a creature of Karl Marx—Nicolai Lenin—labelled in his own person, as the lie it is, the notion that statesmanship cannot be creative. And Lenin's tomb to-day is the visible witness of the spiritual power which the hero exercises in life and after death. The world is too "big" to be controlled not because greatness is an illusion but because the material discoveries of the last century have put to sleep for the moment the faculty in men that responds to greatness. But a century is short, and the memory of mankind is long; and we cannot believe in the lasting dominion of blind forces, we who believe in literature. We are obliged, as regards the function of writers and artists, to accept—and let them call it what they like—the "melodramatic" view: for history bears us out. We are obliged, in a word, to believe in heroes, whether they swagger or not.

And partly because of the light, corroborating our faith, that psychology has thrown upon these blind forces. So little has civilization advanced that we are still savages cowering in fear of a sinister "nature" that exists in reality only within ourselves. We no longer fear lightning and storms and those other phenomena which to primitive man appear as emanations of the Adversary. But we still fear what we imagine to be the "not ourselves" just the same; and, fearing it, we create objects for our fear. We fear poverty, and our fear is responsible for the oppression that seems to justify it; we fear war, and our fear creates war; we fear the loss of caste, we fear the downfall of our nationality, and our fear keeps us in jeopardy. These blind forces, in short, that dominate us and that are, as we suppose, outside of us and beyond our control, are in reality projections of the blind forces in our own spirits. If, for instance, we did not desire wealth, how could they have dominion over us, those who appear to prevent us from acquiring it? Our desire makes us their victims. If we did not fear the loss of caste, how could we lose our caste? The fearless have no caste. If people did not, as members of a nationality, wish to outrival some other nationality, how could an aggressive war occur? The incubuses that sit upon mankind are the reflexes of mankind's own weaknesses. We tolerate them because we fear them, and we fear them because there is something in ourselves that demands what they supply. If we became conscious of that "something," conscious of our wishes and demands, and checked them in the light of the "ideals" to which we pay lip-service every day, these incubuses would collapse like the balloons they are. What happened to "imperialism" in India when Gandhi led the boycott of British goods? What would happen to the "capitalistic system" if humanity suddenly went on a hunger-strike? One does not say that humanity will, or should, do anything of the kind; but humanity might, humanity surely can. There is nothing in the world humanity cannot do; there are few things humanity has not done. History has witnessed crusades, revolts, revolutions, flights, migrations, treks beyond all counting; it has witnessed Reformations and Revivals, holy wars, sudden "returns to nature," movements of purification, revaluations of all known values. History, in fact, has witnessed nothing else. And in every case the poets, priests and prophets have set the tune, composed the martial music.

For literature *awakens*. We Americans are all too familiar with the psychology of advertising: how many of our desires have been awakened by advertising? Without advertising, how many Americans would ever have discovered that four porcelain bathtubs, five kinds of talcum-powder, and six kinds of soap are essential in a civilized household? The brisk young business man of our day (who is not so brisk as he was a decade ago)—"Arrow" collar, "style-plus" raiment, "quality" shoes, "distinctive" necktie, haughty frown and all, is, from top to toe, a creation of the advertisers. The desire to approximate to a certain pattern has been evoked in him from without, and he responds with all the alacrity of a true son of freedom.

What advertising does, literature does also. For who would say that the desires of men can be confined to soap and a haughty frown? In other ages very different patterns of character and behaviour have been placed before the young, and the young have responded with just as much alacrity. Who can count indeed the impulses which, in history, poets have stirred to life, unlocked, as it were, and liberated into the sphere of action? Under the eyes of this generation, Ireland has awakened to the desire to become itself, to direct its own destinies; and what was the fountainhead of that desire but the poets of Ireland? The conditions were ripe, the people had become susceptible, the poets spoke. To what extent was not the character of the Russian Revolution, of the French Revolution, determined by the characters of poets, novelists and philosophers? Who evoked in the French of the Napoleonic epoch that thirst for glory which placed them in the hands of their Emperor? Who convinced the Germans that they were a Chosen Race? Literature is not directly an ethical force; one must see it first of all as a force merely. For poets can play upon human nature, for good and for evil also, as a musician plays on an instrument; they can evoke from it desires that respond to their own desires. Man, in fact, with his whole scale of latent impulses, lies at the mercy of this eloquent agent of what Emerson called the Over-Soul, this Pied Piper of the Unconscious.

The English novelist, Miss M. P. Willcocks, has very justly noted that Balzac "founded a whole over-world of imaginative figures that, acted upon by 'real' life as they were, yet reacted in their turn upon reality itself, and so became directly productive on the plane where men buy and sell, draw up contracts, or engage in trade-warfare. The characters found in the pages of novels or on the boards of the theatre, became the moulds into which action itself was ultimately poured." She is discussing, apropos of Balzac, the "strange interaction between man's acts and man's dreams" and the extent to which the life of trading, fighting and begetting has been, in the forms in which we have known it, the outcome of ideals that have gathered round the stories of great "saviours" and of lesser characters, real and imaginary; and indeed, as Emile Faguet pointed out, the whole tone of French society was altered by Balzac's influence, types and characters arising on every hand, in the generation that followed him, reproducing in life all the traits that Balzac had conceived in fiction. This is merely one of the illustrations of Oscar Wilde's idea that life holds the mirror up to art. "Scientifically speaking," said Wilde, "the basis of life—the energy of life, as Aristotle would call it—is simply the desire for expression, and art is always presenting various forms through which this expression can be attained. Life seizes on them and uses them, even if they be to her own hurt. Young men have committed suicide because Rolla did so . . . Think of what we owe to the imitation of Christ, of what we owe to the imitation of Caesar." And think, let us add, of what we owe to the imitation, in the United States, of great industrial leaders who describe history as "bunk" and philosophy as "ninny stuff"; to the imitation, in Russia, of Nicolai Lenin! It used to be said that the women of England grew perceptibly taller as a result of Du Maurier's cartoons; and no doubt Du Maurier did spread the fashion of a more erect carriage.

Thus writers and artists, and men of action too, when they use words and phrases, play upon us and mould us to their wills. And that is why one cannot understand such contentions, for instance, as Mr. Max Eastman's, that "the real motor forces in social evolution" are "currents of material interest." Who would deny that currents of material interest are indeed forces? That is another matter: it does not conflict with Pascal's observation that history would have been altogether different if Cleopatra's nose had been shorter. During the four years of the war the world was so drugged and confused by propaganda that it lost all power of coherent action. Was any "material interest" at the bottom of it, that humanity allowed itself to be led about by the nose, a nose that lacked the sagacity of Cleopatra's? It was sentiment, sentiment, sentiment all the time: adventure, loyalty, hatred, love, bravado. And what was this propaganda but a kind of literature? Practical men do not spend tens of millions for any commodity unless they think they are getting their money's worth; and who has ever computed the tens of millions that were spent during the war on the written word? Far from proving the truth of Mr. Eastman's contention, the events of recent years prove nothing so much as that the real motor forces in social evolution are not by any means "currents of material interest," but rather currents of feeling, currents, moreover, which, as often as not, lead to the exact reverse of any "interest." The only thing they really prove, in fact, is the infinite plasticity of human nature. For what is the meaning of the power of this propaganda? That human nature is ductile and suggestible; and, for the rest, that the human imagination can be made to work as readily for evil as for good. Granting a single instance of a social change resulting from the influence of the written work, the fact, for instance, that, as a result of Rousseau's agitation, the women of the French aristocracy began once more to suckle their own children, and how can one set a limit to the possible power of artists and writers, their ideas, their visions, their examples?

This was what Shelley meant when he asserted that "poets are the unacknowledged legislators of the world," who, in the end, will be found to legislate in the interests of goodness and beauty. And if it is true that a poet can also be what William Morris called "the idle singer of an empty day," one can still reply: That depends on the poet.

1932

Hugh MacDiarmid

LIFE IN THE SHETLAND ISLANDS

IF the real Robinson Crusoe had the good luck to land on an island where tropical conditions obtained and the problems of securing shelter and food were accordingly at a minimum, I felt justified in preparing for staging my first venture at such a life where both these problems are exceedingly acute by selecting an island which, though uninhabited, is within easy enough distance of other inhabited islands to make it reasonably likely that the waving of a coat would attract attention.

I went further. The adjacent islands, if inhabited, are only sparsely so; a coat or something might be waved for weeks without being seen; besides, my jacket and my raincoat are of a colour that would be practically indiscernible. My shirt is brighter, but the weather would prohibit any undressing for the purpose of removing it and waving it as a flag. I did not trust to such chances of rescue. I arranged with the boatman who took me over from the inhabited island of Whalsay to the uninhabited island of Linga to train his telescope on a given spot on the third day afterwards in the early afternoon, and, if I was seen standing there, to come over and fetch me. If not, to keep on doing so every afternoon thereafter until I was so seen—if I ever was. The boatman suspected that I might commit suicide,

Reprinted by special permission of the author.

but he did not communicate his suspicions to anyone else; he did as he was told; he trained his telescope on the arranged spot in the early afternoon of the third day, but he was a bit of a Nelson. I was not there, as a matter of fact, but even if I had been he could not have seen me, for a thick wall of fog (one of the many little matters I had not foreseen or provided for in the arrangements I made). Nevertheless, he came, and I returned to Whalsay with him.

I took no food with me to Linga, but I took a good supply of the thick black tobacco which is my habitual smoke and plenty of matches. I felt justified in doing this, since it was past the season when birds' eggs are to be found all over the island and even the later period when young birds can be caught by the hand among the rocks. It would be extremely difficult to bring down any of the birds still about. I suppose a more resourceful fellow than myself might have managed to collar one or two of them in their nests during the night, but they nested in places that are precariously enough accessible even by day to one who is less sure-footed than one of the local sheep, and apart from the perils of rock-climbing, I suffer from night-blindness. I had decided if I did catch one to cook it in the way I had heard of gipsies cooking hedgehogs in Dumfriesshire in my boyhood: cover it—feathers, intestines and all the rest of it intact—in a nice thick coating of mud, and put it in the middle of a good-going fire until the mud was baked hard and had begun to crack. Then I would poke the ball out of the fire, let it cool a little, and break off the fired-clay covering, which would bring the feathers and skin away with it and disclose the flesh, done to a nicety.

The contingency did not, however, arise. So far as a larder was concerned then, I was restricted to the chances of rabbits or fish. There are black and blue rabbits on the island, but they are very scarce. As a boy—in a place where rabbits were far more plentiful—I had succeeded in coming up to them and bringing a stick down upon them. I wondered if I could repeat the feat. I never saw a rabbit to attempt it upon, however. There were plenty of nice, fat "sillocks" (first-year saithe) close in to the shore; at times the top of the sea was quite solid with them. I caught four—with a piece of string I found among the flotsam and jetsam in one of the little coves, or "gios," as the Shetlanders call them, and a bent pin. I had not brought the pin of *malice prepense;* it was a pure accident that I happened to have one in the bottom seam of my waistcoat.

But for that I should probably have had nothing to eat these three days; the four "sillocks" were all I did have. Catching them with bent pins is common practice in the Shetlands. They are so easily caught; they practically jump into your hands at times if you hold these an inch or thereby above the surface of the water. Occasionally I saw the dark patches in the water close in, indicating the presence of shoals of mackerel; but you cannot catch mackerel with a bent pin. Nor can you catch a dog-fish with a bent pin; there were any amount of them hard in to the shore. The Shetland people do not eat them; but, under the name of "rock turbot" and other fancy appellations, they sell well in the South of England, and are, as a matter of fact, quite good eating.

I said that, failing birds, I was restricted to the chances of rabbits or fish; there was one other possibility. I feel certain now that I would have killed a sheep (one of this year's lambs) rather than have gone a day or two longer than I actually did without food beyond the four "sillocks." The Shetland lamb season had just begun; one could buy a lamb for five or six shillings. I thought a little of the practical problems involved—I have never seen a lamb butchered—and decided they were not insurmountable. I am not so certain now, however, as I am that, given a day or two longer, I would have killed a lamb, that I would have surmounted the difficulties of killing and skinning and cutting it up quite so easily. My only instrument would have been my pen-knife, which I keep for the twin purposes of cutting up my plug tobacco and digging the dottel out of the bottom of my pipe. I am afraid it would have been a very gruesome business. However, as I have said, the boatman came on the third day. So the contingency did not arise after all.

I slept in a cave in the rocks. It was very cold, and in any case I should say "lay at nights" instead of "slept," because I found the glug-glug of the water against the rocks and the roar of the tides in a little bed of shingle away up at the top of the cave very annoying. There are no trees in the Shetlands; so it was impossible to find any sheltered spot on the surface of the island to lie in; and there is no bracken or long grass, so it was impossible to gather anything to make any sort of bed on my ledge of rock. A little earlier on it would have been possible to read in the open until well after midnight; indeed, there is practically no night. But by this time the long light of the summer-time had given way to the opposite conditions when there is a very short day. I had brought with me a volume of Rilke's poems and Theodora Bosanquet's little book on Paul Valéry; but I did not open either of them. I was too busy; lying for the most part on that rocky ledge with the sound of the sea in my ears and the darkness of the cave (broken only by the yellow flashing of innumerable matches and the red glow of my lit pipe) grateful to my eyes, doing nothing—but what I intended to do, which was sufficiently engrossing to keep me from being lonely or conscious very much of either cold or hunger; for I am a poet myself, or think I am, which explains the whole thing. All the same, I would have killed a sheep. I will yet—and stay on the island till I have eaten the whole of it. Poetry must be served. But it will be a few weeks earlier in the year, and I will also have an eider duck or green cormorant or two and a plentiful supply of mushrooms.

2

The Shetland Islands are fighting (in a curious fashion, as will appear as this article proceeds) a losing battle. The fishing, upon which they principally depend, is in a bad way; the population is rapidly declining; crofts are falling into desuetude and the ground is being increasingly acquired by big sheep-farmers. It is a significant fact that as soon as Shetlanders abandon the calling of the sea they begin to wear an extraordinary excess of clothes and to live in more and more oven-like homes with sealed windows and big fires. A couple of pairs of thick drawers may be necessary for a fisherman, especially in the exposure of the small boats prosecuting the haddock-fishing; but the superimposition of fifteen sets of underclothing on a schoolboy is another matter. Yet a school M.O. found that in one case; and remonstrance with the elderly aunts with whom the boy lived only evoked the obstinate answer that he was a Scotsman and did not understand how cold it was in the Shetlands. As a matter of fact it is much less cold in the Shetlands than it is in Edinburgh, or in the Thames Valley. There is a sharp differentiation in physique and health between the children of those who are still fisher-folk (the vast majority) and those who are not. The former are by far the healthier. It is, indeed, impossible to eke out a decent living in the Shetlands by crofting alone. That is the difference between the Orkneys and the Shetlands. The Orcadian is a farmer with a boat; the Shetlander is a fisherman with a croft.

The Shetlanders know perfectly well that there is no real reason why they should not have a very prosperous fishing industry. But they have never had it. In the old days they lived under conditions of virtual slavery; the laird had to get his share of all the fish they caught, then the minister had to get his, and between them these two gentlemen got the best of the fish. The Shetlanders had to live on the balance and the similarly-taxed crops of their small crofts. Bad seasons put them into debt to the lairds, and they never got their feet clear; nor were the lairds sufficiently enlightened in their self-interest to equip the fishermen in the most effective fashion. They had to work with craft and tackle inferior to that being introduced elsewhere; and any offence meant their expulsion from the islands. Such conditions induced a secret radicalism and an external sycophancy—characteristics which survive in the Shetlanders today in the forms of a hidden preservation of their real lives and an outward accessibility to current conventions generally. This duality makes the Shetlanders very difficult to know to anyone who does not actually live long enough in the Shetlands to win the native confidence and secure acceptance as if island-born. The power of the lairds has almost entirely disappeared, of course; they are poorer than many of the fisher-folk and virtually dependent in many ways on their charity; and it is amusing to observe how the old bland dealing with them on the part of the fisher-folk, masking their true feelings under an even amiability, persists in the present attitude to these superiors in reduced circumstances— an attitude of affected humility and readiness to help, backed with the clear realization that if the wheel of fortune should restore them to any measure of power the gentry, now so innocuous, would instantly manifest again their predecessors' old characteristics of ruthless exaction and injustice. Happily their wings have been shorn away; a "revenge complex" never manifested itself in a subtler and more patient form; the sons and daughters of the victims of an age-long oppression of almost unparalleled savagery know how the heirs of the oppressors are now placed and afford themselves the luxury of being sorry for them, but do not avail themselves of any opportunity of taking political or practical measures at variance with a species of lip-service to the shadow of the ancient status. This negativeness is the outstanding feature of life in the Shetlands. It would almost seem as if the psychology of it were a sense that the traditional oppression had vanished, but that a definite move in any direction might incur other oppressions still more dire. And there is a great wisdom in that. Poor though they may be, and hard though they may have to work, they have now a certain independence —they are self-subsisting in regard to the staples of life; they lead a kind of all-round life rare in these days of the greater and greater division of labour, farming, fishing, building, cobbling, butchering, knitting and what not each household for itself; their time is their own to make of it what they will and can. All their intromissions with organized industry and commerce, and with life as it arises in the form of education, newspapers, radio and other contacts with the outside world, and everything that does not spring directly out of that core of island economy, are marginal to that substantial body of free living, within which they maintain themselves not only materially but spiritually. They may profess the same religious and political and other views and interest as people elsewhere, just as they talk English and not their own old Norse language; but all such professions are only a protective camouflage. On that level they give visitors an impression of quiet candour and good nature; but visitors must not attempt to probe below that to the real nature of their lives. They do not want the latter discussed in any way. So long as writers confine themselves to a rehash of the traditional lore, stories of the Vikings, general descriptive matter, and mere tittle-tattle, they will approve; but they resent any writing that slips below the surface. They do not want to be "disturbed in their warm corner." For that is the essence of the matter. Given the measure of independence they have, the island economy is in curiously surreptitious enjoyment of a measure of Douglasism—of economic nationalism within the present framework of international interdependence and high finance. The degree to which the latter impinges upon them does not, in their particular conditions of living, deprive them of a sufficient field of self-reliance which that system cannot touch. Their fishing industry is a mere fraction of what it might be, thanks to trawler combines, poaching within the three-mile limit, the rigging of the markets by alien financial interests, and the interposition of middleman parasitism of all kinds. But where a Douglasite might contend that an immense access of prosperity was immediately practicable, what the Shetlanders are concerned about is the really extraordinary degree of comfort and well-being obtainable under the existing system in conditions such as theirs where this measure of independence obtains and self-subsistence as the first call on their activities is practicable. They are not going to risk anything that may deprive them of that; they know perfectly well that strangers watching their toilsome lives and little externally-poor cottages have no idea of the degree of comfort that actually obtains in their homes; they have a not-unnatural fear—akin to that which leads a certain type of well-to-do person to dress quietly and avoid ostentation—of "giving the game away." They do not believe they could in essentials be a great deal better off; but for certain easily specifiable lets and hindrances they could be as well off with a great deal less exertion and hardship—but there are perhaps worse things than such exertion and hardship, and a mere increase of monetary wealth without a proportionate enrichment of their actual lives does not attract them—does not, at all events, counterbalance the danger of any active endeavour to secure it. So they argue. Who can say that they are wrong? Who dare advise them to risk anything that might, whatever else it brought them, diffuse or dilute the deep integrity of their lives? Who can assail the shrewdness that realizes the brevity of individual lives in a way that disencourages any attempt to envisage the remote benefits that might accrue from present sacrifices, or the relative unimportance of the few thousands of Shetlanders to those world-affairs that breed the over-riding factors that, in the last analysis, so largely determine the precise width of the margin on which the island economy can continue to operate? They have a real autonomy in basic matters; so they refuse to respond to any denunciation of that centralization of their affairs in London which in all other matters stultifies their local initiative. "Faithful in small things," they are not to be shaken in their allegiance to them by hopes that they could do as well in greater.

Behind these economic matters there lies a very interesting life, in the various aspects of which not dissimilar tactics in dealing with the outside world are discernible. They may speak of the Shetlands as "The Viking Isles" and recall old traditions; but they have really little or no history, and have allowed the old Norse language, which would have differentiated them superficially from the Scots and the English, to lapse. Yet whilst sacrificing the obvious signs of separate raciality, and under a surface appearance of practical at-one-ment with the people of Scotland and England, with whom they share the same language, the same religion, the same education, the same newspapers and broadcast programmes, and other apparent interests, their social spirit is profoundly different. The deep difference does not manifest itself externally; it does not issue in cultural or political movements—it concerns the very texture and inmost essence of their lives. They belong, nominally, to the Church of Scotland, which dispenses them from any necessity to discuss religion; they have allowed themselves to forget their history and ancient speech because they know that by thus converting positive things into negative things they do not weaken them but render them less susceptible of recognition and attack; but their deep hold upon their own essential tradition is maintained in many ways, as, for example, in their sexual and matrimonial customs. How can one prove the latter? They will blandly deny that any such difference exists. Nothing in their appearance—at least nothing at all easy to discern—in the tone of the island life—discloses the fact that in these intimate relationships they pursue a course which would be repudiated everywhere in Scotland and England as "immoral," "dangerous," or "unthinkable." Yet it is so. On certain nights in the week the lads go to their lassies' homes and to bed with them, with the full knowledge and approval of the parents. It is understood that "if anything happens" marriage will follow; and it almost invariably does. As in other peasant communities, where similar customs are known, this simple resolution of the complications of adolescence seems to induce a forthrightness and understanding between the sexes and a complete lack of furtiveness, pretences, discomforts, and general cant and humbug. Or perhaps it is the simplicity of the people which makes the custom possible. Once a young islander goes with a girl he is—almost invariably—with her "for keeps." None of the other girls would have anything to do with him if, after once committing himself, he attempted to "change over." The Shetland practice puts the relationship of the sexes on a natural basis. It is true, of course, that one man may be more suited to a certain woman than to any other woman; but under their system he is perhaps as likely to hit upon his "true affinity" as under any other. What is certain is that the individual differences between men and women who live in hearty contact with hard and essential labour are relatively unimportant set beside the possibility of any average man and woman making an average good job of the business if, having once come together, they determine to play their part by each other. And that is what happens in the Shetlands. Romance in the sex-relation is replaced by a general realistic co-operation which can well dispense with it. And as a matter of fact Shetland couples are extremely faithful and affectionate, and have, moreover, that essential equality which comes from being mutually indispensable in the given way of life, for the degree of independence of which I have spoken is dependent in almost equal measure on the exertions of both partners. Much of the work of the croft devolves upon the woman, while the man is at his fishing. They are literally tireless, these Shetland women, carrying their loads of peat in the "kishies" (as they call the peat baskets) resting on their backs, and knitting as they go. Here too, as everywhere, the "law of compensation" is at work, for the effect of "kishie" carrying on the woman's back is said to ease child-bearing.

These brief notes touch only the fringe of a difficult and little-known subject, and have communicated nothing of my love for these island people amongst whom I live. The few aspects of Shetland life upon which I have commented are only pointers to a "way of living" which, so far as I am personally concerned, makes the Shetlanders by far the most interesting and attractive people in that congeries of very varied groups which constitute the people of Scotland, of whom a recent writer has said: "Though Scotland is a small country, yet there are many Scotlands; South Uist differs more from the Merse, let alone from Motherwell, than Rochdale from Dorset, or even Lille from Béarn."

3

"Scotland's greatest exclave." The claim involved in so describing the Shetland Islands will, no doubt, be hotly contested by the Hebridean enthusiasts, though there can be no challenge if the term "greatest" is taken to mean in superficial area, in present or potential economic value, or in historical interest. But I mean rather more than all that even. I am using the term "greatest exclave" in its strictest sense as well, meaning that the essential traditions, life, problems, and potentialities of the Shetlands are at the furthest remove from the general conceptions bound up in the term "Scottish" and that the greatest ignorance about them prevails on the Scottish mainland itself. They are the greatest of our unrealized possessions—a province capable of greater regional planning than any and of a more distinctive cultural development. My point can be readily established by comparing the tourist traffic to the Hebrides with the almost negligible tourist traffic to the Shetlands; the scantiness and poverty of books or articles about the Shetlands with the constant succession of volumes about the "Immortal Isles" and newspaper and magazine articles on Iona, Syke, Hebridean song, and so forth; the relative familiarity of the Gaelic language to the Norn; and the history and character of the land problem and traditions of the western islands to the general ignorance of the udal system and the very different but not less chequered and tragic history of *Ultima Thule*. The appeal of the Shetlands is not so facile as that of the Hebrides, nor has it been eked out with so many adventitious aids. This is not altogether a misfortune. If the Shetlands are much less known they have at all events escaped the dangers of superficial and general false enthusiasm and have nothing to correspond to "Celtic Twilightism." If the fake-glamour of the Hebrides has become a weariness to the flesh and a real obstacle to their true appreciation, an insistence on the claims of the Shetlands may now prove a useful corrective and help to establish a properly balanced conception of Scotland as a whole. A sense of actuality will serve us better than any artificial allure.

It is all the more regrettable that so few holiday-makers come to the Shetlands since the essence of a holiday is a complete change, and this the Shetland Islands offer to mainland dwellers to a far greater extent than is obtainable anywhere else within easy reach, which is to say, at moderate cost. Superficially even, the Shetlands are quite unlike Scotland, and, unless the visitor has been prepared in advance, he or she may find it difficult to account for the sense of something very different—the sense of something wanting. It may take them a little time to realize that what is affecting them is the total absence of trees and of running water. But one quickly gets accustomed to that, and appreciates that, even if trees and singing streams could be introduced, they would be no improvement; they would simply make the Shetlands like other places we know, whereas, without them, the Shetlands are complete in themselves, and the absence of these usual features of the countryside does not involve any deficiency or monotony. There is no less variety of form and colour; just as we find it difficult in other connections to imagine how we could get on without certain things we are accustomed to, so here it surprises one to discover how easily even the presence of trees and rivers can be dispensed with and how, instead of a sense of loss, we soon realize that their absence throws into relief features we seldom see or underprize because of them—the infinite beauties of the bare land and the shapes and colours of the rocks which first of all impress one with a sense of sameness and next delight one with a revelation of the endless resource of Nature albeit in subtler and less showy or sensational forms than we are accustomed to appreciate in regions of more profuse development. It is in fact the treasures and rich lessons of a certain asceticism the Shetlands provide, and these offset in an invaluable way our normal indulgences in scenic display. But the spirit of the Shetlands is not easily or speedily apprehended; one must accustom oneself patiently to a different aspect of the world, a different rhythm of life, before one can fully understand how its variations from what we have been used to are counter-balanced by its own essential qualities. The lack of ostentatious appearances, the seeming bareness and reserve, make the Shetlands insusceptible of being readily or quickly understood; one must steep oneself in them, let them grow upon one, to savour them properly. It is a splendid discipline.

Though frank and kindly, the Shetland people are like their country; their distinctive qualities and traditions are not seen at a glance, but must be carefully studied to be truly gauged. It is not because they are "clannish" and debar the incomer from intimacy, but simply that the essential differences of their racial and cultural background and mode of life are in themselves elusive and easily missed by the hasty observer. You will hear little of the old Norn speech; you will hear little of the strange beliefs in the trolls and so forth; you will be able to detect still less of the lets and hindrances of their secret adhesions to old customs and ways of thought still effective in their vital practice but seldom consciously admitted, or attributed to their true origins, even by themselves under their quiet but friendly exteriors. They are a secret people, not by active concealment, but because they are so natural and unselfconscious in their unobtrusive but very real differences that these habitually escape the observation of the impatient and uninstructed, and because nowadays most of the Shetlanders themselves have lost most of the obvious manifestations—in language, costume, social habits, and so on—of those essential differences which are as potent as ever in their intimate selves. Outside Lerwick and one or two other small townships which are in no wise typical, one of the signs of this different life and different attitude to life is to be seen in the fact that the cottages, instead of being grouped into little villages or clachans, stand separately, each on its own croft. This does not mean that the people are unsociable—they are far from that—but simply that they are independent and self-reliant; they do not need to stand shoulder to shoulder either for gossip's sake or mutual support against the danger of bogies. This may seem a small thing, but it is very significant, and an understanding of the Shetlands can only be got by slowly and carefully piecing together such little signs and symbols. Another illustration may help to make my meaning clear. Southern city people looking out over a grey Shetland landscape dotted with these little isolated cottages, each by its own scanty patch of vegetation, might conclude that these were the outward signs of a very hard, stoical, and niggardly life, destitute of all the amenities of civilization; but to go into these seemingly poor cottages is to appreciate at once that, despite appearances, there is a "routh of gear," an unexpected degree of comfort, a rich family and social life. So it is with all the outward appearances in the Shetlands; a very vivid and generous life lies behind them, and whatever may be missing of what is taken for granted elsewhere, this different tradition of existence has its own fullness and ample compensations in every respect.

In one respect, however, the outward signs are not misleading. The Shetlands are going steadily downhill; the population is decreasing, there is a passive attitude to adverse conditions, a lack of local initiative or a realization that alien over-control and centralization in London make any attempt at local initiative vain. This negative attitude —this capacity for endlessly tightening the belt and yet preserving a tranquil and apparently contented mien— has, of course, a long and tragic history, and dates back to the times of feudal oppression and Shetland's deprivation of the old Norse laws and liberty. They have at least a strong subconscious feeling that their present affiliations are hopelessly wrong—that their problems and potentialities are being posed against a wrong background and cannot therefore be seen in proper or useful proportion. They are fully alive to their situation both in regard to the fishing industry and the other aspects of their island economy; they know the remedy—but they feel that under present conditions it is inapplicable; they will do nothing. But they entertain this feeling without much, if any, sense of grievance; they are not embittered, only they are used to disappointment and hardship, and (this is the point) accustomed behind the scenes, at their own firesides and in their own personalities to triumph over them with a resource and a quiet puissance of character which is apt to seem incredible to the outsider discerning enough to catch a glimpse of it.

Their case, however, is what that of the Faroe Islands was seventy or eighty years ago. The Faroes were then on the verge of destitution. Since then they have risen to comparative affluence, built up a prosperous and progressive fishing industry and developed a vigorous national renaissance in every aspect of arts and affairs. The Faroes did this by breaking off alien ties opposed to their true national development; and by putting their activities once more upon their natural basis and developing them in accordance with the dictates of a true local economy, they have risen to their present healthy and happy condition. The Shetlands could do likewise, given like courage and enterprise and an effective re-orientation on their true basis. But there is no sign of any such attempt so far. If it does come, the Shetlands may become the theatre of an exceedingly interesting politico-economic-cultural movement; but till it does they will remain Scotland's greatest exclave, the neglected of the neglected, a sphere of lapsed traditions and unapprehended possibilities, a congeries of islands of a forlorn fascination which is to be found nowhere else.

1934

In giving permission to reprint this essay, Mr. Mac-Diarmid asks us to add the following paragraph:

Since the above essay was written, there has been a considerable revival of local patriotism in the Shetland archipelago, carrying with it a fair amount of economic regeneration, including a marked development of the tourist industry and the provision of improved transport services, hotel and boarding-house accommodation, and other facilities for visitors, and a growth of a lively movement for the revival of the old Shetland language. Along with this a strong literary movement has manifested itself and "The New Shetlander" is a monthly organ of a numerous group of young Shetland writers whose work on the whole compares favourably with that of the writers of the Scottish Renaissance Movement on the mainland of Scotland. Many new books, descriptive, scientific, and historical, dealing with Shetland have been published during the past few years. (*1951*)

Edmund Wilson

A. E. HOUSMAN

THE VOICE, SENT FORTH, CAN NEVER BE
RECALLED

WHEN A. E. Housman's *Introductory Lecture* delivered in 1892 "Before the Faculties of Arts and Laws and of Science in University College, London" was reprinted in 1933, Housman characteristically wrote of it as follows: "The Council of University College, not I, had the lecture printed." He described it as "rhetorical and not wholly sincere" and put upon the title-page, "*Nescit vox missa reverti.*"

The little essay is curious in largely evading the questions it raises and taking the direction of a piece of special pleading for the author's own pursuits. Both the sciences and the arts, says Housman, are ordinarily defended by arguments which make their interests appear mutually antagonistic. But the arguments on both sides are mistaken. Science is said to be useful; but what is the use, for example, of a great deal of astronomical research? And the business men who make practical use of the results of scientific study are usually not scientists at all. (They do make use of them, nevertheless; and the results of the most gratuitious researches are always likely to turn out to be useful.) The Humanities, on the other hand, are supposed to "transform and beautify our inner nature by culture." Yet the proportion of the human race capable of

From *The Triple Thinkers* by Edmund Wilson. Reprinted by permission of the author.

being benefited by classical studies is certainly very small, and these "can attain the desired end without that minute and accurate study of the classical tongues which affords Latin professors their only excuse for existing." Not even the great critics of the classics are genuine classical scholars: "When it comes to literary criticism, heap up in one scale all the literary criticism that the whole nation of professed scholars ever wrote, and drop into the other the thin green volume of Matthew Arnold's *Lectures on Translating Homer,* which has long been out of print because the British public does not care to read it, and the first scale, as Milton says, will straight fly up and kick the beam." (We shall look into the assumptions here in a moment.)

The arts and the sciences alike are only to be defended, says Housman, on the ground that the desire for knowledge is one of the normal human appetites, and that men suffer if they do not have it gratified. And "once we have recognized that knowledge in itself is good for man, we shall need to invent no pretexts for studying this subject or that; we shall import no extraneous considerations of use or ornament to justify us in learning one thing rather than another. If a certain department of knowledge specially attracts a man, let him study that, and study it because it attracts him; and let him not fabricate excuses for that which requires no excuse, but rest assured that the reason why it most attracts him is that it is best for him."

This is certainly true in so far as it means that we should follow the direction of our aptitudes; but it seems to imply that there is no difference in value between one department of learning and another or between the different points of view from which the various kinds of research can be conducted. There is no conception in Housman's mind, as there would have been in Whitehead's, for example, of relating the part to the whole, understanding the organism through the cell. Knowledge seems to be regarded by Housman as a superior sort of pastime—"good for man" because it gives him pleasure and at most because "it must in the long run be better for a man to see things as they are than to be ignorant of them; just as there is less fear of stumbling or of striking against corners in the daylight than in the dark." (*The thoughts of others Were light and fleeting, Of lovers' meeting Or luck or fame; Mine were of trouble And mine were steady, So I was ready When trouble came.*) The disillusionment of western man in regard to his place in the universe, finding "that he has been deceived alike as to his origin and his expectations, that he neither springs of the high lineage he fancied, nor will inherit the vast estate he looked for," is described in an eloquent passage; and the activities of the "Arts and Laws and Science" are finally characterized as "the rivalry of fellow soldiers in striving which can most victoriously achieve the common end of all, to set back the frontier of darkness."

In other words, there is no role for creation in Housman's scheme of things. Indeed, if one had read only his poetry, one might be surprised to find that he even believed that it was possible or of any importance to set back the frontier of darkness. In this poetry, we find only the realization of man's smallness on his revolving globe among the revolving constellations and of his own basic wrongness to himself, his own inescapable anguish. No one, it seems, can do anything about this universe which "ails from its prime foundation": we can only, like Mithridates, render ourselves immune to its poisons by compelling ourselves to absorb them in small quantities in order that we may not succumb to the larger doses reserved for us by our fellows, or face the world with the hard mask of stoicism, "manful like the man of stone." For the rest, "let us endure an hour and see injustice done." And now we learn that for Housman knowledge itself meant at most the discovery of things that were already there—of those

sharp corners which it was just as well not to bump into,
of facts that were as invariable and as inert as the astronomical phenomena which are always turning up in his
poems and which form the subject of the poem of Manilius
to which he devoted so much of his life. He does not look
to the sciences and arts for the births of new worlds of
thought, of new possibilities for men themselves. It is
characteristic of him that he should speak, in this essay,
of Milton as a greater artist than Shakespeare, of Shakespeare, in fact, as not "a great artist"—as if the completeness and richness of Shakespeare's dramatic imagination,
a kind of genius which Milton, by comparison, seems
hardly to possess at all, were not important enough to be
taken into account in estimating his greatness as an artist—
as if those stretches of *Paradise Lost* where everything is
dead but the language were not the result of artistic deficiency. Again, the creation of life has no place in the
universe of Housman.

Housman's practice in his own field of scholarship is an
astonishing proof of this. The modern English classical
scholar of the type of A. W. Verrall or Gilbert Murray
is a critic not merely of texts but of the classics in their
quality as literature and of literature in its bearing on history. This school on one of its sides sometimes merges
with the anthropology of J. G. Frazer; and it deals with
ancient Greece and Rome in relation to the life of its own
time, restates them in terms of its own time. The danger,
of course, with a Verrall or a Murray is that, with something of the poet's imagination himself, he may give way,
in the case of Greek drama, for example, to inventing new
plays of his own and trying to foist them on Euripides or
Aeschylus. With Housman we do not run this danger.
Housman is the opposite kind of scholar; he is preoccupied with the emendation of texts. He could never have
been guilty of the extravagances of a Gilbert Murray or

a Verrall, but he was not capable of their kind of illumination. Note his assumption, in the passage quoted above, that "the minute and accurate study of the classical tongues," with which he himself is exclusively preoccupied, "affords Latin professors their only excuse for existing." Have those classical scholars who write history, who write criticism, who make translations—Gibbon and Renan and Verrall and Murray and Jowett and Mackail (to take in the whole field of the classics)—no excuse for existing, then? Is it so certain that, if their literary criticism were put into the scales with Matthew Arnold on Homer, the scholars would kick the beam? Or are such persons not scholars at all? In either case, it is plain that, for Housman, their activities lie outside the periphery of the sphere which he has chosen for himself.

Not, however, that Housman in this limited sphere has left the poet of *The Shropshire Lad* behind him. On the contrary, the peculiar genius which won him a place beside Porson and Bentley, which established him in his own time as almost supreme, with, apparently, only Wilamowitz as a rival, was derived from his ability to combine with the most "minute and accurate" mastery of language a first-hand knowledge of how poets express themselves. "The task of editing the classics," he wrote in his preface to Juvenal, "is continually attempted by scholars who have neither enough intellect nor enough literature. Unless a false reading chances to be unmetrical or ungrammatical they have no means of knowing that it is false." And he himself seemed able with a miraculous sureness to give the authors back their lines as they had written them. So, for example, despite a unanimity of manuscripts which read *"Omnis ab hac cura mens relavata mea est,"* Housman restored to Ovid from an inscription one of the latter's characteristic turns of style: *"Omnis ab hac cura cura levata mea est."* (*"And set you at your threshold down, Townsman of a stiller town"; "Runners whom renown outran*

And the name died before the man"; "By Sestos tower, in Hero's town, On Hero's heart Leander lies.") So, slightly emending the text, he turned a meaningless accepted reading of Juvenal, *"Perditus ac vilis sacci mercator olentis,"* into a characteristically vivid satiric stroke: *"Perditus ac similis sacci mercator olentis"*—the money-chasing merchant, on a stormy voyage, turns as yellow as his bag of saffron. (*"They shook, they stared as white's their shirt: Them it was their poison hurt."*) So, without even an emendation and simply by indicating a new relation between three words of Virgil's, he was able to save Virgil's style in a phrase—*"fallax herba veneni"*—which had always up to then been read as if it had been written with neither style nor grammar: substituting for "the deceitful plant of poison," "the plant that dissembles its venom." (*"And bear from hill and valley The daffodil away That dies on Easter day"; "Lie long, high snow-drifts in the hedge That will not shower on me"; "Snap not from the bitter yew His leaves that live November through."*) Several of his readings, I believe, have been corroborated by the subsequent discovery of manuscripts which Housman had never seen.

To this rescue of the Greek and Roman poets from the negligence of the Middle Ages, from the incompetence and insensitivity of the scholars, A. E. Housman brought an unremitting zeal which may almost be described as a passion. It has been said of the theorems of Newton that they cause the pulse to beat faster as one follows them. But the excitement and satisfaction afforded by the classical commentary of Housman must be unique in the history of scholarship. Even the scraping of the rust from an old coin is too tame an image to convey the experience of pursuing one of his arguments to its climax. It is as if, from the ancient author, so long dumb with his language itself, his very identity blurred or obliterated, the modern classicist were striking a new spark of life—as if the poet could only find his tongue at the touch across Time of the poet. So far is Housman the scholar a giver of life—yet it is only as re-creator. He is only, after all, again, discovering things that were already there. His findings do not imply a new vision.

It was a queer destiny, and one that cramped him—if one should not say rather that he had cramped himself. (Not to dispute, however, with Housman, who thought that human beings were all but helpless, the problem of natural fate and free will.)

The great work of A. E. Housman's life in the field of classical scholarship was his edition of the five books of Manilius, the publication of which alone extended from 1903 to 1930. We are told in a memoir of Housman by his colleague, Professor A. S. F. Gow of Cambridge, that Housman regarded Manilius as "a facile and frivolous poet, the brightest facet of whose genius was an eminent aptitude for doing sums in verse." And the layman may be disposed to assume that by Housman's time the principal Latin poets had already been covered so completely that there was nobody left except third-rate ones like Manilius. But it turns out from Professor Gow that Housman's real favorite was Propertius, and that he had done a great deal of valuable work on him and had at one time contemplated a complete edition. Professor Gow says that presumably Housman saw in Manilius and Lucan (Lucan he seems also to have despised) "more opportunity than in Propertius of displaying his special gifts, and more hope of approaching finality in the solution of the problems presented," but adds that he "cannot help regretting that he [Housman] abandoned a great and congenial poet on whom so much time had already been lavished."

The elegist of *The Shropshire Lad,* then, deliberately and grimly chose Manilius when his real interest was in Propertius. There is an element of perversity, of self-mortification, in Housman's career all along. (Gow tells how up to the time of his death "he would be found reading every word of books whose insignificance must have been apparent in ten pages, and making remorseless catalogues of their shortcomings.") And his scholarship, great as it is in its way, is poisoned in revenge by the instincts which it seems to be attempting to destroy, so that it radiates more hatred for his opponents than love for the great literature of antiquity. Housman's papers on classical subjects, which shocked the sense of decorum of his colleagues, are painful to the admirers of his poetry. The bitterness here *is* indecent as in his poetry it never is. In a prose, old-fashioned and elaborate, which somewhat resembles Pope's, he will attack the German professors who have committed the unpardonable sin of editing the Latin authors inadequately with sentences that coil and strike like rattlesnakes, or that wrap themselves around their victims and squeeze them to death like boa-constrictors. When English fails, he takes to scurrilous Latin. And the whole thing is likely at any moment to give way to some morose observation on the plight of the human race:

"To believe that wherever a best *ms* gives possible readings it gives true readings, and that only when it gives impossible readings does it give false readings, is to believe that an incompetent editor is the darling of Providence, which has given its angels charge over him lest at any time his sloth and folly should produce their natural results and incur their appropriate penalty. . . . How the world is managed, and why it was created, I cannot tell; but it is no feather-bed for the repose of sluggards."

And not only, he continues, has the notion been imposed that "inert adhesion to one authority is methodical criticism," but "rational criticism has been branded with a term of formal reprobation."

"But still there is a hitch. Competent editors exist; and side by side with those who have embraced 'the principles of criticism,' there are those who follow the practice of critics: who possess intellects, and employ them on their work. Consequently their work is better done, and the contrast is mortifying. This is not as it should be. As the wise man dieth, so dieth the fool: why then should we allow them to edit the classics differently? If nature, with flagitious partiality, has given judgment and industry to some men and left other men without them, it is our evident duty to amend her blind caprice; and those who are able and willing to think must be deprived for their unfair advantage by stringent prohibitions. In Association football you must not use your hands, and similarly in textual criticism you must not use your brains. Since we cannot make fools behave like wise men, we will insist that wise men should behave like fools: by these means only can we redress the injustice of nature and anticipate the equality of the grave."

And here is the somber and threatening, the almost Isaian, utterance to which he is moved by the failure of one of the compilers of a German-Latin dictionary to include in the article on *aelurus,* the Latinized Greek word for *cat,* any mention of an instance of its occurrence arrived at by an emendation in Juvenal and believed by Housman to be the first extant:

"Everyone can figure to himself the mild inward glow of pleasure and pride which the author of this unlucky article felt while he was writing it and the peace of mind with which he said to himself, when he went to bed that night, 'Well done, thou good and faithful servant.' This is the felicity of the house of bondage, and of the soul which is so fast in prison that it cannot go forth; which commands no outlook on the past or the future, but believes that the fashion of the present, unlike all fashions heretofore, will endure perpetually and that its own flimsy tabernacle of second-hand opinions is a habitation for ever-lasting."

Even when Housman is saying something positive the emotion is out of proportion to its object: he speaks fever-ishly, seems unnaturally exalted. Here is a passage on Bentley from the preface to the first volume of his Manilius:

"*Lucida tela diei:* these are the words that come into one's mind when one has halted at some stubborn per-plexity of reading or interpretation, has witnessed Scaliger and Gronovius and Huetius fumble at it one after another, and then turns to Bentley and sees Bentley strike his finger on the place and say *thou ailest here, and here.* . . . The firm strength and piercing edge and arrowy swiftness of his intellect, his matchless facility and adroitness and re-source, were never so triumphant as where defeat seemed sure; and yet it is other virtues that one most admires and welcomes as one turns from the smoky fire of Scaliger's genius to the sky and air of Bentley's: his lucidity, his sanity, his great and simple and straightforward fashion of thought."

Transferring Arnold's words for Goethe to Bentley is not perhaps comparing great things with small, but in the sub-stitution for the "physician of the Iron Age" of the physi-cian of mangled texts, there is a narrowing of scope almost comic. The preface to the first book of Manilius, from which the above passage has been quoted, magnificent as it is in its way, has also something monstrous about it.

Yet some acquaintance with the classical work of Hous-man greatly increases one's estimate of his stature. One encounters an intellectual pride almost Dantesque or Swiftian. "You would be welcome to praise me," he writes, "if you did not praise one another"; and "the

reader whose good opinion I desire and have done my
utmost to secure is the next Bentley or Scaliger who may
chance to occupy himself with Manilius." His arrogance
is perhaps never more ferocious than when he is judging
himself severely: when a friend who had ventured to
suggest the publication of a paper on Swinburne which
Housman had read before a college literary society had
been told by Housman that he was leaving directions to
have it destroyed after his death and had retorted that if
Housman really thought it so bad, he would already himself have destroyed it, Housman replied: "I do not think
it bad: I think it not good enough for me." And he put
on the title page of his edition of Juvenal, *"editorum in
usum edidit,"* to indicate that this feat of erudition—according to his own announcement, unprecedented—was
merely intended as a hint to coming scholars as to how
they could go about editing Juvenal in a really thorough-
going manner.

   Is this the spectacle of a great mind crippled? Certainly
it is the spectacle of a mind of remarkable penetration and
vigor, of uncommon sensibility and intensity, condemning
itself to duties which prevent it from rising to its full
height. Perhaps it is the case of a man of genius who has
never been allowed to come to growth. Housman's anger
is tragic like Swift's. He is perhaps more pitiable than
Swift, because he has been compelled to suppress himself
more completely. Even when Swift had been exiled to
Ireland, he was able to take out his fury in his crusading
against the English. But A. E. Housman, giving up Greek
in order to specialize in Latin because he "could not attain
to excellence in both," giving up Propertius, who wrote
about love, for Manilius, who did not even deal with
human beings, turning away from the lives of the Romans
to rivet his attention to the difficulties of their texts, can
only flatten out small German professors with weapons
which would have found fit employment in the hands of

a great reformer or a great satirist. He is the hero of "The Grammarian's Funeral"—the man of learning who makes himself great through the magnitude, not the importance, of his achievement. After all, there was no need for another Bentley.

It is only in the Latin verses—said to have been called by Murray the best since the ancient world—which Housman prefixed to his Manilius, in his few translations from Latin and Greek, and in his occasional literary essays, that the voice of the Shropshire Lad comes through—that voice which, once sped on its way, so quickly pierced to the hearts and the minds of the whole English-speaking world and which went on vibrating for decades, disburdening hearts with its music that made loss and death and disgrace seem so beautiful, while poor Housman, burdened sorely forever, sat grinding and snarling at his texts. Would he have called back that voice if he could, as he recalled, or tried to recall, so much else? There are moments when his ill humor and his pedantry, his humility which is a perverse kind of pride, almost make us think that he would.

At this point Professor Gow is able to throw some further light on his friend. It seems that Housman had marked the following passage from Colonel Lawrence's *Seven Pillars of Wisdom,* which he had come across in a review:

"There was my craving to be liked—so strong and nervous that never could I open myself friendly to another. The terror of failure in an effort so important made me shrink from trying; besides, there was the standard; for intimacy seemed shameful unless the other could make the perfect reply, in the same language, after the same method, for the same reasons.

"There was a craving to be famous; and a horror of

being known to like being known. Contempt for my passion for distinction made me refuse every offered honor. I cherished my independence almost as did a Beduin, but my impotence of vision showed me my shape best in painted pictures, and the oblique overheard remarks of others best taught me my created impression. The eagerness to overhear and oversee myself was my assault upon my own inviolate citadel."

Housman had written in the margin, "This is me." Both had been compelled by their extreme sensibility to assume in the presence of their fellows eccentric or repellent masks. Both had been led by extreme ambition to perform exploits which did not do them justice, exploits which their hearts were but half in: Professor Gow says that Housman's prime motive in undertaking his edition of Manilius was the ambition to "build" himself "a monument." And just as Lawrence was always losing the manuscripts of his books, limiting their circulation, making the pretense of suppressing them altogether; so Housman kept his poems out of anthologies, made the gestures of a negative attitude in regard to the reprinting of his other writings and left instructions that his classical papers, of which Gow says there are something like a hundred, should never be collected in a volume (instructions which it is to be hoped will be disobeyed).

Both were products of the English universities, and it would take an Englishman properly to account for them. But their almost insane attempts to conceal their blazing lights under bushels are recognizable as exaggerations of the Englishman's code of understatement in connection with his achievements and conquests. And both obviously belong to the monastic order of English university ascetics. The company to which Housman refers himself is that of Walter Pater, Lewis Carroll, Edward Fitzgerald and Gerard Manley Hopkins—and, earlier, Thomas Gray.

Hopkins, converted at Oxford, entered the Jesuit order; Pater and Dodgson stayed on there as dons; Fitzgerald and Gray, when they had finished at Cambridge, continued to haunt the place: they remained men of the monastery all their lives. Are their humility, which seems imposed by moral principles, their shyness in relation to the extra-collegiate world, derived from the ages when learning was the possession of pious brotherhoods and shut away between the walls of foundations?

Certainly their failure to develop emotionally is due to that semi-monastic training. All seem checked at some early stage of growth, beyond which the sensibility and the intellect—even, in Lawrence's case, the ability to manage men—may crystallize in marvelous forms, but after which there is no natural progress in the experience of human relationships. Their works are among the jewels of English literature rather than among its great springs of life; and Alice and the Shropshire Lad and Marius the Epicurean are all the beings of a looking-glass world, either sexless or with an unreal sex which turns only toward itself in the mirror of art. Isn't the state of mind indicated by Lawrence in the first of the paragraphs quoted above essentially an adolescent one? We are told, in a recent memoir, that Housman used to rail against marriage and childbearing. "My father and my mother," Housman makes one of his hanged heroes say, "They had a likely son, And I have none."

It would not be true to say of Housman, as it would be of Fitzgerald or Gray, that his achievement has been merely to state memorably certain melancholy commonplaces of human existence without any real presentation of that existence as we live it through. There *is* immediate emotional experience in Housman of the same kind that there is in Heine, whom he imitated and to whom he has been compared. But Heine, for all his misfortunes, moves at ease in a larger world. There is in his work an exhilaration of adventure—in travel, in love, in philosophy, in literature, in politics. Desolate though his accents may sometimes be, he always lets in air and light to the mind. But Housman is closed from the beginning. His world has no opening horizons; it is a prison that one can only endure. One can only come the same painful cropper over and over again and draw from it the same bitter moral.

And Housman has somehow managed to grow old without in a sense ever knowing maturity. He has somehow never arrived at the age when the young man decides at last to summon all his resources and try to make something out of this world he has never made.

1938

Bernard DeVoto

WISDOM LINGERS

FOR the last few days before Christmas the corridors have a blessed quiet and the campus is as solitary as it was in late August. The professors may sleep later in the morning, take an unregardful third highball in the evening, and help the children trim the tree without thinking of tomorrow's nine-o'clock lecture. Optimism comes back, and on December 26th the railroads carry a freight almost as genial as the one that crowded them on December 21st: the scholars are off to their trade conventions. The convention city has been chosen with proper regard to the average fare, hotel accommodations, the neighboring university, and geographical impartiality—not to mention the horse trade by which St. Louis will get next year's convention and Princeton a second vice-president. If it is Chicago this year, it is likely to be Baltimore next year; but if it should be Baltimore then the administration must be induced to put the local delegates on an expense account, at least those who are on committees and those who will read papers.

The professors are joined by their colleagues from the private foundations, from the research departments of the national government, and from the laboratories of big corporations. Post-Christmas week draws the learned to-

From *Minority Report* by Bernard DeVoto. Reprinted by permission of the author.

gether from all over the country, to exchange information and advice, to report on the year's work, to plan for the coming year—and beyond it as far as thought can reach. A layman in search of enlightenment could choose among at least two dozen congregations of wise men. No formula can be given here to guide his choice. The American Association for the Advancement of Science gets the best press and puts on the most interesting show. The American Historical Association has the best time. The American Sociological Society is usually the windiest and always the funniest. The Modern Language Association is the dreariest and most fretful. If none of these suits the layman's taste, however, he may try the Association for Research in Nervous and Mental Diseases, the Seismological Society of America, the Archeological Institute of America, the Association for Symbolic Logic, or the trade organizations of geographers, philologists, speech teachers (*sic*), physicists, geologists, chemists, mineralogists, metaphysicians, anthropologists, economists, paleontologists, psychologists, oceanographers, and many others.

Off stage a convention of the learned is just like a convention of shoe salesmen or investment counselors. In the hotel corridors and the delegates' rooms the same activity goes on, the renewal of friendships, the manipulation of influence for committee appointments and next year's program, reminiscence of livelier days when we and the world were younger, the nurture of candidacies for President in 1943. Anxieties swell and tragedy is close at hand. The dean has given warning that you must produce; perhaps a ten-minute paper will hold him off for another year or a thirty-minute paper turn the corner for good. Or the last year of your appointment is here, the appointment is not going to be renewed, and somewhere in this convention you must find a department head who is looking for talent. Or your feud with the vitalists or the revisionists must be settled now by a redistribution of committees.

Or the inadequacy-feeling that is endemic among the learned comes to a head and can be assuaged only by permission to read a paper—any paper, a paper on any subject, embodying any data and conclusions so long as you are vindicated before your fellows by an exhibition of technique utilized and work done.

For the convention exists, ultimately, that papers may be read. The main body breaks up into sections of specialists, and in the meetings of the sections, so theory has it, scholarship renders account of its trust. Here the results of research are presented, here the progress of knowledge is declared. Here the learned communicate to one another and to the world the end products of their labor, from the earth-shaking to the inconceivably inane. And, since scholars have as much flesh as any man, the inane predominates. The layman can get a picture of the state of learning in America from the specialists' papers, but he will spare himself shock if he assumes that the median line of scholarship must be very much like any other median.

It was the American Speech Teachers who this year heard about recordings of Hitler's speeches. The records reveal that Hitler is frequently angry. His strong emotion and his use of the higher voice-level tend to put the German people in a passive state. Hitler, the paper concluded, frequently reaches a condition bordering on hysteria. . . . The Folklore Society learned that Mexican peasants have a contemptuous epithet for political jobholders. . . . A professor told the Student Union that "every classroom in the nation must be converted into an outpost in the struggle for democracy," and professors were saying things quite as silly as that in all the conventions. . . . Another one told the Archeological Institute that Virgil was the first modern, just as Bruce Barton used to tell Rotary International that Jesus was the first advertising man. . . . The American Sociological Society heard that "American language behavior" is "a societal epiphenomenon, a form of oral hyperkinesia, a kind of chronic and acute but highly contagious blabitis." That means that Americans talk a lot. It is typical of the sociologists' language-behavior and contains a stately academic joke, and it shows that the lust for semantics which recently raged through sociology did not strike inward. . . . Always excepting Professors of Education, sociologists tend to be the most pretentious of scholars. A certain insecurity, a repressed fear that their four-dollar words may not mean anything and that their shiny, scientific-looking gadgets may not make them scientists after all, produces an aggressive clamor that isn't hard to diagnose. They beat gongs to keep the spooks away. . . . Insecurity takes a different form in the Modern Language Association, where professors of literature grieve over the dullest of all papers read during this supercharged week. What depresses these scholars is a realization that their discipline is supposed to deal with literature, whereas of sixty-odd papers annually read to the society only about ten have any bearing on literature and only about five of those understand that it is an art, that it is related to the dreams and heartbreaks and aspirations of mankind, that the odd creatures who write it have the blood and emotions of living men. They feel that culture is in their keeping, just as Professors of Education feel that progress and revolution are in their keeping, and five out of sixty seem a small proportion and they fall into despair.

Well, dispatches come in from the frontiers of knowledge: Solomon's port on the Red Sea is being excavated. . . . The serpents carved on Roman lintels were meant to ward off evil. . . . Amish hymns have been recorded for the phonograph. . . . It is now clear that a British naval officer was lying, a hundred and four years ago, when he claimed to have invaded the Antarctic ice. The map he drew was phantasy and the sea he named after himself was discovered at his desk. . . . White Leghorn chickens have had their feathers colored with pigment taken, in the embryo, from a robin's wing. . . . Professor Yerkes says that his chimpanzees are very much like human beings, and no lover of justice rises to denounce this libel of a mild and prepossessing animal. . . . The Association of American Geographers hears that we have started on the hot-to-cold part of the weather cycle and so may expect the kind of events correlated with that half of the curve. During the next five or ten years, that is, the dictatorships will probably perish. . . . But this heartening news is contradicted at the Geological Society of America, whence word comes that the earth is growing warmer as it continues to emerge from the latest glacial period and that the attempts of the "have-not" nations to get more metals will soon lead to war.

But now of course we are in an area where knowledge wears brighter clothing. The planet Neptune began to be disorderly in 1925 and is now five seconds ahead of where it should be in its orbit. But that may be because the earth wobbles so much that an error was made in the observation—and, considering the earth since 1925, the suggestion sounds reasonable. The metal-bearing ores of the wobbling earth dwindle fast but might be conserved for another century, though because of armaments they probably will not be. But new oil fields are being laid down on the ocean floor off California and will be ready for use in a few million years. Study of the chromosomes has revealed a gene which accelerates the rate of mutation. The discovery helps us to understand evolution, supplies a new instrument for those who are studying cancer, and suggests that a new type of mankind may appear in time to mop up the mess. Photographs in color were taken of the recent lunar eclipse, and the earth's crust is rising toward its pre-glacial level.

A chemical called histamine, which is carried by the blood cells, produces anaphylactic shock and is held responsible for various sensitivity diseases, including asthma. (So the Association for the Advancement of Science heard in Richmond. But papers read to the Association for Research in Nervous and Mental Diseases recorded cures of asthma by psychiatric methods and suggested that some asthma may be psychogenic.) A better analgesic than morphine has been found: cobra venom, which does not produce insensibility but has a pleasant reaction and so fulfils one of medicine's oldest dreams. And the audience at Richmond saw a new kind of microscope. It focuses not light rays but electrons, magnifies up to a million times, and effects separations as small as one twenty-five millionth of an inch. They saw it reveal the shape of the smallpox virus and of the *Staphylococcus aureus,* which no optical microscope can make visible. And while they watched, its fluorescent screen picked out the atomic pattern of a tungsten crystal and with their naked, virgin eyes they could see residual molecules of air shimmer against the sides of the vacuum tube. . . . Elsewhere scholars might fret and chill with doubt of what they were doing, but not these scholars. Here was the advance of knowledge and a tool to carry it farther still.

They are a more serene, more confident group than their colleagues in the social sciences and the humanities. Physical and biological scientists, medical men, even psychologists know what they are talking about, as sociologists and their kin commonly do not. They know it is worth talking about, which is not a conviction that the members carry away from the Modern Language Association. They know that even the humblest paper of the humblest chemist reporting that one hundred compounds which mathematics said in advance could not be produced in the laboratory cannot in fact be produced there will be useful to someone, whereas the reports on cultural vestiges shown in the drawings on outhouse walls in Wilkes-Barre that humble sociologists compose and the studies of Cowper's syntax which the abashed M.L.A. produces will just be dumped forever on the garbage heap of a self-perpetuating vested interest. They see instruments of hope and growth and healing and mastery put at the disposal of the human race, if the race should ever care to take them up, and not even Professors of Education, who claim everything, can claim healing or mastery. And they know that sometimes in small, drowsy rooms where a few aging men gather, papers are read which will ultimately change the face of nature and the form of society. No paper read at the Modern Language Association or the American Sociological Society, past, present, or to come, will ever have any effect whatever on either nature or society.

But, out of their laboratories, the scientists also are uneasy. They were told in Richmond that they must assume responsibility for social changes produced by science (talking like a Professor of the Science of Teaching the Science of Teaching, the speaker remarked that the main duty of our secondary schools is to teach civics and manners, science and discipline) and they are willing and even eager to accept that responsibility—if they can find out how. That, however, is one research for which they have no instruments. One of the foremost physicists in the world tried to tell his colleagues how; but his speech had as little meaning for the layman as if he had been talking about the mathematics of cosmic rays, and had far less meaning for the physicists. Like all other learned societies, the physicists passed resolutions in favour of democracy and against absolutism, and dedicated themselves to free inquiry and social advance, and denounced the perversion of learning to evil ends; but in the bitter glare of the modern world they saw that a physicist was indistinguishable from a sociologist and even from a Professor of Education, except that, a million-power microscope in his hand, he looked more forlorn. He had only his microscope, and it would be quite as futile as a study of cultural vestiges in outhouses or one of Cowper's syntax when he took it out into the freshening winds and the rising waters.

Yet the physicist is not so forlorn as he looks, and the layman reflects, when the week is over, that the other scholars are not so disheartening as they seem in a close-up. It is a mistake to look at them in close-up, unless one sedulously remembers that no human activity is very impressive under a magnifying glass. The average of anything human is—a human average. Measured against eternity, measured against hope and desire, measured against even the scholars' own aspiration and pretense, most scholarly researches do indeed look trivial, futile, and ridiculous. But measured against history, even the slightest of them does not look so bad. For their kind has been certainly the cleanest and by far the most fruitful activity the race has given itself to, and has built the one Republic that has withstood darkness and storm. And when you turn away from human mediocrity to the best, you come close to what is just about the only source of hope the storms have not obliterated. They are plain, imperfect men, plentifully bewildered, plentifully mired in human ignorance and human stupidity, but they do their job, their job goes on in peace, it slowly widens, it moves along. Even the statistician of outhouses or of ethical datives works against chaos, works toward rationality, is a conduit of the mind's freedom, a tender of an imperishable item who, if he should fall, would bring all down with him. And the physicist's microscope may be but a small bastion against the winds and waters but you will find no other quite so large. . . . And they meet in freedom and in peace, and, meeting so, are an earnest and a prayer and—a fortress.

1939

E. M. Forster

NOT LISTENING
TO MUSIC

LISTENING TO MUSIC is such a muddle that one scarcely knows how to start describing it. The first point to get clear in my own case is that during the greater part of every performance I do not attend. The nice sounds make me think of something else. I wool-gather most of the time, and am surprised that others don't. Professional critics can listen to a piece as consistently and as steadily as if they were reading a chapter in a novel. This seems to me an amazing feat, and probably they only achieve it through intellectual training; that is to say, they find in the music the equivalent of a plot; they are follow-ing the ground bass or expecting the theme to re-enter in the dominant, and so on, and this keeps them on the rails. But I fly off every minute: after a bar or two I think how musical I am, or of something smart I might have said in conversation; or I wonder what the composer— dead a couple of centuries—can be feeling as the flames on the altar still flicker up; or how soon an H.E. bomb would extinguish them. Not to mention more obvious distractions: the tilt of the soprano's chin or chins; the antics of the conductor, that impassioned beetle, especially when it is night time and he waves his shards; the affecta-tion of the pianist when he takes a top note with difficulty, as if he too were a soprano; the backs of the chairs; the bumps on the ceiling; the extreme physical ugliness of the audience. A classical audience is surely the plainest collection of people anywhere assembled for any common purpose; contributing my quota, I have the right to point this out. Compare us with a gang of navvies or with an office staff, and you will be appalled. This, too, distracts me.

What do I hear during the intervals when I do attend? Two sorts of music. They melt into each other all the time, and are not easy to christen, but I will call one of them "music that reminds me of something," and the other "music itself." I used to be very fond of music that reminded me of something, and especially fond of Wagner. With Wagner I always knew where I was; he never let the fancy roam; he ordained that one phrase should recall the ring, another the sword, another the blameless fool and so on; he was as precise in his indications as an oriental dancer. Since he is a great poet, that did not matter, but I accepted his leitmotiv system much too reverently and forced it on to other composers whom it did not suit, such as Beethoven and Franck. I thought that music must be the better for having a meaning. I think so still, but am less clear as to what "a meaning" is. In those days it was either a non-musical object, such as a sword or a blameless fool, or a non-musical emotion, such as fear, lust, or resignation. When music reminded me of something which was not music, I supposed it was getting me somewhere. "How like Monet!" I thought when listening to Debussy, and "how like Debussy!" when looking at Monet. I translated sounds into colours, saw the piccolo as apple-green, and the trumpets as scarlet. The arts were to be enriched by taking in one another's washing.

I still listen to some music this way. For instance, the slow start of Beethoven's Seventh Symphony invokes a grey-green tapestry of hunting scenes, and the slow movement of his Fourth Piano Concerto (the dialogue between piano and orchestra) reminds me of the dialogue between

Orpheus and the Furies in Gluck. The climax of the first movement of the Appassionata (the "più allegro") seems to me sexual, although I can detect no sex in the Kreutzer, nor have I come across anyone who could, except Tolstoy. That disappointing work, Brahms' Violin Concerto, promises me clear skies at the opening, and only when the violin has squealed up in the air for page after page is the promise falsified. Wolf's "Ganymed" does give me sky—stratosphere beyond stratosphere. In these cases and in many others music reminds me of something non-musical, and I fancy that to do so is part of its job. Only a purist would condemn all visual parallels, all emotional labellings, all programmes.

Yet there is a danger. Music that reminds does open the door to that imp of the concert hall, inattention. To think of a grey-green tapestry is not very different from thinking of the backs of the chairs. We gather a superior wool from it, still we do wool-gather, and the sounds slip by blurred. The sounds! It is for them that we come, and the closer we can get up against them the better. So I do prefer "music itself" and listen to it and for it as far as possible. In this connection, I will try to analyse a mishap that has recently overtaken the Coriolanus Overture. I used to listen to the Coriolanus for "itself," conscious when it passed of something important and agitating, but not defining further. Now I learn that Wagner, endorsed by Sir Donald Tovey, has provided it with a Programme: the opening bars indicate the hero's decision to destroy the Volscii, then a sweet tune for female influence, then the dotted-quaver-restlessness of indecision. This seems indisputable, and there is no doubt that this was, or was almost, Beethoven's intention. All the same, I have lost my Coriolanus. Its largeness and freedom have gone. The exquisite sounds have been hardened like a road that has been tarred for traffic. One has to go somewhere down them, and to pass through the same domestic crisis to the same military impasse, each time the overture is played.

Music is so very queer that an amateur is bound to get muddled when writing about it. It seems to be more "real" than anything, and to survive when the rest of civilisation decays. In these days I am always thinking of it with relief. It can never be ruined or nationalised. So that the music which is untrammelled and untainted by reference is obviously the best sort of music to listen to; we get nearer the centre of reality. Yet though it is untainted, it is never abstract; it is not like mathematics, even when it uses them. The Goldberg Variations, the last Beethoven Sonata, the Franck Quartet, the Schumann Piano Quintet and the Fourth Symphonies of Tchaikovsky and of Brahms certainly have a message. Though what on earth is it? I shall get tied up trying to say. There's an insistence in music—expressed largely through rhythm; there's a sense that it is trying to push across at us something which is neither an esthetic pattern nor a sermon. That's what I listen for specially.

So music that is itself seems on the whole better than music that reminds. And now to end with an important point: my own performances upon the piano. These grow worse yearly, but never will I give them up. For one thing, they compel me to attend—no wool-gathering or thinking myself clever here—and they drain off all non-musical matter. For another thing, they teach me a little about construction. I see what becomes of a phrase, how it is transformed or returned, sometimes bottom upward, and get some notion of the relation of keys. Playing Beethoven, as I generally do, I grow familiar with his tricks, his impatience, his sudden softnesses, his dropping of a tragic theme one semitone, his love, when tragic, for the key of C minor, and his aversion to the key of B major. This gives me a physical approach to Beethoven which cannot be gained through the slough of "appreciation." Even when people play as badly as I do, they should continue: it will help them to listen.

1939

E. B. White

ON A FLORIDA KEY

I AM writing this in a beach cottage on a Florida key. It is raining to beat the cars. The rollers from a westerly storm are creaming along the shore, making a steady boiling noise instead of the usual intermittent slap. The Chamber of Commerce has drawn the friendly blind against this ugliness and is busy getting out some advance notices of the style parade which is to be held next Wednesday at the pavilion. The paper says cooler tomorrow.

The walls of my room are of matched boarding, applied horizontally and painted green. On the floor is a straw mat. Under the mat is a layer of sand that has been tracked into the cottage and has sifted through the straw. I have thought some of taking the mat up and sweeping the sand into a pile and removing it, but have decided against it. This is the way keys form, apparently, and I have no particular reason to interfere. On a small wooden base in one corner of the room is a gas heater, supplied from a tank on the premises. This device can raise the temperature of the room with great rapidity by converting the oxygen of the air into heat. In deciding whether to light the heater or leave it alone, one has only to choose whether he wants to congeal in a well-ventilated room or suffocate in comfort. After a little practice, a nice balance can be established—enough oxygen left to sustain life, yet enough heat generated to prevent death from exposure.

On the west wall hangs an Indian rug, and to one edge of the rug is pinned a button which carries the legend: Junior Programs Joop Club. Built into the north wall is a cabinet made of pecky cypress. On the top shelf are three large pine cones, two of them painted emerald-green, the third painted brick-red. Also a gilded candlestick in the shape of a Roman chariot. Another shelf holds some shells which, at the expenditure of considerable effort on somebody's part, have been made to look like birds. On the bottom shelf is a tiny toy collie, made of rabbit fur, with a tongue of red flannel.

In the kitchenette just beyond where I sit is a gas stove and a small electric refrigerator of an ancient vintage. The ice trays show deep claw marks, where people have tried to pry them free, using can openers and knives and screwdrivers and petulance. When the refrigerator snaps on it makes a noise which can be heard all through the cottage and the lights everywhere go dim for a second and then return to their normal brilliancy. This refrigerator contains the milk, the butter, and the eggs for tomorrow's breakfast. More milk will arrive in the morning, but I will save it for use on the morrow, so that every day I shall use the milk of the previous day, never taking advantage of the opportunity to enjoy perfectly fresh milk. This is a situation which could be avoided if I had the guts to throw away a whole bottle of milk, but nobody has that much courage in the world today. It is a sin to throw away milk and we know it.

The water which flows from the faucets in the kitchen sink and in the bathroom contains sulphur and is not good to drink. It leaves deep-brown stains around the drains. Applied to the face with a shaving brush, it feels as though fine sandpaper were being drawn across your jowls. It is so hard and sulphurous that ordinary soap will not yield to it, and the breakfast dishes have to be washed with a washing powder known as Dreft.

On the porch of the cottage, each in a special stand, are two carboys of spring water—for drinking, making coffee, and brushing teeth. There is a deposit of two dollars on bottle and stand, and the water itself costs fifty cents. Two rival companies furnish water to the community, and I happened to get mixed up with both of them. Every couple of days a man from one or the other of the companies shows up and hangs around for a while, whining about the presence on my porch of the rival's carboy. I have made an attempt to dismiss one company and retain the other, but to accomplish it would require a dominant personality and I haven't one. I have been surprised to see how long it takes a man to drink up ten gallons of water. I should have thought I could have done it in half the time it has taken me.

This morning I read in the paper of an old Negro, one hundred and one years old, and he was boasting of the quantity of whisky he had drunk in his life. He said he had once worked in a distillery and they used to give him half a gallon of whisky a day to take home, which kept him going all right during the week, but on weekends, he said, he would have to buy a gallon extry, to tide him over till Monday.

In the kitchen cabinet is a bag of oranges for morning juice. Each orange is stamped "Color Added." The dyeing of an orange, to make it orange, is Man's most impudent gesture to date. It is really an appalling piece of effrontery, carrying the clear implication that Nature doesn't know what she is up to. I think an orange, dyed orange, is as repulsive as a pine cone painted green. I think it is about as ugly a thing as I have ever seen, and it seems hard to believe that here, within ten miles, probably, of the trees which bore the fruit, I can't buy an orange which somebody hasn't smeared with paint. But I doubt that there are many who feel that way about it, because fraudulence has become a national virtue and is well thought of in many circles. In the past twenty-four hours, I see by this morning's paper, one hundred and thirty-six cars of oranges have been shipped. There are probably millions of children today who have never seen a natural orange—only an artificially colored one. If they should see a natural orange they might think something had gone wrong with it.

There are two moving picture theaters in the town to which my key is attached by a bridge. In one of them colored people are allowed in the balcony. In the other, colored people are not allowed at all. I saw a patriotic newsreel there the other day which ended with a picture of the American flag blowing in the breeze, and the words: one nation indivisible with liberty and justice for all. Everyone clapped, but I decided I could not clap for liberty and justice (for all) while I was in a theater from which Negroes had been barred. And I felt there were too many people in the world who think liberty and justice for all means liberty and justice for themselves and their friends. I sat there wondering what would happen to me if I were to jump up and say in a loud voice: "If you folks like liberty and justice so much, why do you keep Negroes from this theater?" I am sure it would have surprised everybody very much and it is the kind of thing I dream about doing but never do. If I had done it I suppose the management would have taken me by the arm and marched me out of the theater, on the grounds that it is disturbing the peace to speak up for liberty just as the feature is coming on. When a man is in the South he must do as the Southerners do; but although I am willing to call my wife "Sugar" I am not willing to call a colored person a nigger.

Northerners are quite likely to feel that Southerners are bigoted on the race question, and Southerners almost invariably figure that Northerners are without any practical experience and therefore their opinions aren't worth much. The Jim Crow philosophy of color is unsatisfying to a Northerner, but is regarded as sensible and expedient to residents of towns where the Negro population is as large as or larger than the white. Whether one makes a practical answer or an idealistic answer to a question depends partly on whether one is talking in terms of one year, or ten years, or a hundred years. It is, in other words, conceivable that the Negroes of a hundred years from now will enjoy a greater degree of liberty if the present restrictions on today's Negroes are not relaxed too fast. But that doesn't get today's Negroes in to see Hedy Lamarr.

I have to laugh when I think about the sheer inconsistency of the Southern attitude about color: the Negro barred from the movie house because of color, the orange with "color added" for its ultimate triumph. Some of the cities in this part of the State have fête days to commemorate the past and advertise the future, and in my mind I have been designing a float which I would like to enter in the parades. It would contain a beautiful Negro woman riding with the other bathing beauties and stamped with the magical words, Color Added.

In the cottage next door is a lady who is an ardent isolationist and who keeps running in and out with pamphlets, books, and marked-up newspapers, hoping to convince me that America should mind its own business. She tracks sand in, as well as ideas, and I have to sweep up after her two or three times a day.

Floridians are complaining this year that business is below par. They tell you that the boom in industry causes this unwholesome situation. When tycoons are busy in the North they have no time for sunning themselves or even for sitting in a semi-tropical cottage in the rain. Miami is appropriating a few extra thousand dollars for its advertising campaign, hoping to lure executives away from the defense program for a few golden moments.

Although I am no archaeologist, I love Florida as much for the remains of her unfinished cities as for the bright cabanas on her beaches. I love to prowl the dead sidewalks that run off into the live jungle, under the broiling sun of noon, where the cabbage palms throw their spiny shade across the stillborn streets and the creepers bind old curb-stones in a fierce sensual embrace and the mocking birds dwell in song upon the remembered grandeur of real estate's purple hour. A boulevard which has been reclaimed by Nature is an exciting avenue; it breathes a strange prophetic perfume, as of some century still to come, when the birds will remember, and the spiders, and the little quick lizards which toast themselves on the smooth hard surfaces that once held the impossible dreams of men. Here along these bristling walks is a decayed symmetry in a living forest—straight lines softened by a kindly and hap-hazard Nature, pavements nourishing life with the begin-nings of topsoil, the cracks in the walks possessed by root structures, the brilliant blossoms of the domesticated vine run wild, and overhead the turkey buzzard in the clear sky, on quiet wings, awaiting new mammalian death among the hibiscus, the yucca, the Spanish bayonet, and the palm. I remember the wonderful days and the tall dream of rainbow's end; the offices with the wall charts, the pins in the charts, the orchestras playing gently to pre-pare the soul of the wanderer for the mysteries of sub-division, the free bus service to the rainbow's beginning, the luncheon served on the little tables under the trees, the warm sweet air so full of the deadly contagion, the dotted line, the signature, and the premonitory qualms and the shadow of the buzzard in the wild wide Florida sky.

I love these rudimentary cities that were conceived in haste and greed and never rose to suffer the scarifying effects of human habitation, cities of not quite forgotten hopes, untouched by neon and by filth. And I love the beaches too, out beyond the cottage colony, where they are wild and free still, visited by the sandpipers that retreat before each wave like children, and by an occasional hipsprung farmwife hunting shells, or sometimes by a veteran digging for *Donax variabilis* to take back to his hungry mate in the trailer camp.

The sound of the sea is the most time-effacing sound there is. The centuries reroll in a cloud and the earth becomes young again when you listen, with eyes shut, to the sea—a young green time when the water and the land were just getting acquainted and had known each other for only a few billion years and the mollusks were just beginning to dip and creep in the shallows; and now man the invertebrate, under his ribbed umbrella, anoints himself with oil and pulls on his Polaroid glasses to stop the glare and stretches out his long brown body at ease upon a towel on the warm sand and listens.

The sea answers all questions, and always in the same way; for when you read in the papers the interminable discussions and the bickering and the prognostications and the turmoil, the disagreements and the fateful decisions and agreements and the plans and the programs and the threats and the counter threats, then you close your eyes and the sea dispatches one more big roller in the unbroken line since the beginning of the world and it combs and breaks and returns foaming and saying: "So soon?"

1941

V. S. Pritchett

TWO WRITERS
AND MODERN WAR

And so good-bye to the war. I know not how it may have been or may be to others—to me the main interest I found (and still in recollection find) in the rank and file of the armies, both sides, and in those specimens amid the hospitals and even the dead on the field.

THIS passage comes from *Specimen Days,* from those pages where Whitman described his work in the hospitals during the American Civil War. The interest of Whitman's pages about this war lies in the fact that he is the first to reveal the modern attitude. He stands at the breaking point with the past.

The American Civil War was the first modern war. It is true that the Crimean War, some eight years earlier, has resemblances with the American conflict. There is the awakening of public concern for the care of casualties, a concern which had grown with medical knowledge. But the Crimean War was fought in a small area. It was fought by professional soldiers—the British commander-in-chief directed operations from his private yacht to which he returned to dine and sleep every night—and the casualties, though heavy, were less than half of those suffered in America, where a million men died in the field, the hospitals and the prison camps. The Civil War involved everyone, the armies became conscript armies almost at once. The professional soldiers were put to the task of training the man in the street. Similar conditions, it will be said, existed in the Napoleonic wars—for Napoleon was the first to use conscription on a great scale. But the Napoleonic army was the Grande Armée. The conscript was transformed by the professional and national notions of Glory and the impulse of the Revolution. He was, in a sense, a party man and not a citizen in military dress. And then, when we read the memoirs of those wars, in English or in French, we notice that they are the work of men bent on the military career. They have the professional officer's outlook. Gleig—a subaltern of Wellington's—who wrote an account of his adventures in the Peninsula, is typical of them. One can imagine Gleig reborn in the 'sixties and exclaiming at the moral deterioration of his profession, once it is overweighted by every Tom, Dick and Harry. There is a loss of style and manner, both in action and in the narratives written afterwards. The precise horrors of war are sometimes mentioned in the classical records but, generally, rhetorical clichés are preferred: carnage, slaughter and so on.

If Gleig were to return and read Whitman's notes, he would first be struck by the importance given to the casualties and the hospitals; and then by the unprotected nakedness of human feeling. The classical manner was not inhumane; but it put military dignity and professional virtue first. It was the manner of leaders. War, the most lawless of activities, was given a frame of decorum; you might not always fight by the code of honour, but a code of honour existed and, above all, you spoke and wrote in accord with it. The British troops sacked San Sebastian and fired at the officers who tried to stop them; but Gleig in *The Subaltern* speaks in the voice of a gentleman when he describes and deplores the event. There is no suggestion that war is a human tragedy. This suggestion is not made until the civilian fights. He cannot shrug his shoulders and say, *"C'est la guerre."* He is stunned by his own fears, stupefied by his own atrocities, amazed at his happiness, incredulous at the point of death. When all people are at war, no code, no manner, can contain the experience. The nearest writers to Whitman are Tolstoy and Erckmann-Chatrian—it is interesting to note that they were all writing about war at the same time—but Tolstoy's ironical pacifism and Erckmann-Chatrian's mildness and peaceableness are a branch of the main stream of popular feeling. They are not, like Whitman, the stream itself. The *Histoire d'un Conscrit de 1813* was written in 1864. It has been called *l'Iliade de la peur* and it portrays the pathos of the conscript's situation. The tragedy of the conscript is a passive one: that a quiet, peaceable man like himself should be killed. But in Whitman—as in Wilfred Owen—the tragedy is not passive; it lies not only in what is done to a man but in what he himself does and in what happens to him inside. When we compare these things with the sentiment of Erckmann-Chatrian we see that these authors are propagandists concerned with society. The freshness of their document is deceptive. They describe the Napoleonic wars with wonderful verisimilitude; but the wars are not taken direct from life. These writers have digested the moving simplicities of old men's hearsay. They are propagandists with an uncommonly delicate ear. They write to warn opinion in the fond domestic parlour behind the little shop.

Compared with them, Whitman does not know his mind. He is all over the place. He is the public. It is typical of *Specimen Days* that its first picture of the war is of the news spreading in the streets at night. The emotion of the street catches him. He is not intoxicated with patriotism but he does not deny the message of the pennants and the flags in the street. He is the man in the parlour who goes out into the street and loses his head. He feels the herd instinct. Two great wars have made us guarded, and when we read *Specimen Days* and especially the poems called *Drum Taps,* we resist that old-fashioned war. The sun has faded the defiant and theatrical photograph, and paled the headlines to a weak-tea brown. The uniforms are shabby. We suspect Whitman's idea that out of this a nation is born; it sounds like the cracked bugle and slack drum of propaganda. And yesterday's propaganda puts no one in a flurry. Yet, in all this, the loquacious Whitman is right. It is the bewildering thing in all his work, that this dressed-up egotist with all the air of a ham actor, is always half-right when he is most dubious. He is the newspaper man who reflects the ambiguous quality of public feeling. His virtue is that he begins on the pavement and that, like the streets, he has no shame and no style. Excitement and incantation take the place of it. The soldiers straggle into Washington after the defeat at Bull Run:

"The men appear, at first sparsely and shame-faced enough, then thicker, in the streets of Washington—appear in Pennsylvania avenue, and on the steps and basement entrances. They come along, in disorderly mobs, some in squads, stragglers, companies. Occasionally, a rare regiment, in perfect order, with its officers (some gaps, dead, the true braves), marching in silence, with lowering faces, stern, weary to sinking, all black and dirty, but every man with his musket, and stepping alive; but these are the exceptions. Sidewalks of Pennsylvania avenue, Fourteenth street, etc., crowded, jamm'd with citizens, darkies, clerks, everybody, lookers-on; women in the windows, curious expressions from faces, as those swarms of dirt-cover'd return'd soldiers there (will they never end?) move by; but nothing said, no comments. . . . Amid the deep excitement, crowds and motion, and desperate eagerness, it seems strange to see many, very many, of the soldiers sleeping—in the midst of all, sleeping sound. They drop down anywhere, on the steps of houses, up close by the basements or fences, on the sidewalks, aside on some vacant lot, and deeply sleep. A poor seventeen- or eighteen-year-old boy lies there, on the stoop of a grand house; he sleeps so calmly, so profoundly. Some clutch their muskets firmly even in sleep. Some in squads; comrades, brothers, close together—and on them, as they lay, sulkily, drips the rain."

All that effort to produce one last remarkable phrase—that is Whitman.

After this the reality begins. And the reality, as the first modern war drags on, is the casualty list. In the classical narratives men are merely shot. Sometimes they are blown up. The aftermath was not minutely described. "Bloodshed," "carnage," generalise it. Whitman, too, uses those words but with all his voice. And he went round the hospitals and saw the gangrene, the amputations, the unspeakable wounds. He smelt the ether. Saw the tiptoe walking. The screens put round. He saw the stretcher cases lying out in the rain and glad to be cooled by it. He knew men crawled under bushes to die by inches. He took down the last words and wrote letters for men too weak to write. The men were not sorry for themselves. They talked very little. They had become detached and incredulous. Thousands, he knew, died and were never identified. It struck him, when he saw the burial trenches, that the typical soldier of this first modern war was "unknown."

That discovery marks the beginning of the modern attitude to war. We write as followers, not leaders. And though Whitman likes the heroic act, the message in the leader's eye, enjoys seeing the President ride past with his escort of cavalry and feels the public emotion of the "great

convulsive drums," he writes more surely when he goes
back to the rank and file, when he recovers his sense of
anonymity. (Odd that this huge and often so flaccid egotist should be able to puff himself large enough until he is
identified with all the people and lost in them; it is his paradox.) It is his paradox, too, that doggerel and the real
thing trapes along together like the blind leading the
blind, unable to see, unable to stop. In avoiding literary
jargon, he easily wallowed in the tear-jerking stuff of
small town In Memoriam notices—to emerge from the
bathos with perhaps one line or two worth writing:

"Grieve not so, dear mother" (the just-grown daughter
    speaks through her sobs,
The little sisters huddle around speechless and dismay'd)
"See dearest mother, the letter says Pete will soon be
    better."

Alas, poor boy, he will never be better (nor may-be needs
    to be better that brave and simple soul),
While they stand at home at the door he is dead already,
The only son is dead.

But the mother needs to be better,
She with thin form presently drest in black,
By day her meals untouch'd, then at night fitfully sleep-
    ing, often waking,

In the midnight waking, weeping, longing with one deep
    longing,
O that she might withdraw unnoticed, silent from life
    escape and withdraw,
To follow, to seek, to be with her dear dead son.

  Blake could be simple, but he was never maudlin.
  And there are the curious parallels with the poetry of
the last war, the same mixing of the romantic note with
the realism. We turn from Wilfred Owen's

> I am the enemy you killed, my friend,
> I knew you in this death.

to Whitman's

> Word over all, beautiful as the sky,
> Beautiful that war and all its deeds of carnage must in
>   time be utterly lost,
> That the hands of the sisters Death and Night incessantly
>   softly wash again, and ever again, this soil'd world:
> For my enemy is dead, a man divine as myself is dead,
> I look where he lies white-faced and still in the coffin—I
>   draw near,
> Bend down and touch lightly with my lips the white face
>   in the coffin.

Well, there it is. The set piece has gone, the full-bot-
tomed formal patriotism of the eighteenth century, the epi-
sodic poetry of the early nineteenth. The sense of occasion
has gone. There are no more "incidents from the French
camp," there is no loss of the *Revenge,* no *Charge of the
Light Brigade,* no *Burial of Sir John Moore.* The serving
soldier has been outnumbered and swamped by the civilian
soldier. The profession has been drowned in the classes.
Nor can we attribute the change to a decay of the love of
country—as some critics tried to do at the beginning of
this war—for Whitman was a bombinating patriot, yet
he wrote no pieces of occasion of that kind. *Drum Taps*
describe the general scene, what the unknown and anonymous man did and saw and how filthily he died. Patriotism
has not decayed; but the human being has emerged. He
emerged first of all, it is interesting to observe, in a civil
war, a war of ideas; and in the country which, to so many
people, had seemed the Promised Land, where no formal
tradition of war existed. Whitman himself observed, in
his confused groping way, that a new way of warfare was
necessary to America. A new way of writing about war

certainly emerged; perhaps that is what he was trying to say.

It is worth while turning at this point to an American novelist who is the child of the Tolstoy-Whitman movement, the child of the Crimea and Bull Run. I am thinking of Stephen Crane and his book *The Red Badge of Courage* which was published in the 'nineties. The achievement of Crane was individual and high, but in placing it we must now confess that it came in on the Tolstoy wave; and that but for Tolstoy, it would never have been written. There is an important difference of experience between Tolstoy and Crane. In writing respectively about the Napoleonic and the American Civil Wars, both writers were reconstructing wars they had not seen; but Tolstoy *had* seen the Crimea, he had been a soldier, whereas Crane had seen war only as an intrepid journalist will see it, and the journalist does not go through the mill of soldiering. However adventurous he may be, he is not fully-conditioned. He does not, in the end, feel this is his inescapable fate. He does not look mildly into the blank expressionless features of death; but, dramatically, with face half-averted. One feels that Crane stands apart from his scene and that a great skill has to take the place of an inured contemplation of the subject. Crane is simply the specialist and expert who has narrowed his interest to the relation of a man with himself or a crowd's relation with other crowds in the battle; whereas Tolstoy in his wide survey saw that war was a continuation of peace. One curious common emotion nevertheless unites the master and the disciple. They reject the formal, the professional and rhetorical attitude to war; they reject the illusions of the profession and the traditional litanies of patriotism; but they cannot quite conceal a certain sadness at the passing of these things. In Tolstoy one so often suspects the secret longing of the repentant, the too-repentant soldier; in Crane the faint harking back to romance expresses, I sup-

pose, the reporter's hidden regret that he has not a profound and comprehensive point of view.

The Red Badge of Courage is a *tour de force*. Crane
starts a bugle call and sustains it without a falter to the
end of the book. The scene is a single battlefield in the
American Civil War, and the purpose of the novel is to
show the phases by which a green young recruit loses his
romantic illusions and his innocence in battle, and acquires a new identity, a hardened virtue. War has ceased
to be a bewraying and befogging dream in his mind; it
has become his world and he derives virtue from his unity
with it. There is a second element in the story. To Crane
a battlefield is like a wounded animal. The convulsions of
its body, its shudders, its cries and its occasional repose, are
the spasmodic movements and dumb respites of the groups
of soldiers. There is not only the individual mind in the
battlefield, but there is the mass mind also. Crane watches
the merging of the individual with the herd. There is no
plot in this book; it is a collection of episodes. We do not
know which battle is being described or what are its
objects. The rights and wrongs of the war itself are not
discussed. No civilian and hardly a sight of the work of
man, like a house or a cultivated field, comes into the picture. Few of the characters are named; the central figure
is known simply as "the young man." The enemy are
just the enemy, something fabulous and generally invisible
in the blue smoke line of the engagement, terrifying and
dragon-like at the worst, and at the best a singularity to
be mistrusted. Who wins or loses is obscure. The whole
thing is almost as anonymous as a poem or a piece of
music and has the same kind of tension and suspense. For
we are not specially interested in the mortal fate of the
boy. We do not specially fear that he will be killed, nor
do we privately hope he will cover himself with glory.
Our eyes are fixed on something different in him; on each
adjustment in his character as it comes along. At the end

of this book, we say to ourselves, we too shall know how we shall behave when we discard our illusions about war and meet the reality. Romantically we fear or hope for battle as a way of singling ourselves out and dying; but underneath this day-dream is the awe of knowing that battle is a way of living before it is a way of dying, and one in which we cannot calculate our behaviour in advance. It was one of the discoveries of the unrhetorical attitude to war in literature, that even the men on the right side and in the just cause are afraid, and to Crane— an adventurous man who died young from the effects of going to see trouble all over the earth—the deep fear of fear was a personal subject.

This comes out in the first chapter of *The Red Badge of Courage,* where the young man is seen in the camp listening to the rumours and torturing himself with questions. He feels courageous, but will courage stand? Will he stay or will he run in panic? These are overmastering questions. The first dead do not scare him, nor does the early uproar. He can stand the first attack and face the fear hidden in the wall of forest where the enemy lie, and after the frenzy of the first onslaught he lies for a few moments in the trench overcome by a sense of fellowship with his companions and experiencing with astonishment "the joy of a man who at last finds leisure." But, fixed on their intense personal problem, his heart and mind have not yet understood that while the imagination expects decisive and single answers, reality does not deal in such simplicities. The attack, to everyone's despair, is renewed. The second phase has begun. It is too much. The youth throws down his rifle and runs. Here Crane shows his power as a novelist, for in this part of the story he writes those dramatic scenes and draws those portraits which have given the book its place in the literature of war. This is where the dying soldier, walking white and erect like a rejected prince among his broken court, goes stiffly towards his grave. Crane was an observer of the ways of dying, but this death is one of the most terrible, for it is a progress to death:

"The spectral soldier was at his side like a stalking reproach. The man's eyes were still fixed in a stare into the unknown. His grey, appalling face had attracted attention in the crowd, and men, slowing to his dreary pace, were walking with him. They were discussing his plight, questioning and giving him advice. In a dogged way he repelled them, signing to them to go on and leave him alone. The shadows of his face were deepening and his tight lips seemed holding in check the moan of great despair. There could be seen a certain stiffness in the movement of his body, as if he were taking infinite care not to arouse the passion of his wounds. As he went on he seemed always looking for a place like one who goes to choose a grave. Something in the gesture of the man as he waved the bloody and pitying soldiers away made the youth start as if bitten. He yelled in horror. Tottering forward he laid a quivering hand upon the man's arm. As the latter slowly turned his wax-like features toward him the youth screamed: 'Gawd! Jim Conklin!'

"The tall soldier made a little commonplace smile.

"'Hello, Henry,' he said."

If the boy's horror and quivering seem conventionally over-emphatic in that passage, the rest is not. Writers are always faced by two sets of words before they write: those which will draw a literary curtain over reality, and those which will raise the veil in our minds and lead us to see for the first time. Crane's gift for raising the veil is clear. The presence of "spectre" and "commonplace smile" in that portrait is imaginative observation at its best.

The book is filled with observation of this kind. Some is placed there by poetic intuition:

"The sun spread disclosing rays, and, one by one, regiments burst into view like armed men just born of the earth. The youth perceived that the time had come. He was about to be measured. For a moment he felt in the face of his great trial like a babe, and the flesh over his heart seemed but thin. He seized time to look about him calculatingly.

"But he instantly saw that it would be impossible for him to escape from the regiment. It enclosed him. There were iron laws of tradition and law on four sides. He was in a moving box."

This inner sensation of the experience is matched by wonderful, small phrases of verisimilitude: "His *forgotten feet* were constantly knocking against stones or getting entangled in briars." Or there is this picture—how common it has become in modern realism, which Crane anticipates by thirty or forty years:

"Once the line encountered the body of a dead soldier. He lay upon his back staring at the sky. He was dressed in an awkward suit of yellowish brown. The youth could see that the soles of his shoes had been worn to the thinness of writing paper, and from a great rent in one the dead foot projected piteously. And it was as if fate had betrayed the soldier. In death it exposed to his enemies that poverty which in life he had perhaps concealed from his friends."

The only word a modern reporter would not have written in that passage is the word "piteously."

Toughness, that is to say fear of facing the whole subject, as Crane faced it, has intervened to make the modern writer's picture purely visual and inhumane—one remembers the turned-out pockets of the dead in Hemingway and his bravado about writing a natural history of the dead. The pathetic fallacy abounds in Crane's prose and we hear of "the remonstrance" and "arguments" of the guns; but for all the artiness—which belongs to the 'nineties—there is pity, there is human feeling. There is a background of value and not a backdrop gaudy with attitudes. There is a quest for virtue—what else is the meaning of the young boy's innocent odyssey among his fears, his rages and his shames?—and not as one sees in Kipling, the search for a gesture or some dramatic personal stand which avoids the issue and saves the face. Crane ignores the actor in human beings, the creature with the name on the personal playbill; he goes—at any rate in *The Red Badge of Courage*—for the anonymous voice in the heart.

1946

Christopher Morley

NOTES ON AN ISLAND

I. GENERAL INFERENCE

IT was a warm autumn Saturday, breezy and bright, as the train came down across the Midlands, from Liverpool to Euston. A visitor who has been so long away (seventeen years, and what years) looks close indeed to try to discern what has happened. Field and hedge, locomotive and signal box, cattle and cathedral, all had been through long mortal storm. On the sidings were strings of those gnomelike little goods wagons, each on four spindly wheels with spokes. It is easy to tell, by the spokes, whether the wagons are moving. Not nearly enough of them were. I saw with apprehension that many were filled with turnips and cabbage. The turnips, however, were "swedes," for fodder.

The visitor looks as sharp as a housewife. In back yards the family washing everywhere fluttered, to get the last of the week's air and sun. Washed and washed again, those humble shirts and linens, heroic trivialities of our human woe—and all a dull cloudy oystery gray. England has little soap. I felt ashamed that I had hooked only one small cake from the C.P.R.

England has little soap; not even Soft Soap, for herself or for others. She must get very weary of being praised for stoicism, a tiresome virtue. Like everyone else she would prefer to be loved for what she feels in her heart: frivolity, mischief, and acute artistic sense. It is dangerous to try to make fair report because words in print are often given more heed than they merit. Even when you know a writer is a natural ass there is some wickedness in ink that lends him respect.

It would be easy to answer all questions by saying "A bit grim," because that is obviously what one is expected to say. But, for a traveller like me, England is still astonishingly comfortable. She has relaxed to my own social level; a shabby man can go almost anywhere without embarrassment. I was startled at first, then rather tickled, to see such proletarian figures trotting in and out of the offices in Whitehall. The black Homburg is still emblem of the professions, but would readily be doffed for a platter of Hamburg. I think I was a bit too jocular in chat with Lady —— at an Imperial soirée. She said, "I'm afraid you find us very down-at-heel." I said, "I like it. When your heels were high you had such a habit of putting them on people's necks." That was perhaps less than tactful in an Old Treacle Hand. But I did have a distinct impression in England that no one's boot is on anyone's nape—except of course Economics, which has its heel on us all.

Do not, therefore, say anything that might discourage the tourist. The American's inherited and infatuated curiosity about Britain, his mingled shock and delight when he puts it to proof, are among the island's greatest assets. His innate query is, What is it she has that we haven't got? She has plenty, including beauty that took time, good humor with a very high boiling point, and her unshaken habit of doing things, or not doing them, her own way.

The North American, the world's great Handy Man, is in for many a shudder. A Canadian on the boat train, getting his first look at rolling stock, was baffled by all the little "wagons" shrouded with tarpaulin. "What have they got under all those canvases?" he exclaimed. "Corpses?"

It did seem like it, for a while. The corpse of transportation. Commerce was definitely at pause. The spokes of the little "mineral wagons" weren't spinning. The miners hadn't made up their minds whether to dig or not; nor do I blame them. I know what it feels like to sit down to a typewriter. But one of the first places I visited was Keats's house at Hampstead; and there, behind the mulberry tree where the nightingale ode was written, was a great dump of coal, unloaded in the garden. It was the same everywhere: whatever coal you could get hold of you piled in the garden, or the scullery, or the bowling green, or cloister. That, I said to myself, is England. Remember and revere the nightingale and the poet, but pile up the coal while you can. Elfland—with a Weather Eye.

The weather was unusual; it usually is. British meteorologists have learned not to make Forecasts. They print only what they call a General Inference. But weather seemed loath to bedevil the hardy island further, except with drouth. Tepid Saint Martin went on and on; Hyde Park orators were able to talk off distemper until late November.* The Labor Government was combing thorns out of its hide. Like Br'er Rabbit, it was born and bred in a briar patch; it inherited a skinful of prickly problems, and invented new prickles of its own. Little Mr. Attlee's shanks didn't look comfortable propped on the table in the

* How I wish someone would reread the tragic John Davidson's poem about Indian summer and railway stations (in London)—in his *Fleet Street* (1909; Mitchell Kennerley).

House of Commons. As you know, the Front Benchers show themselves at ease by hoisting their feet on the table. Perhaps the new tables in the House are not quite as wide as those that were blitzed? At any rate the reach is too far; I could see, from my perch (in the tiny balcony intended for Dominion Premiers), that Mr. Attlee had to sit quite on the bottom of his neck to make cantilever. It is an attitude that recalled the phrase that puzzled me as a schoolboy: the Rump Parliament. Mr. Churchill is too thick and too veteran to attempt it. Besides, you can't *lower* (lour) from that posture.

Mr. Eden, deliciously trim and self-aware, can look threatening even while he lolls. He has crural advantage; they are better striped, more debonair. He has his ankles to windward (on the Table) and his mind on the decimal system, whose address is Number Ten, Downing Street.

I must try not to be cheerful. It is fatal for an historian to think too much about things that amuse him.

Golden pause went on and on. It was like the *Ode to Autumn,* with its wonderful line that a boy in Philadelphia thought meant John Wanamaker: "Who hath not seen thee oft amid thy Store?" England was like Sleeping Beauty, stupefied within her quickset hedge, waiting for the cold accipitrine kiss of Sir Stafford. But the island is wary even in swoon. When she opens Parliament, or marries an Heir, she still makes Royalty ride in a glass coach, to be sure there's no deception. A new budget hung, like thunder on the left, over everyone's horizon. (Alas, poor Dalton, who fused his electricity betimes and grounded thunder in the lobby.) Cigarettes were sold, when you could get them, in demi-pack of ten, including such un-kenned brands as "Fifth Avenue." (But there are actually two Fifth Avenues in London: one in Paddington, and one in East Ham.) Streets were dark at night; petrol perished. When you saw old U. S. Army trucks (as you often did) they were placarded behind: "Left Hand Drive:

No Signal." That seemed to me a sort of emblem of the Socialist Government. With which, let me say, I am greatly in sympathy; but its psychological élan has been feeble. During my brief stay in England they sprang upon their glooming public two uncushioned shocks, with no warning: Guy Faux petards under two of England's most revered bulwarks: the House of Lords and the Home Fleet. England was just as much shocked to learn how her Navy had shrunk as we are how ours has grown.

So everyone in England felt like a patient in the dentist's waiting room, reading an old copy of *Punch*. Even lovers of Moby Dick couldn't work up much zest for Antarctic Filet or Esquimaux Cutlet, which were caterers' name for whale; also called whaleburger. Drouth went on, douce but damnable. Farmers' fields were powder. Great cities like Manchester were within twelve days of water famine. English railways, usually the most exact in the world, had disastrous accidents, by fatigue and man-shortage. This was appalling to an American, who always loved English railways as the supreme example of toy trains: he wants to sprawl on the floor and play with them. Even before St. Paul's or Westminster Abbey the American revisits all the old stygian stations. Pseudo-classic (Euston) or pseudo-gothic (St. Pancras) or pseudo-Bankofengland (L'pool Street) they harbor in their gloomy and agglomerated sheds more pressures of human emotion than any cathedrals. I even did what relatively few English have done, took train (in a day of fog) from old Marylebone Station. That is a runway of mortal oddity that the Black Prince, or the Prince of Blackness, would relish. My old friend—dead these many years—Archie Macdonell—used it as starting point for his idyll of English oddity. Archie was a Scot, and the Scot comes near the American in his pawky sense of England's comedy of weird.

The Island was in trance. So was I; I could tell it by my sense of enjoyment and uncouth hilarity. My visit had double purpose: I wanted to see my English grandchild (I walked her in her pram up and down Sloane Street and round Lowndes Square) but I also wanted to see England, my grandmother. I had no prejudice in favor of either. England is about the same age as a nation as I am as a person. It is better for us both to take things easier than we have. England's wise and strategic inpulling of horns (or heels) is like my own. Life, whether of animals or nations, has its limitations. Events are going to move faster, from now on, than either I or she can deal with alone. So I say to the old emboggled men who like to think they're running the world, turn it over to the Young Folks. They'll do better than the official elders. I have nothing against Marshall, nor Molotov, nor the universal mischief Malapropos, except that they're old and tired and deprived. They were never lyric poets, and have worked harder than men should. Put them to bed. I only wish Stassen weren't getting bald so fast. The shrewdest political and oecumenical comment of our lifetime was that of the great Dr. Osler—and how he was razzed for it—to chloroform ambitious men at forty. I know, and you know too, it is men over forty who make trouble.

I don't think it's my fault; but it's usually my fortune, to visit any different civilization just when it's holding its breath. That is always difficult for an American.

The sense of wonder is the most precious, maybe the most exhausting, of mortal emotions. It doesn't last long; man, the coward, prefers to wallow in the familiar and the habitual. There is always wisdom in old catchwords: Nine Days' Wonder. True, for about the Tenth Day one begins to adapt, to osmoze. By then you have lost the fine bouquet of surprise. You no longer gape nor gripe at Britain's unchangeable habits, not even her explanatory interpolation "D'you see?" at every pause of narrative. By the tenth day you have given up trying to get a glass of water at

meals, or preventing the waiter from pouring coffee and
hot milk simultaneously into your cup (spoiling them
both). You have remembered by then the fundamental
lesson in dealing with all traditional peoples: it hurts them
more to do it your way than it would hurt you to do it
theirs. So you put the salt in a pile on the rim of your
plate; never directly on the cabbage or fish to be salted.
You don't ask what the fish is, it's turbot.* You may
speak without offense of any architectural ruins of the
War, but do not, in charity, remark the most painful ruin
of all, the shards and rubble of the noble English Sausage.
It is gone, and (as the Shakespeare monument in Westminster Abbey spells it) "left not a wreck behind." Take
the mustard, let the sausage go. But remember, better
than any mustard (as international condiment) are these
little differences.

Turbot was somehow comic even in Gilbert and Sulli-
van: in *Pinafore,* you remember, "turbot is ambitious brill."
If not turbot, it's bream, plaice, mullet, haddock, cod,
kipper, or bloater; or pilchard; even sprat. If fish is phos-
phorus, as they used to say, Britain will shine in the dark
for centuries to come. We stayed, forty-five happy days,
in a delightful little hotel (unknown to Americans, except
for one Confederate colonel who was there one night and
fled the next morning because there was no interpreter)
which was itself, all glass and porcelain and iridescent reflections, very like a fishbowl. It was like a lens, or specu-

---

* As it was in that great masterpiece of mild Victorian humor,
Burnand's *Happy Thoughts.* I spent much time in London trying to find a copy of *Happy Thoughts* for some young people;
the rising generation in Britain has had no chance to study that
classic portrait of a mind full of fog. One of my pleasant memories is of Mr. John Wilson, dean of the London book trade, running up and down ladders to try to find me a copy which he was
sure lurked somewhere in Bumpus's famous shop. For advanced
students, *Happy Thoughts* is a lifelong favorite of Max Beerbohm's.

lum, or cystoscope, into the very bowels of Britain. There was even a young man there who wore a morning coat for breakfast, put on a gray topper, and took taxi for the Opening of Parliament. From the experienced way he tweezed the hairy vertebrae of his kipper from his gums, I believe he was an hereditary Lord.

It is excellent politics, I said to myself, that these legislators ride the London taxi, which can twirl on a dime and reverse itself in mid-traffic.

But wonder, or strangeness, doesn't endure. I dare say Adam and Eve began to think themselves acclimated in Eden by the tenth day. Probably Karl Marx, up in Hampstead, believed after a week and a half that he was getting the hang of Britain? I think of Marx because 1948 is the centennial of his earnest manifesto, the burthen of which was his anxiety about exploitation; he himself was busy exploiting British lodgings to try to undo British habits. I also think of Marx because he and Keats lived (thirty years apart) in the same street in Hampstead. Marx's boarding house has some terrible stained-glass windows. But Keats, as Shelley implied, wrote stained glass windows.

In those blasted heaths of ruin east of St. Paul's I found stained glass for myself. England's quickening soil for flowers sprouts autumn asters and marigolds and michaelmas daisies, natural rock gardens, in the checkerboard of ruin, so it seems almost like a common land; clumps of yellow and blue autumn wave in chinks of rubble, as Conservatives of the Nineties used to knot the colors on their whips when they went coaching to elections. When the City was blasted it was mixed with ruins older still; it is hard to know what was St. Giles Cripplegate and what was the old Roman Wall. There, moseying round with H. M. Tomlinson (birthright master of East London) I dug two scraps of red and green glass (port and starboard lights for memory) from the brickheaps of St. Giles Cripplegate. They were from a shattered window that had cast colored light on Milton's burial and Cromwell's wedding. Then we went down by Limehouse, Stepney, Poplar, and the East India Docks; even to Blackwall Stairs, where so many first families of Virginia and Massachusetts felt the first stomach of the sea. The old greasy cobbles they trod are still there. Tommy remembers when he netted shrimps there as a boy, but the tide now swells black as Scotch treacle. Shrimps prefer clean water; the only one we saw was a little girl about to do a pilgrim plunge on the slimy ramp. We dragged her back, wiped her nose, and begged her to be wary.

"I can't imagine what you want to see all this for," old Tommy kept murmuring as we rode bus down Commercial Road, among landscapes of damnation. Then he suddenly became showman. "You see that church," pointing to a skeleton of walls. "That's where my wife and I were married." A little farther, another pile of ruin. "That's where my father and mother were married." Somewhere down by Robin Hood Lane (which would have astounded Robin Hood), or maybe Tunnel Gardens, there were more hollows of broken brick. "That was where my grandmother climbed out of the bedroom window and eloped with a young Navy officer." And Tommy's own home in Croydon was wrecked by a buzzbomb. He lives now in Hammersmith, farther upstream than ever before, but still within tidemarks.

It begins to look, I said, as if the Nazis had something against you.

The things not said are often the truest. Tommy didn't say, and probably didn't even think, it was rash of him, long ago, to write a beautiful book called *All Our Yesterdays*. Where are they? But neither of us thought that; we were more interested, both of us, in having lately become grandfathers.

There was other stained glass too. I saw the fourteenth-century windows in the chapel of New College, Oxford, being put together, piece by piece, after wartime burial. They were shown, for the moment, as few have ever seen them, behind a temporary screen, so they transfuse (as intended) only northern light. That is the light historians write by. And there were moments tinctured with the heraldry of chance. The only time we had to take shelter from actual rain was at Westminster Abbey. We retreated, with others, into a closed side-portal (the North Porch) while an April shower (in November) was falling in crystal douche across the sanctuary. But only a few rods away, beyond the street, the sun was shining like Chaucer, and the statue of Abe Lincoln gilded in cheerful bronze, bright as a new penny.

While we're at Westminster, I was sorry to notice they were straightening the bent sword of Richard the Lionheart. That twisted glaive was one of the things I wanted to see. But they had Richard inside a scaffold, evidently fixing him up. Like Shirley (in his glorious hymn they sing in the Abbey when a King dies), I prefer a broken sword in the hand of a stark man. Even more I admire the "poor crooked scythe and spade." See, if you are curious, your "Oxford Book" No. 296. Best of all, in that strong poem, 300 years in print, is the "victor-victim." We know, and well, all victors are victims too.*

We were speaking of the Sense of Surprise. I've been home on Long Island long enough for that awareness to dull. "Then fades the glimmering landscape on the sight." I am no longer startled by the horror of New York com-

---

* I have just remembered: walking through ruins with Tommy, he wanted me to send him Steve Benét's fine inscription for the East River Drive in N. Y. City (at E. 25th Street). In part, Tommy, here it is: "Beneath this East River Drive of the City of New York lie stones, brick, and rubble from the bombed City of Bristol. . . . These fragments that once were homes shall testify while men love freedom to the resolution and fortitude of the people of Britain" (1942).

muting (worse than the electric trains from Victoria or Waterloo), or the high cardiac pressure of commercial radio, or the inordinate adipose of newspapers, or the reluctance of Congress to face anything at par. I even accept, after a few trips to Town, the draggletail look of women in the new ¾ length skirts. Then I think of how many reasons Britain has to be grateful. Little miniature newspapers that you can put half a dozen of them in your coat pocket. Wireless without hysteria; you can be told, in sober and literate barytone, what seems to be happening; even a Royal Nuptial doesn't elicit the pizzicato molto troppo of some aspirin or toothpaste. England is still, in secret, an aristocracy, for the only way you can find out what people are really thinking is by reading the letters to *The Times* or the *Manchester Guardian;* and the only way you can get those papers is by theft or by someone on the list of subscribers going abroad. I was able to get a black-market *Times,* after many visits to the underground newsstand at Knightsbridge, because some regular subscriber went to South Africa. While he was away digging (or raising "ground-nuts"?) in the Witwatersrand, I was reading his paper; I learned about the autumn misbehavior of the chiff-chaff (a Warbler or Lesser Pettychap), and the cleansing of the paintings at the National Gallery, and the fact that the Archbishop of Canterbury isn't responsible for everything said about USSR by the Dean of Canterbury. I wanted greatly to write a Letter to *The Times,* but what was on my mind had nothing to do with birds, edible fungi, or church ritual, so I knew it was futile.

There were many things I'd like to have written to The Papers. I am a good traveller, for my naïveté is absolute and microscopic, but I can take up a good deal of space. I felt it more considerate to impose it on American paper, where pulp is lavish. Also I was having a happily selfish time just meditating it for myself. Some of the letters I wanted to write:

(1) Love and congratulation to the new *Caronia,* launched and christened on the Clyde, in mid-November, by Princess Elizabeth, with young Prince Philip standing by. I was horrified that none of the news stories said anything about the old *Caronia* (launched, I think, about 1904) which was for many years one of the happiest of Atlantic ships. I should guess that about half a million Americans went to and fro in her; I did myself ten times; I even dedicated a book to her once, though a very small one. She looked rather like Lord Halifax, very long for her beam, with an expansion joint amidships to absorb strain. A good idea for all travellers. So I wanted to send her new daughter my love and blessing, and beg her builders to change their minds and give the new *Caronia* two funnels, like the old ship, and a real open fire in the smokeroom, not just electric glass nuggets; and old Nighters, the middle-watch steward. Then, if there had been space, I would have concluded with a meditation: that all kinds of international musing are futile. Unless you love both nations equally, your ideas are crude; and as soon as love enters anywhere, they're just personal fantasy. Yours, Sir, etc.

(2) My delight at finding that a Toilet Saloon was a place where I could get my beard trimmed; *viz.,* a barber. The one I found, on Duke Street (they call it Juke Street), does all the haircutting for Eton College. Like thirty-five years ago, they put you in a windsor chair (Windsor is close to Eton) and you don't even take your coat off. So the little snips of hair go on your coat instead of down your neck. It's what that good man John Wilson, dean of the London book trade, always says of Pearsall Smith: "the art of the snippet." While you are waiting your turn at the Hairdresser you can read, instead of *Life* and *Time,*

the alumni journals of the Royal Lancers and the Queens Bays. I never felt myself so definitely a gentleman. Yours, Sir, etc.

(3) One gets, of course, the notion that all the street cleansers (that's their name) are Anzacs; they wear the wideawake (as we would say, Stetson) pinned up on one side. They look so gloomy, with their little pushprams, you suppose they are Macaulay's New Zealanders come to study the ruins of St. Paul's. (How near they came to being Nazi instead of New Zealand.) But only an American, with his austere literary discipline, is likely to remember Macaulay. Yours, Sir, etc.

(4) The great Johnsonian discovery, made by my Scots son-in-law. We had long been stricken by Boswell's quotation (p. 50, Oxford Press edition) that Johnson, while at Pembroke College, was usually seen "lounging about the college gate." This gave a suggestion of otiose Etonian idleness. Not at all. We visited Johnson's old rooms (now occupied by an American Rhodes Scholar). They are on the stairway above the porter's lodge. So young Sam hung about the lodge because there was always a fire in the porter's grate, and he couldn't afford one in his room. I would have added a few words about my wonderful visit to the Warden of New College, his noble old fourteenth-century kitchen, the Adventure of the Carton of Chesterfields, and the coltsfoot leaves he was drying to use as tobacco; but there wasn't, and never will be, space. Yours, Sir, etc.

(5) The lovely lady who shared with us a television festival—I think Chaucer would have called it a flyting—at a place called Alexandra Palace. It interested me because my grandfather, who had some acuity as realtor, was creeping his way up that plateau from Muswell Hill, about 1868. But what I liked most was Mrs. Halliday's cry of artists' woe: "When you get used to television, the

movies seem so huge and crude and vulgar." All my Lilliput blood rose in joy to that, and I would have wished to say to *The Times* or *M.G.*: "England is a television country. Leave her so." Yrs, etc.

(6) You can see (if you're the kind of reader I like to think you are) why I didn't write these letters. I could have written a letter about Traffic in Oxford compared with Tranquillity in Cambridge; or the Lady with Big Blue Eyes in Berkshire and her cry of anguish, as she showed us her great black shoat in the barnyard: "Piggy! Poor Dear Pig! He's been Taken Over by the Government. And we had him All Fattened for Christmas!" That was in a midland midden that might have been Puck of Pook's Hill. The English go on living their literature, without remembering it's literature. To you and me it's too often something on a shelf. I would have added a brief glimpse of the huge Bengal tiger reaching his bended paw under the bars for a scarlet joint of horse-beef, at the Regents Park Zoo. You get a very good lunch there, by the way, with plenty of macerated potatoes and turnips and thick-skinned Socialist sausage; because you get Children's Priority. In the Socialist State (which none of our American Socialists have been encountered in reality, not even Norman Thomas) children and carnivores get First Pick. Yours, Sir, etc.

(7) Six letters would have wound up a week for *The Times* or the *M.G.*, but there might still be a seventh for the *Sunday Times* (a quite different sheet), to which literary and historical queries are mostly addressed. Here I think I would have dwelt on the Other Pair of Shanks. These were the cotton-stocking shins of Mr. Speaker, sitting on his throne as arbiter of the House of Commons. The Speaker, in grey wig, black robe, and breeks, has his own formality no less than Front Benchers. One leg, even if the hose wrinkle a little, must dandle over the other; by

the vibration of the swinging silver-buckled slipper the student, or Dominion Premier, may guess the undercurrent of debate. Anxiously, as argument trends toward partisan rapids or stagnant riposte, one sees the slipper toss faster, hang looser and looser on the suspensive great toe. Suppose, thinks the Dominioneer, slipper should fall off? The whole of parliamentary decorum depends from one nervous phalange. And what a severity of argument that day: the matter of the Chancellor of Exchequer's gaffe was in debate. The Prime Minister was frozen and terse. The Leader of the Opposition, Mr. Churchill, was all jowls and jalap. Then it became obviously a to-and-fro, a squabble; each side gambiting for party position. The best gambit was (properly) Mr. Speaker's wrinkled shank. Toe, and slipper, swung faster and faster. Mr. Speaker takes no sides but that of House Itself. Suddenly he rose. "I think the House cannot profitably discuss this matter further at the present time." I quote from memory only, but you can enlarge me in Hansard, who is still the carbon paper of British Raj. (November 17, 1947.) There was no razz and no squawk. The House, without further yapping, proceeded to the order of the day. That, I thought, was England; and so were Mr. Attlee and Mr. Churchill, bending double, almost on all fours (more difficult for Churchill), to exchange some parliamentary advertisement during debate; creeping together, across the frontier (two sword-blades wide, by tradition), to confer below the Speaker's line of clairvoyance. You have never seen legislatures (any of them) in action until you have watched Mr. Speaker. Implemented with his scratch wig and his wrinkling hose, he is the emblem of impartiality. Out you go, between Westminster Hall and Westminster Abbey, and hunt long for your cup of tea. Spend a few weeks in England and you'll take tea seriously, or take it anyhow. Yours, Sir, etc.

II. L FOR LEARNER

London and I were a good deal alone together; we planned it that way. The ladies of my house had errands and affairs of their own; except to revisit a few old friends I wanted to listen and look, with gazing fed. Of a thousand glimpses what can one choose to write down? Perhaps nowhere on earth has man's imagination, the gyroscopic spider in his skull, concentered so intricate a web. One no longer remembers, or cares, which was fact and which fancy. One sees Holmes and Watson as clearly in the ruins of Baker Street as Johnson and Boswell (in diuretic urgency) skipping under the roaring busses to that easement in mid-Fleet. Among small pilgrimages, impulsive and random (one should dominate one's worships), some of those best memorable were one way or another associated with that great foursome of London friendship. *Nil Londinii a me alienum puto;* but I think there was a special pleasure in finding that in all dearth of materials the Dictionary House in Gough Square had been given priority. It was in the workmen's hands, and not yet fully repaired, but the shibboleth is "A. Edward Newton." Mention that name Johnsonissimus and Mrs. Phyllis Rowell, the curatrix, throws débris aside. She might tell you how, during the savageries of the blitz, her old mother lay dying in that house. In age and weakness her mind had fused the Doctor and the Deity. Blast and fire were all round them, the exhausted firemen were getting casual soup and sleep on the floors of the Johnson house. A shocking explosion sounded near, and the dying woman said to her daughter: "Don't worry, dear; Our Old Sam won't let us down." The Dictionary House will be open again this spring, in substance as it was, but with one cherished addition: a beautiful little miniature carpenter shop fashioned for Mrs.

Rowell by volunteer fire brigadiers, in memory of their welcome at the Johnson House in intervals from struggle. It is a delicious mimicry, with tiny figures, benches, and tools, carved from chips and shavings. In that house, if anywhere, the visitor feels short of words; but he can hear the Doctor saying: "Madam, this is the triumph of affection united with dexterity."

Boswell would have had much pleasure in noting the neighbors who now have the proximate quarters: The Society of Correctors of the Press. That is, I suppose, a trade union of proofreaders. They are lucky that Johnson and Boswell are no longer on duty. I like to think, by the way, that Bozzy, in the blitz and the buzz, would have come down from bomb-exempt Auchinleck to share Johnson's dangers; and it is not hard to imagine the arguments Mrs. Boswell could have offered against it.

The proper pilgrim does devoir also to the living. There was an extraordinary shock to see, still posted in a stark and fireblacked entry of Kings Bench Walk—in the ruins of the Temple—the nameplate Mr. James Bone. J.B. himself whom the New York *Times* once called "the greatest Londoner since Dr. Johnson," is retired to an abbacy (Abbot's Holt) in Surrey. But not even the gold and russet of autumn landscape, nor the gold and russet prose of his proofsheets (I wonder what the Correctors of the Press make of his handwriting, on the galleys of his forthcoming book about London?), keep him very long on Tilford Common. Last Summer's drouth encouraged a heath fire (brush fire, we would call it) and everything was cinders to his very hedge. Only a miraculous change of wind, and an American girl who was visiting Mr. and Mrs. Bone and derring-did with the garden hose, saved their house. Blitzed out of The Temple, and torpedoed into the North Atlantic, Mr. Bone was only a few inflammable feet of shrubbery from losing another home. "I'm glad we didn't; it would have been thought careless." But every few days the black oilcloth gripsack (you can't buy leather in England; it's all for export) carries J.B.'s proof-sheets and pyjamas up to Fleet Street, where he makes appointment with you at El Vino, last of the sacred pubs.

By James Bone's kindness, and Freddy Bain's, I was able to make the kind of revisit that means most, to the great old "locals" of London River. The Grapes on Lime-house Reach; The Anchor, where Bankside turns round into the Clink; The Angel at Rotherhithe. The Anchor needs perhaps special mention: it has been strongly but-tressed with huge beams after a shaking in the blitz, and the tap marked GIN, that comes right out of the wall, no longer flows (gin is scarce); but the Barclay & Perkins brewery is just behind it, and Johnson's head is still on the beer bottles. Not only that, it is probably the only bar in London that Shakespeare may have drunk in, for The Globe was just behind it. It was rather grim to hear that The Anchor is to be demolished for the new vast Bankside Power House. But there are many kinds of power houses, and they have their various destinies. The Globe had a voltage that is not forgotten. Mrs. Ellen Moy will con-tinue to make her admirably utility sandwiches as long as the house stands. If I were Harvard University, or the General Motors Corporation, I would buy and remove The Anchor and Elley Moy (stone by stone and sand-wich by sandwich) to somewhere in the States; to show the young and jejune what a pub should look like. Alas they couldn't take with it the loveliest of all London's vespasians, opposite the door of The Anchor. You look across the River to the greatest broadside of St. Paul's.

After a wonderful utility lunch (and that means cod, cabbage, and boiled potatoes, and Courage's Stout) at The Angel, Rotherhithe, you go, like Pepys (15 June 1664), to Cherry Gardens pier; and by water, "singing finely." Pepys had his breaks, and made the most of them, but he never travelled, as I did, in Supt. Fallon's launch down river as far as Erith and back to Wapping. It was the course of the Pursuit of the Andaman Islander (in *The Sign of the Four*), and Supt. T. Fallon's fast cruiser (he is head of the Thames River Police) leaps from lump to lump of the stream. Tide runs faster, deeper, and bumpier in London River than any of the old boatmen's madrigals ever told us. Cherry Gardens, I'm sure, is as far downstream as Pepys or Nell Gwynne ever went. If you go in tidal rip as far as Doyle's "melancholy Plumstead Marshes," or further to Gravesend, where Conrad and Marlow used to anchor the yawl, you better be steady with guts. But there is no other way to get a notion of the Courage Stout, and the estuary ebb and flood, and the great web of power-grids, on which London is built.

The India Docks were a commercial appendectomy. You have to get below that twisted gut (the Isle of Dogs) to see the great glands and bowels of service. Docks and ships, chimneys and transmission lines, even the old tawny canvassed sailing barges luffing across, I shall remember them in the rolling heave of grey and green misty sparkle. "Plenty of power round here," said Superintendent Fallon, pointing out various pools of potential. "All we need is a little push from somewhere. It's mostly in the mind, isn't it?"

There was one of Thames's pale-ale-colored sunsets as we came up river. Against the patched old canvas of the barges their men were heaving at huge leeboards and tillers. I was reminded of the Admiralty Appraisal of the *Mayflower* in 1624, when she was beached (or broken up?). The document is preserved in the old Quaker barn at Jordans, Bucks, where some of her timbers perhaps still exist. She had "a suite of sailes more than half worn." They had a right to be.

But the *Mayflower* inventory also listed "five anchors,"

good evidence of prudent seamanship. The same strong old flukes that first hooked Massachusetts bottom. The visitor in Britain will see plenty of things more than half worn, from shirt or collars to railway carriages; he will see enough evidences of disaster, endurance, and fatigue. But more astonishing is how little is really changed. The anchors of temperament are in good holding ground. The British have passed, in their gradual and casual way, through a political and economic shift that would stagger many a tycoon. But the instinctive attitudes are the same. Still the elderly ladies sit muffled in their ancient furs in the glazed hotel lounge, watching to see if you do anything they can identify as "typically American." Still the curly-haired butcher on Sloane Street (I used to watch him through the window) keeps his queue of jaded housewives amused by an incessant patter of cockney comedy. The utility classes of Britain are the most humorous on earth. They have to be; in their oystershell climate they need to secrete pearl-juice. I was wondering why, aboard the C.P.R. liner, the emigrating British flocked with solemn acceptance to a succession of the most appalling Hollywood movies. A man of science, on his way to North America to try to sell British induction coils or something, told me the lurking truth. "They're starved for sunlight and black shadows. They don't pay any attention to the picture for people or plot. They just want to see sunshine and sky." Quite an essay could be written, by the way, on the C.P.R.'s preparatory drill, by movies and magazines, to indoctrinate its British passengers in the North American Way. It was a rough passage, but not even seasickness could discourage the infatuated Britons from those color pictures of ski trails and diving girls, or Bob Montgomery letting himself go as a Tough Guy (Bob Montgomery! who used to be a Collector of Max Beerbohm!) or the color advertisements in *The Magazine Women Believe In.*

How many emigrating grandmothers I saw in the Saloon Lounge, trying hard.

But how, I said to myself 1,000 times, is one small, more-than-half-worn, confused and impure mind—vitiated by love, detachment, skepticism, and indolent habit—to match itself against so large and troubled a panorama? Who could come surgeon-clean? Love and inheritance are themselves fatal to precision. Toynbee or Santayana might perhaps make luminescent (what I call neon-platonist) generalities. I could find few for myself. But I did keep seeing, in London papers, a financial note that Middlewits were up. It took me some time to figure out that had something to do with the Witwatersrand and gold shares. I preferred to take it as a personal hint.

A wise man noted that minnows skip on a turning tide. My own private pantheism believes that minnow can be as testimonial as man; I suspect that the minnow believes it is his own shiny capering that causes the tide to turn. There were plenty of social minnows on the skip, but I was looking for Middlewits. To put it another way, I was listening for the "dialing tone," which the British telephone identifies as "a purring sound." (What is so lonely, so abject-looking, as the British "call-box," sequestered up some dark alley or under a plane tree in a leafy alcove; rectangular relief for the bedtime dog.) It was a pity to be able to get *The Times* so rarely, because it is in Letters to *The Times* that the intelligentsia blow their top; as in the Fourth Editorial they apply the demulcent of Humor-for-the-Few—the kind of prune-and-prism chaffing that no one but Simeon Strunsky has done in America since—well since Washington Irving? Letters to *The Times* are the dialing tone, the purring (or griping) sound of things to come. They are good, sturdy British beefing. Their writers, I said to myself cackling, are old Soup Stock. And they have had to learn, as no American ever did, the lesson of brevity.

The student of civilizations lives by self-denial. In the terrifying baritone of Bill Stern, unconscious energumen of football (feet are the chosen triumph and symbol of the Anglo Saxon), he gets "out of the huddle very quickly now." His own habituated preferences mean nothing. He has to record, and relish (if England is his curiosity for the moment), sponge-bags and bread-sauce, nannies and nappies, bathtubs too deep and whiskies too shallow. But as the ancient immortal saying had it, when the customer complained there was a fly in his whiskey; the barman replied, "That's all roight, sir; 'e won't drown; 'is feet are on the bottom." So are John Bull's, and J. B. Priestley's. I'd nominate Priestley as a thumping good Prime Minister—he has somewhat the same qualities as Churchill—except for his brave, blooming compulsion to grind his teeth in public. At the very moment when every well-meaning American was trying to help the slow-cosseted movement to kick in, Old Candid Jack informed us that all Americans are hysterical sheep; and New York the crass crabmeat of the world. A man from Yorkshire should look less suddenly on New York.

I am trying to say, a visitor (any visitor, anywhere) has to look for the simplest and humblest emblems. In the English crossword puzzles the clues are quite different from our own. You won't find them by travelling in the Queens, and going direct to the Dorchester and the Savoy. You're more likely to twig them in London Transport, or what we in New York call (to British amazement) a Comprehensive Omnibus. It is not distance that separates people; it is being too close. The *Queen Mary-Dorchester* type of visitors is only a flying wedge of the U.S.A. bullying their way a few yards between guard and tackle. If I wanted a real social document I'd hire a man like Bill Stern to live in England, muzzled, for a year, and then report to the U. S. about British Sports. Or I'd hire a commuter from Surrey (under gag for conditioning) to compare the train service from Charing Cross or Victoria with that of the Long Island Railroad. I have seen Victoria on a night of hellish fog; at least they give the season-ticket-holders an empty train to sleep in.

Differences being so subtle, what would you regard as clues in the stunningly chequered crossword puzzle of American-English relatives? I had an amusing dream not long ago, in which by some accident of oblique view I saw a burlesk chorus capering above me; as they stripped and teased I could see their eyes from about course 145 degrees. It was curious to see the actual jelly and bulge of the eye, glittered by the footlights and prominent sideways. My dream continued into sheer farce when a Hokinson matron (who was there as an umpire of public morale) was carried away with excitement and began tearing off her own clothes, to everyone's dismay, and curvetting in the aisle and a percentage of slip. I mention that only because if one doesn't record a dream one forgets to analyze it. What I'm getting at is the sidelong jelly of the eye; things seen in dream or chance. Those are partly clues, partly testament.

We are, as Matthew Arnold said, between two worlds: one dead, one powerless to be born. Arnold enjoyed ribbing the Americans, almost as much as Jack Priestley does; but he begat grandchildren who became highly useful and distinguished Americans. So, more than likely, will Mr. Priestley. From the jackstraws (spillikins) of tumbled memory let me hook out a few slivers.

The methodical good sense of the English. See the signs in country towns: *No Waiting on This Side on Odd Days.* Waiting means parking. The idea is, you park on alternate sides of the street on alternate days. Result, no shopkeeper is permanently hurt by constant car-parking in front of his shop.—And the noble simplicity of putting a large red sign on the bonnet (of the car) of any apprentice driver. L. for Learner. That means, give him the benefit of anxiety—a wide berth.

The stark simplicity of British statement. Almost every day I went past the Royal Artillery Memorial at Hyde Park Corner; at last—and in great peril, dodging the horrors of cloverleaf traffic—I decided to see what was carved on the base of that dead man. He lies in bronze, covered with coat and helmet. When I last saw him a light pall of snow whitened his rest. He symbolizes 49,076 dead of the Royal Artillery Regiment in 1914-18. And the statement: "Here was a Royal Fellowship of Death." It is more than November snow that chills you as you hunt an opening to Knightsbridge among the teeming traffic.

Or would it be Oxford, seen again in snell windy weather—Oxford of the sweet dreaming gasometers—Oxford that, more lucky than any university except Yale, now finds itself only the Latin Quarter of a factory town; like a bishop in Birmingham. So it has something on which to grind its teeth. The traffic on Corn and High is worse than New York's Holland Tunnel. But there, bicycled in pedalled pause, are the flocks of youth—held in leash a moment by some yokel policeman's arm—waiting for signal. The arm descends and they flit off like a flight of starlings, like a wing of airplanes, on their way to lectures by C. S. Lewis or Father D'Arcy. The bells of Oxford have been almost drowned by the lorries. You have to get inside a college quadrangle before you can remember Roger Bacon or Duns Scotus or Matthew Arnold. I went into the front quad at BNC, to try to remember how St. Mary's spire looked from there when they had bonfires (I was thinking of the surly and surrogatory Pater), but all I learned was the B.N.C. 3rd VIII had made a number of bumps; it was chalked on an entry. I wish there were space to tell you of New College: of dear old

Rose, the housemaid at the Warden's lodgings, to whom I gave a can of Canadian beef-cum-mushrooms and said, "This is my calling card." She fluttered her kindly tickle-eye and said, "It will be very welcome, sir." I saw it, next day, in that last of England's fourteenth-century kitchens, surmounting itself in the oven with a great arch of austerity pastry; what we would call a Warden Pye.

Oxford was always a carfax (*carrefour*) of traffic. She breathes, from her stricken towers, the latest enchantments of Lord Nuffield. We stayed, of course, in the last of England's frostbitten inns, the blessed old Golden Cross. That was where Shakespeare stayed, en route to and fro The Globe. His sheets, thanks to Mistress Davenant, were I hope warmer than mine. Postponing those gelations, I sped down St. Aldate's to hear Great Tom (Magnus Thomas) toll his 101 strokes, at 9.5 P.M. I listened, waited, and no booming bronze. Imperious as any outworn scholar has right to be, I questioned the Porter (proper in his round hard hat). "Yes, sir, quite right, sir, but we're still on Summer Time. Christ Church goes on Greenwich Time. Thank you, sir."

The ghost that Oxford has given up can still be found at Cambridge; the ghost of silence. Cambridge is still mute. In her Cavendish laboratories, or where the organ and choir winnow the cool autumn air alongside the chapel of King's, or where the tame hedgehog probes the back lawns of John's with his inquest snout, you can still find the space and silence of academe. Nowhere else, I think, in the world? When new modes of international argument are shown, they are likely to be fissioned from Cambridge. Because Cambridge is bedded in silence, and in unspoiled archways where you see a great swath of scarlet creeper, flung like a doctor of science gown across the grey shoulder of a college.

"Euston always does this to me," said a young woman (a daughter) trying to keep her face under control. You don't know Dark and Damp, Delay, Doubt and Despair, until you've seen a Boat or a Leave Train from what they call the Departure Platform. Worse still there was a posse of the Salvation Army seeing off one of their benevolent brigadiers; he was going out to Save Canada; when his adjutants hymned "God Be With You," etc., it was too terrible. We took it personal. I saw our young woman's face beginning to slip. In our carriage was a young dog emigrating to Canada; he moaned like Manfred. And the Xmas number of the *Illustrated London News,* said W. H. Smith's newsstand, wouldn't be published until tomorrow. I knew that was absurd, because I'd seen it all over town, but thought I wouldn't buy it until getting aboard the train. If you don't read the stories, and no one ever does, the noble color-printing is like prose by Churchill: full of beef and brandy and thrippenny bits.

Yes, a dark day; the first snow had fallen; visibility was low. The great yellow and white gonfalons were already up along the Mall, for the Royal Wedding tomorrow, but in November light they looked more jaundice than gold. Was this the beginning of Another Winter? The Midlands were white with too early snowfall. Mrs. Gaskell, I thought, would have to wear her pattens in Cranford. In the carriage with us was a handsome young R.N. lieutenant, who looked so astoundingly like Prince Philip that I wondered at first had the bridegroom weakened and fled out on his assignment?

Spending most of the long cold journey (as I always do) in the corridor, to study what things look like, I saw that the little spoky wagon-wheels were spinning again. Just in those last few days the Island had got off dead center. Wheels were turning. Chimneys were puffing smoke. Even in the restorong car there was a kind of valedictory nostalgia in turnips and turbot.

It was a long chilly ride. Who but a lover of railways would be moved to think this was one of the latest travels under the great name of the LMS (which I first knew as the immortal L.N.W.R.) before they became National Railways. Even Toynbee, even Sir Stafford Cripps, couldn't have been more intensified to consider, we were among the very last patrons of Private Enterprise. Myself I care little about ownership; I don't much care who hatches the eggs if I can fertilize and lay them. That is the fun; the rest is paper work.

The train was cold; the customs shed was cold (you go through Outbound Customs as well as Inbound, in our new world of fisco-analysis); and when we climbed the snowy gangplank to the *Empress of Canada* we were shocked and shamed. Tea with meat sandwiches (delicious thin sheaves of Canadian rare beef); cheese Eccles cakes, hot water, liquid soap, towels laundered in crisp hundreds on the washroom racks—what had we done to deserve them? I was horrified, and still am. And the piles of toast, of fresh rolls, the tables of ham and turkey and the slicing-master with his shaven blade to curl off such slabs of veal-and-ham and Melton Mowbray. What is there in a tide-tabled gangplank to warrant one's passage from less than enough to too much? I suppose it is somehow credited as "export." It is as silly, and as selfish, as all human history. The rich white-shining outbound ship stands high at her cold and sleety pier. You look through the glassed-in windows of the promenade and see the last fourgons of baggage loaded aboard by chilblained men; do you wonder why people wonder? As I saw the great platters of rolls and buns I thought of the little old lady in Cambridge, who brought to every meal her little paper bag of crusts, saved from the day before.

We had fixed our sailing date long before Elizabeth and Philip did. I was sorry it had to be the night before the Wedding; but how tickled they were at our little glass hotel because they still had time to sell our rooms to four royalists. I felt in my simple way that two people's wed-

ding is their own affair. I had found some of the ante-
nuptial and millinery details hard to take. The description of Elizabeth's camiknickers (an exclusively British
lingerie) fitted with "little kicks of frosty lace" gave me
no comfort at all. I only hoped that she herself, poor soul,
was not required to read the description of her bridal bed-
gown, in oyster silk. These were all in those scurvy little
afternoon penny papers, where England shows her peasant
psyche worse than we do. England does it in four pages,
and takes it seriously. We do it in sixty-four pages, and
roar from laughter. As in Thomas Hardy, too much of
anything, even butchery, becomes comic.

The *Empress* ran into bad weather as soon as she was
over the bar. The next morning, beyond the Mull of
Kintyre, we were plunging in a nice old North of Ireland
swell. It was drizzle and dour; those who had wrestled up
from their berths were blanketed and supine in deck
chairs. Then the BBC came on. In their earnest mode, so
much more effective than American hysterics, the report-
ers along the Mall, along Whitehall, in The Abbey, told
us about it. Sturdy British matrons, prostrate with seasickness, rallied up from their rugs; wizened Indian colonels
strode the scuppers to hear. We heard the cheer, the cry
of the British folk. I am, I think, a faithful reporter. Balancing against the leeward rail, I listened. There was
something maenad in that cry. It was more than a salute
to two bashful and earnest young people. It was the voice
of a race that had long had nothing to cheer. It rose about
privations and queues and cold beds. It rose above the
stately unsteamed homes of England; above discomfort
and dearth. It was strange to hear it there, in the grey-
green stormy waters north of the islands, in their own
approved element of struggle. The beautiful white ship,
loaded with good hope, buried her bright nose in dark
northern gale. The voices of the air, the yell of stubborn
millions worn by patient endurance, were not identifiable

even as men, women, or children. They were the cry of an enduring race. Coal, for the first time, was over target. Steel was on the up and up. Themselves, by themselves if needed, could get round Cape Stiff. Despair was never their cup of tea.

As I heard that mixed and diapason roar, I thought of their great alien spokesman, Joseph Conrad. (They will never be good spokesmen for themselves.)

"You were a good crowd," he said. "As good a crowd as ever fisted a heavy foresail . . . or gave back yell for yell to a westerly gale."

I thought of that, and walked forward, alone, to smell the western sea.

1948

James Thurber

IVORYTOWN, RINSOVILLE, ANACINBURG, AND CRISCO CORNERS

THE last time I checked up on the locales of the thirty-six radio daytime serials, better known as soap operas, that are broadcast from New York five days a week to a mass audience of twenty million listeners, the score was Small Towns 24, Big Cities 12. I say "score" advisedly, for the heavy predominance of small towns in Soapland is a contrived and often-emphasized victory for good, clean little communities over cold, cruel metropolitan centers. Thus, daytime radio perpetuates the ancient American myth of the small town, idealized in novels, comedies, and melodramas at the turn of the century and before, supported by Thornton Wilder in "Our Town," and undisturbed by the scandalous revelations of such irreverent gossips as Sherwood Anderson and Edgar Lee Masters. Soapland shares with the United States at least five actual cities—New York, Chicago, Boston, Washington, and Los Angeles—but its small towns are as misty and unreal as Brigadoon. They have such names as Hartville, Dickston, Simpsonville, Three Oaks, Great Falls, Beauregard, Elmwood, Oakdale, Rushville Center, and

From *The Beast in Me and Other Animals* by James Thurber. Reprinted by permission of the author.

Homeville. "Our Gal Sunday" is set in Virginia, but no states are mentioned for the towns in the other serials.

The differences between small-town people and big-city people are exaggerated and oversimplified by most serial writers in the black-and-white tradition of Horatio Alger. It seems to be a basic concept of soap-opera authors that, for the benefit of the listening housewives, distinctions between good and evil can be most easily made in the old-fashioned terms of the moral town and the immoral city. Small-town Soaplanders occasionally visit, or flee to, one of the big cities, particularly New York, out of some desperation or other, and they are usually warned against this foolhardy venture by a sounder and stabler character in tones that remind me of such dramas of a simpler era as "York State Folks" and "The County Chairman." A few months ago, Starr, a young, selfish, and restless wife who ornamented "Ma Perkins" with her frets and tears, ran away to New York. She promptly met two typical Soapland New Yorkers, a young woman who talked like Miss Duffy in "Duffy's Tavern" and an underworld gent with a rough exterior and a heart of gold. This type of semi-gangster threads his way in and out of various serials, using such expressions as "on the up-and-up," "baby doll," and "lovey-dovey stuff," and, thanks to some of the women writers, the fellow has become a kind of extension of Editha's burglar. In "Rosemary," a conniving chap named Lefty actually conceived a fond and pure devotion for a little girl. But the Soaplanders do not have to come to New York, as we shall see, to become entangled with the Misses Duffy and the Lefties and all the rest.

A soap opera deals with the plights and problems brought about in the lives of its permanent principal characters by the advent and interference of one group of individuals after another. Thus, a soap opera is an endless sequence of narratives whose only cohesive element is the eternal presence of its bedevilled and beleaguered principal characters. A narrative, or story sequence, may run from eight weeks to several months. The ending of one plot is always hooked up with the beginning of the next, but the connection is unimportant and soon forgotten. Almost all the villains in the small-town daytime serials are émigrés from the cities—gangsters, white-collar criminals, designing women, unnatural mothers, cold wives, and selfish, ruthless, and just plain cussed rich men. They always come up against a shrewdness that outwits them or destroys them, or a kindness that wins them over to the good way of life.

The fact that there are only two or three citizens for the villains to get entangled with reduces the small town to a wood-and-canvas set with painted doors and windows. Many a soap town appears to have no policemen, mailmen, milkmen, storekeepers, lawyers, ministers, or even neighbors. The people live their continuously troubled lives within a socio-economic structure that only faintly resembles our own. Since the problems of the characters are predominantly personal, emotional, and private, affecting the activities of only five or six persons at a time, the basic setting of soap opera is the living room. But even the living room lacks the pulse of life; rarely are heard the ticking of clocks, the tinkling of glasses, the squeaking of chairs, or the creaking of floor boards. Now and then, the listener does hear *about* a hospital, a courtroom, a confectionery, a drugstore, a bank, or a hotel in the town, or a roadhouse or a large, gloomy estate outside the town limits, but in most small-town serials there are no signs or sounds of community life—no footsteps of passers-by, no traffic noises, no shouting of children, no barking of dogs, no calling of friend to friend, no newsboys to plump the evening papers against front doors. A few writers try from time to time to animate the streets of these silent towns, but in general Ivorytown and Rinsoville and Anacinburg are dead. This isolation of soap-opera characters was brought about by the interminability of daytime serials, some of which began as authentic stories of small-town life. The inventiveness of writers flagged under the strain of devising long plot sequences, one after another, year after year, involving a given family with the neighbors and other townsfolk. Furthermore, the producers and sponsors of soap opera and the alert advertising agencies set up a clamor for bigger and wider action and excitement. The original soap-opera characters are now often nothing more than shadowy and unnecessary *ficelles,* awkwardly held on to as confidants or advisers of the principal figures in the melodramas that come and go in chaotic regularity. Even "Mrs. Wiggs of the Cabbage Patch" followed the formula and degenerated into radio melodrama after six months. Its heroine spent her time dodging the bullets of gangsters and the tricks and traps of other scoundrels from the city.

If the towns in Soapland are not developed as realistic communities, neither are the characters—except in rare instances—developed as authentic human beings. The reason for this is that the listening housewives are believed to be interested only in problems similar to their own, and it is one of the basic tenets of soap opera that the women characters who solve these problems must be flawless projections of the housewife's ideal woman. It is assumed that the housewife identifies herself with the characters who are most put-upon, most noble, most righteous, and hence most dehumanized. Proceeding on this theory, serial producers oppose the creation of any three-dimensional character who shows signs of rising above this strange standard. Advertising agencies claim— and the record would appear to sustain them—that a realistically written leading woman would cause the audience rating of the show to drop. The housewife is also believed to be against humor in the daytime—in spite of the long success of the truly funny "Vic and Sade"—on the ground that comedy would interfere with her desire to lose herself in the trials and tribulations, the emotional agonies and soul searchings, of the good women in the serials. The only serial that deliberately goes in for comedy now is "Lorenzo Jones," whose narrator describes it as "a story with more smiles than tears." The lack of humor in most of the others is so complete as to reach the proportions of a miracle of craftsmanship.

The principal complaint of audience mail in the early days of the serials was that they moved so swiftly they were hard to follow. Surveys showed that the housewife listens, on an average, to not more than half the broadcasts of any given serial. Plot recapitulation, familiarly called "recap," was devised to slow down the progress of serials. "We told them what was going to happen, we told them it was happening, and we told them it had happened," says Robert D. Andrews. The listeners continued to complain, and action was retarded still further, with the result that time in a soap opera is now an amazing technique of slow motion. Compared to the swift flow of time in the real world, it is a glacier movement. It took one male character in a soap opera three days to get an answer to the simple question "Where have you been?" If, in "When a Girl Marries," you missed an automobile accident that occurred on a Monday broadcast, you could pick it up the following Thursday and find the leading woman character still unconscious and her husband still moaning over her beside the wrecked car. In one sequence of "Just Plain Bill," the barber of Hartville said, "It doesn't seem possible to me that Ralph Wilde arrived here only yesterday." It didn't seem possible to me, either, since Ralph Wilde had arrived, as mortal time goes, thirteen days before. Bill recently required four days to shave a man in the living room of the man's house. A basin of hot water Bill had placed on a table Monday (our time) was still hot on Thursday, when his customer stopped talking and the barber went to work.

Soap-opera time, by an easy miracle, always manages to coincide with mortal time in the case of holidays. Memorial Day in Hartville, for example, is Memorial Day in New York. Every year, on that day, Bill Davidson, Hartville's leading citizen, makes the Memorial Day address, a simple, cagey arrangement of words in praise of God and the Republic. One serial writer tells me that the word "republic" has been slyly suggested as preferable to "democracy," apparently because "democracy" has become a provocative, flaming torch of a word in our time. For Soapland, you see, is a peaceful world, a political and economic Utopia, free of international unrest, the menace of fission, the threat of inflation, depression, general unemployment, the infiltration of Communists, and the problems of racism. Except for a maid or two, there are no colored people in the World of Soap. Papa David, in "Life Can Be Beautiful," is the only Jew I have run into on the daytime air since "The Goldbergs" was discontinued. (Procter & Gamble sponsored "The Goldbergs" for many years, and the race question did not enter into its termination.) Lynn Stone and Addy Richton, who have written several serials, were once told by a sponsor's representative to eliminate a Jewish woman from one of their shows. "We don't want to antagonize the anti-Semites," the gentleman casually explained. They had to take out the character.

Proponents of soap opera are given to protesting, a little vehemently, that serials have always promoted in their dialogue an understanding of public welfare, child psychology, and modern psychiatric knowledge in general, and that this kind of writing is supervised by experts in the various fields. There was an effective lecture on the dangers of reckless driving in "The Guiding Light" one day, and I have heard a few shreds of psychiatric talk in a dozen serials, but I have found no instances of sustained instruction and uplift in soap opera. During the war, it is true, at the behest of government agencies, many writers worked into their serials incidents and dialogue of a worthy sociological nature. Charles Jackson, the author of "The Lost Weekend," who wrote a serial called "Sweet River" for more than two years, brought to his mythical town factory workers from the outside and presented the case for tolerance and good will. Social consciousness practically disappeared from serials with the war's end, and Soapland is back to normalcy. Three weeks after Charles Luckman's food-conservation committee had begun its campaign, Ma Perkins invited a young man who had not been satisfied by a heavy breakfast to "fill up on toast and jam." It was just a slip. The script had been written before the committee started work. But, after all, there is plenty of bread in Soapland, which never has scarcity of production.

A study of the social stratification of Soapland, if I may use so elegant a term, reveals about half a dozen highly specialized groups. There are the important homely philosophers, male and female. This stratum runs through "Just Plain Bill," "Ma Perkins," "David Harum," "Life Can Be Beautiful," and "Editor's Daughter," a soap opera not heard in the East but extremely popular in the Middle West, whose male protagonist enunciates a gem of friendly wisdom at the end of every program. ("Life Can Be Beautiful," by the way, is known to the trade as "Elsie Beebe." You figure it out. I had to.) Then, there are the Cinderellas, the beautiful or talented young women of lowly estate who have married or are about to marry into social circles far above those of their hard-working and usually illiterate mothers. (Their fathers, as a rule, are happily dead.) On this wide level are Nana, daughter of Hamburger Katie; Laurel, daughter of Stella Dallas; and my special pet, Sunday, of "Our Gal Sunday," who started life as a foundling dumped in the laps of two old Western miners and is now the proud and badgered wife of Lord

Henry Brinthrop, "England's wealthiest and handsomest young nobleman." Christopher Morley's famous Cinderella, Kitty Foyle, also lived in Soapland for some years. Mr. Morley was charmed by the actors and actresses who played in "Kitty," but he says that he never quite gathered what the radio prolongation of the story was about. Kitty eventually packed up and moved out of Soapland. The late Laurette Taylor received many offers for the serial rights to "Peg o' My Heart," which was written by her husband, J. Hartley Manners, but it is said that she rejected them all with the agonized cry, "Oh, God, no! Not that!" On a special and very broad social stratum of Soapland live cores of doctors and nurses. You find scarcely anyone else in "Woman in White," "Road of Life," and "Joyce Jordan, M.D." The heroes of "Young Dr. Malone," "Big Sister," and "Young Widder Brown" are doctors, and medical men flit in and out of all other serials. The predominance of doctors may be accounted for by the fact that radio surveys have frequently disclosed that the practice of medicine is at the top of the list of professions popular with the American housewife.

A fourth and highly important group, since it dominates large areas of Soapland, consists of young women, single, widowed, or divorced, whose purpose in life seems to be to avoid marriage by straight-arming their suitors year after year on one pretext or another. Among the most distinguished members of this group are Joyce Jordan, who is a doctor when she gets around to it; Helen Trent, a dress designer; Ellen Brown, who runs a tearoom; Ruth Wayne, a nurse; and a number of actresses and secretaries. For some years, Portia, the woman lawyer of "Portia Faces Life," belonged to this class, but several years ago she married Walter Manning, a journalist, and became an eminent figure in perhaps the most important group of all, the devoted and long-suffering wives whose marriages have, every hour of their lives, the immediacy of a toothache and the urgency of a telegram. The husbands of these women spend most of their time trying in vain to keep their brave, high-minded wives out of one plot entanglement after another.

All men in Soapland must be able to drop whatever they are doing and hurry to this living room or that at the plaint or command of a feminine voice on the phone. Bill Davidson's one-chair barbershop has not had a dozen customers in a dozen years, since the exigencies of his life keep him out of the shop most of every day. In eight months, by my official count, Kerry Donovan visited his law office only three times. He has no partners or assistants, but, like Bill, he somehow prospers. The rich men, bad and good, who descend on the small town for plot's sake never define the industries they leave behind them in New York or Chicago for months at a time. Their businesses miraculously run without the exertion of control or the need for contact. Now and then, a newspaper publisher, a factory owner, or a superintendent of schools, usually up to no good, appears briefly on the Soapland scene, but mayors, governors, and the like are almost never heard of. "The Story of Mary Marlin," just to be different, had a President of the United States, but, just to be the same, he was made heavily dependent on the intuitive political vision of his aged mother, who, in 1943, remained alive to baffle the doctors and preserve, by guiding her son's policies, the security of the Republic.

The people of Soapland, as Rudolf Arnheim, professor of psychology at Sarah Lawrence, has pointed out, consist of three moral types: the good, the bad, and the weak. Good women dominate most soap operas. They are conventional figures, turned out of a simple mold. Their invariably strong character, high fortitude, and unfailing capability must have been originally intended to present them as women of a warm, dedicated selflessness, but they emerge, instead, as ladies of frigid aggressiveness. The writers are not to blame for this metamorphosis, for they are hampered by several formidable inhibitions, including what is officially called "daytime morality," the strangest phenomenon in a world of phenomena. The good people, both men and women, cannot smoke cigarettes or touch alcoholic beverages, even beer or sherry. In a moment of tragedy or emotional tension, the good people turn to tea or coffee, iced or hot. It has been estimated that the three chief characters of "Just Plain Bill" have consumed several hundred gallons of iced tea since this program began, in 1932. Furthermore, the good women must float like maiden schoolteachers above what Evangeline Adams used to call "the slime"; that is, the passionate expression of sexual love. The ban against spirituous and amorous indulgence came into sharp focus once in "Just Plain Bill" when the plot called for one Graham Steele to be caught in a posture of apparent intimacy with the virtuous Nancy Donovan. He had carelessly upset a glass of iced tea into the lady's lap and was kneeling and dabbing at her dress with his handkerchief—a compromising situation indeed in Soapland—when her jealous husband arrived and suspected the worst.

The paternalistic Procter & Gamble, famous for their managerial policy of "We're just one big family of good, clean folks," do not permit the smoking of cigarettes at their plants during working hours except in the case of executives with private offices. This may have brought about the anti-cigarette phase of daytime morality, but I can adduce no evidence to support the theory. The supervision of Procter & Gamble's eleven soap operas is in the tolerant hands of the quiet, amiable William Ramsey, who smokes Marlboros. In daytime radio, the cigarette has come to be a sign and stigma of evil that ranks with the mark of the cloven hoof, the scarlet letter, and the brand of the *fleur-de-lis*. The married woman who smokes a cigarette proclaims herself a bad wife or an unnatural mother or an adventuress. The male cigarette smoker is either a gangster or a cold, calculating white-collar criminal. The good men may smoke pipes or cigars. A man who called on the hero of "Young Dr. Malone" brought him some excellent pipe tobacco and announced that he himself would smoke a fine cigar. As if to take the edge off this suggestion of wanton sensual abandon, a good woman hastily said to the caller, "Don't you want a nice, cold glass of ice water?" "Splendid!" cried the gentleman. "How many cubes?" she asked. "Two, thank you," said the visitor, and the virtue of the household was reestablished.

Clean-living, letter-writing busybodies are unquestionably to blame for prohibition in Soapland. When Mrs. Elaine Carrington, the author of "Pepper Young's Family," had somebody serve beer on that serial one hot afternoon, she received twenty indignant complaints. It wasn't many, when you consider that "Pepper" has six million listeners, but it was enough. The latest violation of radio's liquor law I know of occurred in "Ma Perkins," when a bad woman was given a double Scotch-and-soda to loosen her tongue. Letters of protest flooded in. The bad people and the weak people are known to drink and to smoke cigarettes, but their vices in this regard are almost always just talked about, with proper disapproval, and not often actually depicted.

As for the sexual aspect of daytime morality, a man who had a lot to do with serials in the nineteen-thirties assures me that at that time there were "hot clinches" burning up and down the daytime dial. If this is so, there has been a profound cooling off, for my persistent eavesdropping has detected nothing but coy and impregnable chastity in the good women, nobly abetted by a kind of Freudian censor who knocks on doors or rings phones at crucial moments. Young Widder Brown has kept a doctor dangling for years without benefit of her embraces, on the ground that it would upset her children if she married again. Helen Trent, who found that she could recapture romance after the age of thirty-five, has been tantalizing a series of suitors since 1933. (She would be going on fifty if she were a mortal, but, owing to the molasses flow of soap-opera time, she is not yet forty.) Helen is soap opera's No. 1 tormentor of men, all in the virtuous name of indecision, provoked and prolonged by plot device. One suitor said to her, "After all, you have never been in my arms"—as daring an advance as any of her dejected swains has ever made in my presence. Helen thereupon went into a frosty routine about marriage being a working partnership, mental stimulation, and, last and least, "emotional understanding." "Emotional understanding," a term I have heard on serials several times, seems to be the official circumlocution for the awful word "sex." The chill Miss Trent has her men frustrated to a point at which a mortal male would smack her little mouth, so smooth, so firm, so free of nicotine, alcohol, and emotion. Suitors in Soapland are usually weak, and Helen's frustration of them is aimed to gratify the listening housewives, brought up in the great American tradition of female domination. Snivelled one of the cold lady's suitors, "I'm not strong, incorruptible, stalwart. I'm weak." Helen purred that she would help him find himself. The weak men continually confess their weakness to the good women, who usually manage to turn them into stable citizens by some vague and soapy magic. The weak men and the good men often confess to one another their dependence on the good women. In one serial, a weak man said to a good man, "My strength is in Irma now." To which the good man replied, "As mine is in Joan, Steve." As this exchange indicates, it is not always easy to tell the weak from the good, but on the whole the weak men are sadder but less stuffy than the good men. The bad men, God save us all, are likely to be the most endurable of the males in Soapland.

The people of Soapland are subject to a set of special ills. Temporary blindness, preceded by dizzy spells and headaches, is a common affliction of Soapland people. The condition usually clears up in six or eight weeks, but once in a while it develops into brain tumor and the patient dies. One script writer, apparently forgetting that General Mills was the sponsor of his serial, had one of his women characters go temporarily blind because of an allergy to chocolate cake. There was hell to pay, and the writer had to make the doctor in charge of the patient hastily change his diagnosis. Amnesia strikes almost as often in Soapland as the common cold in our world. There have been as many as eight or nine amnesia cases on the air at one time. The hero of "Rosemary" stumbled around in a daze for months last year. When he regained his memory, he found that in his wanderings he had been lucky enough to marry a true-blue sweetie. The third major disease is paralysis of the legs. This scourge usually attacks the good males. Like mysterious blindness, loss of the use of the legs may be either temporary or permanent. The hero of "Life Can Be Beautiful" was confined to a wheel chair until his death last March, but young Dr. Malone, who was stricken with paralysis a year ago, is up and around again. I came upon only one crippled villain in 1947: Spencer Hart rolled through a three-month sequence of "Just Plain Bill" in a wheel chair. When their men are stricken, the good women become nobler than ever. A disabled hero is likely to lament his fate and indulge in self-pity now and then, but his wife or sweetheart never complains. She is capable of twice as much work, sacrifice, fortitude, endurance, ingenuity, and love as before. Joyce Jordan, M.D., had no interest in a certain male until he lost the use of both legs and took to a wheel chair. Then love began to bloom in her heart.

love with a millionaire, can a woman married to a hope-
less cripple, can a girl who married an amnesia case—can
they find soap-opera happiness and the good, soap-opera
way of life? No, they can't—not, at least, in your time
and mine. The characters in Soapland and their unsolvable
perplexities will be marking time on the air long after
you and I are gone, for we must grow old and die, whereas
the people of Soapland have a magic immunity to age,
like Peter Pan and the Katzenjammer Kids. When you
and I are in Heaven with the angels, the troubled people
of Ivorytown, Rinsoville, Anacinburg, and Crisco Corners,
forever young or forever middle-aged, will still be up to
their ears in inner struggle, soul searching, and everlasting frustration.

1948

ABOUT THE ESSAYISTS

HENRY DAVID THOREAU (1817-1862), individualist, ascetic, rebel, and nature-lover, one of the most fascinating and original figures in American literature, is best known for his *Walden or Life in the Woods* (1854), in which he describes his two and a half years of living in a solitary hut on the shore of Walden Pond. This essay, describing his objectives and method of living during the period, is a central chapter in *Walden*.

OLIVER WENDELL HOLMES (1808-1894) is one of the great personalities in American literature. A distinguished doctor whose medical theories were often in advance of his time, he was also a prolific and versatile writer on a great variety of themes. His *Autocrat of the Breakfast Table* (of which the essay here printed is the opening) originally appeared as a series of essays in *The Atlantic Monthly* in 1857 and 1858. His writing is marked by a highly individual kind of humor and a genial wisdom which is often ironic and never merely "soft."

The lectures, poems, essays and journals of RALPH WALDO EMERSON (1803-1882) constitute a fascinating record of the thought of an idealist nature-lover with a strong (though highly individual) religious and even mystical cast of mind. Emerson was already a towering figure on the American intellectual scene when his essay, "Illusions," appeared along with Holmes' first *Autocrat* paper in the first issue of *The Atlantic Monthly*.

WALTER BAGEHOT (1826-1877) was a versatile Victorian writer and editor whose work is too little known among Americans today. Banker, economist, political thinker, historian, and literary critic, he possessed an eager, original mind and a lively prose style. His *The English Constitution* (1867) remains one of the most perceptive studies of the subject, and his *Literary Studies* show a critical and historical awareness that is still highly impressive. The essay here printed was written as a review of *The Letters and Works of Lady Mary Wortley Montagu,* edited by Lord Wharncliffe.

MATTHEW ARNOLD (1822-1888), poet, critic, and apostle of culture, was ever concerned with the problem of educating the middle classes of England to an awareness of the proper nature and function of literature, and with leavening the lump of English belief in material progress with the "sweetness and light" he found so prevalent in the civilization of ancient Athens. In his efforts to substitute for Biblical fundamentalism an esthetic awareness of the Bible's greatness and a feeling for great poetry as the real source of a tenable modern religion, he faced theological and sociological as well as more strictly literary problems. This essay, the preface to the second edition of his *Essays in Criticism, First Series* (1869), sums up much of his critical thought. Arnold's criticism is frequently controversial in tone, and the references to personalities in this essay illustrate his views at the same time they show his skill in extricating himself from the embarrassing predicaments in which the very articulate airing of his views sometimes involved him.

ROBERT LOUIS STEVENSON (1850-1894), novelist and essayist, is something more than the mere artful prose stylist he is so often considered. Even in this early essay the language is carefully molded to fit the sensibility, and the cadence of the sentences and rise and fall of the paragraphs project a mood persuasively and interestingly.

Like Stevenson a Scot, ANDREW LANG (1844-1912), was a poet, folklorist, historian, anthropologist, literary critic and essayist of great versatility. He was also a good Greek scholar and collaborated with S. H. Butcher in the famous Butcher and Lang translation of the *Odyssey* and with Leaf and Myers in the long-standard translation of the *Iliad.* Lang was a man of letters *par excellence,* who wandered widely and happily in a great variety of literary and historical fields. The essay here printed shows him in lighter vein, but its tone is characteristic of much of Lang's less formal writing.

WALTER HORATIO PATER (1839-1894) is generally remembered as a quiet and scholarly lover of beauty who wished everybody, in his words, to burn with a hard gem-like flame. He was also, however, a historian and critic of real substance, and in addition to such well-known works as his philosophical romance,

Marius the Epicurean, and his *Studies in the History of the Renaissance,* Pater produced literary essays in which critical sensitivity is nicely blended with historical awareness. The essay here printed shows his characteristic perceptiveness: his remarks on Shakespeare's *Richard II* are some of the most acute that have ever been made on that play.

Best known as an accomplished writer of clever light verse, HENRY AUSTIN DOBSON (1840-1921) was also a keen student of eighteenth century English literature and wrote many critical and historical essays which combine charm with scholarship. If Dobson failed frequently to penetrate very far beneath the surface, it was from choice rather than from any intellectual lack. The essay here printed shows the peculiar grace with which he could treat historical and biographical subjects.

FRANK MOORE COLBY (1865-1925) was an American editor, historian and economist with a gift for prose style and a remarkable sense of humor. Like Stephen Leacock, also a professor of economics, he developed an original and impressive species of humorous essay in the intervals between more serious writing; the essay here printed is a good example of his easy skill.

One of the great wits of English literature was GILBERT KEITH CHESTERTON (1874-1936). He loved to reach orthodox conclusions by the most outrageously unorthodox ways, and his essays display a brilliance in the manipulation of paradox that has rarely been equaled in English prose.

WILLIAM JAMES (1842-1910), the distinguished American psychologist and philosopher, had perhaps the clearest and most persuasive style of any philosopher since David Hume. His famous lecture on pragmatism, here printed, is an excellent example of his luminous philosophical prose. He and his brother Henry James have rarely been matched among modern writers in their differing contributions to the life of the intellect.

HILAIRE BELLOC (1870-   ) is generally classified with Chesterton among modern English essayists: both were Roman Catholics and defended their religious position with unconventional wit, and both were ardent lovers of the English scene. Belloc is at his best in writing of some of the more elemental aspects of the English countryside.

HENRY BROOKS ADAMS (1838-1918), scion of a distinguished family of American statesmen, is remembered today chiefly for his autobiographical work, *The Education of Henry Adams* (of which the essay here printed is a chapter), an American classic valuable both as a revelation of a particular kind of intelligence and as a document illustrating an important transitional period in American and European political, social, and cultural ideas.

BERTRAND RUSSELL (1872-   ) is the distinguished logician, mathematician, and philosopher whose freely inquiring mind has ranged widely throughout his fruitful career as a writer. This is one of his better known essays, illustrating the less specialized aspect of Russell's mind. His "field" is mathematical logic, to which he has made distinguished contributions, but he has also written illuminatingly on historical, political, and ethical questions.

JOHN JAY CHAPMAN (1862-1933) talked and wrote with a fierce brilliance that could be illuminating and sometimes perverse. In reply to a letter from Chapman, his friend William James once wrote, "You are the only reincarnation of Isaiah and Job and I praise God that He has let me live in your day." Abandoning the legal profession early in life, Chapman wrote in his own highly individual vein of Greek literature, Dante, Shakespeare, and Emerson. His letters and his scattered essays on subjects literary, philosophical, and religious show a nimble, bristling mind in action.

MAX BEERBOHM (1872-   ), who belongs among the great English wits, has enlivened the English literary scene with polished ironical essays for well over half a century. Equally distinguished as essayist, satirist, parodist and caricaturist, he is probably best known for his caricatures of late Victorian personalities.

GEORGE SANTAYANA (1863-   ), American philosopher of Spanish birth, is one of the most distinguished thinkers of the present century. The essay here printed is characteristic of his skill in combining incisive logic and a naturalistic bent with a firmly held theory of values.

STEPHEN BUTLER LEACOCK (1869-1944) was a Canadian professor of economics who is much better known to the general public as a humorist. His short stories and essays constitute a *genre* of humorous writing all their own, as the present example will show.

HENRY LEWIS MENCKEN (1880-   ), journalist, essayist, satirist, and student of the American language, has become a legend during his lifetime. With *A Book of Prefaces* (1917) and the volumes of collected essays belligerently entitled *Prejudices,* he early won an enormous reputation as a social and literary iconoclast. Mencken's decade as editor of the *American Mercury* was the most influential period in the career of a writer whose vituperative manner has sometimes overshadowed his essential seriousness and learning.

EDWARD MORGAN FORSTER (1879-   ) is the distinguished British novelist whose individual vision and quiet perceptiveness are manifested in his essays as in his fiction. His best known novel is *A Passage to India,* but recently there has been a revival of interest in his other novels, which include *Howard's End* and *A Room with a View.*

THOMAS STEARNS ELIOT (1888-   ), the distinguished American-born poet and critic, is now a British citizen. This essay shows him turning his highly developed sense of poetic craftsmanship to the work of one of his favorite seventeenth century "metaphysical" poets, a group whom he is largely responsible for restoring to high critical esteem.

LYTTON STRACHEY (1880-1932) is best known for his *Eminent Victorians* (1918), witty and iconclastic biographies of Cardinal Manning, Florence Nightingale, Dr. Thomas Arnold, and General Gordon, and for his lively *Queen Victoria,* written in similar vein. His urbane, sophisticated, critical and historical writing set a new fashion in English prose, against which some contemporary historians are trying hard to rebel.

ROBERT LYND (1879-1949), the wise and genial essayist who wrote under the pen-name of "Y.Y.," is known to two generations of Englishmen for his prolific but consistently brilliant contributions to a variety of British periodicals. During the years immediately preceding his death he was writing regularly for *The New Statesman and Nation.*

CHARLES EDWARD MONTAGUE (1867-1928) was a journalist and novelist whose liberal mind and satirical pen combined to make a first-rate essayist. Too little known today in America, he is typical of the best type of cultivated British journalist who, at the end of the last and the beginning of the present century, made a career of letters without being either vulgarly popular or snobbishly esoteric.

REBECCA WEST is the pseudonym of Cicely Isabel Fairfield (1892-   ), essayist and novelist, perhaps the most brilliant of living British women writers. She has recently won new fame for her remarkable reporting of significant trials, both in England and America.

Novelist, essayist, and critic of both life and letters, JOHN BOYNTON PRIESTLEY (1894-   ) has managed throughout his fruitful career to combine popular appeal with literary integrity. His is in many ways the voice of intelligent middle class England. His popular fame began with the novel *The Good Companions* (1929). During the war his broadcasts were notable for their mixture of liberal principles with quiet common sense.

VIRGINIA WOOLF (1882-1941) is best known for those brilliant novels in which she filtered reality through a delicate personal sensibility. But there was a more robust side to her nature, illustrated by many of her widely ranging essays, which display a searching intelligence and sharp observation. Her best known novels are *Mrs. Dalloway* and *To the Lighthouse,* and the two volumes of *The Common Reader* contain many of her best essays.

ALDOUS HUXLEY (1894-   ), one of the great ironists of modern English literature, is best known as a novelist, though he is a born essayist and expresses himself most naturally and effectively in this medium. His best known novels are probably *Point Counter Point* (1928) and *Eyeless in Gaza* (1936); but he has also written copiously on a great variety of topics, including art, literature, politics, ethics and religion.

VAN WYCK BROOKS (1886-   ) is the American critic and literary historian who is best known for his literary history of New England. One of the few modern American critics to cultivate a literary style, he has remained aloof from the newer critical movements to champion certain conservative values in literature.

HUGH MACDIARMID is the pseudonym of Christopher Murray Grieve (1892-   ), the brilliant Scottish poet and essayist who almost single-handed produced a new flowering of Scots poetry in the present century. An aggressive, flamboyant, colorful personality, he has long been the leading figure in modern Scottish letters.

EDMUND WILSON (1895-   ) is one of America's leading literary critics whose studies of nineteenth and twentieth century writers have done much to clarify modern critical notions about late nineteenth and twentieth century literature. He has assimilated much of modern sociological and psychological thought and uses it fruitfully in interpreting literary figures. His *Axel's Castle* (1931) was a milestone in the understanding of the aims of new literary directions.

BERNARD DEVOTO (1897-   ), professor, editor, and critic, is one of the few genuine essayists still operating full time in America. He has been running "The Easy Chair" in *Harper's Magazine* for over fifteen years. His trenchant studies of American society and literature include *Mark Twain's America, The Year of Decision,* and *The Literary Fallacy.*

ELWYN BROOKS WHITE (1899-   ) is another of the few genuine American essayists, best known perhaps for his association with *The New Yorker.* His quietly witty observation finds expression in a restrained, carefully modulated prose which is justly distinguished among modern American writing. The essence of his style and attitude are to be found in *One Man's Meat.*

VICTOR SAWDON PRITCHETT (1900-   ) is one of the most civilized and perceptive of modern British literary critics. His essays on the novel are especially distinguished, and his articles in *The New Statesman and Nation* are a model of candid, informed critical writing. His novel, *Mr. Beluncle,* appeared in 1951.

GEORGE ORWELL is the pseudonym of Eric Blair, whose death in 1950 at the early age of forty-seven was a severe loss to English letters. His incisive, original mind stood alone in his time. The appearance of his apocalyptic *Nineteen Eighty-Four* shortly before his death led V. S. Pritchett to speak of Orwell as "the conscience of his generation."

CHRISTOPHER MORLEY (1890-   ) is the American novelist and essayist whose genial wit and deliberate cultivation of gusto are exhibited in his prolific writing as in his personality.

JAMES GROVER THURBER (1894-   ), the great American cartoonist and humorist, distills a wild humor out of a fundamentally pessimistic view of the universe. His methods, in both his drawing and his writing, are wholly original: an apparent abandonment to sheer absurdity hides an ironic commentary on some phase of human behavior. This essay is more obviously satirical in intention than much of his work, but it does show his ability to use humor as a critical weapon.

NOTES

In the interests of pleasurable and unimpeded reading the editor has deliberately undertaken no systematic annotation of the essays, but the following notes may provide occasional orientation.

Page 13 Harivansa: the Sanskrit epic poem celebrating the life and adventures of Krishna (also sometimes called Damodara), great deity of later Hinduism who was worshiped as an incarnation of Vishnu. The moral and religious parables of the East powerfully affected Thoreau's thought.

Page 47 "qu'un état de vapeur était un état très faûcheux, parcequ'il nous faisait voir les choses comme elles sont": "that a misty state is a very troublesome one because it makes us see things as they are." The paradox in the statement has puzzled some commentators, but was doubtless intended.

Page 91 "Insanam vatem aspicies": "You will look upon the mad priestess." These are the words of the oracle at Delos, who tells Aeneas he will reach Italy safely after many vicissitudes, and there at Cumae will hear of his further fate from the prophetic Sibyl. Thus Walpole's earlier mention of drawing "Virgilian lots."

Page 92 Mr. Wright: Ichabod Charles Wright (1795-1871) was not only a Homeric scholar but also, as Arnold calls him in his lecture On Translating Homer, "the conscientious and painstaking translator of Dante."

Page 134 "Nemo potest Thetidem simul et Galatean amare": "No one can at the same time love Thetis and Galatea."

Page 157 Messrs. Dewey, Schiller and their allies: Some of the scholars named along with John Dewey and the German chemist, Wilhelm Ostwald (1853-1932), are perhaps less familiar names today than they were in James's time. The American-born philosopher, Ferdinand C. S. Schiller (1864-1937), spent the bulk of his career at Oxford and became the leading English exponent of Pragmatism, which he preferred to call "humanism." Shadworth Hodgson (1832-1912) was a founder and the first president of the Aristotelian Society of London. Christoph von Sigwart (1830-1904) became the distinguished German logician of Tübingen. Ernst Mach (1838-1916) was an eminent Austrian physiologist and psychologist.

Page 243 Dr. Elsie Clews Parsons: Mrs. Parsons (1875-1941) did eventually achieve a place in "Who's Who in America." In her later years she turned her attention more and more to the backgrounds and culture of the Indians (*American Indian Life,* 1925; *Kiowa Tales,* 1929), and was president of the American Anthropological Society at the time of her death.

Page 258 Pallida Mors aequo pulsat pede pauperum tabernas,/ Regumque turris: Pale Death beats with equal foot on the huts of the poor and the palaces of kings.

Nobis, cum semel occidit brevis lux,/Nox est perpetua una dormienda: We, when once the brief light of day sets, must sleep through everlasting night.

Page 259 Le squelette était invisible/Au temps heureux de l'art païen! : The skeleton was invisible in the happy time of pagan art!

Page 263 Necessité faict gens mesprendre/Et faim saillir le loup des boys: Necessity makes people misapprehend and hunger leap (like) the wolf from the woods.